I0086124

Anonymus

Archaeologia

Miscellaneous tracts relating to antiquity

Anonymus

Archaeologia
Miscellaneous tracts relating to antiquity

ISBN/EAN: 9783742828460

Manufactured in Europe, USA, Canada, Australia, Japa

Cover: Foto ©Lupo / pixelio.de

Manufactured and distributed by brebook publishing software
(www.brebook.com)

Anonymus

Archaeologia

ARCHAEOLOGIA:

O R,

MISCELLANEOUS TRACTS

RELATING TO

ANTIQUITY.

PUBLISHED BY

THE SOCIETY OF ANTIQUARIES OF LONDON.

VOLUME XII.

LONDON,
Printed by J. NICHOLS, Printer to the SOCIETY;
Sold at their APARTMENTS in SOMERSET PLACE; and by Meſſieurs WHITE,
ROBSON, LEIGH and SOTHEBY, BROWN, and EGERTON.
M DCC XCVI.

[v]

T A B L E

OF

C O N T E N T S.

CONTENTS.

vii

AR-

ARCHAEOLOGIA:

o r,

MISCELLANEOUS TRACTS, &c.

I. *Antiquities discovered in* Derbyshire. *In a Letter from* Hayman Rooke, *Esq.* F. S. A. *to the Rev. Dr.* Pegge, F. S. A.

Read November 21, 1793.

DEAR SIR, *Mansfield Woodhouse, Dec.* 27, 1793.

THE following account of some Roman antiquities lately discovered near Hopton, which Mr. Gell was so obliging as to reserve for my inspection, I did intend to have had the honour of presenting to the Society ; but, as it will be rendered more acceptable by the addition of your learned observations, I shall solicit for its admittance into your interesting account of Roman antiquities *(Derbeiescira Romana)*, which I hope you intend to continue. I am, dear Sir,

Your sincere and obliged humble servant,

H. ROOKE.

N° 1. Pl. I. is an iron head of a spear, found in a romantic valley which extends about three miles, where Mr. Gell is now making a road from Hopton Moor to Ible.

N° 2. appears to be the head of an arrow found near the above.

N° 3. seems to be an iron dagger found in removing the earth in the same valley.

N° 4. an iron head of a spear, much corroded with rust, found in making the new road.

N° 5. is another iron head of a spear the size of the drawing found near the above in June, 1792.

N° 1. Pl. II. was found in November, 1791, in the same valley, and about three feet under ground; this very singular-shaped instrument appears to be marble, of a light colour, tinged with yellow, and a mixture of pale red and green veins, and, what is very extraordinary, it still retains a fine polish; the edges are thin, rising gradually to about the thickness of half an inch in the middle; from its shape and size it could not have been used as a weapon, but I think it might very possibly be the instrument used by the Aruspices, who examined the entrails of the victims that were sacrificed, which were always carefully surveyed.

It is very remarkable, that these spear-heads should be found covered with stones three feet below the surface in this sequestered valley, where there are no traces of a Roman road or remains of Roman barrows; but, as Mr. Gell's letter to me on this subject will be more satisfactory than my conjectures, I shall here send you a copy of it : " I should not dare to venture a conjecture with any Antiquary excepting yourself, whose candour I have so frequently had occasion to experience, and which I must now trespass upon again by risking an opinion of the means of these implements coming to the strange

4   place

3   4

Antiquities found in Derbyshire

MUSC
CELL
PRAE · C·III
LIBRIT

place where they are discovered ; in my almost daily solitary
rides down the valley, my thoughts have been almost always
employed (when near the place) upon their being found in
a situation where it is impossible there could have ever been
either camp, station, or habitation of any kind, except, perhaps, an hermitage, where no traveller ever set his foot before the present time ; that they should be found here is
certainly extraordinary ; but, as you have clearly proved
that the Romans have been in this neighbourhood, it may
be fairly concluded, that, in their attempts to proceed farther, they met with interruptions from the Britons, who,
most probably, attacked them in this defile with showers of
stones, and this appears to me the most probable method of
accounting for their being covered with stones of the size
for the purpose of throwing."

About a mile South of the above-mentioned valley, on a
rising ground near Hopton, is a very large barrow called
Abbot's Low, the circumference of which is 196 feet. As
the labourers were preparing this for a plantation, they discovered an urn, which Mr. Gell was so obliging as to
order should not be touched till I came to Hopton. In
May last we proceeded to examine the urn, and after removing the stone, N° 2, which covered it, and clearing
away the ground to the depth of five feet from the top, and
about eighteen inches below the natural soil, I got a distinct
view of the urn, which was four feet three inches in circumference, made of coarse baked earth, and full of burnt bones
and ashes, in attempting to take it up, it fell to pieces. See
the shape of the urn in drawing N° 3. The stone which
covered this urn, see N° 2, measures on the top two feet six
inches by one foot eight inches, and about nine inches thick,
it appears to be a soft yellowish free stone, and much cor-

roded ;

roded; in rubbing off the dirt from the top, which had filled up the interstices of the letters, I discovered an inscription, a fac simile of which is on the stone N° 7. There evidently appears to have been more letters above, but they are now so defaced by time, that nothing can be made out, though very possibly they might have been the letters of the prænomen; the inscription seems to be intended for *Gellius Præfectus Cohortis Tertiæ Legionis Quintæ Britannicæ*, but it does not appear, by any Roman author, that the fifth legion was ever in Britain, though Mr. Gordon mentions [a] a stone with the V. legion upon it, found in the fort at Girot hill in Scotland; he says, " I likewise found another very rare and curious stone with the following letters upon it, *Leg*. V. from the letters, two angular borderings appear on each side of the stone, so close and plain, that it leaves no room to doubt of its being read *Legio Quinta*; nor is there any space whatsoever for another letter to have been put in. I take this to be an invaluable rarity of its kind, being the only stone that ever I found in the island of Britain with the name of the fifth legion impressed upon it." ▷ LEGV ◁

But Horsley seems to be of a different opinion. He says: " But though there be no space between the letters and the angular borderings on each side, yet why may it not be read *legio victrix*, and by it be meant the *legio sexta victrix?* which, by the following inscription *(Legio sexta victrix fecit)* appears to have been at this very fort; as there was no room for VI. and V. *(sexta* and *victrix)* it is more likely that the number should be omitted, than the honourable title or epithet; especially since in this case the title would sufficiently distinguish them without the number. Besides, the *legio quinta* is a legion unheard of in Britain [b]." Hence I think

[a] Gordon's Itinerarium Septentrionale, p. 56.
[b] Horsley's Britannia Romana, p. 200.

there

there is great reason to suppose, that this (V) on the stone which covered the urn, was intended for *vi.rices*, the title of the sixth legion, which probably remained some time in Derbyshire before they marched to the North.

The finding of an inscription on a rough undressed stone covering an urn in a barrow, is, I think, a curious discovery, for I do not recollect, in any account that has been written on Urn Burial, or on Sepulchral Inscriptions, that one has been found in a similar situation; it is also remarkable, that the prefect's name should be Gellius, and that the urn which contained his ashes should be deposited in a barrow on Mr. Gell's estate. Could Mr. Gell's family be descended from this antient Roman?

The Peak of Derbyshire abounds also with natural curiosities. Drawing N° 3 is part of a remarkable large horn; the pith, or slough, only remains, the horny part being entirely rotted off; circumference at (a) one foot four inches, at (b) one foot ten inches, length from (c) to (d) one foot eight inches; it was found in making the tunnel of the Cromford canal, near Butterly; from the great size this horn must have been of when perfect, I think it cannot be appropriated to any species of animals now extant in this country.

Drawing N° IV. is a piece of pure native lead perfectly refined, it evidently appears, from the number of pendent drops, to have been melted and formed by a subterraneous fire; it was found hanging by the top (a) to the roof of a small cavity about thirty yards deep in a mine near Alport; it weighs two pounds five ounces, and is the size of the drawing. It has been observed by naturalists, that native gold and silver have been found in mines, but a specimen of native lead has never, till now, been discovered.

H. Roman

II. Roman *Antiquities at and near* Bradburn *in the County of* Derby. *In a second Letter from* Hayman Rooke, *Efq. to the Rev. Dr.* Pegge.

Read December 12, 1793.

Mansfield Woodhoufe, Auguft 27, 1793.

DEAR SIR,

WHEN I was laft at Hopton, I went again to examine thofe three fingular fculptured ftones in the church-yard at Bradburn; two of thefe (fee plate III. N° 1 and 2) are fixed in a wall fo near together as to form a narrow pafs, the common way of making ftiles in Derbyfhire; the other is placed as a corner-ftone in the foundation of the porch, which evidently appears to be coëval with the church.

On examining the grounds round the church-yard, I plainly traced a ditch and vallum on the North and on the Weft fide, where they extend acrofs the Afhbourn road through fome meadows to a valley. They are alfo diftin-guifhable on the Eaft fide, but on the South fide there are hardly any traces of either, having been deftroyed by build-ings and fences; this inclofure takes in a hill, near the fum-mit of which the church was built; the apex plainly appears to have been floped down on the fide next the church, to level the ground for the foundation. There is, I think, great reafon to fuppofe, that this fpot might have been an expro-ratory

Antient Stones in Bradbourn Church Yard.

the inclofures ; on the North fide they may be traced near
400 yards ; on the Eaft and Weft fides I could difcern but
very little of the ditch and vallum, at leaft not fufficient to
afcertain the fize of the camp ; within this enclofure and
near the top, is what they call the *Lombard piece*, where,
about twenty years ago, an urn was found which contained
near eighty coins, chiefly Denarii, moft of them of the Upper
Empire ; here are alfo the remains of feveral fmall enclofures,
but they are now fo deftroyed by taking away the ftones for
walls, that I could only get the exact dimenfions of one,
which enclofes a fpace of twenty feven yards by ten ; but, as
they were more perfect when Mr. Pilkington examined them
fix or feven years ago, I fhall give you his account of them.

    " About half a mile North of the village may ftill be feen
" fome faint veftiges of a Roman encampment or ftation,
" at a place called *Lombard green*, it is of an oblong form,
" and occupies a fpace of about half an acre. It confifts of
" feveral divifions made by walls, the foundations of which
" are in many parts ftill vifible ; the fize and fhape of thefe
" divifions are various, they are oblong, femi-circular, and
" fquare, the number is about twelve ; perhaps there might
" formerly have been more, for thefe do not all lie together.
" This fuppofition is rendered very probable by confidering,
" that the ground has been difturbed at different times by
" the miners in purfuing veins of lead ore. It was a circum-
" ftance of this kind, from which it was difcovered, that this
" was a Roman encampment [b]."

    Here is, my dear Sir, a large field for conjecture, and I
fhall venture to trefpafs on your patience by hazarding one
or two. Might not this ftation have been the *Parvus Vicus*
of the Romans, whence the village of Perwich took its

    [b] View of the prefent State of Derbyfhire, vol. II. p. 284.

name? which is situated in a bottom half a mile South of
the station. The *Lombard piece* might possibly have been the
quarters of an auxiliary cohort of the Lombards before they
invaded Italy upon the decline of the Roman empire. It is
true, we do not find this cohort mentioned in any of the inscriptions found in Britain, nor is it to be met with in the
Notitia. *Horsley* tells us, "there are eight cohorts mentioned both in inscriptions and the Notitia; fourteen are found
only in inscriptions, and nine in the Notitia only, which
make the whole number of cohorts in Britain thirty-one, but
it does not appear that these cohorts were all in Britain at
the same time, because some of them relate to different
ages [c]." Nor do we know, with any certainty, what
auxiliary cohorts belonged to each legion. I think it is not
improbable, that the above-mentioned corps might have been
an equestrian cohort; we find "that the word *ala* is sometimes used by the best Roman writers to express the whole
body of auxiliary forces, both horse and foot, but most frequently denotes only the auxiliary horse[d]." There were eight
of these *alae* in Britain, one of them, the *Ala Petriana*, appears to have taken its name from the station *Petriana*, or
Cambeck fort. The Lombard cohort might possibly have
been removed soon after its arrival at *Parvus Vicus* to one of
the stations *per liniam valli*, and there change its name.

Where no certain conclusion can be deduced from scattered
remains of remote antiquity, conjectures may be allowable,
the probability of these I shall now leave to the consideration
of a more learned Antiquary.

I am, dear Sir,
Your affectionate,
and obliged humble servant,
H. R O O K E.

[c] Horsley's Brit. Rom. p. 91.   [d] Ibid. p. 92.

III. *An Attempt to illustrate the Figures carved in Stone on the Porch of* Chalk Church. *By the Rev.* Samuel Denne, F. A. S.

Read February 6, 1794.

THERE having been published in Bibliotheca Topographica Britannica [a] an engraving of the porch of Chalk church from the correct pencil of Mr. Tracy, Mr. Clarke declined sending a view of it, when he transmitted for the inspection of the Society his other drawings of different parts of that edifice [b] ; but it was my desire that he would favour me with the delineation now exhibited *, conceiving it to be a suitable accompaniment to them. And I had, as an additional motive for my request, the hope of obtaining a satisfactory elucidation of the subject represented from a person, who, I knew, was very conversant in architectural embellishments. In this instance, however, I did not succeed, Mr. Clarke acknowledging in his answer, that he could not account for a sculptured relief so improperly placed. Nor did Mr. Thorpe propose an illustration of it, he observing on these strange and whimsical ornaments, that " such chimerical dressings convey little, if any, meaning or design, and seem to have been merely the effects of rude caprice, and fantastical humour of the architects and sculptors of those times." But, as I suspect, the terms *chimerical, little meaning*

[a] N° VI. part I. plate III. N° III. p. 13.
[b] Engraved in vol. XI. pl. XIV. XV. p. 365, & seq.
* See plate IV.

7

or

Figure carved in Stone
on the porch of Chalk church, Kent.

or *design, rude caprice,* and *fantastical humour,* may not be
strictly appropriate; the objects carved not being merely the
creatures of the imagination of the artist, but worked from
the life, with an endeavour to perpetuate countenances and
actions not unfrequently displayed in this cemetery.

Wakes, or anniversaries, on the festival of the saint to
whom the church was dedicated, and fairs, which origi-
nated from them, were in former ages usually kept in church-
yards, and sometimes in churches; by which, as was a matter of complaint, "Goddes house was made a tavern of glut-
tons [c]." We read also of *scotales* and *giveales,* appellations
deemed by several writers to be always used synonymously,
but between which, I think, I can occasionally trace marks
of distinction.

Scotales were, as the word imports, maintained by a joint
contribution of the resorters to them. Thus the tenants of
South Malling in Sussex, which belonged to the archbishop of
Canterbury, were, at the keeping of a court, to entertain
the lord or his bailiff with a drinking, or an ale, and the
stated quotas towards the charge were, that a man should pay
three pence halfpenny for himself and his wife, and a widow
and a cottage three halfpence. And in the manor of Terring
in the same county, and under the same jurisdiction, it was
the custom for the tenants named to make a *scotale* of sixteen
pence halfpenny, and to allow out of each sixpence three
halfpence to find drink for the bailiff [d].

Common scotales in taverns, at which the clergy were not
to be present, are noticed in several ecclesiastical canons.
They were not to be published in the church by the clergy or

[c] Kennet's Parochial Antiquities, p. 613.
[d] Somner's Treatise on Gavelkind, p. 29.

the

the laity [*e*]; and a meeting of more than ten persons of the
same parish or vicinage was a scotale that was in general prohibited [*f*]. There were also common drinkings, in the mentioning of which the prefix *scot* was omitted, and instead of
it was inserted a word which denoted the special purpose
which occasioned the compotation. *Leet-ale, bride-ale, clerk-
ale, church-ale,* are instances in point. To a leet-ale it is
likely all the resiants in a manerial district were contributors;
and the expence of a bride-ale was probably defrayed by the
relations and friends of a happy pair, who were not in circumstances to bear the charges of a wedding-dinner. The
clerk's ale was in the Easter holidays, and was the method
taken to enable clerks of parishes to collect more readily their
dues; or, as it is expressed in Aubrey's MS History of Wilts,
as cited by Mr. Warton in his History of English Poetry, " it
was for the clerk's private benefit and the solace of the neighbourhood [*g*]."

Mr. Warton has likewise copied from the Dodsworth MS.
the following extract from an old indenture made before the
Reformation, which shews the design of a church-ale. " The

[*e*] A. 1223. Constitut. Ricardi Poore, epi. Sarum. Prohibemus quoque ne
denunciationes scotallorum fiant in ecclesia per laicos, nec in ecclesiis, nec extra
ecclesias per sacerdotes, vel per clericos, Wilkins' Concil. Magn. Britan. v. I. p. 600.
    A. 1229. Constitut. W. de Bleys epi. Wigorn. ne sacerdotes ad tabernam accedant, nec in ecclesiis hujusmodi potationes denoncientur. Ibid. p. 614.
    A. 1237. Constit. Alex. (de Stavenby) Coventr. Episc. Item inhibemus sub
poena dimidie marcæ, ne quis sacerdos ad tabernam eat, vel tabernam teneat,
vel scotales. Ibid. p. 641.——A. 1240. Constit. W. de Cantilupo epi. Wigorn.
Et quod nollus clericus intersit compotationibus quæ vocantur scotales. Ibid.
p. 672.
    [*f*] A. 1256. Constitut. Ægid. de Bridport epi. Sarum. Commones autem
compotationes declaramus, quoties numerum denarium excesserant ejusdem parochiæ, in qua cervisia venalis extiterit, vel etiam vicinarum in tabernis hujusmodi,
vel infra septa ejusdem domicilii potandi gratia commorantur. Ibid. p. 719.
    [*g*] Vol. III. p. 128, note *f*.

" pa-

" parifhioners of Elvefton and Okebrook, in Derbyfhire,
" agree jointly to brew four ales, and every ale of one quarter
" of malt, betwixt this and the feaft of St. John the Baptift
" next coming. And that every inhabitant of the faid town
" of Okebrook fhall be at the feveral ales. And every huf-
" band and his wife fhall pay two pence, every cottager
" one penny; and all the inhabitants of Elvefton fhall have
" and receive all the profits and advantages coming of the
" faid ales to the ufe and behoof of the faid church of El-
" vefton. And the inhabitants of Elvefton fhall brew eight
" ales betwixt this and the feaft of St. John Baptift, at which
" ales the inhabitants of Okebrook fhall come and pay as be-
" fore rehearfed. And if he be away at one ale, to pay at
" oder ale for both, &c."

The different ales above fpecified were, as I already remarked, fupported by joint contributions, and moft of them,
in a greater or lefs degree, compulfory. But the *giveales,*
which I have principally in view, were the legacies of indi-
viduals, and from that circumftance entirely gratuitous:
though fome of them might be in addition to a common
giveale before eftablifhed in the parifh [*b*].

If

[*b*] " St. Mary's in Hoo. Teft. Will. Hamond. Alfoe I will, that fpecially any feoffees and executors fee that the yeovale of St. James be kept for ever, as it hath bin here aforetime." Sudwell's extracts of gifts to charitable ufes from wills in the regiftry of the diocefe of Rochefter, printed in Thorpe's Antiquities, page 41. " Hoo. Teft. Thomas Bridle, of Cievall houfe, lying at Grenehill, proou wardens and the brethren of the Gerall." Ibid. p. 47. " Hoo Allhallows, Teft. John Devell. Alfo I will that the geavale of Alhallows in Hoo have one acre of land after my wife's deceafe to maintain it withal, called Pilehland, and that to be done after the olde cuftom of olde time." Ibid. p. 48. " Jo. Bromley, fubtrahit de la gideale aviiis, a lumine beatæ Mariæ apud Woldham." Acta Archid. Roffen. 1514, Sept. 28, fol. 73. a.—" Thomas Gate et Rogerus Gilwyn, tifu' apud Woldham.—Habent ad proband. quod Johannes Beauley, gen. fubtraxit de la
Gif

If an adequate judgement can be formed from Stowell's Extracts of Wills entered in the Register's office of the diocese of Rochester, testamentary giveales must have been very numerous in England. In several clauses the word occurs [*i*]; but, when the bequest was of malt or of barley, the use to which it was to be converted is obvious.

A dole of bread, with, now and then, a small quantity of cheese and other *corrodies*, is also mentioned in the same bequest [*k*]. Charity was suggested as a pretence for collecting some of the scotales; but, in the testamentary giveales, the dif-

Gif Ale contionat' afque diem Jovis in vigil. S. Catharine ; quo die comparavit Job. Beasley—et quoad de la Gif Ale dicit, quod obtulit parochianis isti quarter. brasii poct. Angl. quater via. iiid. et quod omnino recufabant." Ibid. fol. 86. b. 91. a.

(*i*) " Snodlandi Teft. John Holman. Item volo, &c. unam acram terræ, imperpetuum—inveniend. inde annuatim de proventibus duos buffiel' brafei, et unum buffiel' frumenti pro quadam giveale paroch' de Snodland in fefto purific'." Thorpe's Antiquities, p. 39.—" Hoo. Teft. Petri Samfon. Alfoe I will that Harrie Compton have 1 acr' et dim. land, to the intent that he keep a yevale every other year on the feaft of St. Michael, at every time to be difpended vi. buffiel of wheate bread, and a buffiel of maulte in ale, &c." Ibid. p. 39.—" St. Mary's. Teft. Tho. Tomys. Alfo I will and give that Joane my daughter fhall have houfe and land, with condition, that fhe, or elfe fome other in her name, keepe or doe a yevall upon St James's day, and to this yevall I bind this land whoever have it without end." Ibid. p 40.—" Hoo. Teft. Serph. Sprake. Alfoe I will, that Alice my wife fhall have my houfe and land, and marfh, doeing yearely the charge of a yeveale at Alhallon tide for evermore." Ibid. p. 43.

[*k*] " Hoo. Teft. Stephen Jacob. I will that my heires fhall have five yards of land lying in Longfeld, and five yards in Pettefield, upon condition that they make a yearly geveall on Trinity Sunday of 5 buffiels of wheat, and 1 feame of barley, and aid in cheefe." Ibid. p. 41. " Watringbury. Teft. James Williams xxiii. iiiid. for ever. Churchwardens, and 4 or 6 of the parifhioners to be inferted in lands to the ufe of his will." Ibid. p. 43.—" Cowling. Teft. Thomas Love. To his heirs made for evermore, to this intent, to keepe and maintayne in the church of Cowling to the value of 4 buffiel of wheat and 4 buffiel of mault, and avid. in cheefe or fifh, &c." Ibid. p. 43.

tribution

tribution of them to the poor was frequently enjoined, though from the largeness of the quantity brewed it must have been intended, that neighbours, who were not of the indigent class, should participate in them [*l*].

The most luxurious treat of the kind recorded in Stowel's Extracts was at East Greenwich, pursuant to the will of John Champnis, who bequeathed three shillings in bread, two shillings in spice-bread, a barrel of ale, a gallon of malmesey, two pounds of comfits, and twenty pence in cheese, six shillings and eight pence in wood and cole, six shillings and eight pence in money, and twenty pence to the ——— and wardens to see it donn for ever [*m*]. That the poor had the spice-bread, comfits, and Malmesey wine, is not so probable a surmise, as that the wardens and their friends were regaled with this choice fare.

Giveales differ likewise materially from the common scot-ales in their having been so much blended with notions and practices of a superstitious tendency: for the bequests were frequently to the light, or altar of a saint, with directions for singing of masses at the obit, trental, or anniversary of the death of the testator [*n*]. Lands were settled for the per-

---

[*l*] " Freindsbury. Test. Joh. Toppe. Item voluit quod un' ver' et un' virgat' terre que jacet apud Westbuth.—ollam cervisæ ad refœcionem vicinorum in vigil' S. Joh'is Bapt'ti' singulis annis imperpetuum." Ibid. p. 39.

[*m*] Thorpe's Antiquities, p. 47.

[*n*] A. 1524. Jan. 1. Gardini Luminis S. Hildeford de Swankomb, contra Rob. Clark et Agneton uxor' ejus pro 4 quarter. brasei." Acta Archid. Roffen. fol. 49. a.—" Lumini Sti. Nich. de Cobham, et beatæ Mariæ debentur multa quarter. ordei et brasii." Ibid. fol. 91. a.—" Freindsbury. Test. Will. Marchant. Item, volo quod Rob. rios filius meus habeat tres acres terre ad terminum vitæ suæ, sub conditione quod disponat annuatim in die anniversarii mei iii bushel' frumenti et 1 bushel' brasii in exequiis; et post decessum dicti Roberti volo quod supradict. tres acre remaneant ecclesiæ de Friendsbury predict' imperpetuum. Ita quod ejusdem

perpetual payment of the legacies fo appropriated, and in
confequence became vefted in the crown by the ftatute of
1 Edward VI. which will account for its now being very difficult to trace the lands enfeoffed, and for the general difcon-
tinuance of the giveales, which were to be fupported by the
profits of them. The parifh of St. John Baptift in the Ifle of
Tenet is, however, poffeffed of upwards of fifteen acres of
land acquired by a legacy bequeathed for a giveale by Etheldred Barrow, in the year 1513, there not having been any
directions for the performance of maffes. Mr. Lewis has not
mentioned the fpecial ufe to which the rent of this land
is applied, but from the manner of writing it may be

dem cuftodes ecclefie difponant annuatim, &c." Thorpe's Antiq. p. 40.—
" Cliffe. Teft. Rob. Quikerell. I will that a flate be made by my feoffers of and in
all my lands in Cowling, to twelve or more perfons, as the wardens and parithio-
ners of Clire will name, under condition that the faid wardens fhall employ for ever
all the faid lands and tenements, to doe an obit in Clive church, and as much bread
as will be made of three bufhels of wheat, as much ale of 4 bufhels of mault, in cheefe
and. for ever, &c." Ibid. p. 42.—" Shorne. Teft. Will. Hawke, I bequeath
to John Hawke, my brother, xiii acres of land, and to his heirs for ever, with
this condition, that the faid John hold and keepe, or make to keepe yearly, in the
church of Shorne, an obit yearly, &c. And I will there be fpent in bread 4
bufhel of wheat, and a quarter of mault in drink, &c." Ibid. p. 43. " Hoo. Teft.
Joh. Winbray. Firft, I will that A. my wife have my houfe for terme of her
life, and fhe to keepe an obit every yeere, and to be fpent in bread a bufhel of
wheat, and in ale a bufhel of malt, &c." Ibid. p. 44. " Shorne. Teft. Joh.
Hawke. I will that an obit be kept yearly in the parifh church of Shorne on
Reliche Sunday, by the heir of the time being of my land, a quarter of mault,
&c. and half a quarter of wheat, &c. for ever." Ibid. p. 45.—" Stoke. Teft. Joh.
Hamond. Item, I will that always be kept an obit once a year in lent, of a
quarter of wheat and a quarter of malt, from heir to heir, for evermore, out of
lands in Ofterland borowe." Ibid p. 45 —" Halftow. Teft. Rich Francis. An
obit every Paffion Sunday for ever of 6 bufhel of wheat, and 6 bufhel of mault."
Ibid p. 49.—" Freindfbury. Teft. Joh. Devenifh. I will that every yeare per-
petuall John Devenifh doe an obit for me of 6 bufhel of wheat and 3 bufhel of
mault, and the faid land to pay it, whoever occupy it, from yeare to yeare."
Ibid. p. 50.

inferred,

inferred, that there is not every year on St. James's day a distribution of a quarter of malt, and six bushels of wheat and victell according thereto, notwithstanding the testator [*n*] willed, that such a yearly yeovale should be mainteyned while the world endureth.

Scotales were generally kept in houses of public resort, but the ale at giveales was first dispensed, if not in the church (which however sometimes happened [*o*]), yet in the church-yard;

[*n*] History and Antiquities of Tenet, p. 155, and Append. p. 74. In the page referred to of the History, it is expressed *her* will, Mr. Lewis not having attended to the clause in which Etheldred Barrow bequeaths a legacy to the Light, of which he was a brother, " Item cuilibet lumini cujus sum *frater* duos modios ordei."

[*o*] A. 1516, April 18. Injungitur D'no Joh. Thompson, cur' de Hoo, quod de cætero non permittat aliquas potationes fieri ecclef. sub pœna juris. Item Rect' de Halstow.—Curat' de Sanct. Maria, et vic' de Stoke. Act. Cur Confist. Ruffen. fol. 164. Perhaps these injunctions might have reference to common scotales, and not to testamentary giveales at obits, which were to be distributed in the church, as were those noticed in the underwritten bequests. " Halstow. Test. Will. Love—In omnibus annis sequent' viz. quolibet anno circa anniversar', &c. tres modios frumenti et tres modios brasii pro pane et cervis' in ecclef. distribuend' per heredes meos in perpetuum duratur."—Thorpe's Antiq. p. 42. " Hadlow. Test. Jam. Goffe. I will that the yearly profits of a field shall be bestowed in bread and ale amongst poor people in the church of Hadlow." Ibid. p. 43. " Halstow. Test. Joh. Sharnwell. I will eight bushels of wheat and five bushels of malt to be distributed in the church or church-yard." Ibid. p. 45.—" Bromley. Test. Joh. Hasledg. Certain lands entailed on condition to keepe yearly in Bromley church of llis. 4d. bread and beer to the poor, &c." Ibid. p. 47.—" St. Margaret. Test. Jane Smith. A yearly obit on Monday next after Midlent Sunday viiid. to the vicar, to the clerk iiid. two bushels of wheat for bread, and peas, and too of white herrings, and half a seame of mault, to be brewed yearly, the bread, peas, &c. to be delt in St. Margaret's church to poor people that will come to take it." Ibid. p. 50.— " Hoo. Test. Edward Pratt. I will that my executors shall receive and take the

yard; and had not this mode been adopted of inducing persons to assist at the celebration of private masses, and to repeat Ave Marias and Pater Nosters, for the health of the founders and their relatives, a principal design of the institution of them would probably have been frustrated.

Evident then is it that a man in high glee over "a stoup of strong liquor," was not in former days an unusual sight within the precincts of a church; unquestionably not, as I apprehend, in Chalk church-yard, William May, of that parish, having provided a copious giveale for a very small district which had very few inhabitants. In his will, which was dated the 24th of May, 1512, are some memorable items concerning his funeral which were not minuted by Stowell [*p*]. To every godchild he had within the county of Kent, or elsewhere, he gave six bushels of barley; and he directed, if four of these children were able, they should bear him to the church, and every of them have sixpence for his labour. He further willed, that his executors should buy two new torches against his burial for x sh. [*q*]; that four poor men should be paid

profits of the land I have hired of John Love, of Halshow, for the space of nine years, and they to give yearly during the said term 9 bushel of wheat in bread and 10 bushel of mault in drink, on Midlent Sunday, in the church of Hoo." Ibid. p 51.

[*p*] Thorpe's Antiq. p. 46.

[*q*] My friend, Mr. Fountaine, who favoured me with the additional notes from the will of William May, hinted a doubt, whether by mistake of the register in copying the will the torches are not over-rated. But great as appears to be this charge of wax taper, or torch, some centuries ago, it may be supported as the true reading by sundry authentic evidences." A. 1458, Sept. 18. "Lawrence Joys of Rochester was found guilty in the Bishop's court of the crime of adultery, and the sentence was, that he should offer a torch as high as himself, " *at tomam pro longitudinis*," at the tomb of St. William, and another torch at the tomb

paid two-pence apiece for bearing thefe torches, and that
the three men who fhould fing at his burial fhould have for
their labour three pence apiece, and as much at his month's
mynd [r]. To the highth altar he bequeathed twenty-pence,
and he willed that an honeft prefte fhould fynge for his foull
and his friends, as fhortly as he may be goten, half a yere,
and have for his labour five markes. He willed at his burial
there fhould be thirteen preftes, and every prefte to have
then, and alfo at his month's mynd, fix-pence for his labor.
He likewife willed, that his wife make every year for his foull
an obit, and to make in bread fix bufhels of wheat, and in
drink ten bufhels of mault, and in cheefe twenty-pence, to
give to poor people for the health of his foull; and he ordered, that after the deceafe of his wife his executors and feoffees fhould continue the obit before rehearfed for evermore.

tomb of St. Blaze in the bifhop's chapel." AQ cur. confil. p. 356. " A.
1458. Dec. 20, Walter Crepehogg, who had countenanced and promoted a clan-
deftine marriage, was adjudged to be whipt three times round the market at Rochefter, and as often round his parifh church, carrying in his hand, as a penitent,
a torch value vis. viiid. which he was to prefent at the altar in Rochefter cathedral, and he was to prefent a torch of the fame value at the image of St. Blaze
in Bromley." Ibid. p. 363. a. A. 1464. Teft. Thomas Blackinden. " Item
do et lego unum novum le torche ad pretium vis. ardent. in dicta ecclefia [St.
Nicolai, Tenet) in falutem animæ meæ, ac parentum et amicorum meorum."
Lewis, Hift. and Antiq. p. 53. It is obfervable, that William May directed there
fhould be two men to carry each torch.

[r] A. 1225, in a provincial council held in Scotland, it was ordered, that
no layman fhould fing at the burial or obfequies of the dead. " Item ad funera
et exequies mortuorum laicorum cantus vel choreas fieri prohibemus, cum non
deceat de aliorum fletu ridere, fed ibidem potius de hujufmodi dolere." Wilkins, Concil. v. I. p. 617. This prohibition implies it to have been a practice
in that country, as it certainly was in England; and moft probably, the perfons who had exercifed their vocal talents at the celebration of a mafs of Re-
quiem, became afterwards ballad fingers at the Gifeafe.

Give-

Givcalcs on obfequies, as well as on the anniverfaries on the dedication of churches, were in other refpects merry-makes, at which there was a free, perhaps a licentious indulgence in the games and fports of the times; though playing with the ball, finging of ballads, diffolute dances, and ludicrous fpectacles in churches and church-yards, fubjected the frequenters of them to pecuniary penalties and ecclefiaftical cenfures, excommunications not excepted [*s*].

In

[*s*] A. 1223. Conftit. Ricardi Poor ep'i Sarum. Adhuc prohibemus, ne chorex vel turpes et inhonefti ludi, qui ad lafciviam invitant, fiant cœmeteriis. Ibid. p. 600. A. 1240. Conftit. W. de Cantilup. ep'i Wigorn. Ad fervendam quoque tam cœmeterii quam ecclefiæ reverentiam, prohibemus, ne in cœmeteriis vel aliis locis facratis—ludi fiant inhonefti, maxime in fanctorum vigiliis, et feftis ecclefiarum, quod potius in dedecus fanctis cedere novimus quam honorem, præfumptoribus et facerdotibus, que hæc fuftinuerint fieri, canonice coercendis. Ibid. p. 666. A. 1287. Synod. Exon. diœc. a Petro de Quivil epifcopo. Et quia in cœmeteriis dedicatis multa fanctorum et falvandorum corpora tumulantur, quibus debetur omnis honor et reverentia; facerdotibus parochialibus diftricte præcipimus, ut in ecclefiis fuis denuncient publice, ne quifquam luftas, choreas, vel alios ludos inhoneftos in cœmeteriis exercere præfumat, præcipue in vigiliis et feftis fanctorum, cum hujufmodi ludos theatrales et ludibria fpectacula introductos per quos ecclefiarum coinquinatur honeftas, facri ordinis deteftantur. Quod fi aliqui poft factam denunciationem, ludos hujufmodi, quamquam improprie dictos, eo quod ex eis crimina oriuntur, exercuerint, prædicti facerdotes eorum nomina loci archidiacono vel ipfius officiali denuncient, ut ipfi pro fuis demeritis canonice puniantur. Ibid. vol. II. p. 140. A. 1308. Conftit. fynodal. per Henricum Woodloke, epi Winton.—Præcipimus et in ipfis (cœmeteriis) in fanctorum feftivitatibus aut aliis luftæ non fiant, aut choreæ ducantur, vel alii ludi fpectabiles habeantur. Ibid. p. 295. " By a mandate of the bifhop of Winchefter in the regifter there, were forbid ballad-finging, the exhibiting of fhows, and other profanations in the church-yard, on pain of excommunication." Not. Reg. W. Wykam. " *Ad pilas ludere, saltes diffolutos ferre, cantus canere videmus, ludibriorum spectacula ferre, et alios ludos celebrare.*" The Environs of London, vol. I. p. 248. A. 1363. Conftitutions of John Thoreby, arch-

In the church-yard of Chalk, therefore, the sculptor who had directions to ornament the porch, if he was of a humourous cast, had a choice of subjects for his chisel; and we accordingly perceive that he selected the portrait of an antick fool, or vice, dressed in character, and grasping a jug. He is described by Mr. Clarke as wearing a short coat or jacket, with large buttons and a belt (to which seems to be suspended a pouch), and on his head a cap, or hood pointed, the end falling over his right cheek, though this is somewhat broken. He is squatted beneath the base of a neat recess that has a pointed arch, is adorned with roses, and was certainly designed to contain the statue of the tutelary saint of the church. In the center of the moulding above the nich is a shocking distortion of the human form, noticed by Mr. Thorpe, as being in the attitude of a posture-master, or perhaps it may be as properly described by the words, a tumbler caricatured. On each side of this figure is a human head, and on their faces, as well as on the visage of the jovial tippler, Mr. Clarke observes, the sculptor seems to have bestowed such an indelible smirk, that however they have suffered by the corrosions of time and weather, nearly to the

archbishop of York.—2. Whereas some, being turned to a reprobate sense, meet in churches on the vigils of saints, and offend very grievously against God and his saints, whom they pretend to venerate, by minding hurtful plays and sanities, and sometimes what is worse; and in the exequies of the dead turn the house of mourning and prayer into the house of laughter and excess, to the great peril of their own souls—we strictly forbid any that come to such vigils and exequies, especially in churches, to exercise in any way such plays and uncleanlinesses.—And we strictly enjoin all rectors, &c. that they forbid and restrain all such insolencies and excesses from being committed in their churches and church-yards by the sentence of suspension and excommunication according to the canon, &c. Johnson's Collection.

lofs

loss of features, it is yet visible. All three are represented as
beholding with delight the feats of the tumbler; and Mr.
Clarke intimates, that the figure below from the grin of self-
approbation on his countenance may be the fool by whom
the posture-master was usually accompanied, who, to heighten
the mirth, had seized the jug while his principal was exer-
cising his talents.

Chalk church being dedicated to the Virgin Mary, it may
be concluded that her image was in the nich, and from its
having been placed in the center of these ludicrous figures,
the presumption is that the humours of the church-ale, or
give-ale, here displayed, might have been realised on a public festival of the saint to whose honour the people were af-
sembled, or on a parochial holiday, when a private mass was
performed at her altar.

When this porch was erected cannot be ascertained. Its
not being bonded to the contiguous wall shews it to be a
building not coëval with the church; and that it might be
finished after the institution of William May's anniversary
give-ale is a conjecture not destitute of plausibility [s].

But if we reflect that a devotional homage to the statue
was expected, nay required from all who passed under it
into the church, it must be matter of astonishment that objects so unseemly, so disgusting, should be here exhibited.
Notorious however is it, that, architectural dressings, far
more indecorous, are to be seen within sacred edifices, and in

[s] Mr. Clarke has suggested, upon sufficient grounds, that formerly this church
had a South aile, where was most probably placed the principal door of entrance, with a porch. And on the diminishing of the church it might be judged
more convenient to construct a new porch at the West end.

5   those

those parts which were deemed most holy, in different countries, where the rites of the Romish worship prevailed.

In the church of St. Spire at Corbeil there are grotesques under the seats of the stalls [u] : and Dr. Moore, after mentioning that on the pillars and cornices of the church at Strasburgh, the vices of monks are exposed under the allegorical figures of hogs, asses, monkeys, and foxes in monkish habits, who perform the most venerable functions of religion, observes, that upon the whole this cathedral is considered by some people as the most impious, and by others as the merriest Gothic church in Christendom [w].

Under the seat of each stall in the chapel of Henry VII. in Westminster abbey are carvings so very indecent, and so satyrical on ecclesiastics, that a gentleman who inspected them a few years ago found it difficult to persuade himself, that a congregation of St. Benedict should ever suffer them to appear within their sacred walls ; he, in this favourable opinion of the monks, being influenced by a perusal of the rigid rules of their order, without attending to the laxity in their observance of them. And though in this instance it may be allowed, that as this chapel was built by king Henry VII. the architects and workmen were not subject to the controul of the abbat and his brethren ; the plea will certainly not avail in the case of the prior and convent of Christ Church, Canterbury, who, instead of preventing, as was manifestly in their power, must have countenanced as glaring a violation of decency in their cathedral near the high altar, and the shrine of their darling saint, Thomas Becket. For the fence of iron work at the West end of Trinity chapel, has at

[u] Antiq. Nat. by Millin.
[w] View of Society in France, &c. vol. I. p. 370.

the

the top a rail or cornice of wood, painted with those ridiculous and trifling fancies with which the monks were every where fond of making the preaching order of friers appear as contemptible as they could [x].

The Statue of Mary at Chalk church was demolished by the Iconoclasts of the last century; though possibly there might not be at that time an inhabitant of the parish in whose mind the image would have excited an idolatrous propensity. But the grotesque figures escaped the hammers of these conscientious reformers; whose pious feelings were not hurt with the view of a toper and a scaramouch carved on the frontispiece of the vestibule of a house of Prayer; notwithstanding, in their own conceits, they held purer doctrines, and were more sanctimonious in their devotions, and stricter in their morals, than other men.

Wilmington, Jan. 6, 1794.   SAMUEL DENNE.

[x] Walk in and about Canterbury, p. 261.

IV. *Mr.* ASTLE *on the Tenures, Customs, &c. of his Manor of* GREAT TEY. *In a Letter addressed to the President.*

Read May 22, 1794.

MY LORD,

HAVING observed several singular tenures, customs, and usages, in my manor of Great Tey, in the hundred of Lexden and county of Essex; I conceive that illustrations of the most remarkable may be acceptable to the Society of Antiquaries.

This manor was paramount to, and had jurisdiction over many other manors in very early times. These were held by various Rents and Services, as well civil as military.

The military services were abolished in the reign of king Charles the Second, but most of the ancient rents are still paid. The lords had both courts-leet and courts-baron, wherein they held pleas of different kinds. This manor is of considerable extent, being about seventeen miles in circumference; the lands, which are mostly arable, are remarkably productive, and have long been in a high state of cultivation. The ancient possessors of this estate seem to have considered both convenience and security in the disposal of their lands. On an elevated spot, which commands an extensive prospect over a great tract of country, stood the lord's mansion in the centre of the manor, which was surrounded by a mote; this house was occasionally the summer residence of the lords Fitz-Walter from the reign of king John to that of king Henry VI. Several manors and lands were granted to knights and to freemen to be holden of the lords of this manor, on various conditions, and by different rents and services, the most remarkable of which shall be mentioned hereafter.

The free tenants were chiefly placed on the Southern part of the manor, towards the great Roman road leading from Kelvedon to Colchester, or that leading from Coggeshall, to the same place. The base tenants or villani were placed in the Northern part, and were in a great measure surrounded by the lord's demesnes, and by the lords of Bacons and Flories ; the lands on the North of the manor are most of them copyhold at this day. On the North-east side of the capital mansion, at the distance of about a mile and a half, stood the mansion house of the lords of *Bacons*, which in early times was a sub-infeudation made by one of the great lords of Tey, to a vavasour or rear vassal. This manor was held by knight's service, homage, fealty, suit of court, a reasonable aid to marry the lord's daughter, and by the rent of £.1. 6s. 6d. payable half-yearly, which is paid at this day by Charles Alexander Cricket, Esq. the present possessor of this estate [a].

On

[a] In the 11th of Edward I. the manor of Bacons was held of the lord Fitz-Walter by Roger Fitz-Richard, by the rents and services above-mentioned. In the reign of Edward III. it was held by the family of Bacon. In the next reign it was possessed by the family of Calthorpe, whose descendants enjoyed it till the 3d of Edward VI. when, on the death of Sir Philip Calthorpe, knight, it descended to his daughter and heir Elizabeth, wife of Sir Henry Parker, knight. In the 9th of queen Elizabeth she and Sir John Woodhouse, her second husband, sold the same to John Turner, gent. from whom it descended to Margaret his daughter and sole heir, who was first the wife of Thomas Smith, esq. by whom she had four sons and six daughters ; she was afterwards married to Sir Stephen Poule, knight. On her death it descended to her eldest son and heir, Stephen Smith, esq. whose descendants possessed it till 1724, when Thomas Smith, dying without issue, left them to his niece, Mary Tendring, who devised

4   them

On the West side of the lord's mansion, at about the distance of a mile, stands the manor house of *Flories*, which has for ages been held of this manor by knight's service, homage, fealty, suit of court, and by the yearly rent of 11s. 3d. which is still paid [b].

The manor of Uphall is on the South-west part of this manor, which, with its demesnes, came into the possession of the lords Fitzwalter in the reign of king Richard II. when it was absorbed in the paramount manor, and the estate is to this day a part of the demesnes of the manor of Great Tey.

A capital messuage and half a carucate of land, called Trumpington's, was likewise within the said manor. In the 13th of Edward I. Robert de Trumpington held this estate

them to her cousin Thomas Alexander Smith, esq. who, in 1747, devised the same to Charles Alexander, from whom it came to the present proprietor.

[b] This manor was enjoyed by the possessors of the manor of Bacons till the death of Margaret Smith, sole daughter and heir of John and Christian Turner, when her son John Smith had Flories, who, November 1, 1645, sold it to William Stubbing, of Great Tey, gent. who, April 19th 1650, with Rose his wife, sold it to Christopher Scarlet, who, by his will dated September 23d in the same year, devised it to his son Thomas Scarlet; but, in 1657, Stephen Smith, esq. commenced a suit against the said Thomas Scarlet for the manor, which suit continued till November 12th 1664, when it was determined they had an equal right, and the courts were held in their joint names. The said Thomas Scarlet, by his will dated December 4th 1705, devised this estate to his nephew Thomas Scarlet, who, April 23d, 1713, sold it to John Little, who held a court jointly with Thomas Smith, August 31st in that year. On the 23d of March, 1714, the said Thomas Smith for a valuable consideration conveyed all his manerial rights to the said John Little, referring to himself the site of the manor of Bacons, with the demesne lands and the farms thereto belonging. Mr. Little held his court as sole lord of the manor May 2d, 1714. After his death it descended to his daughter Mary, who was first married to Thomas Bridge, gent. and afterwards to ―― Foster, whom she survived, and by her will devised the same to Thomas Stock, of Halstead, gent. for his life, and after his decease to Samuel Sharn of Hatfield Peverell, gent. who is the present possessor.

E 2

by

by the service of finding the king one horse, one sack of canvas, and one broche in his army in Wales, during forty days, at his own charge. By an inquisition taken the 30th Edw. I. it appears, that this estate was held of the king *in capite* [c]. In 1398 it was given to the priory of St. Botolph in Colchester, and after the dissolution it was granted to Lord Chancellor Audeley, and since that time it has been part of the demesnes of the lords of Great Tey.

The following fiefs were held of this manor by knight's service, homage, fealty, suit of court, and by several rents and services.

Ramsey Hall. Two-third parts of the manor of Ramsey Hall in Essex were held of the manor of Great Tey, by the third part of a knight's fee, and by the third part of 10s. payable at the end of every twenty-four weeks for castle ward, and by homage, fealty, and suit of court [d]. *Parker's* or Roydon Hall. *Lagenhoe* in Essex. The tenement of Avenells in Gamlinghay. The master of Martinage Hall holds the manor of *Martynage* in Gamlinghay in the county of Cambridge. The master of Pleshy College in Essex, held in Pleshy

[c] Morant's Hist. of Essex, vol. II. p. 207.

[d] In an ancient extent of the manor made 12 Edward I. A. D. 1284, it appears, that Robert de Vere, earl of Oxford, held three fees in Ramsey, Gosfield, and Beauchampe, by the farm or rent of 2s. payable every 24 weeks. In the 48th Edward III. the countess of Oxford paid to the lord Walter Fitz-walter, lord of Tey, as an aid to marry his daughter three pounds for the said three fees. On the 25th of November, 19th Richard II. ten shillings were paid for Castle Guard, and the further sum of 10s. were also paid on the same account. In the 22d of Henry VI. John earl of Oxford paid at the end of 24 weeks, 2s. In the 11th of queen Elizabeth William Ayloffe, esq. was distrained for his relief of 100s. due on the death of William Ayloffe, his father, for the manor of Ramsey-hall, held of this manor as a knight's fee, and for a rent of 2s. payable at the end of 24 weeks for Castle Guard silver.

half

half a knight's fee. *Westley Manor* in Cambridgeshire. *Steeple Morden*, alias Bryse's Fee in Cambridgeshire. The estates called Vernons in Wake's Colne, formerly possessed by Hugh de Crepping, and afterwards by John de Vernon, are held of this manor by knight's service, homage, fealty, and suit of court, under the rent of 3*d*. at Easter, and the like sum at Michaelmas, a pair of gilt spurs at Pentecost or 12*d*. and three pounds of pepper, and one pound and a half of cummin; and the possessor of these estates was to find one man to attend the Justices itinerant in Essex at his own cost.

The lands called Sompnors in Aldham were held by knight's service, homage, fealty, suit of court, and by the yearly rent of 5*s*. and the proprietor was to find one man at his own cost, to attend the Justices itinerant in Essex.

The tenement called Georges was held by knight's service, fealty, suit of court, and paid scutage 20*s*. 6*d*. when scutage was to be levied. Many other estates were held by knight's service of this manor, by homage, fealty, and suit of court; but as there is nothing remarkable in their tenures they are omitted.

In ancient times rents in kind were paid by several of the free tenants within the manor. The Cressfield family paid yearly one pound of cummin for certain lands called Cookes, containing twenty-five acres [*e*].

[*e*] This family possessed estates in this county in very early times. In the Clause roll of the first of Edward II. A. D. 1307, is a writ directed to Walter de Gloucester, the king's escheator on this side Trent, to grant seisin to Andrew de Cressfield of all the lands of his father Robert Cressfield, who held of the king's father in *capite*, the said Andrew having obtained his full age, and done homage. The estate called Pope's has been enjoyed by the posterity of the said Andrew Cressfield, and descended in the direct line for several centuries until the year 1782, when Edward Cressfield, Doctor in Divinity, dying unmarried, devised it to me, I having married the heir general of the family.

The

The Upcher family paid yearly a gilly-flower for land called Langley.

The family of Pudney paid annually a red rose at Midsummer, for a cottage and a garden called God-sons. This was probably a gift from a lord to his godson.

The Motcham family paid a quit-rent of 6*d.* and a dish of honey, or 8*d.* in lieu thereof.

There were also other rents, as capons, hens, geese, eggs, and a plough-share, for Collops tenement, two years together, and the third year none, and two seams of wheat within fourteen days after Hallowmass.

The villani or copyhold tenants belonging to this manor were bound by their tenures to plow the lord's land, to mow his grass, to reap his corn, and to cut underwood in his woods for fire. They were also obliged to make the lord's fences round his woods within the manor, who furnished the materials for making them by permitting the tenants, whose lands border thereon, to enter one rod within the woods, and to cut the underwood for that purpose; and after they were repaired, the tenants were allowed to take the overplus of the underwoods so cut, to their own use; and from this service grew a custom, which prevails at this day, called *rod fall*, which the tenants now claim as a privilege. Many particulars concerning the villain services and customs of this manor are fully exemplified in a survey made thereof in the year 1593, by a jury on oath consisting of forty-eight persons, composed of both free and copyhold tenants, in which survey is inrolled many charters and records relating to the manor.

These villain services are also referred to by several inquisitions remaining in the Tower of London. I shall only mention a few of them. By an inquisition taken in 1326, after the death of Robert Lord Fitzwalter, the jury found that he held on the day of his death, in his demesne, as of fee, the manor

manor of Great Tey in the county of Essex, and that there were
within the said manor 500 acres of arable land worth 12*l.*
10*s. per annum*, the value of each acre 6*d.* and that there were
20 acres of meadow, which were worth *per annum* 60*s.* and 10
acres of pasture, of the yearly value of 10*s.* and 10 acres of
wood and underwood, which were worth *per annum* 3*s.* 4*d.* and
there were 2070 villain services, called Winter Works, to be performed annually by the base tenants or copyholders of the manor, between the feast of St. Michael and the gules of August,
which were of the annual value of 4*l.* 3*s.* 4*d.* the value of each
man's labour one halfpenny *per diem*; and also 580 villain
services, called Autumnal Works, to be performed by the
copyholders of the manor, between the gules of August and
the feast of St. Michael, which were valued at 48*s.* 4*d.* the
value of each day's labour 1*d.* and there were 60 days
ploughing to be done by the customary tenants, which were
of the value of 30*s.* &c. [*f*] By this inquisition it appears,
that the state of agriculture must have been very low at this
period, the arable land being valued at only six pence *per*
acre. The comparative value of the meadow was as six to
one, and that of the pasture as two to one. By another inquisition taken 2 Edw. III. after the death of the Lord Robert
Fitzwalter, lord of this manor. " Juratores dicunt, &c.
" quod est ibidem de servitiis & consuetudinibus villanorum
" ij mil. c opera Yema'is que valent ijd. vijs. vjd. pretium operis
" obolum. Item, sunt ibidem 680 opera Autumpnal' que
" valent 48*s.* 4*d* pretium operis 1*d.* Item, sunt ibidem 60
" arurae quae valent 30*s.* pretium arurae 6*d.* Item, sunt ibi-
" dem viij *Au opes* que valent ij *s.* [*g*]" By the same inquisi-

[*f*] By the survey of the manor abovementioned it appears, that in the reign
of king Henry V. several villain services were commuted for by rents, which is
the reason why many small copyhold estates pay large quit-rents.

[*g*] Esc. 2 Edw. III. n. 59. A. D. 1328.

tion

tion it was found that capons, hens, and eggs, were annually paid to the lord.

Several singular customs prevailed in this manor, which appear to be worthy of observation. In one of the manor books I find the following entry.

"Memorandum. Anno Dom. 1613, Robert Audeley, Esq.
" then lord of the manor of Much Tey, required of the cus-
" tomary tenants or copyholders, a duty due to him, as he
" and his steward Ezekiel Rayner affirmed, of forty shillings,
" called *Onziell*, which of long time had not been paid,
" and no copyholder could remember any such duty in their
" time demanded ; whereupon the tenants required of the lords
" a day until the lord's court next following. The tenants re-
" teyned for their council Mr. Wakering of Kelvedon, and Mr.
" Beriffe of Colchester. The lord by his steward then shewing to
" these counsellors all such rolls as they supposed would have
" proved that this duty of *onziell* ought yearly to be paid ;
" the counsellors' answer was, *viz.* That it did appear to
" them to be true, that in the time of Mungomery, who was
" then lord of the said manor, his copyholders which held
" of that manor paid him that duty of forty shillings *per an-
" num*, called *onziell*, during his life, and were still to con-
" tinue payment of the same, so long as the said manor con-
" tinued in that blood unsold, (which seemed to them to be
" the meaning of the word *onziell*) ; but after his death one
" Wiseman marrying Mungomery's widow, and the said
" Wiseman purchasing the manor of Mungomery's heirs, who
" sold the same, the said duty of forty shillings *per annum*,
" called *onziell*, ceased payment, and so hath continued ever
" since, as being no such duty due to the lord."

These opinions manifest, that neither the lord's steward nor the counsel understood the nature of the claim ; for it is

called

abfurd to fuppofe, that an ancient right or cuftom could have been annihilated by an alienation of the manor, but ftill it was difficult to difcover, what this cuftomary payment of *anziell* or *ouziell* was [h]. On infpecting the old furvey of the manor above mentioned, I found, that the word was written unzeld, which, in an inquifition remaining in the Tower of London, hereafter to be quoted, will appear to be a tallage, payable by ancient cuftom, called unʒeſd or unʒelo, as it ought to have been written ; but the Saxon letters having long been difufed, the Norman fcribes adopted the Gothic ʒ, a character which was familiar to them, inſtead of the Saxon ʒ, to them unknown. This word unʒelo is frequently to be met with in the ancient records, charters, and grants of the Emperors and Princes of Germany, whereby they difcharged their vaffals from the payment of *ungelds* [i]. Gaffar in Annal. Augfburg. has the following paffage, which feems a probable etymology : " Tributa feu collectæ, quas plebs fuo idiomate " ungeltam, hoc eſt indebitum appellare confuevit." The people feem to have thought it a payment which ought not to have been made. Skinner, in his Etymologicon, explains this word *infolutus*, which he derives from the Saxon negative Un and Gildan folvere. Somner cites the fame word in his Gloffary from John Brompton's Chronicle, which is explained unpaid. In Germany this word is ſtill written *ungeld*, *umbgeld*, *angeld*, *omgelt*, and it is often made fynonymous with *tributum* [k]. The inquifition above alluded to, which

[h] At firſt I fuppofed that there might have been a cuftom which obliged the bafe copyholders to feed the lord's young hawks, for *ewal* or *eſol* is an obfolete French word for a bird, and *eſelr* is a little bird, particularly a hawk, fee Cotgrave in his French Dictionary; but this fuppofition is proved by records to be erroneous.

[i] See Du Cange's Gloffary.

[k] See Adeling's German Dictionary, voc. Ungeld.

was taken at Chelmsford in the first year of the reign of king Henry the Sixth, A. D. 1422, after the death of Humphry lord Fitzwalter, shews, that ungelb or unʒelb, as it was corruptly written, was a tallage of forty shillings to be annually paid to the lord, according to ancient custom, at the feast of St. Michael [*f*], which was an arbitrary tax imposed on the base tenants of this manor by one of its ancient possessors before the Conquest, and I am inclined to think so, because the word is Saxon, derived from the Teutonic or German. It is well known, that it was customary for the chieftains among the Germans, and for the great lords in the times of the Saxons, to subject their villani of the lower order to arbitrary impositions. Thus it appears, that the payment of ungelb was a tallage paid to the lords of the manor in ancient times, long before the family of Montgomery acquired it, and therefore it could not have been a personal payment to Sir John Montgomery for his life only, as was suggested by the council.

Many estates in this manor were subject to the *Marcheta Mulierum*, which custom has commonly been supposed to be a right which the lord had, of passing the first night after marriage with his female villain. The best historians of

[*f*] Inquisitio capta apud Chelmesford, in com. Essex, coram Johanne de Kirkeby, Escaetore, Domini Regis, per sacramentum, Johannis Semy, & al'. Qui dicunt, &c. quod manerium de Magna Tey eum pertinentiis, in Comitatu predicto, et alia materia, &c. in manu domini regis devenerunt, ratione minoris etatis Walteri fil' Walteri, &c. Et dicunt quod omnia predicta materia de Magna Teye, ac manerium de Uphalle, &c. tenentur de domino rege ut parcell' baroniae de Baynard's Castle, per servicium militare. *Et que quid m materia de Magna Teye, fuit, &c. Et Tallagium confuetam, de quodam antiqua confuetara, vocat. unʒelb* &c. solvend'. ad festum sancti Michaelis per ann. et placita et perquif. curiae, &c. Esc' 1 Hen. VI. n. 56.

4   Scot-

Scotland, also Dr. Plot, Bayle, and others [*n*], as well as several foreign authors, have given many marvellous and indecent particulars concerning this custom, which some writers have asserted was not abolished in Scotland till the reign of Malcolm the Third; but, on diligent inquiry, I am of opinion that this kind of intercourse between the lord and his female villain never existed. Many of the relations concerning this custom are too absurd to deserve attention. The materials, collected by the writers who endeavour to support the opinion above referred to, tend to the establishing a system, in support of which much reading has been misapplied.

I will not trouble your lordship or the Society with entering into particulars, but will proceed to inquire what this custom really was, which prevailed not only in many manors in England, Wales, Scotland, and the Isle of Guernsey, but also on the Continent.

I am persuaded that I shall be able to prove to the satisfaction of the Society, that the *Marcheta* was a compact between the lord of a manor and his villain, for the redemption of an offence committed by the unmarried daughter of his vassal; but more generally it was a fine paid by a sokeman or a villain to his lord, for a licence to marry his daughter, and if the vassal gave her away without obtaining such licence, he was liable to pay a fine. This was sometimes termed *Maritagium*, but that word must be distinguished in this sense, from the same word in its more general import. There are two records quoted by Sir Henry Spelman which explain this custom. Extenta manerii de Wivenho (Com. Essex), 18 Dec. 40 Edw. III.

[*n*] Boethius's Hist. vol. III. p. 35. Plot's History of Staffordshire, p. 178. Bayle's Dict.

" Ric-

" Ric. Burre tenet unum mesuagium et debet talliagium,
" sectam curiæ, & merchet, hoc modo, *quod si maritare vo-*
" *luerit filiam suam cum quodam libero homine, extra villam, fa-*
" *ciet pacem domini pro maritagio, & si eam maritaverit alicui*
" *custumario villæ, nihil dabit pro maritagio.*"

" Placita coram concilio domini regis. Term' Mich. 57
" Hen. III. Rot. 4. Suffolk. Johanna Deakeny attachiata fuit
" ad respondend. hominibus de Berkholt, quare exigit ab eis
" alia servitia, &c. Unde dicitur quod tempore regis H.
" (Henry II.) avi regis, solebant habere talem consuetudinem,
" quod quando maritare volebant filias suas, solebant dare
" *pro filiabus suis maritandis* duas Oras, quæ valent 32 de-
" narios, &c. postea veniunt homines et concedunt quod de-
" bent dare *merchetum* pro filiabus suis maritandis scilicet 32
" denarios." Bracton mentions this as a villain custom.
" Qui tenet in villenagio talliari potest ad voluntatem do-
" mini. Item dare *merchetum*, ad filiam maritandum, & mer-
" chetum vero pro filia dare non competit libero homini, inter
" alia propter liberi sanguinis privilegium [n]."

The probable reason of the custom appears to have been
this. Persons of low rank residing on an estate were generally
either *ascripti glebæ*, or were subjected to some species of ser-
vitude, similar to the *ascripti glebæ*, the tenants were bound to
reside on the estate, and to perform several services to the
lord. As women necessarily followed the residence of their
husbands, the consequence was, that when a woman of low
rank married a stranger, the lord was deprived of part of his
live flock; he therefore required a fine to indemnify him
for the loss of his property. In process of time this compo-

[n] Bracton, 4. T. l. c. 28. 2. T. l. c. 8. f. 2.

sition

sition was thrown into the aggregate sum of quit rents, as appears by the ancient survey of this manor above referred to.

The following instances extracted from the records of different manors will elucidate this custom, and tend to confirm what has been said concerning it. By the custom of the manor of Brayes, in the county of Warwick, the tenants were not to marry their daughters, or make their son's priests, without licence from their lord. Blount, p. 247, edit. 1784.

A villain in Clymeshond in Cornwall, was not to send his son to school, nor marry his daughter, without the prince's licence; and, when he died, the lord was to have all his chattels. Ib. 250.

By the custom of the manors of Thurgarton and Horsepoll, in the county of Nottingham, every nief or the villain who took a husband, or committed fornication, paid *marchet* for redemption of her blood 5s. 4d. and the daughter of a cottager half a marchet; and, in Fiskerton and Moreton, in the same county, every she native who committed fornication paid as aforesaid, to the lord, in lieu of *marcheta mulierum*. Ibid. 264. The *marchet* of Howel Dha was the fine for the marriage of a daughter. Ib. 268. In the manor of Brug or Burg, in the county of Salop, when a customary tenant married his daughter out of the manor, he was to pay the lord 3s. Also he was to give for every lierwyte 2s. Ib 267 [a] Further particulars on the *marcheta* are to be found in Sir David Dalrymple's Annals of Scotland, vol. I. Appendix.

The Guildhall, where the lord's courts have been immemorially held, is an ancient structure, which for several ages

[a] Lierwyte or Lairwyte is from the Saxon Lagan, concubere, to lie together; and Fine merited, a fine imposed upon offenders in adultery and fornication, and payable to the lord of the manor.

has

has been granted by copy of court-roll to trustees for the use of the poor of the parish, the lords reserving to themselves the right of holding their courts therein according to ancient usage.   Near to the Guildhall there is a field called the Play-field or Playing-place, where the young men exercised themselves in archery and other manly diversions [*p*] ; the herbage is at this day held by copy of court-roll ; but, in the year 1727, John Lay, the copyhold tenant, forbid the inhabitants to play in the said field as formerly, and in order to prevent them broke it up, and sowed the same with oats, notwithstanding their remonstrances ; whereupon they assembled on Trinity Monday, made bonfires, and diverted themselves as usual, and of course destroyed the oats. Lay indicted them for the trespass, the inhabitants joined issue, and pleaded, that they and their predecessors had used the said field as a common playing place, time whereof the memory of man was not to the contrary, and the cause was tried before Lord Chief Justice Eyre, at the assizes at Brentwood, on Friday August 19th, 1728. The defendants proved, that for upwards of seventy years the young people of Tey, and of the neighbouring parishes, had used the said field as a common playing place every Trinity Monday, which was the time of holding the fair at Great Tey, and they produced an arrow which had been used in

---

[*p*] In 11 Hen. VII. A. D. 1496, John Warren surrendered to Robert Knight, and others, the herbage of a piece of land, containing one rood, for the enlargement of a common playing place, " pro architenentibus licitis, ex intentione per " dominum istius manerii ex antiquo sic concessum." Tenend. pro annal Reddit. 2d. In the 34th of Queen Elizabeth Samuel Motcham was admitted to the herbage and pasture of the common playing place, per Reddittum 2d. " et per-nittendo architenentes sagittacios, et lusores villæ prædictæ ibidem habere uti et gaudere loca sua, more solito et consueto, absque impedimento seu vexatione, secundum verum intentionem prædicti Johannis Warren donationis inde." Survey of the Manor made 35 Eliz. A. D. 1593.

shooting at butts in the said playing-place above sixty years before, which butts were standing in the memory of most of the witnesses, and that the plaintiff and his predecessors were only admitted to the feeding and pasturage, and that the lord of the manor and another magistrate, refused the plaintiff a warrant against the young men for playing in the said field. The defendants were found not guilty, and the Lord Chief Justice Eyre said, that he did not think an action of trespass would hold, but that the defendants might justify their action of right. Upon the hearing of this cause a question arose, whether townsmen could be witnesses, the Chief Justice allowed of them, because it was not only the parishioners of Great Tey, who had a right to play in the said field, but those of other parishes.

I shall conclude by giving your Lordship, and the Society, a short account of the descent of the manor. In the Saxon times this manor was possessed by earl Alfgar, who was succeeded by his daughter Ælflede, or Ægelflede, the wife of Brithnorth duke of the East Angles, and after her decease by Æthelflede her sister, who was married to duke Æthelstan, on whose death it was given to the monastery of Stoke near Neyland, which was the burying-place of the family, and perhaps, says Tanner, founded by some of them. Earl Alfgar lived in the tenth century [q]. At the time of the Survey it was possessed by Eustace earl of Bologne; from earl Eustace it came to his third son, Eustace, also earl of Bologne, whose daughter Maud brought it in marriage to her husband Stephen earl of Blois, afterwards king of England. King Stephen gave it to his third son, William earl

[q] See the testaments of the two daughters of earl Alfere, in Wotton's short View of Hickes's Thesaur. London, 1708, 4to. p. 60. 63, and Tanner's Notitia, p. 508.

of

of Mortain and Surrey, who granted it to Richard de Lacy, Lord of Diss in Norfolk, and Chief Justice of England in 1162, who died without issue male January 14th, 1179. Maud, his eldest daughter, was married to Walter Fitz-Robert, great grandson of Gislebert earl of Eu in Normandy, who came into England with the Conqueror, and ancestor of the noble family of Fitzwalter. This lady brought Great Tey, and many other estates in the counties of Essex, Norfolk, and Suffolk, to her husband Walter Fitz Robert, on whose death, in 1158, his estates descended to Robert Fitz Walter his son, whose descendants enjoyed this manor, with other large possessions, till the death of Robert lord Fitzwalter in 1432. Soon after it was possessed by Sir John Montgomery, knight. Sir Thomas his son succeeded him, who died January 2d, 1494, without issue, whereupon his sister Philippa brought this manor to her husband Francis Bryan, esq. who, in 1532, had licence to sell it to Thomas lord Audeley, Lord Chancellor of England, in whose family it continued till the 24th of June, 1704, when Henry Audeley, esq. sold this manor, with its demesnes and dependencies to George Cressener of London. In May, 1771, his son, George Cressener, esq. his Majesty's Minister Plenipotentiary to the Electors of Mentz, Triers, and Cologn, and to the Circle of Westphalia, with other necessary parties, conveyed the said manors and estates to

Your Lordship's

most faithful and

Battersea-Rise,   most obedient Servant,
May 22, 1754.

                    THOMAS ASTLE.

                           V.

V. *An Account of some Druidical Remains in* Derbyshire. *In a Letter to the Right Honourable* Fre-
derick Montagu, F. A. S. *By* Hayman Rooke, *Esq.*
F. A. S.

Read March 13, 1794.

DEAR SIR,

IN this letter I have ventured to describe some Druidical
remains in Derbyshire hitherto unnoticed, which, if you
think sufficiently interesting to be communicated to the Society, I must beg you will do me the honour to present to
them.

The investigation of monuments of remote antiquity, is an
interesting pursuit to an Antiquary; and undoubtedly the
most ancient we have in Britain are those of the Druids,
whose religion was, most probably, that of the Patriarch Abra-
ham, brought into this island by a Phœnician colony soon
after his time. Dr. Stukeley was of this opinion, and observes,
that " the Druid Philosophers and Priests are never spoken
" of in antiquity but with a note of admiration ; and are
" always ranked with the Magi of the Persians, the Gymno-
" sophists of the Indians, the Prophets and Hierophants of
" the Egyptians, and those sort of Patriarchal Priests, whose
" orders commenced before idolatry began, from whom the
" Pythagoreans, Platonists, and Greek Philosophers, learned
" the best things they knew [a]."

[a] Stukeley's Preface to Stonehenge.

As the Druids never committed their sacred mysteries to writing, the only clew we have left, by which we can trace the religious rites and judicial ceremonies of this extraordinary order of priests and magistrates, is their rock monuments and temples; which, notwithstanding the lapse of time, are still to be found in great numbers variously dispersed in this kingdom.

Though these that are left give sufficient evidence to an accurate observer, of their having been formed partly by art, and made occasionally to move; yet there are many people who seem to think the rocking stones, rock idols, and other singular shaped rocks, to have been formed by some violent convulsion in nature, and are merely the effect of chance.

In my Druidical researches I have carefully examined above thirty rocking stones; and they all plainly appeared to have been formed by art, particularly those among Brimham rocks [b]. Toland tells us how these rocking stones were contrived, as mentioned by Sir Robert Sibbald in the Appendix to his History of Fife and Kenross. " That gentle-
" man speaking of the rocking stone near Balvaird (or the
" Bards town), I am informed, says he, that this stone was
" broken by the usurper Cromwell's soldiers; and it was
" discovered then, that its motion was performed by a yolk
" extuberant in the middle of the under surface of the upper
" stone, which was inserted in a cavity in the surface of the
" lower stone [c]."

Most of those that I have examined have had their bottoms sloped off, some towards the centre of the stone, others have

[b] See a description of these curious Druidical Monuments in Archæologia, vol. VIII. p. 210.

[c] Toland, vol. I. p. 106.

had

A Rocking Stone, on Ashover Common, Derbysh.   A Rock Idol, called the Turning St.

had three sides sloped, and some only two; by this artful contrivance the stones could only be put in motion from some particular parts.

There is in the Peak of Derbyshire a very remarkable rocking stone, called by the country people *Robin Hood's Mark*; it stands on the edge of a declivity near the top of a hill on Ashover common, looking down upon Overton hall, an estate of Sir Joseph Banks, Bart. the respectable President of the Royal Society, who will undoubtedly preserve this curious Druidical monument.

Fig. 1. plate V. represents the South view of this rocking stone, which, from its extraordinary position, evidently appears not only to have been the work of art, but to have been placed with great ingenuity; the two upper stones (a and b) have been shaped to fit exactly with the two upright stones (c and d) on which they rest; and so artfully contrived, that the lower stone (b) moves with the upper stone (a). It measures about 26 feet in circumference.

That this is a Druidical monument formed by art, cannot, I think, be denied; we are assured that the Druids were well skilled in the art of magic, by which the superstitious Britons were led implicitly to believe in the miracles performed by these rocking stones.

At about two hundred yards North of this rocking stone, is a singular shaped rock called the *turning stone*. See fig. 2. plate V. It stands on the edge of a hill on Ashover common; height nine feet. It was a very ancient practice among the Britons to make three turns round their sacred rocks and fires, according to the course of the sun. Martin, in his account of the Western isles, says, " that in the Isle of Barry there is one stone about seven feet high, and when the inhabitants come

near

near it, they take a religious turn round according to the ancient Druid custom." Hence there is great reason to suppose,
that the above-mentioned stone was a rock idol to whom the
Druids offered up their devotional rites.

The augurial seat, or rock chair, is another curious Druidical monument, which was never taken notice of till I difcovered thofe on Harborough rocks [*d*]. In my vifits at
Wingerworth, the elegant and hofpitable manfion of Sir
Henry Hunloke, Bart. I had frequent opportunities of ex-
ploring that neighbourhood, and Sir Henry very obligingly
shewed me fome rocks upon his eftate called *Stone-edge,* or
more properly *Stainedge* cliff, at the Eaft end of the moor,
about two miles and a half from Wingerworth, and four
from Chefterfield.

On examining the rocks upon this cliff, which is rather
difficult of accefs, I found a large flat rock with five rock bafons on the top, evidently cut with a tool. Fig. 3. plate V.
is a view of the cliff where (a) is the flat rock with the bafons.
Fig. 4. plate V. is a plan of the top of that rock; the furface
is 59 feet by 57, the rock bafon (a) is 3 feet diameter by 2,
and 1 foot three inches deep; that marked (b) is three feet
diameter, (c) 3 feet 5 inches diameter; the two fmall oval
bafons are about 1 foot 8 inches in length, and each has a
little channel to carry off the water when it gets near the top.

There is fomething remarkable in the chafms and little
holes on the outfide of thefe rocks, as may be feen in the
perfpective view fig. 3. They appear to have been formed
by art, and were probably intended for the myfterious purpofes of auguration, to which the fituation is well adapted.

[*d*] See an account of thefe and other augurial feats in Archæologia, vol. IX.
p. 207

Ae

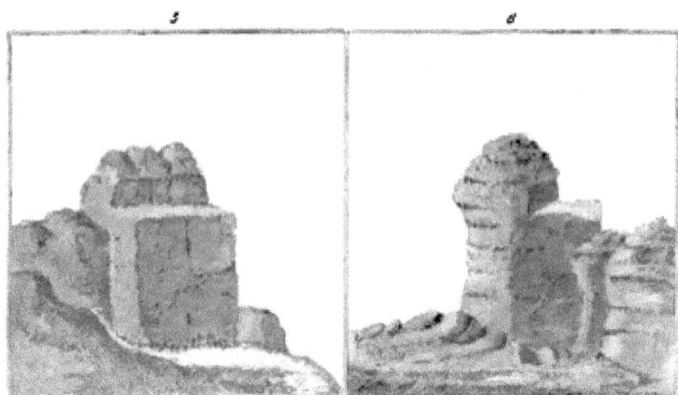

Two views of an Augural seat on Stanedge Cliff near Wingerworth

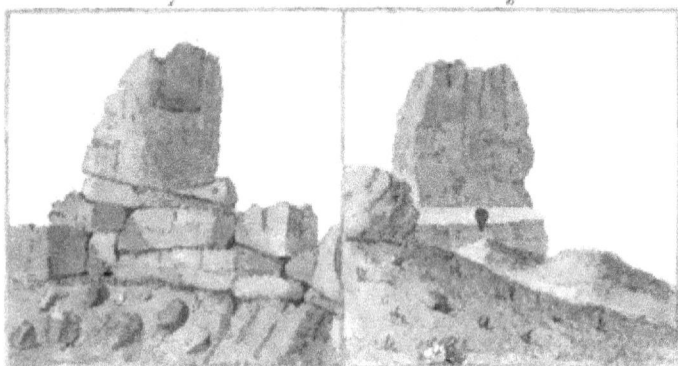

Two views of another Augural seat on the same Cliff.

At about 140 yards East of the rock basons and in the same cliff is an augurial seat cut in a rock ; see two views of this seat in plate VI. fig. 5 and 6 ; height 16 feet.   At the distance of 30 yards East of this rock is another augurial seat, two views of which are represented in fig. 7. and 8.

The view fig. 7 is taken from the bottom of the cliff; its elevated situation made every attempt to measure it impracticable, but it bears the same proportion to the other, allowing for the distance in perspective.

Fig. 8 is the back part of the same rock, where there is another seat with a rock bason cut in the middle of it, evidently the work of art, which is also visible in shaping the front part, fig. 7, and where the stone (a) plainly appears to have been cut like a wedge to support the rock under which it is placed.

The mark of the tool is plainly to be perceived in forming, in a rough manner, these rocks for their occasional augurations.   The rock basons seem necessarily connected with these augurial seats, as I observed in a former paper [e].

Dr. Borlase tells us, that " the Druids were the Magi of the " Britons, and had a great number of rites in common with " the Persians ; now one of the chief functions of the Magi of " the East was to divine, that is, to explain the will of the " Gods, and foretell future events ; the term *magus* signi- " fying among the ancients not a magician in the modern " sense, but a superintendant of sacred and natural know- " ledge [f]."

We are well assured that the Druids divined by augury, from the observations they made on the flight of birds and other ominous appearances.

[e] Archæologia, vol. IX. p. 208.
[f] Antiquities of Cornwall, chap. xxi. p. 138.

The [catchword]

The above-mentioned learned author fays, "The Druids
" also (as we have great reason to think) pretended to pre-
" dict future events, not only from holy wells and running
" streams, but from the rain and snow water, which, when
" settled, and afterwards stirred either by oak-leaf or branch,
" or magic wand, might exhibit appearances of great in-
" formation to the quick-sighted Druid, or seem so to do to
" credulous enquirers, when the priest was at full liberty to
" represent the appearances as he thought most for his pur-
" pose [g]."

From the number of rock basons we meet with among
other Druidical monuments it is evident, that they used
this fort of hydroman.y ; and from the rock bason being annexed to the above-mentioned feat it seems as if the Druids
thought it a necessary part in their mysterious rituals of auguration.

At the South-west end of Stanton moor, in the Peak, and
in Hartle liberty, is an assemblage of rocks, which stand on
the summit of a circular hill called *Graned Tor*, but more
commonly known by the name of *Mock Beggar's Hall*.
When I had the honour of communicating to the Society
some years ago an account of the Druidical monuments in
that neighbourhood, I had not an opportunity of examining
this Tor with that accuracy which is necessary in the investigation of these ancient monuments ; but having been since
in the vicinity of these rocks, at the house of my worthy
friend Bache Thornhill, esq. to whose politeness I am much
indebted, I frequently examined every accessible part of this
Tor, and, notwithstanding the many large rocks that have
fallen from the top, there is sufficient evidence of its having

[g] Antiquities of Cornwall, p. 140.

been

N.W. View of Grame Tor, or Mock Beggars Hall, at the S.W. end of Langton ...

Nº 10.

In my account of the Brimstone rocks, I gave drawings of two that have apertures cut through them; in which there are rock basons [h]. These sheltered basons are very remarkable, and seem to have been so contrived, that no water could get into them but what had been first filtrated through their sacred rocks, which the Druids would look upon as having been divinely purified.

On the other side of the rock (f) in fig. 9, Plate VII. is an exact circular hole, as is seen in fig. 11, Plate VIII. which is a South view of the Tor. I found there was no possibility of getting near enough to examine this rock, but I should suppose, from the little channels on the other sides, that there are rock basons on the top.

There are many large rocks scattered about, which must have fallen from the top, where, when they stood erect, filling up every part of this elevated Tor, the effect must have been sublimely striking to the superstitious Britons, who had been taught to venerate those sacred rocks.

That the Druids had fixed upon this hill for the celebration of their religious rites, I think cannot be doubted; it was usual to inclose their places of worship, and here a fence of large rough stones now plainly appears to have surrounded the rocks near the bottom of the hill.

Fig. 12, Plate VIII. is a South-east view of three remarkable hills at the South end of Stanton moor, on which there are Druidical monuments (a). Carcliff rocks on the top are a rocking stone and several rock basons [i]; at the foot of these rocks at (b) is a hermitage [k]. The rocks marked

[h] Archæologia, vol. VIII. No. 4 and 8, plate 16.
[i] See a description of these in Archæologia, vol. VI. p. 112.
[k] Ibid. p. 112.

I   (c)

been a curious group of Druidical monuments. Fig. 9, Pl. VII. is a North-weſt view of Graned Tor; the rock marked (a) with four rock baſons, is 29 feet in circumference, and plainly appears, from its preſent poſition, to have fallen from the top. The three ſtones (b, c, d,) ſeem to have been placed by art; and the uppermoſt is, I think, very likely to be a rocking ſtone, but there was no poſſibility of getting near enough to make the experiment. Whilſt I was taking a drawing of this Tor, an old man who ſtood by, told me that he remembered when he was a boy, his grandfather's pointing to the ſtone (b), and ſaying, it had always been called the Great Altar, and that ſeveral other rocks had names, but he had forgot what they were. We are led by traditional accounts to form probable conjectures: and, as the Heathens always placed their altars on their higheſt ground, there is great reaſon to ſuppoſe that this elevated rock was a Druidical altar.

At the bottom of the third rock from the top, marked (d), is a large rock baſon of an oval ſhape, diameter 4 feet by 2 feet 10 inches, which evidently appears to be cut with a tool; the rock (c) is placed ſlopingly againſt the rock (d), and forms a kind of cavity, big enough to hold three or four people, in which is the rock baſon above-mentioned.

Fig. 10 is a near view of this aperture, whence there is a very extenſive proſpect, of courſe well calculated for the purpoſe of divination.

We have reaſon to ſuppoſe, that the Druids had the rite of water luſtrations, and the prieſt might purify his hands in this holy-water, which had never touched the earth before he officiated at the high altar.

6   In

A view of Grand Tar.

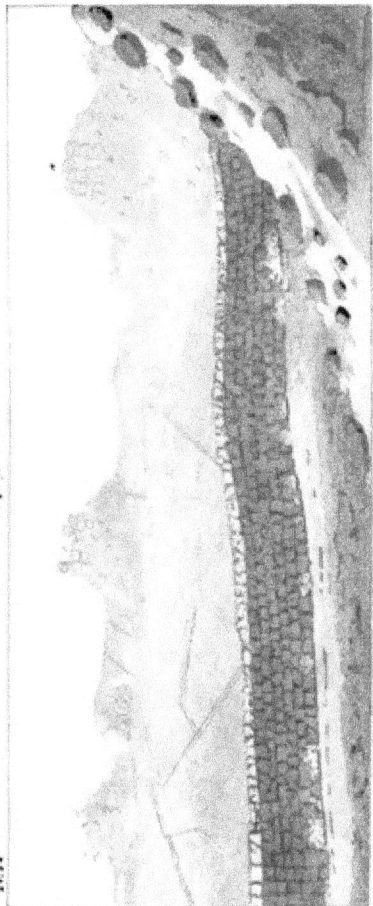

A View of these Hills near Barton Mines on which there are Cumberland Beacons etc.

(c) form Graned Tor, or Mock Beggars Hall; the hill (d) is Dutwood Tor, where (e) is a rock canopy that hangs over an augurial feat; on the top of this Tor are three rock bafons, evidently cut with a tool [*l*].

This view was taken from near the bottom of the hill (f), on which there are feveral large rocks called Bradley rocks; on the top is a large rocking ftone [*m*].

I flatter myfelf you will agree with me in lamenting, that thefe curious remains of antiquity fhould have been fo much neglected, and that the want of attention, in not making accurate obfervations on the form and conftruction of thefe rock monuments, fhould occafion a difbelief of their being Druidical.

　　　　I am, with great refpect,

　　　　　　Dear Sir,

　　　　　　　　Your fincere and

　　　　　　　　　　much obliged

　　　　　　　　　　　　humble Servant,

　　　　　　　　　　　　　　H. ROOKE.

[*l*] See Archæologia, vol. IX. pp. 209, 210.
[*m*] Ibid. vol. VI. p. 111.

VI. *An Epistolary Dissertation upon the Life and Writings of* ROBERT WACE, *an Anglo-Norman Poet of the 12th Century. In a Letter to the Earl of Leicester, President of the Society of Antiquaries.*

Read December 4, 1794.

MY LORD,

IT was under the reign of Henry the Second of England that there flourished a celebrated Anglo-Norman poet named WACE, whose works, at that time the delight of the monarch and his court, are at present to be esteemed as one of the most ancient monuments of French literature ; but inasmuch as France owes these precious relics to a king of Great Britain, and as their author was born in a country which has continually remained since the Conquest under the power of the English, you will, doubtless, my Lord, peruse with some degree of satisfaction a memoir upon the life and writings of this Poet. The discussion will probably be deemed interesting, both upon account of its novelty, and from the circumstance of this writer being altogether unknown to the English Biographers ; besides, most of those learned men who have written upon his works have been entirely mistaken, either in the series of them which they have given, or in the opinions which they have adopted relating to them. It is my object, my Lord, to correct their errors ; and I shall endeavour

deavour to do this with that diffidence which should ever
guide the man of letters, and whilst it prevents criticism from
degenerating into satire, will, doubtless, render it more worthy of your approbation.

The Poet Wace was born in the Isle of Jersey, and although
the precise time of his birth is unknown, it is easy from his
own works to ascertain it in a manner not very distant from
the truth. This author informs us that he had seen three
Henries, all Kings of England and Dukes of Normandy; so
that he lived under Henry I. Stephen, Henry II. and Henry
the eldest son of the latter, who was crowned king in his father's
life-time, and died before him in 1183: he also mentions
that he was *clere lisant* under these three monarchs; from
which it may be inferred that he was born in the beginning
of the reign of Henry I., that is, in the early part of the 12th
century.

Monsieur Huet, Bishop of Avranches, in his *Origines de
Caen*, page 412, assures us that the Christian name of *Wace*
was *Robert*; and Ducange in his Dissertations upon the History of St. Louis, page 108, gives him that of *Matthew*. It
is impossible for us to determine upon which side the error
lies; the poet, who often names himself in his works, has
not amongst all those which we have perused, both in France
and England, once mentioned his Christian name. Upon
all these occasions he styles himself *Maitre Wace, Clere-lisant,*
or *Clere de Caen*; nevertheless the opinion of Monf. Huet has
prevailed, and is adopted by all the French and English
Literati.

La Rocque in his History of the House of Harcourt [a],
and Fevret de Fontette in his French Historical Library [b],

[a] T. III. p. 13 and 35.   [b] T. III. p. 369.
H 2   main-

maintain that Wace lived under William I.; but this is
an error the more manifest, as it is refuted by the Poet's
own evidence, who declares that he lived under the three
Henries, and he would have been equally particular had
he been the Conqueror's subject [c]; besides, no skilful critic
will regard the style of Wace as that of a writer of the
11th century; and since he himself in relating the history of
William I. observes, that he had collected the facts from the
mouths of those who were witnesses, or had taken them from
the memoirs of those times, there is additional evidence that
they did not happen during his own life, and that he cannot
therefore be deemed contemporary with the Conqueror.

Monsieur de la Curne, in his Dissertation on the principal
Monuments relating to the History of France, has said that
Wace did not live before the 14th century [d], an anachro-
nism too obvious to need a serious refutation.

Wace commenced his studies at Caen, a city which at that
time had many celebrated schools. Some of these had been
established about the middle of the 11th century by Lanfranc,
Abbot of Caen, and afterwards Archbishop of Canterbury.
If we are to form a judgment of them from the great men
whom they have produced, they were equally famous with
those which he originally founded in the Abbey of Bec [r].

To the schools of Lanfranc may be added those which
were afterwards opened in the same city by the celebrated
Arnould, a man, who was raised by his talents to the pa-

[c] Treis reis Henriz vi et conoui,
    Et chose fisant en sue tens sui,
    Rei d'Engletere la garnie,
    Et duc so ent de Normendie.

[d] Mem. de l'Acad. des Inscript. t. XV. p. 582.

[e] Neustria Pia, p. 655. Henry's History of England, vol. III. b. iii.

triarchal

triarchal feat of Jerufalem. There was bred the celebrated Roger de Caen, whom he carried with him to the firft crufade, and who has left us a hiftory of it which is written in a ftyle but little inferior to that of Tacitus [*f*].

It was about this period that the young Wace was fent from Jerfey to Caen. After finifhing the firft part of his education, he travelled in France to complete it. Here, as he informs us, he remained fome time ; but it does not appear who were his other tutors, or in what places he received their leffons ; whether it was however from being diffatisfied with his fituation, or from the natural predilection of his countrymen in favour of the Englifh government, it is certain that he returned to Caen. Henry I. often kept his court in this city ; he had embellifhed it with many fumptuous edifices which ftill remain, and in this place Wace fettled. Hitherto he had not written any thing, and here it was that he made his firft Effay [*g*].

It is difficult to afcertain the firft fpecimen he exhibited of the literature of his time. We know that he had compofed many works, that he tranflated others into the language of his country, and that he particularly applied himfelf to the compofition of light poetry and of Romances.

It was in the latter kind of writings that he excelled moft. He affures us that he compofed a great number of Romances ; and, as moft of them have been preferved, it is

[*f*] See this hiftory in Martene's Thefaurus Anecdotorum, and in Muratori's Collection of Italian Hiftorians.

[*g*] En Ifle de Grefai fui nez,
A Caen fus petiz portez,
Iloques fui a letres mis,
Pois fui longues en France apris.

3 natural

natural to conclude that they were held in the same estimation
by his contemporaries as they have been by posterity [*b*].

It is proper to remark in this place, that the word *Romance* is not always to be understood as applicable to those
chimerical tales which have no other basis than the imagination of the inventor. During the 12th, 13th, and even the
14th centuries, every thing that was written in French or
Romance, or that was translated into that language, was
generally termed a *Romance*. Philip de Than, the most ancient of the Norman poets, and William another poet of the
same country, composed in verse a work upon the natural
history of animals, and each of them called his works a *Romance*. Richard d'Annebaut, likewise a Norman poet, translated into verse the Institutes of Justinian, which he says he
has *romanced*. Samson de Nanteuil versified the proverbs of
Solomon; Helie de Winchester, Cato's distichs; and both
of them call their translations a *Romance*.

We are not then to consider the Romances of Wace as the
offspring of a fertile imagination which has created events
for the purpose of embellishing them with the charms of
poetry; on the contrary they are monuments of antiquity
of the most respectable nature, inasmuch as they form for
the most part a precious repository of the Norman and
Anglo-Saxon history. When this poet wrote the history of
events which preceded him, he drew his materials from memoirs which then existed. He often cites the authors upon
whose faith he advances his facts, and of whom many have

[*b*] Quant jo de France repairai,
A Chaen longues conversai,
De romina faire m' entremis,
Mult en escris et mult en fis.

not

not been preferved to us. When he wrote the hiftory of his own times, he always relied upon the teftimony of eye-wit-neffes, or related what he himfelf had feen. In general he ufes the greateft candour in his narrations, and though he may fometimes appear to deal a little in the marvellous, he takes care to obferve that he has found what he advances fo written, and that he gives it in the fame manner.

After fo authentic a profeffion of veracity, fome modern authors who have treated Wace as a fabulous writer, may at leaft be accufed of inaccuracy ; but in commenting upon his works we fhall perceive, that either from their not having fufficiently inveftigated them, or from their having copied from each other, they have committed a great many errors. Even the celebrated Huet, and the learned Tyrwhitt, the only perfons who have fpoken of Wace with any degree of accuracy, are not exempt from miftakes in their opinions of the life and works of this author. This we fhall have occa-fion to obferve in the courfe of the following details.

The work which we have thought fit to place at the head of the writings of Wace is his tranflation in verfe of the fa-mous *Brut of England*. This poem is fo called from Brutus the great grandfon of Æneas, and firft king of the Britons. In it the poet often names himfelf, particularly at the begin-ning and end. He compofed it in the year 1155 ; and, accord-ing to Layamon, a prieft of Ernly upon Severn, who lived at this time, he prefented it to Eleanor the wife of Henry the Second [*i*].

This tranflation contains the hiftory of the kings of Great Britain, almoft from the deftruction of Troy to the

[*i*] Bibl. Cotton. Calig. A. IX.

2

year 689 of the common æra. Walter, archdeacon of Oxford, had imported the original from Armoric Britain, Geoffrey Arthur, otherwise called Geoffrey of Monmouth, translated it into Latin, and Wace into French verse.

Until this time there had been no idea whatever of the history of these British Kings; it had been unknown to venerable Bede. William of Malmsbury and Henry of Huntingdon, when they wrote their histories of England, had unsuccessfully made the most exact researches concerning this early period; and it was not until the year 1139 that the latter of these historians became acquainted with the *Brut* for the first time. Travelling this year to Rome with Theobald Archbishop of Canterbury, he resided some time in the abbey of Bec, of which this prelate had been abbot; there he met with the famous Robert de Thorigni, afterwards abbot of Mount St. Michael. This ecclesiastic, who was then composing his additions to the chronicles of Eusebius, St. Jerom, and Sigisbert, soon formed a connection with Henry of Huntingdon; and, in the course of conversation upon their respective works, presented him with the Latin translation of the history of British Kings, otherwise called the *Brut*, by Geoffrey of Monmouth. As the author of this work had taken care to make his chronology of these Kings accord with that of the Jews and the Romans, he gave to his fabulous history a very delusive appearance of reality; besides at this time criticism was hardly called into existence, and error was adopted in proportion as it was enveloped in the fascinating garb of the marvellous. Henry of Huntingdon made a Latin analysis of this work, and transmitted it to one of his friends in England [k], but this extract was not

[k] Bibl. Reg. 13 C. XI.

sufficient : and, as Geoffrey had tranflated the *Brut* into
Latin, Wace rendered it into French verfe ; Layamon, and
Robert de Brunne a Gilbertine monk, ufed the latter tranfla-
tion for their Englifh poetical verfion ; and, finally, Rufti-
cien de Pife tranflated it into French profe. In the Britifh
Mufeum are to be found feveral copies of Wace's *Brut*.

The firft is in the Royal Library, 13 A. XXI. and written in
the 13th century. The compiler of the catalogue in the account which he has given of this work in p. 218, informs us
that Wace continued the *Brut* till the reign of William Rufus.
This is an error which Mr. Cafley would not have fallen into
if he had only turned over the manufcript. He would have perceived, in p. 141, that Wace finifhed the *Brut*, as Geoffrey
Arthur had done, at the death of Cadwallader, about the end
of the feventh century ; after which follows the continuation
of this romance by Geoffrey Gaimar to the reign of William
Rufus.

The fecond is in the Cotton Library, Vitellius A. X. and
alfo written in the 13th century. The author of the catalogue of this library has committed the fame error, in not
having remarked that Wace had a continuator. This is,
however, the more difficult to perceive, becaufe the continuator and his tranfcriber have not only incorporated the two
works in fuch a manner that no title or other mark of diftinction feparates the refpective parts of the two poets, but
they have even fuppreffed the four laft lines in which Wace
has named himfelf and finifhed his work. This continuator
is not the fame as the former ; after having related fome
interefting facts during the reign of the Conqueror, and
which are not to be found elfewhere, he paffes with great
rapidity to his fucceffors as far as Henry III. whom he only

Vol. XII. I names,

names, and not to the reign of Edward I. as the author of
the catalogue had conceived.

The third is in the Harleian Collection, No. 6508. It is
written in the 14th century, but contains only Wace's *Brut*
without the supplement. The transcriber has written the
name of the poet *Gouce* and *Gace*, according to the French
practice of frequently substituting the G for the W.

Lastly, there is a fourth copy of the *Brut* in the library of
Corpus Christi, or Benet College, Cambridge, of which an
extract is given in the catalogue [*l*]. In this manuscript,
which is of the 14th century, the poet is called *Wace*.

With respect to the French manuscripts of this work, there
is a very superb one in folio in the Royal Library at Paris,
which, in the opinion of connoisseurs, is supposed to be coëval with the author. There are, without doubt, in the
same library many other copies; but, as the catalogue of
French manuscripts is not yet finished, it is impossible to say
what that precious collection contains upon the subject.

According to what has been advanced by Fauchet, Galland, La Combe, Gebelin, La Ravaliere, and other French
literati concerning *Wace's Brut*, it is certain that many other
copies of the work exist in public and private libraries at
Paris; but the discussion of the errors into which almost all
these writers have fallen in treating of this poet, will easily
demonstrate that the manuscripts they used were faulty, and
posterior to those which have been here enumerated.

Fauchet was the first who fell into a mistake concerning
the author of the *Brut* in French verse, in ascribing to him
at the same time the different names of *Eustache*, *Huistace*,
and *Wistace*. Whether it was that he had read his manu-

[*l*] Nasmith's Catal. p. 32.

script

script falsely, that he conceived the name of Wace to be a diminutive of *Euftache*, or in short that the manuscript was really interpolated, which appears most probable, he placed at the head of the French poets an *Euftache* who never existed, and deprived of that honour the poet Wace, who had a more genuine and less disputable right to it [*m*].

And yet, with a small portion of criticism, and the slightest notion of the principles of French poetry, Fauchet might have easily perceived his manuscript was faulty, and have corrected the error. Indeed, if in the first place the verses themselves which he has cited from the manuscript to prove that Euftache was the author of the *Brut* be considered, it will immediately be seen that they are written in the modern style, and not in the native purity of the ancient Norman language. Again, if it be remarked that the verses in this poem are always masculine of eight syllables, and feminine of nine, in all the old manuscripts, one shall be surprized to find, that in Fauchet's manuscript those wherein the poet is called *Huiftace* and *Wiftace* are masculine of nine syllables, a practice absolutely contrary to that which the poet has invariably pursued throughout his work ; whereas by substituting the name of *Wace*, as it is found in the ancient manuscripts, the verses acquire their precise and necessary measure.

But Fauchet was not the only person who was insensible that an ignorant or unfaithful transcriber had altered his manuscript. Monsieur Galland, in his treatise upon some of the ancient poets [*n*], likewise placed *Maiftre Euftache*, author of the *Brut*, at the head of the French poets. This he did

[*m*] Recueil de l'origine de la langue et de la poésie Franç. liv. II. p. 81.

[*n*] Mem. de l'Acad. des Inscrip. t. II. p. 728.

upon

upon the faith of a manuscript that had belonged to Tristan
de St. Amand, and was then in the library of Monsieur Fou-
cault. So far, however, from thereby supporting Fauchet's
mistake, this learned man was in possession of the means of
attacking it with advantage, and he actually does speak of
another collection which contained the *Romance of the Kings
of England*, by *Maistre Gasse*. Now, by comparing this second
manuscript with the first he might have seen that the verses
he has cited from it were the verses of the *Brut*; that he had
consequently two copies immediately before him; that they
only differed in the words *Eustache* and *Gasse*; and that in
short the variation arose from an error of the transcriber, which
the rules of criticism and poetry would have enabled him to
have easily corrected. But the more easy it was to get at the
truth, the more it seems to have escaped Monsieur Galland.
He perplexed the affair in such a manner as to make of
Eustache and *Gasse* two authors essentially different, and to
ascribe to the first the *Brut d'Angleterre*, and the *Roman des Rois
d'Angleterre* to the second, whilst they were literally one and
the same work.

Without penetrating more deeply into the subject, Monsieur de la *Ravaliere* has revived the imaginary *Eustache*.
He even attempts to prove that he was born in Poitou; he
contends that the manner in which the poet celebrates the
courage of the natives of this province in their combats
against Brutus, at once discovers his origin; and that a
writer cannot in this manner extol any other persons than his
countrymen; but, as in all these arguments he seems to have
forgotten that the poet only discharges the office of a translator, it is not difficult to perceive the fallacy of his logic, or
the improbability of his opinions [o].

[o] Révolutions de la langue Franç. à la tête des poésies du Roi de Navarre.
t. I. p. 145.

It

It is with concern that we find in Mr. Warton's History of English Poetry the existence of this *Eustache* renewed and defended [*p*]. This learned man had immediately before him the valuable manuscripts of the British Museum which refute it, together with Layamon and Robert de Brunne, who, in the 12th and 13th centuries, attest their having translated the *Brut* into English verse from the work of *Maitre Wace* [*q*]; and yet he prefers to these most weighty and decisive authorities that of Fauchet, who wrote at the end of the 13th century, and trusted to manuscripts equally faulty and unfaithful.

It is not worth while to take up more time in refuting the same error repeated by M. Rigoley in his Bibl. Franc. de la Croix du Maine et de du Verdier, vol. IV. p. 245; by le Court de Gebelin, in his preliminary discourse to Vol. V. of his Monde Primitif, p. iv. by La Combe, p. xvii. of the Preface, vol. II. of his Dictionnaire du vieux langage; by Mallieu in his Histoire de la Poësie Françoise, p. 109; and by la Borde, in his Histoire de la Musique Françoise, vol. II. p. 138, &c. We are persuaded that these Literati, in other respects men to be held in much esteem, have implicitly followed each other, without examination or previous discussion of the subject.

The learned Benedictines, editors of the New Collection of French Historians, admit that Wace is the author of the translation of *Brut* into verse; they confess that *his name has been differently given by ancient and modern historians*; and, embarrassed without doubt by the confusion of names ascribed

[*p*] History of English Poetry, vol. I. p. 62.

[*q*] Ibid. Cotton Calig. A. IX. Otho C. XIII. Robert de Brunne, in appendice ad Chronic. Pet. de Langtoft, t. I. p. xcviii.

to

to our poet in various parts of the manuscript copies of his works, they are of opinion that the names of *Wistace*, *Huistace*, *Huace*, *Gace*, *Gasse*, *Guase*, *Waice*, *Waise*, and even that of *Wace*, are all of them corruptions of the word *Eustace*, the true name to be adhered to [r].

But this decision being hazarded upon no foundation, and without proofs, we shall take the liberty of making a few observations upon the opinion which has been given by these learned compilers.

In the first place, we admit that modern writers have expressed the name of our poet in various ways; all of them have copied Fauchet, and have even added to his errors; but we shall venture to defy the reverend Fathers to cite a single ancient historian who has called him otherwise than *Wace*; and we have in our favour the testimony of Layamon and Robert de Brunne, who always call him so.

With respect to the manuscript copies of his works, we oppose against the Benedictines all those in the British Museum. The authority of these is so much the stronger, in as much as the poet being an Anglo-Norman, his works were better known in England and Normandy than elsewhere; so that his name never underwent any other alteration in those countries than by substituting the G. for the W. or *Gace* for *Wace*, in like manner as we find *Guillaume* for *Williaume*. If it was corrupted in the French manuscripts, it was upon account of its being less known in France, where the works of our poet were at first held but in little estimation. The king of Navarre is the only person among the old writers who has cited them [s]; but, as they are not in general favour-

[r] Nouvelle Collection des Historiens de France, tom. XIII. p. 220.
[s] Poesies du Roi de Navarre, t. II. p. . . . .

        I

                                        able

able to the kings of France, flattery without doubt, and perhaps rivalry, were the causes of restraining the pens of other writers from doing the same ; and to this alone, and not to a defect of merit, Monf. de la Borde ought to have ascribed their silence concerning this author (*t*). Besides, it must be granted that the protection which Henry II. of England afforded to men of letters, contributed much to the progress of the Romance or French language : it is to him that we owe the histories of Normandy by the poets *Wace* and *Benoit*, the several translations of the *Brut of England*, with those of the *Romances of the Round Table* ; in a word it was from England and Normandy that the French received the first works which deserve to be cited in their language. The first manuscripts of *Wace* that found their way into France preserved in that country their native purity, such as the *Brut* in the royal library, which has been already spoken of, and in which the poet calls himself *Wace*, as he does in those preserved in the British Museum. Monsieur Lancelot, who had examined many others of the same age, found in all the same denomination ; but afterwards, when copies began to multiply in a country where the poet had not been known, every transcriber altered his name : and thence the very numerous variations which have deceived modern writers and occasioned their repeated mistakes. Such were, we apprehend, the real causes of the corruptions in the name of *Wace*.

But we cannot agree with the Benedictines, that this name is to be derived from that of *Euftache* ; and, for the purpose of objecting to them an authority which precludes any reply, we beg leave to cite our poet himself, who, speaking of *Euftache d'Abbeville*, one of the knights who came over with

[t] Hist. gener. de la Musque Franc. t. II. p. 13ᵗ.

William.

William I. at the Conquest, calls him *Wiestace d'Abbeville*, and not *Wace d'Abbeville.* [u]

Before we finish this article, it will be proper to notice the equally erroneous opinions of Wanley and Nicolfon [w]. Layamon having declared that he had rendered the *Brut* into English verfe after the poetic tranflation of a French clerk whom he called Wace, both thefe bibliographers, upon infpection of his manufcript (Bibl. Cotton. Caligula A. IX.), read *Wate* inftead of *Wace*; whence they inferred that *Wate* was a contraction of *Walter*; and that Walter de Mapes, Archdeacon of Oxford, having firft brought over the *Brut* into England, it was he that had originally tranflated it into French verfe.

But, in the firft place, it is evident that they took the C in Wace for T, and it is a very eafy matter to be convinced of this falfe reading by examining the manufcript in queftion, and thofe in which Wace is alfo named. Again, it is no where proved that Walter, Archdeacon of Oxford, was a Frenchman by birth; and if this Walter be Walter de Mapes, which we do not believe, it is clear from the evidence of all the English Biographers that he was born in Great Britain, which by no means agrees with the *French Clerk* mentioned by Layamon.

From what has been advanced concerning the tranflation of *Wace's Brut*, it manifeftly appears, that it was the fate of this author, for more than two centuries, to have his name mutilated by the unfkillfulnefs of tranfcribers, and of courfe to be but little known in the Republic of Letters. All the fubfequent writers, to the hiftorian Fauchet, who was the firft that mentioned this poet, have increafed the obfcurity by

[u] Bibl. Reg. 4. C. XI.   [w] Nicolfon's Engl. Hiſt. Library.

freſh

frefh miftakes. The learned Mr. Tyrwhitt was the firft perfon who attempted to clear up a fubject which from time to
time became more involved in darknefs, and to vindicate our
author from the errors or injuftice of modern writers. By
means of found criticifm, the authority of the manufcripts in
the Britifh Mufeum, and the teftimony of Layamon and Robert de Brunne, he proved, beyond the poffibility of a doubt,
that Wace was the author of the tranflation of the *Brut* into
French verfe [x]. Laftly, Dr. Burney, by means of the rules
of French poetry alone, demonftrated the want of fidelity in
the manufcripts which had mifled Fauchet and all other
writers, who, as he had done, drew their materials from
faulty and imperfect copies [y].

Wace's fecond work is the Hiftory of the Irruptions of the
Normans into England and the Northern Provinces of
France. No Bibliographer whatever has fpoken of this Romance, which is written in verfes of eight fyllables. The
author appears to have extracted all his materials from the
chronicles which exifted in his time, fome of which have
been publifhed in Duchefne's Collection of Norman Hiftorians. The opening of this poem is interefting from its details ; the author difcovers a prodigious knowledge of the hiftory of nations and the revolutions of empires : he gives an
ample nomenclature of the various names which were fucceffively born by thofe nations, as well as the countries and cities
which they inhabited. In a word, he fhews that the hiftories of
Greece and Rome were familiar to him ; and he commends
with much gratitude thofe learned perfons who by their in-
duftry had preferved the valuable materials of ancient hiftory,

[x] Chaucer's Canterbury Tales, vol. IV. p. 57.
[y] Burney's Hiftory of Mufic, vol. II. p. 230.

and who, in their own writings, had constituted those of modern history.

This Romance ought naturally to precede those of the Dukes of Normandy. There are two copies of it in the royal library at Paris, one of which had belonged to the President Bigot; but this last is very imperfect. A third, which was in the collection of André Duchesne, passed into the Colbertine library. Monsieur Lancelot, in his account of the Royal manuscripts and those of Colbert, has given a copy of this Romance, with the variations in the margin; this last copy is also in the Royal Library at Paris.

The third performance of Wace is the famous *Roman du Rou*. This name is derived from *Rollo* or *Raoul*, the first Duke of Normandy, who is the hero of the history, and not from the surname of *Roux*, given to William the Second, as Messrs. la Borde [z] and la Ravaliere [a] have intimated. This Romance is to be found at the end of the Romance of the first Irruptions of the Normans in the manuscripts already cited, as well as in the copy collated by Lancelot. It is written in verses of twelve syllables, otherwise called *Alexandrine*. Wace frequently names himself in this work, and informs us, that he composed it in 1160.

Messrs. La Combe [b], La Ravaliere [c], La Borde [d], and Warton [e], after depriving our poet of the glory of having first translated the *Brut* into French verse, have conceded to him that of being the author of the *Roman du Rou*; but they

[z] Hist. de la Musique Franc. t. II. p. 138.
[a] Poeties du Roi de Navarre, t. I. p. 154.
[b] Dictionn. du vieux langage, Pref. t. II. p. xviii.
[c] Poeties du Roi de Navarre, t. I. p. 151.
[d] Loco citato.
[e] Loco citato.

4   have

have at the fame time maintained, againſt every ſemblance
of probability, that the latter work was a continuation of the
former. What is ſtill more ſurprizing, the Benedictines,
thoſe men ſo profoundly verſed in the knowledge of hiſtory,
have likewiſe imagined the *Brut* to contain the firſt period of
the Engliſh Monarchy, and the Roman du Rou the ſecond [ƒ].
On our part we candidly own, that it ſeems impoſſible to
trace the ſlighteſt connection between the two works. For
indeed, what affinity can there exiſt between truth and fic-
tion, between a chimerical hiſtory of the Britiſh Kings and
the authentic hiſtory of the dukes of Normandy ; or between
Cadwallader the laſt of the kings, who died in 689, and
Rollo the firſt Duke of Normandy, who only began his reign
over that province in 912 ? In ſhort, what relation between
the hiſtories of England and Normandy before the famous
epoch of the Conqueſt in 1066, when the two countries were
firſt united under one Sovereign ? A man muſt either have
never read theſe works, or have peruſed them to little purpoſe, before he could have ventured upon ſuch paradoxes.
In a word, he muſt have been totally ignorant of Engliſh
hiſtory to have ſuppreſſed in this manner the long reign of
the Anglo-Saxon Monarchs.

Monſieur Huet, and ſeveral others after him, have given
out that Wace dedicated his *Roman du Rou* to Henry II. ; but
we can take upon ourſelves to aſſert, that among all the manuſcripts of this work which have come to our knowledge,
no one is preceded by a dedication. It is true indeed, that
at the beginning of his fourth Romance of the Dukes of Normandy, the poet confeſſes it was only *for the honour of Henry* II.

[ƒ] Nouvelle Collect. des Hiſtoriens de la France. loc. cit.

K 2   that

that he had undertaken the histories of Rollo, of William
Longsword his son, and Richard I. his grandson; but this
motive, equally honourable to the monarch and the poet,
being but vaguely expressed in a work absolutely different
from the *Roman du Rou*, and posterior to it by more than
ten years, cannot in strictness be termed a dedication.

There is no copy of the *Roman du Rou* in the British Museum, as the learned Mr. Tyrwhitt has maintained [g]. Monf.
la Ravaliere in his History of the Revolutions of the
French Language [h], had justly asserted, that the *Roman
du Rou* was written in Alexandrine verse, or lines of twelve
syllables. Mr. Tyrwhitt, in order to refute this, professed to
have consulted a manuscript of the *Roman du Rou* Bibl. Reg.
4 C. XI. which he says is written in verses of eight syllables
only. But in this he was too precipitate. Mr. Tyrwhitt, no
doubt, contented himself with a simple inspection of the
manuscript; and, without further examination, imagined he
had got over the difficulty. But if he had only read the two
first pages of the work, he would have perceived from Wace's
own expressions, that this manuscript does not contain the
Roman du Rou; it contains indeed nothing more than a continuation of the Romance of Duke Richard I. and that of his
successors, till the sixth year of Henry I. The poet, before
he enters upon his subject, takes care to announce, that he
had already in his former works given the histories of Rollo,
or *Rou*, and of William Longsword, as well as a great part
of that of Richard I [i]; he refers to these as works of which
                                                    he

[g] Chaucer's Canterbury Tales, vol. IV. p. 78.
[h] Poefies du Roi de Navarre, t. I. p. 153.
[i] Pour l'onur al secunt Henri,
    Ki del lignage Roul nasqui,

Ai

he shall make no further use. Many other English writers as well as Mr. Tyrwhitt have been perfuaded of the exiſtence of the *Roman du Rou* in the British Muſeum, Bibl. Reg. 4 C. XI. But it is enough to have peruſed the beginning of this manuſcript in order to be convinced of the contrary. Again, it is certain, that the *Roman du Rou* is not written in verſes of eight ſyllables, but in Alexandrines, as Monſieur de la Ravaliere has maintained [£]. Extracts from it may be ſeen in Pere L'Abbé's Chronological Alliances, vol. I. ; in the Diſſertation upon the Right of Dependance which the Dukes of Normanly claimed from Britany, page 167; in Du Cange's Remarks upon the Eſtabliſhment of St. Louis, p. 188 ; in p. lv of the preliminary Diſcourſe to vol. V. of Gebelin's Primitive World ; and in La Combe's Dictionary of the old French Language, vol I. p. 357.

Wace's fourth work is the Romance of William Longſword the ſon of Rollo. It is the leaſt extenſive of any of the poet's writings, on account of the ſhort duration of that prince's reign. This is alſo written in Alexandrine verſe. It is to be found in the Royal Library at Paris, at the end of the *Roman du Rou*, among the ſame manuſcripts, and in the copy collated by Lancelot.

> Ai jeo de Raol lunges cunte,
> Et de ſun riche parente.
> De Guilleaume lunge eſpee,
> Avum leſloiſe avant menee.
> Tant que Flameng cume felun,
> Le torrent par traïſun;
> De Richard ſon fiz avum dit,
> Ki ſun pere leiſſa petit.

[1] Loco citato.

The

The fifth is the Romance of Duke Richard I. son of William Longsword. It is a great deal more ample than the preceding works, because the minority of this prince supplied the author with deeds of great importance, and because his reign was as long as it was brilliant. This history is likewise written in Alexandrine verse, and occurs in the manuscripts, and in the copy of Lancelot already mentioned. Although it contains the most remarkable events of Duke Richard's government, it cannot be regarded as a finished work, the poet having passed over in silence many important matters; but in the course of our details upon Wace's sixth work, the motives which induced him to leave this Romance imperfect may probably be found.

The sixth is one of the longest; it contains, in nearly 12000 lines, the remainder of the History of the Dukes of Normandy. Wace resumes it at Duke Richard I. and continues it to the sixth year of the reign of Henry I. that is, to the famous epoch when this monarch, having taken his brother Robert prisoner, became thereby the peaceable possessor of England and Normandy. It appears then, that Mr. Warton has been guilty of a mistake, in asserting, that the Romance of the Dukes of this province went no farther than William Rufus [*l*].

This work has given occasion to a variety of historical and learned remarks. It appears in the first place, that Wace abandoned the plan which he had till then pursued, that is, he declined making any longer a separate Romance of the history of each Duke, but determined to unite into one work the remainder of the History of Normandy. He begins this

[*l*] History of English Poetry, vol. 1. p. 62.

with

with the same introduction which he had placed at the head of his History of the first Irruption of the Normans; but we may perceive that he has retouched and augmented it considerably. He then gives a series of the works which he has already composed upon the three first Dukes of Normandy. He resumes the thread of their history till Duke Richard I. and gives some new and interesting details concerning that prince; he even presents us with some facts which he says historians had not dared to commit to writing, because they tarnished the memory of that Duke, and were only known by tradition.

Another instance in which the poet deviated from his plan, was in giving up his Alexandrine verses for those of eight syllables. He certainly found these last better adapted to the narrative style; at the same time we do not perceive in this Romance that elevation of ideas, that gravity of elocution, which are to be met with in the Alexandrine verses, and are oftentimes worthy of admiration in his preceding works.

The author names himself several times in this Romance, and as he speaks in it of Henry the Second's eldest son, whom he informs us he saw crowned in the life-time of his father, it may be thence concluded, that he composed it after the year 1170, when this event took place [*m*].

Notwithstanding the honours which our poet had received, and the very flattering invitations to continue his Romances of the Dukes of Normandy, it appears that he remained several years without writing. In those days authors do not seem to have made glory the sole object of their ambition. Wace complains much of the Mecaenases of his time, who confined themselves to barren compliments, and did not even give

[*m*] Roger Hoveden, Annales, ad ann. 1170.

him

him fufficient to defray a month's wages of his amanuenfis ; he
reminds them of happier days, in which the barons and their
ladies knew how to honour and reward the hiftorian who confecrated their names in his works, and tranfmitted them to
pofterity. But, though difappointment had compelled him to
abandon his pen, emulation induced him to refume it. Henry II. entered into an engagement with a poet named Benoit,
to reduce into verfe the whole hiftory of the Dukes of Normandy. Wace, jealous no doubt of the glory which this
poet was about to acquire, was defirous at leaft of fharing it
with him. Endued with an extenfive facility in writing, and
having already taken a part in the work, he did not hefitate a
moment in abfolutely completing it. He alfo in concluding it
recommends the poet Benoit to avoid fatiguing himfelf to no
purpofe in the continuation of his own work ; he informs him
that he has fung in his ftead, and that, the wifhes of the monarch being fulfilled, he may give up the tafk which had
been allotted to him. Benoit, however, far from taking
the advice of his competitor, determined to purfue the fame
career, and to leave him nothing more than the glory of having preceded him.

It is then to this fortunate rivalry that we are indebted for
the greateft part of the hiftory of the Dukes of Normandy
by Wace. It is to be found at the end of the Romances of
the three firft Dukes in the manufcripts, and in the copy of
Lancelot before cited. The Benedictines, in the XI. and XIII.
volumes of their hiftorians of France, have printed feveral
fragments of this Romance, which they very improperly con-
found with the *Roman du Rou.* They inform us, that they
originally intended to print the whole of it, but have preferred the giving a profe tranflation made during the thirteenth
cen-

century, under the title of a *Chronicle of Normandy*. It is extremely to be regretted, that learned men have neglected the original for a copy far lefs interefting, and of neceffity a great deal more verbofe.

Laftly, this work is to be met with in the Britifh Mufeum. Bibl. Reg. 4 C. XI. It is written in the thirteenth century. This is the manufcript which feveral learned men have fuppofed to contain the *Roman du Rou*. Montfaucon [n], and after him Mr. Cafley [o], have erroneoufly given it the title of the Hiftory of England ; whereas the author profeffedly details in it the Hiftory of the Dukes of Normandy to Richard I. and only treats of the other when there is an immediate connection. It is certainly this defective title which has induced fo many learned men to believe, that the *Roman du Rou*, and the Hiftory of the Dukes of Normandy, were a continuation of the *Brut*.

The feventh work of our author is a fort of *compendium*, or abridged chronicle, of the Hiftory of the Dukes of Normandy. It is compofed in the afcending manner, that is, it begins with Henry II. and goes backwards to Rollo. It is written in Alexandrine verfe, and is to be found in the Royal Library at Paris in Monfieur Lancelot's copy before defcribed.

The eighth is a hiftory of the Origin of the Feaft of the Conception of the Holy Virgin. This feaft is very ancient and famous in Normandy. There is a tradition generally received in this province, that it was eftablifhed by William the Conqueror. It was called *The Feaft of the Normans*. To render it more brilliant, poetical games were eftablifhed in honour of it ; and whilft in the different provinces of

[n] Montfaucon, Catal. MSS. Regis Angliæ.
[o] Bibl. Reg. MSS. Catal. 4 C. XI.

France they celebrated the literary sports, so well known by
the name of *Puys d'Amour*, where those who best sang of the
beauty which inflamed them, received a crown in reward,
the Normans celebrated their *puy de la conception de la Sainte
Vierge*, and distributed prizes for the choicest pieces in verse
that were composed in honour of the *Queen of Heaven*. These
ancient establishments exist no where at present but among
the Carmelites at Rouen, and in the University of Caen. In
every year upon the eighth of December the authors of the
Pieces Couronnées receive rings of gold, pens and jettons of
silver, with branches of palm and laurel.

Wace is undoubtedly the first writer of French verses upon
this Feast. The authors of the Catalogue of the Duke de la
Valliere's library had originally ascribed his work to Gace
Brulez, who did not live till the thirteenth century [*p*]; but,
on further consideration, they have acknowledged, that it
was the author of the Roman du Rou who composed it, and
have pointed out the sources whence the poet drew the materials of his history [*q*]. The work is written in verses of
eight syllables. It is to be found in the Royal Library at Paris,
at the end of Monsieur Lancelot's copy of the Romances of
the Dukes of Normandy.

Wace's ninth work is *a life of Saint Nicholas*, in verses of
eight syllables, from which the learned Hickes has given
several extracts in his *Thesaurus Literaturæ Septentrionalis* [*r*].
There is a manuscript copy of it in the library of Trinity
College, Cambridge; another in the Bodleian library at Oxford; and a third in the possession of Mr. Douce, a member

[*p*] Catal. de la Biblioth. de Monsieur le Duc de la Valliere, N° 2738.
[*q*] Suppl. de ce Catal. N° eodem.
[*r*] Hickesii Grammatica Anglo-Saxonica, pp. 145, 149, &c.

2   of

of the Society of Antiquaries. The poet names himself at the end of the work, and says he composed it for the gratification of Osbert the son of Thiout.

The tenth is the *Roman du Chevalier au Lion.* Fauchet ascribes it to Chretien de Troyes, as do likewise the authors of the Catalogue of the Duke de la Valliere's library, who have certainly followed him; but Messrs Galland, la Ravaliere, and la Borde [*s*], conceived it to be Wace's; they even cite some verses from it, which undeniably prove that the work was composed by this poet in 1155. Both these opinions may be reconciled by supposing that Wace rendered it into French verse, and Chretien de Troyes into prose, in like manner as he did the Romance of Perceval le Galois.

It appears that our poet also composed several branches of the *Romance of Alexander.* De Bure ascribes to him some of those which are to be found in a manuscript copy in the Duke de la Valliere's library, N° 2702. It is true, that Wace's name is again disfigured there into *Iface* and *Euface*; but, as Pasquier has wisely remarked, if our ancestors had written a good book, and it became necessary to copy it, this was done, not in the plain and simple language of the author, but in that of the transcriber. See the proofs which he has given in his Recherches, liv. VIII. chap. 3.

Mr. Tyrwhitt has suspected, and not without some reason, that Wace is the *Robert Guasco,* author of the *Martyrdom of St. George,* who is mentioned by the Abbé le Bœuf [*t*] as one of the oldest French translators; and it is, probably, this work which has induced the authors of the

[*s*] Locis jam citatis.
[*t*] Mem. de l'Acad. des Inscript. t. XVII. p. 729.

Gallia

Gallia Christiana to call him *Guasco* [v], and occasioned Monsieur Huet's assertion, that his Christian name was *Robert.* And, lastly, la Roque, in his History of the House of Harcourt, vol. III. p. 13, has printed a piece in verse upon the origin of this family, and ascribed it likewise to our Wace.

The authors of the *Gallia Christiana* have asserted, that he also composed a poem upon the Kings of France, the Dukes of Normandy, the earls of Poitou, and other Princes [w]. No Bibliographer has ever spoken of this work ; and, after much enquiry, we are persuaded that Wace never wrote it. It is true, that in the course of his historical Romances he often speaks of the Kings of France, and sometimes of the Earls of Poitou ; but it is only in those instances where their history has an intimate connection with that of the Dukes of Normandy which he did compose. It is certainly of this latter history that the learned editors mean to speak ; but, having examined it with too little attention, they have mistaken the work, and given it an inaccurate title.

Wace has also mentioned some light poems which he composed ; these he terms *Lais* and *Serventois* : but we do not know that any of them have come down to us.

Such a multitude of works from the pen of the same author engaged the attention of Henry II. who, to reward his merit, bestowed on him a canonry in the cathedral of Bayeux. Monsieur Lancelot in his explanation of the tapestry of Queen Matilda preserved in the treasury of that cathedral, has contended that Wace borrowed several facts which he could not have found elsewhere from that valuable monu-

[v] Gallia Christiana, t. XI. p. 363.
[w] Ibid.

ment.

ment [x]. It is certain, that, by means of the works of our poet, Monfieur Lancelot has very happily explained all the circumstances deferibed in the tapeftry; but we do not perceive how it is to be thence inferred, that the poet is neceffarily indebted to it for feveral of his deferiptions. Wace is fo exact in citing his authorities, that his filence refpecting what this monument prefented him with, is, in our opinion, a certain proof that he did not make any ufe of it. Befides, the tapeftry of Matilda only exhibits events relating to the Conqueft of England; and this author had lived with fo many eye-witneffes of it, that it is not to be wondered at, that, intending to write its hiftory, he fhould have made the moft minute refearches, and have detailed upon this fubject facts which are to be met with in no other hiftorians whatever. In fhort, he informs us that his own father was prefent at the battle of Haftings; he relates the particular circumftances of it which he had learned from him; and he expreffes himfelf throughout the whole with fo much candour, that we are convinced he would have mentioned this tapeftry if he had derived from it the leaft affiftance.

Dumoutier, in his *Neuftria pia,* fays that Wace was canon of Caen [y]; but it is certain there was no chapter then eftablifhed in that city. That of St. Sepulchre, which ftill remains, was not founded till 1219 by William Acarin [z]. It is true, that upon the 7th of March in the year 1153, Philip de Harcourt, Bifhop of Bayeux, founded three new canonries in his cathedral church, and to endow them, annexed the parifh churches of Notre Dame, St. John, and St.

[x] Mem. de l'Acad. des Infcript. t. VIII. p. 608.
[y] Neuftria pia, p 318.
[z] Origines de Caen, par Monf. Huet, p. 223. edit. of 1706.

Peter,

Peter, belonging to the city of Caen; perhaps Wace being afterwards provided with one of these benefices, might have been called *canon* of Caen, because the chief place of his prebend was situated in that city; this conjecture acquires the greater probability on account of a practice still existing in Normandy of describing every canon by the name of the place appropriated to his canonry.

Monsieur Huet, and almost every one of those who have spoken of our Poet, have maintained that he had been clerk of the chapel to king Henry II. Wace, however, mentions nothing concerning this dignity, although he minutely describes all the favours which that monarch conferred upon him; he is even so attentive upon this subject, that he assures us the king gave him many things, but had promised him more. Besides, as the title of Clerk of the King's Chapel was a very honourable one, which generally led the way to a Bishopric, we may presume from his silence that he was not invested with it. Monsieur Huet has certainly been misled by the description of *Clerk*, which Wace often assumes; but he should have remarked, that he never calls himself *clerc du roi*, but always *clerc de Caen*, or *Clerc lisant*, a title which then signified nothing more than a learned man, and which was even given to laymen, since Henry I. was surnamed *Beauclerc*.

Such, my Lord, are the ideas which I have been able to collect concerning the life and writings of this author. With respect to the advantages that may be derived from his works, they will certainly furnish any one who may think it worth while to peruse them, with new light upon the history, the government, and the manners and customs of the Normans.

The

The Antiquary will at firſt remark with aſtoniſhment, that their language in Wace's time has been preſerved even to our own days in the countries of Lower Normandy. He will perceive their progreſs in the various arts; their attainments in that of war; their arms and their military cuſtoms; their method of attacking caſtles and ſtrong holds; the ſtate of their marine and their commerce; the height to which they have carried architecture and other ſciences, together with the monuments they have left us. The genealogiſt will find many curious and intereſting facts relating to ancient families; he will feel himſelf rewarded in the peruſal of the names of the knights who were preſent at the battle of Haſtings; and of the noble actions by which each of them ſignalized his valour. In a word, the hiſtorian will learn with pleaſure many circumſtances and details which are not to be found in any other writer.

I remain, my Lord,

with the moſt profound reſpect,

Your Lordſhip's moſt humble

and obedient Servant,

London, 16th *June*, 1794.   D E L A R U E,

Royal Profeſſor of Hiſtory in the Univerſity of Caen.

VII.

VII. *Particulars of the Expence of the Royal Household in the Reigns of* Henry VII. Henry VIII. *Queen* Elizabeth, *&c.*

Read March 6, 1794.

IF we compare the expences of the Royal Household in former times with those of later dates, and observe the alteration of the value of money, and the progressive rise in the cost of provisions, the result will probably be, that the expence of His present Majesty's Household is not more than it was in the time of Queen Elizabeth, and is much less than it was in the time of her successor.

The articles contained in the very curious wardrobe account of Edward the Second published by the Society seem rather to relate to his extraordinary expences and preparations for war in Scotland, than to what we should properly call the expences of the household. The amount of the latter is, however, to be collected from the conclusion of the account, which, after stating the whole expences of the articles in that book to be £.53,178 15 1

adds, " Summa totalis exituum et expensarum garderobe per istum librum de anno 28, *una cum expensis hospicii Regis ejusdem anni* — — 64,105 0 5

Deduct then the above sum — 53,178 15 1

and the household expences will be 10,926 5 4

What

What might be the expence of Richard the Second I do not know; but, according to Holinſhed, it muſt have been enormous, as he ſays there were 300 ſervitors in the kitchen, and every other office furniſhed at the like rate, and that *ten thouſand* perſons had meat and drink allowed them.

From the Pipe rolls it appears, that the greateſt expence of Henry VII. was about £. 15,000 *per ann.* but this was afterwards leſſened, and towards the end of his reign was reduced to about £. 13,000 [a].

Henry the Eighth, a prince fond of expence, began with about £. 16,000. *per ann.* and went on encreaſing till in his 30th year the expence was £. 22,000.; in the 33d year it got up to £. 34,000. and the 37th to £. 40,000.

In the beginning of Queen Elizabeth's reign, ſhe reduced her expence a little below what her father ended with, but, at the concluſion of her long reign, it was increaſed to £. 55,000.

[a] A certificate of King Henry the Seventh's expences of his houſehold of the years following:

		£.	s.	d.			Henry VIII. £.	s.	d.
A°.	2	14,374	10	0½	A°.	1	16,160	10	11
	4	15,168	6	11¼		4	17,597	4	0¼
	7	14,612	16	1		7	18,302	16	6¼
	10	14,620	9	6¼		10	18,489	15	9½
	13	14,422	14	4¾		13	22,674	11	9¾
	16	13,180	16	0¼		16	19,740	16	2¼
	19	13,248	10	5¼		19	21,412	17	5¼
	23	13,024	19	6¼		23	24,908	14	0¼
						27	23,461	10	8
						30	22,339	5	4½
						33	34,168	6	5½
						37	40,014	9	8

 A lit-

A little before her death she was very uneasy at finding her houshold expences run so high, and the following account of a conversation which she had on the subject with Mr. Brown, one of the officers of her green-cloth, is truly characteristic of her. She died shortly after, and before any thing had been done to correct the abuses complained of.

The original of this paper is amongst some that were collected by Sir Julius Cæsar. It is indorsed.

> " The late Q. Matie speeches often tymes to R. Bro: for houshold causes."

> Richard Brown's s'vice to the late Queene, and her M^{ts}. speeches and com^d at sundrie times to him for houshold causes knowen to some of the Lo: in Councill and White-staves.

" The houshold charges abridged from £.50,000 to £.44,000 *per ann.* for in two offices onlie £.2,000. *per ann.* abated.—Larder—Poultrie—her Matie has notwithstanding told Browne, that in the beginning of her raigne lesse than £. 40,000. defrayed the charge. Browne answered, that all provic'ons then weare cheaper. The Queen said, that may bee soe, and I save by the late compoc'on [b] (as I am informed) £. 10,000 *per ann.* and therefore I charge yo^u examyne the difference of some yeare in the beginninge of my raigne with one yeares expences now, and lett me understand yet.

" An examinac'on and conference was made betweene the third yeare and the 43th yeare, yt was found that in bread, beare, wyne, wood, coles, wax-lights, torches, tallow-lights, and some meete, and other allowances of incidents, necessaries, carriages, wages, &c. to the some of £. 11,000. *per*

---

[b] A composition paid by the counties in lieu of purveyance.

ann.

own. at the leaſt, more was ſpent in aᵒ. 43ᵗⁱ. then in aᵒ 3ᵗⁱ Regⁱ. and no ſufficient warrant for the increaſe, whereby ytt did playnlie appeare, that the booke ſigned by her Maᵗⁱᵉ for the honorable allowance to all ꝑſons was not exceeded.

" The Queenes Maᵗⁱᵉ being informed of this difference, and being therewith moved greatlie, ſaid, And ſhall I ſuffer this, did not I tell yoᵘ, Browne, what yoᵘ ſhould ſynd, I was nevʳ in all my government, ſoe royallie, with numbers of noble-men and la: attended upon, as in the beginninge of my raigne, all offices in my coᵗ being ſupplied, wᶜʰ now are not, and all thoſe then ſatiſfied with my allowance, agreed uppon by my councell and ſigned by me, wᵗʰ that care as by all former princes hath bene uſed. And ſhall theſe now that at-tend, and have the like allowances, not reſt contented, I will not ſuffer this diſhoᵘⁱᵇ. ſpoile, and increaſe that noe prince ever before me did, to the offence of God, and great grea-vance of my lovinge ſubjects, who, I underſtand, daylie com-playne, and not without cauſe, that there is increaſe daylie of carryadges and of ꝓviⁱᵗⁱon taken from them, at low prices, and waſtfullie ſpent within my coᵗ to ſome of their undoings, and now myſelf underſtanding of yt, they may juſtlie accuſe me, to ſuffer yt, with many other diſcontented ſpeeches, delivered with great vehemencie, complayninge of the weak-neſſe of the whiteſtaves to ſuffer yt, and accuſinge herſelf for makinge ſoe ſlender choice, with many more ſpeeches, &cⁱ But my ſpeedie order for reformacᵗon, ſhall ſatiſfie my lovinge ſubjects greeved, for I will end as I beganne with my ſubjects' love."

In another hand is written,

" yt ys no marvell thoughe thoſe grevanᵗⁱ were compl. in parliamᵗ."

"Thoſe

" Thofe that are neareft me, and have dailie great benefit by
fuits, have thefe waftfull increafes daylie, but my whiteftaves
and thofe of my greencloth, by whom all good orders and
hono.ble allowances fhould be mayntcyned, are principal
falters herein, for noe increafe can be without their privitie
and unlawful warraunt, whereby I fynd the difference of officers now, and in the beginninge of ow.r raigne.

" Whereupon her Ma.tie. gave ftraight charge and comandm.t
to Browne [c] forthwith to repayre to the Lo: Treafurer,
Lo: Admiral, and the whiteftaves of the howfhould (w.th
Browne did), that order might be taken to abridge all meffes
of meate, and other expences, more than the booke figned doth
allowe, and further faid, myfelf will fpeke unto them, and geve
them charge, and then let me fee or learn, what he in my houfe
that dareth breake and difobey my orders and comanadem.t
figned, with verie bitter fpeeches, that thee would cleanfe her
co.rt, and not fuffer fuch a number of pfons and famylies more
than are to bee allowed to bee kept within the co.rt, where-
uppon her Ma.tie fent certen noates to the white ftaves, to be
put in p'efent execuc'on, in the meane tyme, before the ef-
fectinge whereof yt pleafed God to take her Ma.tie to his mercie."

Oeconomy was not one of the virtues poffeffed by James
the Firft (if indeed he poffeffed any), and when he came to the
land of plenty, he had no idea of limiting his expences. The
eftimate for the firft year was £.76,954. 2 s. 5 d.¼, befides
£.16,000. for the prince, making together £.92,954. 2 s. 5 d.¼;

[c] In the margin is written in another hand,
        " batt ye befte of them wole have byn contente w.th lefte
        " then my book allowethe, rayther, &c."
        " butt I will fend fome of them home yff my comis
        " be not better regarded."

4   In

In his fourth year his houſehold expence was £. 97,421. 2s. 3d.
From Michaelmas in his ſeventh year to Michaelmas in the
eighth year, it was £. 129,863. 9s. 0d½. and yet the king had
corn and cattle ſerved by the ſeveral counties at under prices,
that the farmers might get rid of purveyors, the benefit of
which was eſtimated to the king at £. 38,000.

Prince Henry's expences kept pace with his father's.
At the firſt eſtabliſhment of his houſehold, 20th July,
1 James I. anno 1603, he had ſervants   70

A few weeks after a ſecond book was ſigned, when
they were encreaſed to   104

In the next year they amounted to   141
beſides ſervants of theſe ſervants who had intruded
themſelves into the court   130

The 141 ſoon multiplied into   215
beſides workmen of various ſorts, and 13 extraordinary.

In 1608 they were   233
and with the maſters, the number of ſervants alſo encreaſed [d].

The book ſigned by his Royal Highneſs in 1610 gives
the names of 297 with wages, 129 without,   426
beſides various workmen, among whom is Inigo Jones,
as ſurveyor of the works [e].

The following letter, the original of which is amongſt
Sir Julius Cæſar's papers, mentioned above, will ſhew the
conſequence of this want of management.

It is indorſed

" To the right honorabl my very good Lord the Erl of
Dorſet, Ld High Treaſurer of Englande."

[d] Sir Julius Cæſar's papers.
[e] Ordinances of the Royal Houſeholds, p. 317.

Right

Right honorabell my very good Lord :

"According to my duty I have beene always carefull to save al needlesſ expenſe in the Prince's houſe. But the continual increaſe of new ſervants dayly ſent hether by warrante procured without my knowlege, has brought the charge ſo farr out of frame, that it [ſ] hard to conceive a courſe how to leſſen it, ſeing the neceſſary increaſe of many moor will follow the Prince's advancement in years and dignitie. Notwithſtanding leaſt I ſhould ſeeme to bee careleſs, or over curious to ſearch into other mens actions, if it ſhall pleaſe your Lᵖ to commande mee by a letter, to call the officers of this houſehold to adviſe of ſome redreſs, unto further inconveniences, I hoope both to give your Lᵖ good accounte of the preſent eſtate of our expenſe, and to make ſome overture how to reforme, or at leaſt to prevent futur accidents. The note that I ſent your Lᵖ : conteining a breefe of ſuch orders as I deſir to bee ratified for avoyding confuſion and diſorder in the table, I beſeech your Lᵖ to conſider of, and to propounde them not ſimply as a ſute of myne, but as a matter generally requiſite for the better government of his Highnes houſe. And as my duty always binds mee I reſt,

St. James,   Your Lᵖ aſſuredly to commande,
Jan. 27.   THO. CHALONER."

Sir Thomas Chaloner, in a letter to Sir Julius Caſar, dated 7 Nov. 1607, mentions ſome of the above circumſtances, ſays he would (at the firſt) have undertaken to maintain the (Prince's) houſe to the king's honour for £8000. yearly, provided they might have good payment of the money ; that in the firſt year he diſmiſſed of unneceſſary dependants on the

[ſ] It is ſo in the original.

2   houſe

houfe at leaft 3 fcore, whereof many had paſſports to return
to their own country, and he utterly refuſed all fuitors who
addreſſed themſelves to him to obtain ſome place about the
Prince, and then he complains of the great encreaſe, without
warrant, as well as with, and of the number of fuitors waiting for places. He fays, that for the want of ready money,
the purveyors are forced to take up meate on truſt, and then
ferve it out fo fmall and ill, at a price fo high, that the king
had better borrow money at 20 *per cent.*

It feems that king James's fervants took much pains in endeavouring to leſſen his enormous expence, and formed various projects for that purpofe. They obtained an account of
the French king's houſchold expence, which was not fo great
as King James's. The heads of it were as follows :

		Sterling.		
The Table and Kitchen	————	35,718	3	6
The ftables	———— ————	7,620	0	0
Domeſtic officers	———— ————	9,000	0	0
The office of plate	———— ————	8,180	0	0
The Treaſurer of the chamber	————	12,893	5	0
The gardes du corps	————	5,400	2	0
The provoſt of the houſehold	————	3,000	0	0
The hounds and falcons	———— ————	3,642	14	0
	Total	85,454	4	6

In 1622 King James's expence was reduced to 78,995 7 8
but he foon after made additions to it.

The

		£.	s.	d.
The houshold expence of King Charles II. from 1 October, 1663, to the last of September, 1664, was　———		57,275	1	0½
to which is to be added for the Duke of York		10,000	0	0
* The houshold of King James II. in 1687				
Houshold coffers	76,118　6　6½			
Stables　———	14,336　19　1½	90,455	5	8
† King William and Queen Mary, 1 Oct. 1691, to the last of Sept. 1693　———		114,685	7	3½
King William alone from 1698 to 1699		90,735	1	2½
Queen Anne, 2 years, Oct. 1703—1705		167,421	4	2
the average　———　———		83,710	12	0
1 year, Oct. 1712—1713		89,044	6	10
King George I.　Oct. 1715—1716		75,619	7	7¼
1713—1724		86,097	19	2½
King George II.　1730—1731		118,487	2	1½
1731—1732		124,806	17	6½
1 Jan. to the last of Dec. 1759		138,290	10	2¼

At the accession of his present Majesty a considerable reduction was made in the houshold expences. An increase attended the increase of his family, but they were again reduced in 1763.

* This account is taken from a book in the possession of the rev. T. Wright, one of the Secretaries to the Society.

† In this and the subsequent reigns the expence of the stables is included in the total sum.

IX.

VIII. *Extract from a Proclamation made in the 20th Year of the Reign of King* Henry VIII, *for dividing certain Lordships and Towns to be annexed and knit into divers Shires near the Marches of* Wales. *Communicated by the Rev. Mr.* Wrighte, *Secretary.*

Read November 6, 1794.

BY virtue of this proclamation the lordships, towns, parishes, commots, hundreds, and cantreds of *Oswestry, Whitington, Masbrook, Knoking, Ellesmere, Downe,* and *Churbury* hundreds, in the marches of Wales aforesaid, and every of them, and all and singular honours, lordships, castells, mannors, towns, hamlets, lands, tenements, and hereditaments, lying and being within the compass or precinct of the said lordships, towns, parishes, &c. were united, annexed, and joined to the county of Salop, and the lordships of Oswestry, Whitington, Masbrooke, and Knoking, were thus united, to be called and known by the name of the hundred of Oswestry and county of Salop, &c. and the lordships of Ellesmere were united to the hundred of Purihill, and those of Downe to the hundred of Churbury. By a subsequent statute made in the 34th and 35th of the same reign, the town and hundred of Aberton, before part of Montgomeryshire, were likewise annexed to the county of Salop.

To the above extract, were added some conjectures concerning the situations of certain Roman stations in that part of the country.

According to the second iter of Antonine, the distance, " *Deva Uriconio*," or from Chester to Wroxeter, is M. P. LIII, thus:

Deva Leg. xx *Victrix*.

Bovio, M. P. X.	Bangor, Flintshire.
Uriconio, M. P. XI.	Wroxeter,
Mediolano, M. P. XX.	Middle, } Salop.
Rutunio, M. P. XII.	Rowton,

The distance from Chester to Wroxeter by the direct road through Shrewsbury and Ellesmere, according to Patterson, is 45 miles, allowing therefore for the difference between English and Roman miles, 45 English being nearly equal to 49 Roman miles, it follows, that the second iter of Antonine proceeded almost in a direct line, *Deva Uriconio*, and consequently, we are not to look for the intermediate stations very far wide of each other.

Deva Bovio, M. P. X.

Since Mr. Horsley's time traces of the Roman road leading through Eccleston and Old Ford have been discovered, where the road seems to have been divided, one branch going directly towards Bangor in Flintshire, and the other through Stretton and Malpas to Wirs Wall near Whitchurch, on the borders of Shropshire, where it joined the road leading to *Condate Mediolano*.

Bovio Mediolano, M. P. X.

From Bangor the road seems to have gone along *Trench lane* to Ellesmere, and from thence in a direct line to *Middle* in Shropshire.

Mr.

Mr. Horſley was not ſatisfied in this place, and choſe rather to fix Mediolanum at *Drayton*. His reaſons for giving the preference to Drayton were examined and compared with thoſe of other Antiquaries who have ſought for the ſituation of Mediolanum either between the Dee and the Severn, where Major General Roy ſuppoſes it to have been, or between Cheſter and Wroxeter, where Mr. Horſley himſelf was diſpoſed, he tells us, to look for it, or to the South or South-Eaſt of Cheſter, according to Mr. Whitaker, all of them pointing directly to the ſituation of *Midille*, where, in the opinion of Dr. Tilſton of Cheſter, we ought to place *Mediolanum*.

In confirmation of this opinion an account was then given of the traces there diſcovered of a Roman road before noticed by Mr. Percival (Archæol. vol I.), leading from Kinderton through Nantwich and Whitchurch to Wroxeter, which of courſe muſt have paſſed by Middle.

Mediolano Rutunio, M. P. XII.

From Middle the Roman military way, inſtead of proceeding in a direct line through Shrewſbury to Wroxeter, took a ſhort circuit to Shrewſbury; and as Camden, Gale, Baxter, and others, are unanimous in their opinions, that Rutunio was at this place, it was not thought neceſſary to ſay much in confirmation of it. " Nec in hoc falſi eſſe poſſumus," ſays Camden. *Rowton*[*], adjoins to *Wattleſbury*, a clear proof that the couſe of the Watling-ſtreet paſſed through that part of the country.

Rutunio Uriconio, M. P. XI.

---

[*] Rowton is placed at the Buſhwalls, a camp near Hawkſtone and the river Raden. Gent. Mag. vol. LXV. p. 725.

From

From Rowton the Roman road has lately been traced to Wroxeter through *Stretton* by *Edge* and *Lea Crofs*, in the parifh of *Pontefbury*, about fix miles from Shrewfbury, where a Roman teffelated pavement was difcovered in November, 1793, and a drawing of it by Thomas Telford exhibited to the Society.

At Wroxeter the Roman road divides, one part going through the Strettons to Brandon camp in Herefordfhire, the *Bravinium* of Antonine; the other towards Staffordfhire through *Uxacona* or Okenyates in Shropfhire. A fketch of the courfe of the abovementioned roads was exhibited at the fame time.

IX. *Defcription of a Carving in the Church of* Long
Melford. *By* Craven Ord, *Efq.* F. A. S. *In a Let-
ter to the Right Honourable the Earl of* Leicefter,
Prefident of the Society of Antiquaries.

Read December 4, 1794.

My Lord,

AS the ornaments of churches have of late been confidered
in the different publications of this Society, give me
leave to communicate a drawing [a] of a *Table* (as we find
thefe carvings called in ancient wills) now remaining in the
North wall of the church of Melford, in the county of Suffolk, and which a few years ago was dug up from beneath
the pavement, where it is not improbable it had lain many
years.

This carving is of alabafter, richly gilt and coloured, and
reprefents the offerings of the Wife men [b].

Similar reprefentations from the Scriptures, or remarkable
paffages in the lives of the Saints, were not very uncommon
in our parochial churches, as we learn from wills, but few

[a] Plate IX.

[b] Their names and offerings are mentioned in a charm againft the falling
ficknfs.

    Jafper fert myrrham, thus Melchior, Balthafar aurum.
    Hæc tria qui fecum portabit nomina regem,
    Solvitur a morbo, Chrifti pietate, caduco.

of

of them at prefent are to be met with, many of them, no doubt, like this, having been buried at the Reformation.

Sometimes thefe hiftories are reprefented by paintings on board. All thefe bore the name of Tables, *Tabulæ.*

In 1458 money was bequeathed, " ad novam *tabulam* de " alabaftro de hiftoria Sanctæ Margaretæ in the church of Dunwich in Suffolk." Four marks were bequeathed to buy a *table* of alabafter of nine female faints in Saint Peter's church, Norfolk [c].

In 1510 Robert Clerk wills to be buried in the church, and a *table* " of Saint Thomas of Ynde [d], which I have caufed " to be made; I will have it ftand in Hatfield church, " Norfolk."

Befides thefe *tables* and ftatues of faints, there ufed to be a more harmlefs imagery than of divine perfons, the walls and windows of our churches being fometimes ornamented with *moral reprefentations*; as over the North door of the North aifle of Windham church, Norfolk, is a painting on the wall, reprefenting naked people in a boat in great danger, and feveral others fuffering for righteoufnefs fake; on the right hand, and on the left, the devils, fome offering a can of drink, others a purfe of money, encouraging finners to their own deftruction.

[c] A drawing of this Table may be feen in Mr. Carter's Specimens of Ancient Sculpture, vol II. plate 8.

[d] Saint Thomas, according to the legend of Antiquity, preached the Gofpel in India. At the end of the 9th century, his fhrine (perhaps in the neighbourhood of Madras) was devoutly vifited by the ambaffadors of Alfred. Saint Thomas is faid to have fuffered martyrdom near that city. There the Portuguefe founded an epifcopal church under the name of Saint Thomé, and there the faint performed an annual miracle till he was filenced by the profane neighbourhood of the Englifh. See La Croix, tom. ii. p. 7—16.

In

In a North window of Heydon church, Norfolk, are painted many young swearers, drunkards, dice-players, and other profligate livers, with a representation of hell, and such sinners in its flames. From the mouths of the youths are labels with oaths. After which is a moral representation.

If these slight notices should induce any person to enter more largely into the consideration of the *ornaments of our churches*, I have no doubt much curious information might be collected of the several religious customs, and modes of thinking that prevailed in former times.

I have the honor to be, my Lord,

With great respect,

Your Lordship's most obedient,

Bloomsbury square,
Dec. 4, 1794.   humble Servant,

C R A V E N   O R D.

X. *Account of a* Roman *Sepulture lately found in* Lincolnshire. *By Sir* Joseph Banks, *Bart. K. B. P. R. S.*

Read December 11, 1794.

THE Urn and stone Chest, of which the annexed drawing is a representation*, were found on the 26th of October last at Ashby Puerorum in Lincolnshire, by a labourer employed in cutting a ditch, to separate the cultivated part of a ploughed field from a road which passes along one side of it. The top of the stone chest lay three feet below the surface of the ground, no elevation whatever was observable in the soil over it, and the road near which it lay is not an ancient highway, having been set out as such under the powers of an Enclosure Act a few years ago.

The lid of the chest fitted the sides neatly, and rather hung over the edges, so that when it was removed no dirt of any kind had gained admittance within, during the long period of time which had elapsed since it was deposited in the earth.

As all the dimensions are accurately marked on the drawing, it is needless to repeat them; the chest is of freestone, such as is found in abundance on Lincoln heath; the urn is made of strong glass well manufactured, greenish, but not more so than green window glass usually is. When found it was perfect in all respects, and had not suffered any of that decay which generally renders the surface of Roman glass of a pearly or opaline hue; for the surface was as smooth and as firm as if it had newly come from the fire.

* Plate X.

3

It

It was nearly quite filled with small pieces of bones much burned, many of them being white throughout their substance. Among them were the fragments of a small lacrymatory of very thin and very green glass; it had probably been broken in consequence of the curiosity of the finder, as he acknowledged his having poured out the contents of the urn upon the grass, in hopes of meeting with money, before he brought it to his employer.

The circumstances attending this sepulture clearly prove it to have been Roman. It is, however, singular that the place chosen for depositing the remains of the deceased was not, as was customary with that people, near to a highway, and that it does not appear to have been the burial place even of a family; for, although the trench in which the chest was found has been cut quite across the field, no traces of a body having been buried in any other part of it were observed.

Horncastle (the *Banovallum* of Stukeley), where evident remains of Roman buildings are still left, is the nearest Roman station, and is about five miles distant from Ashby. No traces of that people have been observed nearer to the place where the urn was found, except that a few coins of brass or copper dug up some years ago in an orchard at Stainby, about half a mile distant, are said to have been Roman, but these were not preserved, and as no recollection can now be traced of the names of the emperors by whom they were struck, it must remain doubtful whether they were Roman or not.

The neighbourhood is pleasant in the extreme; a dry sandy soil moderately fertile, hills gradually rising in slopes, and commanding from their tops an extensive and varied proſpect, and briſk rills of tranſparent water running along the bottom of almoſt every valley, render it a place peculiarly adapted for the ſituation of a country houſe. As no people have ſhewn more taſte in chuſing agreeable ſpots for the ſituation of their villas than the Romans have done, it is far from improbable that the ſite of an ancient Roman villa will ſome time be diſcovered not far from the field where this ſepulture was found; and as the ſize of the urn, and the excellence of the glaſs, a coſtly material in the time of the Romans, prove the family that made uſe of it to have been opulent, it is probable that the teſſelated pavements, which are frequently unimpaired by the lapſe of time, will prove to be of an elegant taſte, and of coſtly workmanſhip.

XI.

XI. *Short Notices relating to the Parish of* Llanvetherine
in Monmouthshire. *Communicated by the Rev. Mr.*
Wrighte, *Secretary,* February 5, 1795.

*L*Lanvetherine is an obscure village in Monmouthshire, about
five miles from Abergavenny, and ten from Monmouth.
It takes its name from the patron St. *Veterinus*, to whom the
church is dedicated. The parish is of very considerable extent, but not proportioned. It is supposed to contain above
2,000 acres of land, which are here called *Covers*: three
covers make two statute acres. The parish register begins
1690. The church itself is not very antient, and the only
thing remarkable about it is a large square stone placed against
the South wall of the chancel, whereon is rudely cut the effigy
of a Saint in a long gown and hat, bearing in his left hand
something resembling a small box or basket, and in the other
a label, whereon is inscribed in Roman characters S. VETE-
RINUS. No account of this Saint could be obtained on the
spot, except that the stone abovementioned was discovered
many years ago in digging a grave in the church yard, and
placed where it now stands. From the mutilated inscription
round it it appears to have belonged to the grave of some
former rector of the parish, the words *Jacob* and *P'son Lc.*
being still legible.

The *Veterani* or *Vavassores*, it is well known, were feudal
vassals of greater and inferior rank, of which the following
account may be gathered from Du Cange: *Vavassores vel
Vavasores generatim sunt vassi feudales. Alii sunt majores,
alii minores. Majores sunt qui regis vel regni valvassores appel-*

O 2   *lantur luntur iidem qui capitanei, qui a ducibus, marchionibus, & comitibus: minores vero qui a majoribus valvasoribus feuda accepissent.* Concerning the etymology of the word, says Bracton, " *nihil melius dici potest quam,* vas fortitum ad valetudinem." By *Veterinus* may therefore be meant some great feudal baron, the founder of the church, to whom it was dedicated, as having bequeathed money for the building and endowment of it ; neither does there seem any thing very extraordinary in this. Churches were always dedicated to God, and not to Saints, Martyrs, or Founders, though sometimes distinguished by their names for a memorial of them. The naming of a church, says Mr. Bingham, by the name of a Saint or Martyr was far from dedicating it to the Saint or Martyr, though it served for a memorial of him among the living ; and so far was an honour to his memory, though dedicated only to God and his service : and this is farther evident from this consideration, that churches were sometimes named from their founders, who certainly did not intend to dedicate churches to themselves. In proof of this last assertion, Mr. Bingham refers to several authors, and we have an instance, perhaps, before us in confirmation of it.

In such obscure parts of the kingdom antient customs are frequently retained. As an instance of this it may be noticed, that the common people of this parish tie a dirty cloth about their heads when they appear as chief mourners at a funeral. The same custom likewise prevails in different places.

XII.

XII. *Mr.* Denne's *Observations on a Triple Stone Seat at* Upchurch *in* Kent. *In a Letter to Mr.* Gough.

Read February 19, 1795.

DEAR SIR,

MR. Thomas Fisher has favoured me with the inclosed delineation * of a triple stone seat in the chancel of the church of Upchurch, a parish in East Kent, situated between Rainham and the river Medway; and, as, to the best of my recollection, these stalls differ in form from any specimen hitherto exhibited to the Society of Antiquaries, I am inclined to believe that this representation of them may not be unacceptable.

Had the drawing passed under my inspection before I had concluded my remarks on stone seats in general, I should certainly have offered it as an instance in point to corroborate the notion I had advanced, that the stalls yet extant in the chancels of many of our parish churches, were not originally constructed for the conveniency of the officiating clergy, but for the use of the impropriators, who had unquestionably a right of admission into the chancel during the celebration of divine worship.

The church of Upchurch belonged to the Premonstratensian abbey of Lisle Dieu in Normandy, and that religious house seems, at an early period, to have acquired an appropriation of it; because when archbishop Wittlesey, in the year 1369,

* Plate XI.

augmented

augmented the portion for the maintenance of a perpetual vicar
to five marks *per* year, it is set forth in the instrument of or-
dination, that it had been for some time appropriated. The
hospital of St. Catharine near the Tower appears to have
had a temporary interest in this church; but king Henry the
Sixth, in the 17th year of his reign, at the request of archbishop
Chicheley, granted the appropriation of Upchurch, and the
advowson of the vicarage, to the newly established college of
All Souls in Oxford, in which body they still remain. In the
eighth year of Richard the Second this church was valued at
£.23. 6s. 8d. and the parsonage now consists of a house,
other buildings, yards, &c. and of eighty-two acres of glebe
land, of which seventeen are arable, sixty-four of meadow,
or fresh marsh, and two salt marsh, together with the tythes
of more than 500 acres of land [a].

By the munificence of the founder the college is also entitled
to a capital manor farm in the parish, situated at a small distance westward from the church. It is called Horsham, and
contains upwards of 1000 acres of land [b].

As the society had in this district possessions so ample and
beneficial, the management of the estate must often have required the superintendance of some of its principal members.
During their abode, when they resorted to church, there
cannot be a doubt of their having placed themselves in the
chancel, which was to be repaired at the expence of the impropriators; and, as it may be reasonably concluded, in the
stalls under review. But, concerning these stalls, it is observable, that the fellows of a college were satisfied with those
of a very plain construction, whereas in the neighbouring
church of Chatham, a triple seat, embellished with a profu-

[a] Hasted's History of Kent, vol. II. p. 545.   [b] Ibid. p. 543.

fion

sion of the said sculpture, was prepared for the accomodation of the canons of Leedes priory [c].

To men of high rank, and to patrons of livings only, was there an indulgence of fixed seats in a church ; but, in former times, as well as in the present age, parishioners would often dispute about seats, two or more being claimants of the same seat. In order to stop a practice so scandalous, and that frequently occasioned an interruption of divine offices, it was decreed in a synod of the diocese of Exeter, held under its prelate Peter de Quivil, in the year 1284, that, with an exception to noble persons, and to patrons, no one should in future claim any seat, but that whoever first entered a church for the purpose of devotion, he might chuse at his pleasure a place for praying [d]. This constitution is cited with the view of contrasting with it a letter upon the same subject, written in 1625, by Dr. Buckeridge, who then presided over the diocese of Rochester, but was in 1628 removed to Ely. The original letter is kept with the records of the city of Rochester, from which a transcript was made by Mr. Fisher, and on the perusal of it one is somewhat surprized to meet with such restrictions and prohibitions so earnestly pressed by a bishop in the 17th century.   The letter was addressed " To " the right wor¹ my very loving friends the Major of Ro-

[c] Vetusta Monumenta, vol. III. Pl. IV. and Archæologia, vol. X. pp. 301, 310.

[d] Wilkins, Concil. Magn. vol. II. p. 140. Item audivimus, quod propter sedilia in ecclesia rixantur multoties parochiani, duobus vel pluribus unum sedile vendicantibus ; propter quod grave scandalum in ecclesia generatur, et divinum sæpius impeditur officium ; statuimus quod nullus de cætero quasi proprium sedile in ecclesia vacans vendicare, nobilibus personis et ecclesiæ a patronis dentaxat exceptis ; si qui orandi causâ primo ecclesiam introierit juxta propriæ voluntatis arbitrium sibi eligat orandi locum.

" chester,

" chester, Mr. Dyer, vicar, and the churchwardens of the
" p'ifh of St. Nicholas in Rochefter theis be——

" After my very hartie commendac'ons I have bin moved
" by Sir Robert Crayford, and fome others, concerninge feats
" in yo' p'ifh church of St. Nicholas, in wch I coulde have bin
" content that yo' felfes, amongft yo' felfes, fhould have foe
" difpofed therein, that I fhould rather have approved yo'
" judgment then given any direc'on at all. I know there are
" certen knights, and ladies, and others, inhabitinge in other
" neighboring parifhes, who, out of devotion to the preaching
" of the Gofpel, reforte to yo' church, who cannot clayme
" any right of feats therein, yet I hold it fitt, that when
" they doe come, they fhould have places anfwerable to their
" rancke and quality. flor myne owne p'ticular opinion I
" doe not thincke it fitt that men and weomen fhould be
" placed in the fame feats, neither that weomen fhould be
" allowed to fitt in the chauncell, wh^{ch} was inftituted for
" clarkes. If you thinke good you may difpofe of fuch knights
" in the feats in the quier. And it had bin fitt (for the avoyd-
" ing all contenc'on about higher roomes in fuch publique
" affemblies), that you had referved two of the principall and
" higheft pewes, on one fide of the church, where fuch la-
" dies, and others, that are ftraungers, might fett, when they
" had come to yo' church, wch if you have done I muft much
" approve, and com'end yo' judgment, if otherwife, it is not
" yet to late to make fome fuch difpofic'on to the contents
" of yo' owne parifhoners, and fuch ftraungers, as reforte
" unto you, wherein I forbeare further to intermeddle,
" not doubtinge but that herein you will obferve decency,
" and order, according to all mens' ftates and quality. And
                                                           " foe

" foe I comend to the protec'ion of the Almighty, and re-
" maine,

" from my lodginge in   " Your affured poor ffreind,
" Durham howfe London,
" this fourth of Aprill,   " JO. ROFFENS."
" 1625."

             I am, Dear Sir,

Wilmington,
27th Oct. 1794.   truly yours,

             S. DENNE.

P. S. Wifhing for fome farther information refpecting the chancel of Upchurch church, I applied to Mr. Fifher, from whom I received the underwritten anfwer :

" I cannot find that I have any memorandums of this church ; but I can neverthelefs take upon me to fay, that there are no arms or cyphers on the fcreen behind the ftalls. Indeed I imagine, that fcreen to be of fubfequent erection. The backs of the ftalls are certainly broken off ; but, as I apprehend, from the plainnefs of their conftruction, they were never defigned to fupport ftone canopies, perhaps they terminated, like the ancient Gothic arm-chairs, thus (B). Pl.XI.

" The area oppofite the arch feen beyond the ftalls is not paved, but is covered with a few loofe boards, from which I fufpect that the altar did not ftand clofe to the Eaft wall, but on the verge of the prefent remaining ancient pavement. Mr. Hafted, I find, mentions the monument in the North chancel, of which the accompanying is an unfinifhed view, and the painted glafs there feen is, I apprehend, the glafs he alludes to ; I do not recollect any other in the church. It

Vol.   P   difplays

displays nothing but Gothic tracery, wherefore I imagine it will not merit your attention. The door which appears on one side of the monument leads by a winding stair-case to a Gothic vault under this chantry chancel, full of bones, which I believe to be coëval with the chancel itself, and may, perhaps, have some relation to the monument. This church has three different chancels; that on the North side contains the monument and stained glass. The middle or great chancel, the stalls, and three steps leading up to the altar, besides which there is a South chancel very spacious, with the stone, anciently the altar, lying in the pavement, as also a few words of an old inscription in French, and a singularly small monumental arch in the North wall. Mr. Hasted, I imagine, noticed the great chancel and nave under the descriptions of one aile, and specifically mentions the two other chancels, because it is probable they are additions to the church of a later date."

XIII. *Account of Sepulchral Monuments discovered at* Lincoln. *By the Reverend* John Carter, F. A S. *In a Letter to* John Pownall, *Esq.* F. A. S.

Read May 25, 1795.

Sir,

INCLOSED I send you, for the information of the Society of Antiquaries, a letter I have received from the Reverend Mr. John Carter of Lincoln, accompanied with very neat and accurate drawings of some curious and sepulchral antiquities lately discovered in the same field to the East of that town, in which former discoveries had been made of the like ancient sepulchrals, an account of which I communicated to the Society in 1791. See Archæologia, vol. X. p. 345.

It was my wish to have presented these papers in person, but my severe and painful indisposition deprives me of that advantage *.

If this communication should be thought worthy of publication in the next volume of the Archæologia, it may remain with the Society; if not, I am to request it may be returned to,

Sir,
        Your most obedient humble Servant,
To the Rev. Mr. Wrighte.   JOHN POWNALL.

* Mr. Pownall died July 17, 1795.

        DEAR

Lincoln, *April* 13, 1795.

DEAR SIR,

I Have taken the liberty of transmitting to you drawings of
some farther discoveries of Roman interments at Lincoln,
since those which you communicated to the Society, and of
which they published an account [a]. In the latter end of
February last, as the workmen were employed in removing
the earth, towards the East side, contiguous to the same
quarry, in order to get at the stone below, they met with the
remains of Roman sepulture exhibited in the inclosed sketches.
I was not present at the time of the discovery, but went to
the place a day or two after, as soon as I heard of it ; and
from the account of the workmen, and the relation given me
by the quarry-man who was engaged in the work himself,
and seems to have been very attentive in marking the particulars, I have drawn up the following, which I have reason
to believe a pretty accurate statement of the manner and position in which these remains were discovered.

About five feet and a half from the surface, placed East and
West, was found the complete skeleton of a man ; the bones
were very large and well preserved : the skull was perfect,
and every tooth remained firm in the head.　At his right arm
was placed fig. 4. Plate XIII. full of earth and bones ; at his left
was fig. 1. a jar, of very fine glass, on which there appeared
a coat of silvering.　It was full of earth, and had fig. 2. a
stylus stuck into it.　The inverted end of this is broad and

[a] Archæologia, vol. X. p. 345.

rather

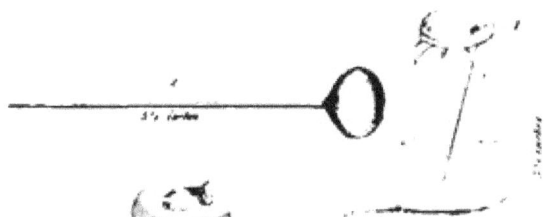

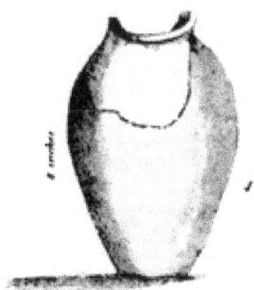

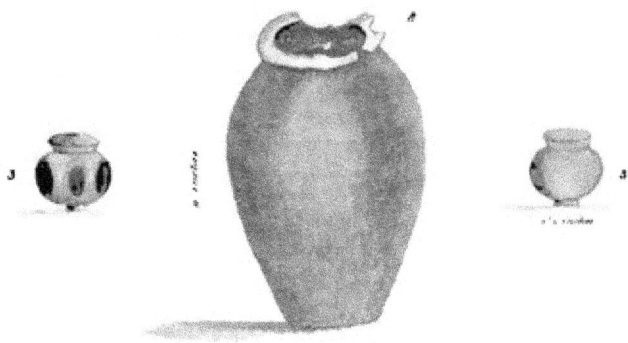

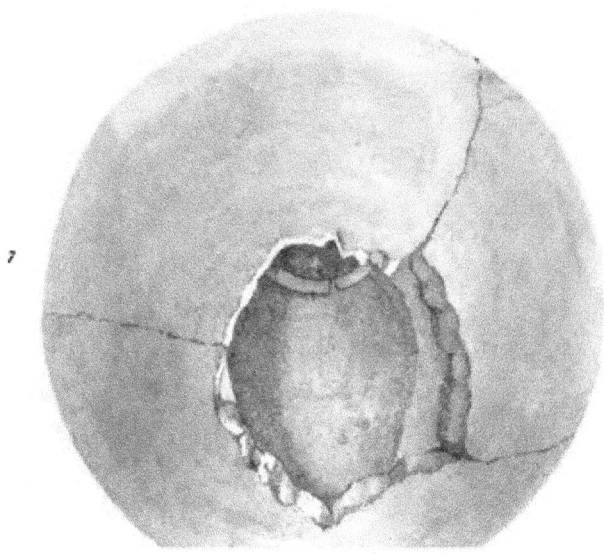

rather concave, and probably may have been used occasionally
as a spoon.   It is of mixed metal, but not at all corroded, and
when found was as bright as it had been on the day when it
was put into the ground.   The soil is of a dry sandy nature,
which is the reason, no doubt, why this and the human
bones have been so surprizingly preserved through so many
centuries.   Figures 3. 3. appear to me to be two specimens of
the *simpulum*, the one of black ware and indented, the other
plain and red.   The latter was found at his head, the other
at his feet.   There were more of these which had been placed
round the body, but the rest were all broken.   From these remains, discovered with the body, I should suppose the deceased to have been of consequence : and, if one may judge
from the glass jar, probably used in libations, and the other
sacrificial utensils, I should conjecture he was one of the sa-
cerdotal rank.

At the foot of this were found two skeletons, placed North
and South, one above the other, the lowest about three
feet, and the other about one foot and a half from the
surface.

Fig. 7. Plate XIV. was dug up at the same time, at the distance of between three and four feet to the right from the remains first described.   It exhibits a mode of sepulture of which
I do not ever remember to have seen any account.   It is a
hollow globe of coarse earthen ware of eighteen inches diameter, with an aperture of nine inches, just large enough to
admit fig. 8, which was placed within it in the manner represented in fig. 7.   The workmen came to the upper part of
this globe at about a foot from the surface, and, though it did
appear cracked, were desirous of taking it up as perfect and
entire as they could.   But when lifting it out of the ground
it

it slipt from them some how or other, and rolled down the declivity, and had nearly overset one of the men in its passage. It was unfortunately broken all to pieces at the bottom [*b*]. But the parts were carefully preserved, and I had them joined together, in order to get the drawing taken; and I dare say you will think with me, that it forms a very curious receptacle for the ashes of the dead. It is a species of *conditorium*, of which I do not remember to have read any description in any ancient or modern author. The *fictiles sarcophagi*, enumerated by Mr. Gough [*c*], perhaps come the nearest to it; but they, if you except the *obrendaria* or *obruendaria*, were all used for the reception of the body entire. Pliny, in treating on the art of pottery and working in clay, has observed, that " many of the dead chose to be interred in earthen *folia*, and that Marcus Varro was buried so among leaves of myrtle, olive, and black poplar, after the Pythagorean custom [*d*]." It is not easy to determine precisely what was the form of those; but from the usual sense of a tub, vat, or vessel, affixed to *folium*, we may conceive they were coffins of the cylindrical, or tun-fashion, *generally* used for interment [*e*]; I say generally, because the specimen before us is a proof of

[*b*] Indeed both this and the urns were very tender, when dug up and exposed to the air, as it was just upon the breaking up of the frost.

[*c*] Sep. Mon. I. Introd. xxv. xxvi.

[*d*] Nat. Hist. XXXV. 12. cited ibidem.

[*e*] Q. Curtius, speaking of the sepulchre of Cyrus, says " *folum*, in quo corpus jacebat, velavit," lib. X. cap. I. 31. " Ubi Pitiscus in loc. annotat *folum* proprie est alveus, in quem lavatori descendebant" Græci σορον vocant." The word *folum*, as applied to vessels, seems to be derived from being q *folum*, de uno ligno factum, scooped out of one piece of wood. Hence another resemblance to the *folia fictilia* mentioned by Pliny, which were most probably sometimes all of one piece, as was this earthen globe.

the fame fort of farcophagus, with a little variation in the fhape, being fometimes applied to the reception of the *afhes* of the dead, and that there were other fpecies of the *folia fictilia* adapted alfo to urn-burial.

Mr. Fardell remembers, that about thirty-five years ago, a fmall fort of *Kiftvaen*, or box formed of four ftones with a cover of the fame, in which was enclofed an urn, was found in the fame quarry, more to the Weft. It was preferved a confiderable time by Mr. Wood, who then occupied the quarry, and kept it for the infpection of the curious. This, the excavated ftone in the poffeffion of Dr. Gordon, and the earthen globe juft defcribed, afford three fuch fingular fpecimens of urn-burial, as I think I may pretty confidently affert have not been difcovered in any other Roman cemetery. They were all undoubtedly ufed for perfons of diftinction; and the intent of the enclofure feems to have been to prevent their afhes mixing with the common earth.

Two or three days after thefe difcoveries were made, the workmen found another fkeleton, placed Eaft and Weft, at the depth of five feet and a half, which, from the fmallnefs of the bones, was fuppofed to be that of a female. On one fide of the head, towards the breaft, was placed fig. 5. This jug has a hole in it at the bottom. Nothing was found in it, but it had been enclofed in an urn, which was broken to pieces.

Fig. 6 was placed over the head, but nearer the furface, and filled with earth, afhes, nails, and bones. Fig 9 was at the feet; it is of a coarfer and darker fort of glafs than fig. 1. and holds four quarts. No coins were found, or any other memorial, which might lead to a conjecture towards afcertaining the date of their interments. There were pieces of black and yellow pitch in a broken urn near the top

I   of

of the larger bottle, and many more scattered up and down the ground.

Dr. Gordon was inclined to conjecture, that the room, discovered 100 yards to the West [*f*], was the common *ustrina* to the cemetery. Against that supposition, I think it evident, that these bodies were burned on the spot from the quantity of pitch found here, which, with paper and other combustible materials, was usually stuffed into the funeral piles, to make it the more easily catch fire, and to assist the flames in more rapidly consuming the body. I picked up pieces of lead also, which were probably melted off some of the funeral *dona*, such as cloaths, ornaments, arms, &c. generally thrown into the pile during the conflagration.

I have thought it remarkable, that the Romans, who confessedly borrowed their ceremonies at funerals, both with regard to cremation and interment, from the Greeks, should not also have adopted their method of placing the body in the ground. Their fashion was East and West [*g*], that of the Romans North and South. One of the workmen, who has been employed in these quarries for a number of years, and has during that time dug up a very great number of skeletons, told me, that except in a very few instances (of which there are two in the present memoir), he has always found them placed in a direction North and South. When different positions have occurred, they have been usually referred to times posterior to the introduction of Christianity, which in general may be true. But I cannot help thinking,

[*f*] Archæologia, vol. X. p. 348.

[*g*] The Ægyptians turned the body to the East, and the Athenians to the West. Plutarch, in Solon. Kennet's Antiq. of Rome, book V. p. 10.

that

that some of these may be ascribed to a much earlier period, where the party have desired to be interred *more Græco*. This however is only the rude conjecture of one not much versed in this sort of researches, and therefore I am certain will meet with the more indulgence from you. I thought, however, that these sketches would form a sort of supplement to the discoveries in the same place in 1791; and that though you might not think them of sufficient consequence to shew the Society, they might afford some amusement to yourself.

      I am, with great regard,

         Dear Sir,

            Yours, sincerely,

               JOHN CARTER.

John Pownall, Esq.

XIV. *Observations on Paper-Marks. By the Rev.* Samuel Denne, F. A. S. *In a Letter to Mr.* Gough.

Read May 21, and June 4, 1795.

DEAR SIR,

NOT long since, when Mr. Thomas Fisher had an opportunity of examining sundry letters and other papers deposited in a room over the Town Hall in Rochester, he was induced to sketch the paper, or water-marks, as they are sometimes called. His fac similes of this kind are sixty-four [a]; of which two are from writings dated in 1473, seven from those of the sixteenth century, and the residue from those of the seventeenth, with an exception of one of the year 1712. There is not one that has *a star of eight points within a double circle*, the device of John Tate, supposed to have been the first Paper-maker in England, and who is recorded to have had, if I mistake not in the reign of Henry VII, a mill at Hertford [b]. Nor is there more than one device (*viz. a hand open surmounted by a star* [c]) that is to be found in the collection engraved for the second volume of Original Letters published by Sir John Fenn [d]. This circumstance

[a] See Plates XV. XVI. XVII. XVIII.
[b] Original Letters, by John Fenn, esq. &c. Preface, page xx. note; and British Topography, vol. I. p. 482.
[c] Plate XV. Nº 3 and 4.
[d] Vol. II. Pl. XIII. p. 41.

may

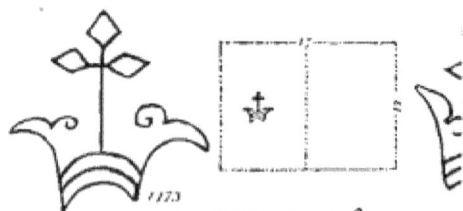

chd oñ bisa principibus wor dñi grunnasiñ qdicat myst dñi debat bru Snodecimo. _____

Snodecimo. _____

Dniatis di tempore boiit Le Anno ꝝ CC iiij Snodecimo ..

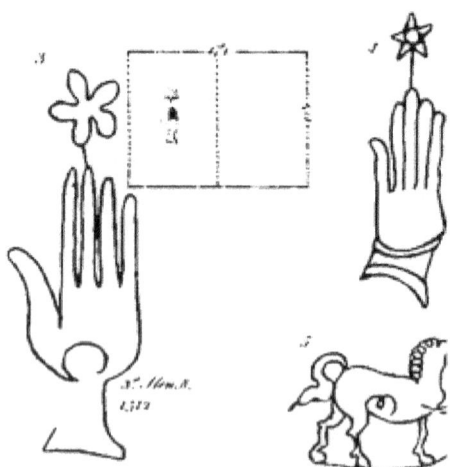

173 & 2. taken from the Irish Book.

may be, however, attributed to thefe original letters having been written on paper made abroad.

Mr. Fifher has fpecified the qualities of the papers, and he has alfo noticed with exactnefs their fizes; concerning which there is, in general, but a trifling difference in their dimenfions from thofe of the Pafton papers.

A fheet for the year 1649 has for a device a large hat [*d*]; and if an allufion to the fafhion of the times was intended, it would denote the broad-brim beaver worn by the puritans and republicans of that age. Four croffes are exhibited in a fheet of the year 1651 [*e*]; and on a fheet of the year 1657 a regal crown is difplayed [*f*]. As thefe fymbols were equally obnoxious to the then ruling powers, one can no otherwife account for the appearance and fufferance of them than on the fuppofition of the papers having been fabricated out of the kingdom. A fleur de lis under the crown ftrongly implies that this paper might be imported from France.

NESSON [*g*], a mark of 1584, was doubtlefs the name of the maker, but I am not aware what perfons were meant by COMPANY [*b*] in 1698. Many of the fheets have letters on them, probably initials of the names of the makers, which thofe who are acquainted with the hiftory of this manufacture may be able to appropriate.

Plate XV.

No. 1. Stout even paper, very hard and ftrong, and brown, but moft probably with age; taken from the leaves of an old

[*d*] Plate XVII. N° 31.
[*e*] Ibid. N° 33.
[*f*] Ibid. N° 34.
[*g*] Plate XV. N° 7.
[*b*] Plate XVIII. N° 46.

Q 2   da damaged book, indorfed *Cafh Book*, written in Latin, from which the two lines are engraved.

2, 3. Very ftout, rough, rather brown.

4. Even and rather thin, but very yellow.

5. Even, white, ftrong, rather thick.

Thefe five from the above book.

INDEX to PAPER MARKS, ranged according to Dates.

Plate XV.

No. 1, 1473. Stout even paper, very hard and ftrong, rather yellow with age.

   2, about 1473. Very ftout rough paper, rather brown.

   3. about 1512. Ditto. ditto.

   4. about 1512. Even, ftrong, white paper, rather thin.

   5, 1530. Even and rather thin, but yellow.

   6. 1558. 1603. Thin, rough, pretty white.

   7. 1584. Even, rather thin, and yellow with age.

   8. 1591. Brief paper, even and thin, but yellow with age.

   9, 1591. Ditto. ditto.

  10, 1601. A ftrong white paper, rather thin.

  11, 1608-9. Very ftout rough, rather brown.

  12, 1609. Very thin, white, and tolerably even.

  13, 1611. Thin, fine paper.

XVI.

  14, 1618. Stout, even, rather brown.

  15, 1623. even, fine.

  16, 1625. Brief paper, very ftout and fine, rather dark.

  17, 1625. Brief paper, coarfe, thin, very brown.

  18, 1625. Tolerably ftout, yellow with age.

19.

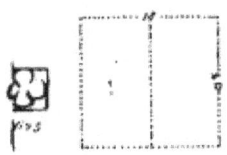

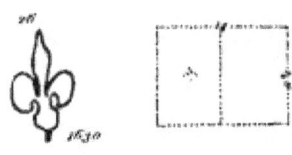

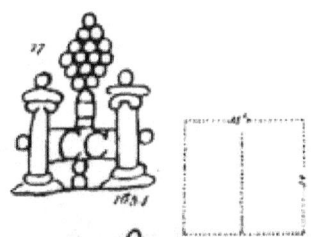

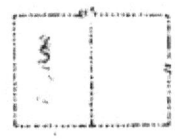

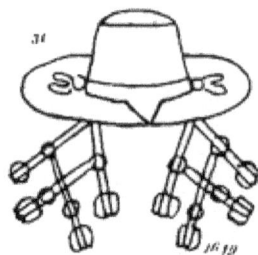

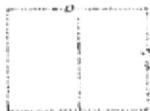

POTT Paper Marks.
Plate XIX.

1, 1604.
2, 1607.
3, 1609.
4, 1611.
5, 1611.
6, 1612.
7, 1618.
8, 1618.
9, 1621.
10, 1622.
11, 1623.
12, 1623.
13, 1624.
    1624.
14, 1635.
15, 1643.
16, 1663.
17, 1663.

Numbers 1, 2, 3, 4, 5, 6, 7, 10, 11, 17, are tolerably ſtout papers; 2, 3, 4, 5, 6, are alſo even; 8, 9, 12, 13, 14, 15, 16, are thin and ſomewhat fine, particularly 8, 12, 15, which are very thin. They are all yellow, but chiefly with age.

REMARKS.

It is probable the poſt horn [a] was the mark of a paper now called *Poſt* paper, one deſcription of which preſerves it at the preſent day, together with its texture and ſize little altered. The fleur de lis [b], of the Demy, which alſo retains

[a] Plate XVII, Nº 39, 40.
[b] Plate XVII, Nº 34. Plate XVIII, Nº 45.

6

its

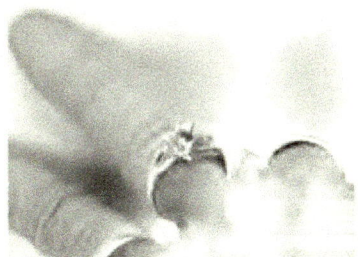

Its primitive device, and nearly its proportions. The hand
also [c], I suppose, gave name to paper now called *Hand* paper,
but which has materially altered in size and texture. There
is little doubt that the *Fools cap* [d] gave name to the paper
now distinguished by that singular epithet, although it has
resigned its mark, and adopted various others, as Britannia
and the Cap of Liberty on a pole, the latter, I apprehend,
peculiar to that manufactured in Holland. The flagons, or
pots [e], of which seventeen specimens are collected of different makers, characterise paper now denominated *Pot* paper, which also retains its proportions and size, but has ex-
changed its mark for that of the arms of England.

Having been favoured by Craven Ord, esq. with the sight
of impressions of eight or nine wooden cuts of paper marks
(not all regularly numbered), two of them on black grounds;
and probably belonging to some former work on printing;
one consisting wholly of ox heads and stars, another of hands
and stars, and a third of flaggons; I have compared them
with the plates at the end of the second volume of the Paston
Letters, and with the engravings from the delineations of Mr.
Fisher; and these circumstances have occurred to me.

The ox head, sometimes surmounted by a star, is on the
paper on which Fust printed some of his ancient books, was
a favourite paper mark, and perhaps as ancient as any of
the *Caput Bovis*, an embellishment much in request. Mrs.
Piozzi, in Observations on a Journey through France, &c.
at p. 198, thus expresses her sentiments: "The tomb of
Cecilia Metella, wife of the rich and famous Crassus, is beautiful, and still called *Capo di Bove* by the Italians, on account
of its being ornamented with the *ox head and flowers*, which

[c] Plate XV. N° 3, 4, and 13.   Plate XVII. N° 32.
[d] Plate XVI. N° 36.   [e] Plate XIX.

now flourish over every door in the new-built streets of London;" but the original of it she relates from Livy, and concludes, that from that time the ornament called *Caput Bovis* was in a manner confecrated to Diana, and her particular votaries ufed it on their tombs.

The open hand was likewife a very ancient paper mark, and much more frequently and for a longer time ufed than the ox head, which will account for a fort of paper having, as obferved by Mr. Fisher, acquired that denomination.

Of the Pafton Letters there are only two on which the paper-mark is what Sir John Fenn terms a flaggon or chalice [f], the latter is however an improper word. In Mr. Ord's plate there are fifteen flaggons, but No. 4 and 6 are of the fame pattern; and in Mr. Fisher's collection are feventeen of what he calls *flower pots*, though they have more the appearance of drinking veffels. The flaggon in the Pafton plate is almoft plain, and not furmounted by a crefcent, a ftar, or any other figure, as moft of the flaggons in the other collections are, and many of them are not a little embellished; but it is obfervable, that there is not an exact refemblance between any two numbers in thefe two plates. The flaggon, or rather pot, feems therefore to have been intended to denote the paper of a particular quality or fize, and the manufacturer thought it advifenble to add his own private mark.

Mr. Ord's plates have feveral marks totally different from any noticed by either Sir John Fenn or Mr. Fisher, and they are judicioufly arranged; but, unluckily, as the *date* of each mark is omitted, it is impoffible to fix with precifion the age of the refpective papers; but the marks are accompanied with initials and merchants marks, and fomething like figns.

[f] There is a chalice in Mr. Ord's Plate IV.

Not

Not one horn is to be feen in the Pafton Letters. In Mr.
Ord's plates there are feven with this fymbol, and in Mr.
Fifher's two, one of the year 1670, the other of 1679. Sup-
pofing thofe in Mr. Ord's collection to have been nearly co-
eval with Mr. Fifher's, as this is the device of what is called Poft
paper, it fhould feem that it was not fo denominated till after
the eftablifhment of The General Poft, when it was the general
practice of the boy who conveyed the mail to blow his horn.

The Fool's cap is not in either the Pafton Letters or Mr.
Ord's Plates. The date of that device in Mr. Fifher's is as late
as 1661. In not one of the collection is the Cap of Liberty difcernible, though now, as Mr. Fifher has obferved,
the Fool's cap paper has for its mark Britannia, or the Ram-
pant Lion fupporting the Cap of Liberty on a pole; but
query his authority for apprehending that the latter is peculiar to that manufactured in Holland.

The marks on the paper ufed by Caxton and other early
printers, engraved by Mr. Ames in his Typographical Antiquities, are the ox head and ftar, the p, the fheers, the hand
and ftar, a collared dog's head reverfed with a trefoil over him,
the holy lamb, a ring furmounted by a ftar, a fhip, a crown,
and a fhield with fomething like a bend.

" Bartholomeus de proprietatibus rerum" was the firft book
printed on paper manufactured in England, and came out,
without date, about the year 1495, or 6. The maker of this
paper was John Tate, junior, as I fuppofe, by the Prohemium
at the end of the faid book [g]. The mark of the faid paper
is a wheel; the paper itfelf is extraordinary fine and good [h].

[g] " And John Tate the yonger, joye mote hem broke,
Which late hathe in England doo make this paper thynne,
That now in our Englith this boke is prynted ioue."
[h] Herbert, p. 4. note d.

VOL. XII. R Mr.

Mr. Fisher copied several of the papers, particularly six letters which had a reference to the proposed arrivals of King Charles the First at Rochester, at the time of his marrying the Princess Henrietta of France. It appears from the first of these letters, that the King had intended sleeping at Rochester as he went to and as he returned from Dover, and it contained an order to the mayor to secure all the lodgings for the accommodation of the retinues of their Majesties. This letter, or warrant, was signed by nine privy counsellors, whose autographs Mr. Fisher delineated *. There are three letters from Dr. Balcanquall, dean of Rochester, upon the same occasion. In the first of them he expresses an apprehension, left, in consequence of the King's having delayed his journey, he may have incurred a needless expence for the provisions he had directed to be sent from Boxley to the deanery: and in the second he apprizes the mayor, that when he with his select band waited on their Majesties, it would be expected that presents should be offered to both the King and the Queen; and a caution explicit is given, that the speech to the King should be very concise. A fac simile is taken of the Dean's seal as well as his autograph †. The seal has impressed on it an anvil, and a hand with a hammer uplifted. The motto is *Ferendo Ferior*. Whether this were the armorial bearing or the crest of Dr. Balcanquall's family, the little knowledge I have in heraldry will not warrant me to determine; but the motto is not unapt for a polemick, and as the Dean was sent to the synod of Dort as a representative of the Church of Scotland, it may be presumed that he was a zealous controversialist.

There are besides two letters from Lord Conway, a principal secretary of state. One of them is an order for a strict pro-

* Plate XX. 1.   † Ib. 4. 5.

6

pro-

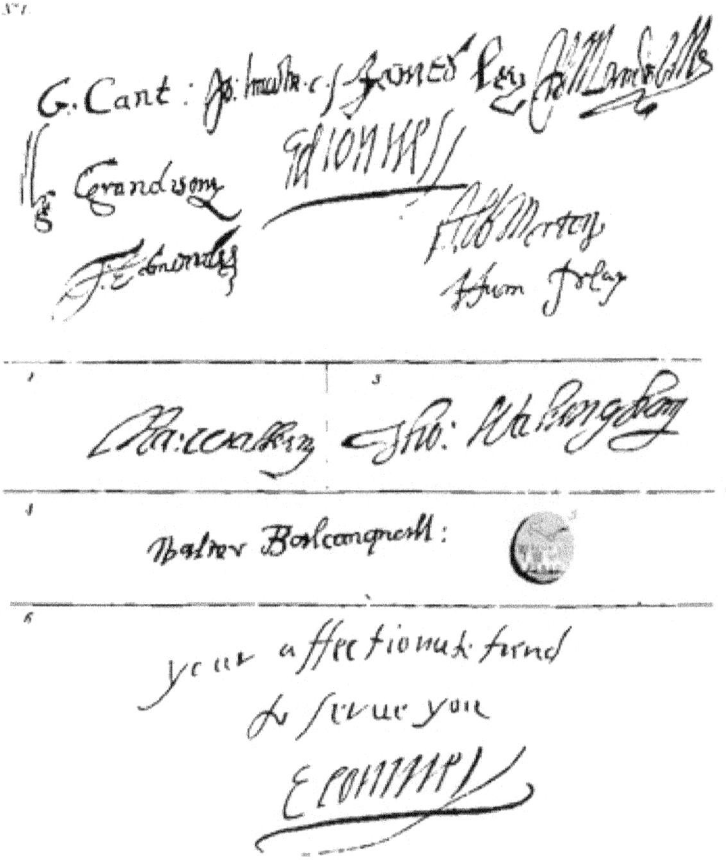
G. Cant:
Grandison
your affectionate frend
to serve you

profecution of fome men taken up on fufpicion of robbing a
courier from the French ambaffador; and, in the other letter the fecretary enjoins a fufpenfion of the trial of a fervant of
count Enno, of Eaft Friefland, who had been imprifoned for
killing a man. The fecretary figns himfelf E. Conwey, and
not Conway, the mode of fpelling generally ufed by the family. From the autograph, which comprizes the fix concluding words of the fecond letter, it fhould feem that the
farcaftic ftricture of King James, of his having a fecretary
that could not write, was not wholly unmerited. This is
advanced on the authority of Lord Clarendon, in whofe Hiftory of the Rebellion *, vol. I. p. 64, is this paffage: "Sir
Dudley Carleton was put into the place of Lord Conway, who
for age and incapacity was at laft removed from the fecretary's
office, which he had exercifed many years with very notable
infufficiency; fo that King James was wont pleafantly to fay,
that 'Stenny (the Duke of Buckingham) had given him two
very proper fervants; a fecretary who could neither write
nor read, and a groom of his bedchamber, who could not
trufs his points;' Mr. Clarke having but one hand."

Imagining that none of thefe letters are in print, I have,
with Mr. Fifher's confent, tranfmitted copies of them, together with the autographs and his delineations of the paper-
marks. And fhould you concur in opinion with me, that the
reading of the epiftles, and an infpection of the figns manual
and devices, are likely to afford amufement for an evening to
the Society, no apology can be wanting for my taking the
freedom of defiring you to convey them to the Secretary Mr.
Wrighte.

I remain, dear Sir,

Wilmington, Your faithful and obliged Servant,
14th Nov. 1794. SAMUEL DENNE.

* Edit. Oxford, 1707, 8vo.

Copies

Copies of Letters referred to in Mr. DENNE's Letter to Mr. GOUGH.

No. I.

AFTER o' hartie comendac'ons. Wheras his Matie intendeth to make repaire to his castle of Dover upon the 16th of this p'sent moneth, attended thither wth a greate traine both for quallitie and nomber, being the place appoynted by his highnes for the landing and first recepc'on of Madame Henriette, doughter of ffrance, now his Matie Royall Consorte, who, as we understand, comes over lykewise, attended wth a full traine, his Matie intending lykewise in his way to Dover to lye at Rochester the 13th of this p'sent month, we takeing into consideraçon, that the concourse and resorte of people thither (usuall upon lyke occas'ons) cannot but fall out to incomodateing and disfurnishing, both for lodging and otherwise, of the traine and retinue aforesaid, unto both their Maties, unless some fitt and tymely caution be had therin, have therfore thought good hereby to authorize and require you to give peremptorie and expresse order, that from the foresaid 13th of this p'sent, dureing his Maties aboade at Rochester (as well in his iorney to Dover, as in his retourne back againe), noe p'sons whatsoever, not being inhabitants of yo' towne, shal be suffered to take up any lodgings w^thin the same, unless onely for the King and Queen's traine and retinue, and untill they be first sufficiently pr'vided for and accommodated by the R^l Harbinger and the rest unto whom that service app'tains. Hereof you are not to fayle upon paine of his Maties high-

high difpleafure, and as you will anfwer the contrarie at yo'
p'lls. And foe we bid you hartely farewell: from Whytehall
the 6ᵗʰ of May, 1625.

Yoʳ loveing ffrends,

G. cant.	Jū : lincoln.	James ley	W. Mandeville.
Grandifone		Ed. Conwey
T. Edmondes		Alb. Morton
		Hum. Play.

May' and Magiftrates
of Rocheſter.

No. II.

Right Woᵘ

THE K' Ma' havinge this daie altered his tyme of cominge
into Kent, maketh me (in refpeſt of my attendance) defyre
yᵉ troble in countermaunding fuch fuſions as by form' warrant you have geven for yᵉ neigbbors meetinge before me, as
deputy clarke of the m'keit for the berge, I now not being
able to attend that fervice but accordinge to the dayes fett
downe in this p'cept; whᵗʰ I pray may be executed accordingly, and the former p'cept fent you for the purpos may doe
no execuc'on: fo I fhall thanke you for this courtefy, and be
traſtable to yʳ will in things fitting and refonable, and ftill
remayne

at yᵉ Wᵗʸ depofall,

xiii May, 1625. CHA: WALKERY*.

The King will be at Rocheſter on Friday the xxᵗʰ of May,
and not before, for foe is warninge this day geven at Whitehall.

To the right worᵏ the mayor and other
principall officeⁿ of the cittie of Rocheſter.

* See his Autograph, Plate XX. 2.

No. III.

No. III.

SIR,

I am sorrie that I am so unfortunate in my provisions, and I am either so mistaken, or my letters so slow; for sure I gave no other direction but that they should be in readiness against the tyme I sent for them, I pray yow let no tyme be made account of for the king's comming till I send you woord; it is now delayed till the next Thuirsday. and for any thing I can learne is lyke to be put of longer; for fear of further mistaking, command John Hall presently to send a messenger to Mrs. Wyat at Boxley, with a note signifying the delay of the King's comming, and that, therefore, no provisions be sent to Rochester till they hear from me, for unles a messenger be presently dispatched, they will perhaps be sent on Monday morning: Thus, with the remembrance of my best love and my wyfs, I rest,

Savoy, this 20 of   Your verie loving freind,
   May, 1625.   WALTER BALCANQUALL.

(Received the 21 of *May* att
8 of the clock att night.)

For my worthy and much respected freind,
   Mr. Dyer, preacher at Rochester.
                    hast! hast!

No. IV.

No. IV.

Worthy Mr. Maior,

ACCORDING to my promis I do write unto you, and fend you all the news that we have at this time; the King is gone this day to Dover, and it is feared he will go to Hulleine, but I hope he will not. The Queen is not expected to land till Monday next; but then the King will make all poffible hafte he can towards London, tarienge but on night at Canterbery, and another at your town. I will go to-morrow to Dover, wheare I will remember you to your noble frende Sir John Hipefley, and will, as occafion ferveth, ftill advertife you efpecially any thinge that may concerne you or the city. I pray let this letter enclofed be fent away for Darford for my father with all fpeed, for it concerns the King's fpeciall fervis. And fo, with my kind love remembered to you and all our frendes, I reft

Canterbery, this Thurfeday	Your affured frende
night late, being the fecond	to do you fervis,
of June, 1625.	Signed THO. WALSINGHAM *.

For his Maj[ts] fpecial fervis—To the Right
Worfhipfull my very loving frende the Maior
of Rochefter, theife—Hafte, hafte, poft hafte,
   THO. WALSINGHAM.

* See his Autograph, Plate XX. 3.

No. V.

No. V.

My Woorthy Freinds,

IMMEDIATELY upon the receipt of your letters I addreſſed myſelfe to my L. Chamberlain, whom I found with the King. I made his L. acquainted with your letters ; the King believeth your cittie to be free of the plaigue, having teſtimonie thereof under your hands. For his intertainment by you, his Maᵗⁱᵉ expecteth the ſame intertainment from you which he had from Canterbury, and meaneth to give you the lyke. Out of his coach his Maᵗⁱᵉ will not ſturre, but looketh to be receaved by you with your ſelect band ; a ſpeech (which yow muſt take order to be verie ſhort), and for a preſent to himſelfe and the Queen. I knowe it is expected ; but I have no direction to ſay any thing of it. This night, by God his grace, the Queen landeth ; for yeſterday by two of the clocke ſhe was certainely at Bulloigne. Wee ſhall all be with you on Monday, or on Tueſday, as I rather think, at fartheſt ; but whether of the two, I ſhall not fail before that tyme to advertiſe. In what I am nowe or ever ſhall be able to doe you ſervice, I hope you will doe me ſo much right as to p--ᵗ your ſelfe of the willing induſtrie of

Canterbury, this 9 of   Your faithful frenid and Servant,
June, 1625.   WALTER BALCANQUAL

For the Right Worᵖ my woorty freinds,
Mr. Mayor, and the Aldermen of the
citie of Rocheſter.

theſe.

No. VI.

No. VI.

SIR,

THEIR are newes juſt nowe come to the King that the Queen is within fight of Dover, and readie to land ; on Tueſday or Weddinſday at fartheſt they will both come through your cittie. I make no queſtion you will doe your beſt for their intertainment. God keep you according to the wiſhes of Canterbury the 12.　　Your moſt reſpectful freind, of June, 1625.　(Signed) WALTER BALCANQUALL.*.

No. VII.

May it pleaſe yo*

I have received informac'on, that ſome of thoſe men w⁰⁰ robbed the currier ſent from the ffrench ambaſſador are now taken. I muſt lett yo* know, that that action brought a verie great inconvenience to his Maᵗʰˢ buſineſſes then in hand, and that yo* may judge how fowle thoſe acts are, even that breake the ordinary trafficke and com'erce of the highwaies, and much more when they reach to perſons that are compriſed wᵗʰin the publicke faith, as the meſſengers of Kings are, even amongſt the camps and gards of fouldiers, ennemies to the Kings of thoſe meſſengers. There is information given, that there was a ſpectacle found, wᶜʰ was a part of thoſe things taken from the ffrench poſt. His Majᵗ pleaſure is, that you make a carefull and ſtraight examinac'on of the parties, and

* See Plate XX. 4.

all circumftances, and that you fend thofe examinac'ons unto mee, one of his Maties principal fecretaries of ftate. And that yo^u doe at the com'ing of the judges to inquire of the ffacts of life and death, and before thefe p'ties fhall be called to an-fwere, inform the Judges of his Ma^u pleafure, by fhewing them this l'tre ; for his Maties pleafure is to require a ftrict ac-count in this caufe, the fact com'itted not onely upon a ftran-ger, but upon a perfvn in publicke employment, and in a more extraordinary manner in his Maties protection than other men. I fhall not doubt of yor care, and yor faithfulnefs ; and I fhall be readie to improve yor affections to juftice, and obe-dience to his Maties directions to yor moft advantage. And wth the offer of my fervice, I remaine

London, March   Yo^r affured loving friend,
9th, 1624.   EDW. CONWEY.

(To the Mayor and Juftices of Rochefter.)

No. VIII.

S^r

I do much wonder at what is told mee by this meffenger coming yefterday from Rochefter, that yo^u had then received no l'res from mee concerning the fonne of one Fredericken Heren, a prifonner there for killinge a man, concerning whom I fignifyed unto yo^u fome dayes fince his Maties pleafure, that yo^u fhould certifie the manner of that fact, and the pro-ceedings that have been thereupon. And in the meane time to caufe him to bee kept in the fame manner as nowe hee is, w^{th}out anie proceedings againft him untill his Ma^{ts}. pleafure be knowne. I am further nowe to give yo^u knowledge, that

5   his

his Ma⁺, at the inftance of his good coufen count Enno, of
Eaft Frizeland (whofe fervaunt the prifoner is), hath a great
inclinac'on to fhewe him favour and grace as by lawe may be
affoarded. And accordingly yo⁰ are to be carefull that there
bee noe proceedinge or tryall againft him upon anie p'text
whatfoever, untill yo⁰ have made retorne of yo' certificate,
and receaved his Ma⁰ᵗ pleafure thereupon. Whereof yo⁰ may
in noe wife fayle. And foe I remayne,

Court at Alderfhott   Your affeftionate frend
   July 25. 1625.   to ferve you,
                      E. CONWEY*.

Yo⁰ muft fhew this l're to the Judges, or
anie other whom it may concerne to ftay
all proceedings   E. CONWEY.

The meffenger had other occafions, and foe I have
addreffed it to yo⁰ by poft

     To the Mayor of Rochefter on his Maj'r* fervice.

         * See Plate XX. 6.

S 2   XIV.

XIV. *An Essay towards a History of the* Venta Icenorum *of the* Romans, *and of* Norwich Castle; *with Remarks on the Architecture of the* Anglo-Saxons *and* Normans. *By* William Wilkins, *of* Norwich,

Read June 11, 18, 25, 1795.

HISTORIANS affert, that the *Belgæ* [a], or *Attrebatii*, a people of Gaul, were the firft emigrants who fettled in the Southern parts of this ifland long before the Roman eagle was advanced hither. Little can be learned relating to them or the ancient Britons before Cæfar's invafion, which was fifty three or fifty four years before Chrift. About that time, we learn, that the kingdom of the Iceni, whofe inhabitants were called *Cenimagni*, comprehended the counties of Norfolk, Suffolk, Cambridge, and Huntingdon, and that they, with other kingdoms in this ifland, fubmitted by their ambaffadors to Cæfar; and that afterwards, in order to keep the people in fubjection, the proprætor Oftorius Scapula, who was fent hither about the year of Chrift 47 [b], eftablifhed garrifons, and difarmed the fufpected people in various parts of the ifland [c]. Perhaps the beft idea that can be formed of Britain is given us in Virgil's firft paftoral:

"Et penitus toto divifos orbe Britannos [d]."

[a] Gibfon's Camden, p. 58.
[b] Brady's Hiftory of England, p. 14.
[c] Camden, p. xlvi.
[d] Divided from the world the Britifh race.

The

The Iceni, who are represented as a stout and courageous people, were the first who revolted from the Roman government; but having no armour to defend themselves, or any knowledge in the art of war, they were soon after defeated in a bloody battle. Under the reign of Nero, when the propraetor Suetonius Paulinus, who succeeded Veranius in the government of Britain, Anno 58 or 60, was engaged in the island of Mona (now Anglesea), the Iceni, whose queen Boadicia and her daughters had been treated by the Roman tribunes in the most ignominious manner, in concert with the Trinobantes [e] and other nations, again revolted [f] with a determination, if possible, to free themselves from the Roman yoke, and at Malden, Verulam [g], and other places, which they passed through, they severely retaliated their wrongs on the Romans and their allies in this war; to the number of seventy thousand being put to the sword without distinction. Boadicia's army, however, consisting of between two and three hundred thousand, were soon after defeated by Suetonius, who had with him the fourteenth legion, some companies of the twentieth, and the nearest auxiliaries, together amounting to about ten thousand men well armed, who slew about eighty thousand of the Britons, and Boadicia, rather than fall into the hands of the enemy, is said by Tacitus, to have poisoned herself [h]. Cerealis was afterwards sent by Vespasian, and after him by Julius Frontinus, who was equally successful in authority and reputation; but Julius Agricola, who governed in the reigns of Vespasian, Titus,

[e] Inhabitants of Middlesex and Essex.
[f] A. D. 62.
[g] A Roman town near St. Alban's in Hertfordshire.
[h] Dio Cassius affirms she died of sickness.

and

and Domitian, diftinguifhed himfelf moft in rendering Britain ufeful to his country, by civilizing its inhabitants, and
gradually incorporating them as a part of the Roman empire [*i*].

To guard the fhore, which was frequently invefted by the
Saxons, and to keep in fubjection the inhabitants, who were
often revolting, the Romans thought it neceffary to appoint
a number of military eftablifhments in this neighbourhood,
namely, Gariononum [*k*], Sitomagus [*l*], Branudonum [*m*],

[*i*] Hume's Hiftory of England.

[*k*] Burgh Caftle near Yarmouth, where was ftationed the captain of the Sta-
blefian Horfe, who was ftiled Gariononenfis, under the command of the count
of the Saxon fhore, called *Comes Tractus Maritimi*, through Britain, who had under
him nine maritime towns placed on the South and Eaft coaft of the ifland, and the
foldiers in garrifon were about 2,200 foot, and 200 horfe *. There are few remains of Roman buildings in Britain in fo good prefervation as Gariononum;
moft of the walls are now ftanding, and it is altogether a very fine fpecimen of
their favourite military architecture; its form is a parallelogram of 214 yards in
length, and 107 yards in breadth, containing 4 acres 2 roods.

[*l*] Thetford, famed for being the feat of the kings of the Eaft Angles.

[*m*] Brancafter near Burnham, another maritime ftation; here was ftationed the Captain of the Dalmatian horfe. Camden fays, "it contained fome
8 acres." Gibfon, his annotator, "there are plain remains of a Roman camp,
" anfwering the figure of that defcribed by Cæfar (Comment. de Bell. Gall. l. 2).
" 'Caftra in altitudinem pedum 12 vallo foffaque duodeviginti pedum, munire
" jubet,' all the dimenfions of it fhew it was not made in a hurry, but was re-
" gular and defigned on purpofe for a ftation upon that Northern fhore againft the
" incurfions of the Saxons." When I was there in 1788 the walls were all erafed,
but on the fummit of the foffe are ftrewed numberlefs pieces of Roman tiles
and urns. W. W.

* Thefe numbers from the Notitia, written in the reign of Theodofius the younger,
A. D. 410, allow only 267 to each ftation, which could not, by any means, be fufficient to defend them; probably the Britifh allies, of which great part of the army
was compofed, are not included.

VENTA

VENTA ICENORUM [n]: and ad Tuam [o], befides other fub-
ordinate Stativa Hiberna, and Caftra Æftiva; Caftor by
Yarmouth, Caftleacre caftle, Elmham and Buxton in Norfolk were probably of thefe defcriptions, where numbers of
coins and Roman burial-urns have at various times been difcovered.

We have Camden's authority for calling VENTA ICE-
NORUM the moft flourifhing city of the kingdom of the Iceni;
yet it is pretty certain, that Sitomagus fubfequently became,
from its central fituation, the capital of the kings of the
Eaft Angles.

The Roman *ftativa* here, in the midft of fmall fwelling
hills, is clofe to the banks of the Tefe [p], which,
though now a fmall river, there is every reafon to fuppofe
to have been in thofe early times of much greater confequence, and moft probably navigable for Roman fhipping,

[n] Caftor, by Norwich, the flourifhing city of the Iceni. Camden, p. 385.

[o] Tafeburgh, 7 or 8 miles South from Norwich, and 5 from Caftor; where
is ftill a fquare entrenchment containing 24 acres. The name of the town fhews
its original to have been the *Burgh* or Fortification on the River *Tuas* or *Tife*,
and accordingly Dr. Gale, in his Commentary on Antoninus's Itinerary, p. 109,
tells us this river was called *Tife*, and that the ftation *ad Tuam*, mentioned in the
Peutingerian Tables, was here; and indeed the parifh church ftands in the fortification, the dimenfions of which are ftill vifible, and an advantageous fituation it
was to guard the pafs of the river leading to *Caftor*, being on the fummit of a
very high hill, commanding the adjacent country, and hanging over the river,
which turns Eaftward, and makes a commodious finus or bay for fuch veffels
as come up hither. Bloomfield, vol. III. p. 136.

[p] The river Tefe joins the Wenfum at Troufe*, about 3 miles to the
North-eaft, where, conjoined with another fmall ftream, it takes the name of
YARE †.

* Troë oufe.
† Garienn.

35

as history informs us of a large extent of flat country in the
Eastern and North-eastern parts of Norfolk, and the adjacent
parts of Suffolk, which was entirely overflooded; but from the
difference of the rise of the tides upon this coast, or the
embankments to the North [q], which have since taken
place, or probably from both, a very considerable quantity
of rich fertile country of many thousand acres area, and even
the ground upon which the town of Yarmouth now stands,
as well as other towns of less consequence, was the bed of the
Æstuary of the Yare prior to the year 1040.

The North, East, and South sides of the station have
banks raised from a vallum of considerable depth, and the
West side has a bank raised from the river. On these were
built the walls, some remains of which are still visible, particularly on the North side.

The superficial area of the station is about thirty-five acres.
It is much superior to any other in this part of England, and
forms a parallelogram [r], with the corners rounded like
those at Burgh, Chesterford, and Dorchester.

The Eastern end, in which was the *porta prætoriana*, is
1120 feet in extent, and the North and South sides, in which

[q] See Act of Parliament, Anno Septimo Jacobi I. 1609, vol. III. cap. 20,
which enumerates 74 parishes in Norfolk, and 15 in Suffolk, subject to inunda-
tions caused by Spring tides assisted by strong Westerly winds.

[r] This nearly agrees with the form of encampment described in Cæsar's
Commentaries; and, according to the author of the Travels of Anacharsis the
younger *, who quotes Herodotus †, was also in use by the Persians, and probably by the Grecians, some centuries before Mardonius, Xerxes's general, at the
battle of Platæa, caused a space of ten stadia ‡ square to be surrounded with a deep
ditch, and likewise with walls and wooden towers.

* Introduct. Travels in Greece, p. 301.
† Ib. IX. cap. 15.
‡ More than a mile.

were

2

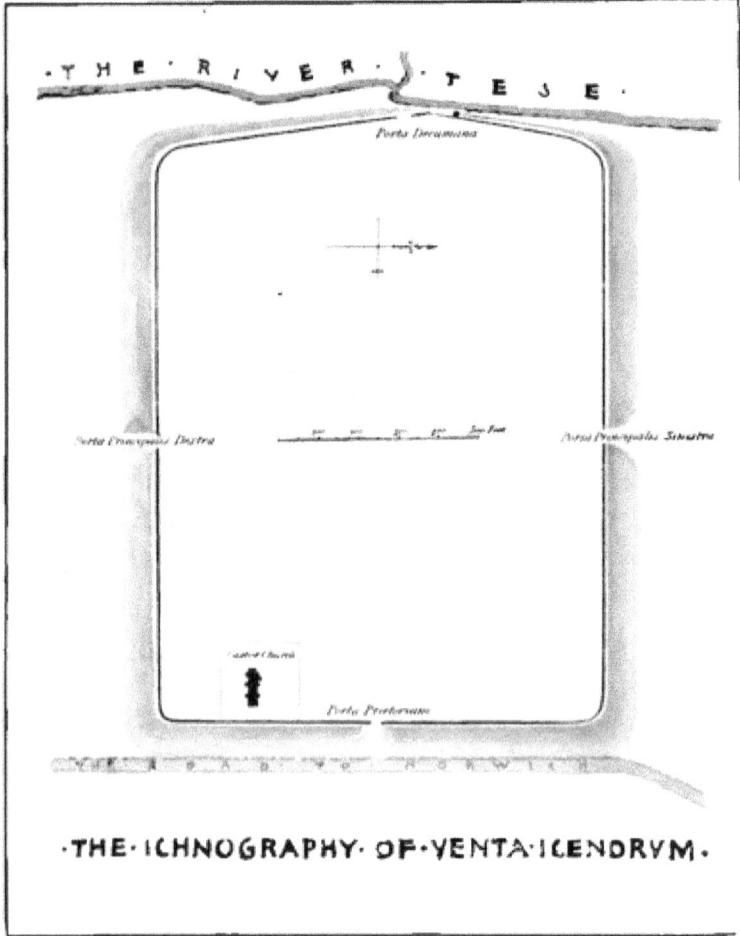

·THE·ICHNOGRAPHY·OF·VENTA·ICENORVM·

were the right and left hand gates, are 1349 feet in length. The
Weft end is not exactly parallel to the Eaft (See Plate XXI.),
but is brought to an obtufe point between the *porta decumana*
and the remains of a folid tower, now ftanding clofe to the
river, preventing the probability of an affault in that quarter,
which, in a ftation of this magnitude, muft have been of great
confequence, and by means thereof they could get to the river
unmolefted. This tower, although much wafted by time, and
the river wafhing againft it, is ftill 33 feet in circumference,
and is built with flints and mortar, in irregular ftrata with
Roman tiles, like the remains of Burgh caftle, Chefter-
ford, St. Albans, &c. &c. The Romans employed in their
camps and armies artificers and workmen of all forts who
not only worked themfelves, but fuperintended thofe lefs
fkilful, in manufacturing bricks, teffellæ, lime, and mortar ;
and thofe ftations whofe vicinity afforded the beft materials for building, from the uncommon hardnefs of their
bricks, and the durable though fimple method of incorporating the lime and fand for mortar and cement, have bid defiance to all weather, though in the moft perifhable fituations.
Several parts of Norfolk are noted for producing the hardeft
and beft bricks in the kingdom; in the neighbourhood of
Caftre particularly is found excellent earth for that very purpofe, and from the denfity of the bricks ufed in this ftation,
moft probably no pains were fpared in mixing the earth, and
moulding them with the clay in a ftiffer ftate than is ufual at
prefent ; and as the country at that time, probably, afforded
firing in plenty, the well burning them made only the difference of the trouble in felling wood. There are not many
tiles to be found in the remaining walls ; but from a piece of
the ruin I obferved in the Northern loffe, almoft buried in

earth and overgrown with grass, it appeared as if the walls had been faced, like those of Burgh castle: for it is composed of three alternate courses of tiles [s], and a thickness of from eighteen inches to two feet and upwards of flints and pebbles cemented with mortar [t]. The neighbouring fields at a few feet from the surface yield excellent chalk; rough sand and rubble are also to be found here in abundance, so that, as Dr. Higgins observes in his experiments on calcareous earths, " chance furnished all that skill could aim at, in the choice and preparation of this article," the most important in holding the walls of the ancients together, as they were unassisted with bond-timber. It may be observed here, the roughness of the mortar, which is mixed with shingle, some of which measures an inch and more in diameter, accounts for the thickness of the joints between the tiles, which varies from three quarters to two inches.

Roman coins are very frequently found within the walls, and in the adjacent grounds, several of which I have in my possession, and the ploughmen, who were working in the Eastern end of the station, sold me two which they had found the preceding day, one of Constantine, and one of Dioclesian.

On the decline of the Roman empire, A. D. 446, most of the forces, which consisted of British auxiliaries as well as Romans, were withdrawn by Maximus and Constantine.

[s] The external angles of Caster church, which stands in the South-east corner of the station (see Plate XXI.), are built with tiles from the ruins; they measure 18 inches long by 12 inches broad, and from 1½ inch to 2 inches in thickness.

[t] The workmen employed in building walls with these materials were called *caementarii*. Mr. Essex's remarks on brick and stone buildings in England. Archæologia, vol. IV. p. 94.

Britain

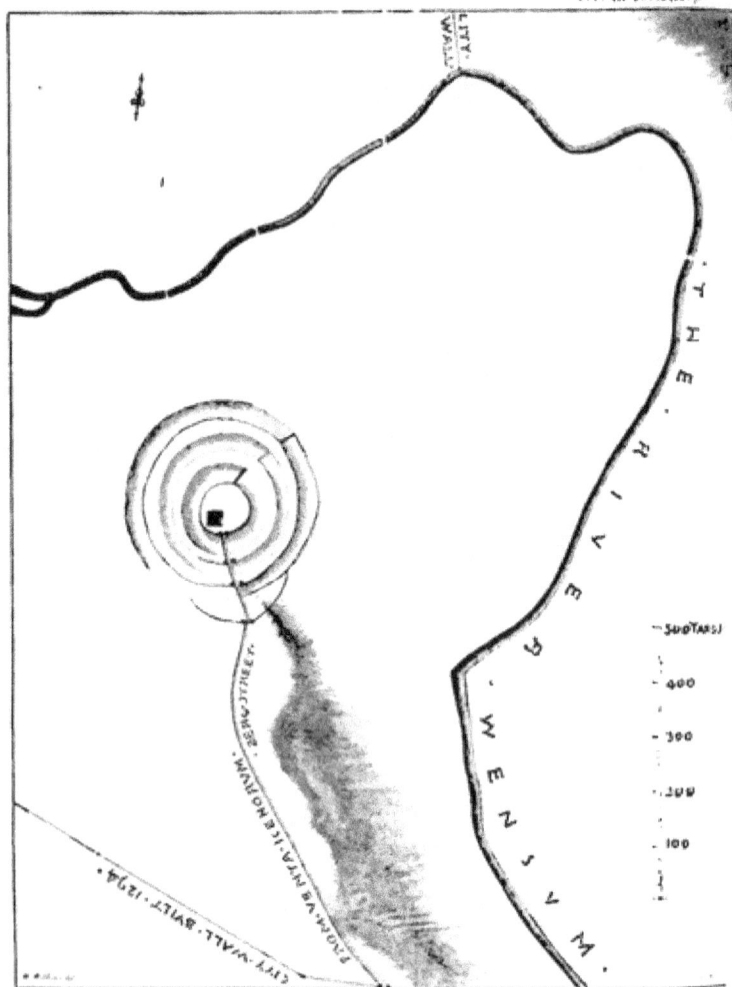

·SITE·OF·THE·NORTH·WIC·PRIOR·TO·THE·BVILDING·OF·THE·CITY·

Britain now having loft thefe her beft foldiers and the affiftance of the Romans, after having been fubject to them near
four hundred years, became a weak people and an eafy prey to
the Picts and Scots until the reign of Vortigern prince of Dum-
nonium, who invited the Saxons for affiftance ; but the Saxons
foon after repaid themfelves by difpoffeffing the Britons after
many battles ; and eftablifhing three new kingdoms. Uffa [u]
was the firft Saxon king who (A. D. 575) affumed the dominion
of the Eaft Angles, containing Norfolk, Suffolk, and Cam-
bridgefhire, whofe inhabitants were from him called Uff-
kinks, and it appears that Norwich was founded about this
æra, and was called in Saxon Noɲðþic, or Northwic [v], from
its relative fituation to the ancient Venta Icenorum, being
about three miles to the North of it, on a cape bounded by
the river Wenfum, which at this point makes an acute winding
from the Weft to the South-weft. See in plate XXII. a
map of the cape prior to the building of Norwich. The fite
of the building is alfo fhewn with the fuppofed road from
Venta Icenorum, which was the principal entrance for fome
centuries afterwards, and what is now called Ber-ftreet [w].

It is probable, the Roman ftation at Venta Icenorum was
about this time deferted. The elevated fite of Northwic, fo
well accommodated to the Britifh and Saxon modes of fortification, its fuperior conveniency for navigation, and its command of the rich adjacent country, were objects not to be
overlooked ; and in fact we find in A. D. 642, it was one of

[u] The eighth in defcent from the famous Woden. From Uffa the fucceeding
kings here were called Uffkings. Malmfb. lib. I. Indeed moft of the Saxon
princes were reputed to have fprung from Woden. Hume's Hift. of England.

[v] Gibfon's Camden, p. 385.

[w] Ber, Burg, &c ; ftreet, i. e. the ftreet leading to the caftle.

T 2 the

the feats and a royal castle of Anna the seventh king of the
East Angles. Tonbert, whom Bede calls a prince of the South
Girvii [x], in the year 652 married Etheldreda [y] the daughter of king Anna, by which marriage the Isle of Ely was fettled on her in dower [z], and after the decease of Tonbert,
part of the possessions annexed to the monastery which she
founded at Ely, were held by Castle-guard service of the
castle of Norwich [a]. This circumstance, which is noted by
Bede, Speed, Spelman, and other historians, shews the antiquity of the castle ; and the sum of money paid afterwards

[x] North and South Girvii were two provinces belonging to the East
Angles, what is now called the Isle of Ely. Tonbert was the proprietor, as appears by his making it a marriage fettlement ; by which it descended to the princess Etheldreda on the decease of her husband, A. D. 955. Bentham's Ely,
p. 47.

[y] Inning, now a small village in Suffolk, bordering on Cambridgeshire,
was also one of the feats of king Anna, where St. Etheldreda, the foundress of
the church, and first abbess of Ely, was born about A. D. 630. Ibid. p. 45.

Holkham in Norfolk was another feat of king Anna, where St. Withburga
his youngest daughter was fent to nurse. The place was sometime called With-
burgstowe, and a church was built in memory of her at the death of her father,
A. D. 654-5. Ibid. p. 76.

This village has since recovered its ancient name of Holkham, where the late
earl of Leicester built a magnificent palace, which descended to the family of
Thomas William Coke, Esq. one of the present members of parliament for the
county of Norfolk.

[z] Desponsatus itaque biennio ante interfectionem patris sui. MS. Lib.
Elien. lib. I. cap. 4. Bentham's Ely, p. 46.

[a] These lands must have been liable to Castle-guard service before they were
granted to Ely monastery ; for by the laws of the Saxons *, lands granted to
the church were not liable to secular services, unless they were first imposed on
them when they were given to secular men. Bede, l. IV. cap. 26, p. 198.

* Ethelwolph, son of Egbert, ordained, that riches and lands due to the holy
church should be free from all tribute or regal services. Bede's Hist. Eccles. lib. III.
cap. 11.

3   by

by Hervey the first bishop of Ely [b] for the king's transferring the service of those who held of the church by knight's service from Norwich castle to the Isle of Ely: shews also the great possessions appertaining to Norwich castle in king Anna's times.

Little can be learned relating to the castle of Norwich, from the time of king Anna to the reign of king Alfred the Great, but that there were frequent conflicts with the Danes, who, in A. D. 866 [c], formed a considerable army in the kingdom of the East Angles, and in 870 wintered at Thetford, and soon after slew Edmund king of the East Angles in an engagement where his army was routed.

The castle of Norwich from its situation, so near the German ocean, was generally the first object of the Danish invasions, and we find it frequently in their possession.

It is said in the life of king Alfred [d], that he found the walls of the Saxon castles, which were of earth [e], incompetent for defence against the Danes, and that he accordingly im-

[b] £.1000 Bentham's Ely, p. 132. See Carta Regis Henrici I. de acquistatione de wards Militum in Castello Regis de Norwic. Ex iisdem MSS. Bentham's Appendix, N° xviii.

[c] Saxon Annals.

[d] Asserius Menevensis de vita et gestis Regis Alfredi. Edit. Francoforti, 1603.

[e] Stone for buildings was in use with the Saxons prior to this time, and particularly so in the kingdom of the East Angles, the conventual church at Ely in the time of the Heptarchy, 673, the chapel at Orford, and the Saxon church at Dunwich, both in Suffolk, of whose foundation there are no records. Their plans are similar to that at Ely, and from Dunwich being the seat of Felix, the first bishop of the East Angles *, it is probable, that both the buildings at Dunwich and at Orford were built about that æra, 630 or 636, or soon after, possibly by his successors.

* At Dunwich there was Felix first bishop
Of th' Angle, and taught them the faith,
That is full hye in heven I hope. Harding, cap. 91. Weever, p. 717.

printed

proved their fortifications with brick and ftone bu ldings, and
that the royal caftle at Norwich in particular was repaired in
this manner by h m. " Among his other accomplifhments,
he was fkilful in architecture, and excelled his predeceffors in
elegance of building and adorning his palaces ; in conftruct-
ing large fhips for the fecurity of his coafts, and erecting
caftles in convenient parts of his kingdom. Indeed architecture before this time had been almoft wholly confined to religious ftructures ; but now it was by Alfred, and his two immediate fucceffors, chiefly applied to military purpofes, in
erecting fortreffes and towers, and in building and repairing
walled towns, which became neceffary to curb the infolence
and perfidy of the Danes [f]."

About A. D. 8 8 King Alfred obtained, at Ethandun in
Effex, a victory over Godrum [g] king of the Danes, to
whom he granted peace on condition of their leaving England,
but afterwards, on Godrum's converfion to Chriftianity,
king Alfred being his fponfor gave to him and his
people, who were alfo converted, the kingdom of the Eaft
Angles to hold in fealty, and the caftle of Norwich was his
royal feat. This was not long enjoyed by the Danes ; for this
forced converfion had but little influence on Efric, the fucceffor to Godrum, who joined the feditious Ethelwold, and
was flain in a battle againft king Edward furnamed the elder,
in 905 [b]. The kingdom of the Eaft Angles became now
again fubject to the Saxon kings, and the caftle of Norwich
continued a royal caftle in quiet poffeffion of the Saxon line
through the reigns of Athelftan, Edmund, Edred or Eldred,

[f] Denthiam's Remarks on Saxon Churches, p. 27.
[g] Godrum, Gothrom, or Gutheum. Brady's Hift. of England, p. 115.
[b] Brady, Ib. p. 117.

Edwin,

Edwin, Edgar, and Edward the martyr [i]; but, in king
Etheldred's reign the castle and town are said to have been
utterly destroyed by Swane [k] king of Denmark, who invaded
Norwich with a fleet in the year 1004 [l]. Ulfkettel earl of
the East Angles endeavoured to draw his forces together as
soon as possible in order to repulse the Danes before they
reached Thetford, and he sent a messenger to the neighbouring
country with command to burn the Danish shipping, whilst
the men were advancing into the country. This order was by
some means neglected; but though the Danes accomplished
their design of destroying Thetford without any check from
Ulfkettle, yet in their retreat from Thetford he met them
with a considerable detachment, and gave them battle; a
sharp engagement ensued, attended with great slaughter on
both sides, and had the whole of the Anglian army been in
the field, the Danes would, most probably, never have
reached Norwich; as it was, they reached their ships and
returned home again for that season. Norwich continued in
this desolate state until A. D. 1010 [m], when the Danish in-
vaders came once more, and fought another battle with
Ulfkettle at a place then called Rigmere near Ipswich, which
terminated in favour of the Danes, who from this time possessed themselves of the whole province of the East Angles.
The next year the Danish earl Turkell [n] expelled Ulfkettel,
and held the government of this province until Canute be-

[i] Various coins executed in Norwich in these reigns are mentioned in
Blomefield, p. 4.
[k] Or Sweyne.
[l] Chron. Sax. p. 133.
[m] Chron. Sax. p. 139.
[n] Or Turkell.

came sole monarch in 1017, who continued him in his go-
vernment, and committed to him the custody of Norwic.
Roger Bigod was made constable of the castle by William the
Conqueror about the year 1077, and the family of the Bigods
continued in that office, with little intermission, until Roger
Bigod, his fifth successor, surrendered it to king Edward the
Third in 1225; but in 1273 it was again granted to the
Bigods, and in 1293 Roger Bigod, as earl of Norfolk, was
constable of the castle, where the sheriff of the county [*o*] was
to keep criminals in safe custody till the coming of the Justices itinerant and jail delivery; notwithstanding the constables often refused the sheriffs that power, until an act of parliament in the 14th year of Edward III. [*p*], that the sheriffs
should have the custody of the same goals and prisoners as
they used to have, yet for a long time after this the king did
nominate a constable to the castle, in respect to its defence, in
his name; for, in 1354, 29 Edward III. Roger Clerk was
constable of the castle. In 1312 Thomas de Brotherton [*q*]
had a charter of the king in tail general of the honors [*r*]
of Roger Bigod, marshal of England and earl of Norfolk [*s*],
and by virtue of this charter he was constable of the castle of
Norwich.

[*o*] Royal castles were frequently committed to the sheriff, who was called
Custos, or Keeper of the Castle; but barons, &c. were called Constables of the
Castles, and exercised royal power within their jurisdiction; which sheriffs never
did, without a special writ for so doing.

[*p*] Gurdon's essay on Norwich castle.

[*q*] Second son of King Edward I. by his second wife. Blomefield, vol. I.
p. 56.

[*r*] The honour of Hugh Bigod earl of Norfolk was 125 fees, that is, 85
thousand acres. Madox's Baronia Anglicana, cap. 3.

[*s*] Blomefield, vol. I. p. 56.

In

In 1327 king Edward confirmed Brotherton's honours, and he was continued conſtable of the caſtle. The office ſtill continued, though frequently abridged by grants to the corporation of Norwich; and we find that in 1470 Sir John Paſton was in expectation of it [t].

Having briefly given the hiſtory of the caſtle, I ſhall now proceed to explain the ſite and manner of the fortifications, and to give a deſcription of the keep and the ſtile of architecture in which it is built.

Canute, who was cautious in ſecuring his Anglian poſſeſſions, built ſeveral ſtrong forts and caſtles. It is conjectured, and indeed it is moſt probable, that the preſent caſtle was built by him [u]. Although the building is of Daniſh workmanſhip, it is notwithſtanding in the taſte of architecture practiſed by the Saxons long before England became ſubject

[t] "For my maſtyr the Erle of Oxynforthe bydeth me aſe and have. I trow my brodyr Sir John ſhall have the conſtabylſhip of Norwych caſtyll wt xxx of fee; for all the lordys be agreyd to it." John Paſton's Letter to his Mother, dated 11 Oct. 1470, 10 Edward IV. See Sir John Fenn's Letters, vol. II. p. xxxvi.

[u] "Under the grand portal of the Eaſt front of the caſtle are two impoſt ſtones, from which the great arch ſprings, which have each a lion in baſſe relievo; and as Mr. Camden aſcribes the building to Bigod from the two lions carved in ſtone there, from theſe very lions I rather take Canute to be the builder of it; for he bore for coat armour *leo paſſans guardant*, and a carver that was not nicely verſed in heraldry, might, inſtead of *guardant curve lions paſſant regardant*, or *ſalient*, which poſtures are ſo widely different from *paſſens* to the moſt curſory view, that the extremity of careleſſneſs could hardly produce ſuch a miſtake." Gurdon's Antiq. of Norwich Caſtle.

I do not quote this paſſage of Mr. Gurdon in proof of the age of the building, becauſe I ſhall afterwards endeavour to ſhew that this part was built by one of the Bigods; the main tower, however, was moſt likely built by Canute, or ſome of his predeceſſors.

VOL. XII. U to

to the Danes, and it is the best exterior specimen of this kind of architecture extant.

The altitude of the promontory on which the keep of this castle is built appears to be chiefly the work of nature, excepting what has probably been thrown out from the inner vallum; for it may be observed, that the ground from the castle for the best part of a mile Southwards is nearly level with the upper ballium, although it dips to the West, and most rapidly to the East. See plate XXII. towards the river.

The area of the whole castle, including the three ditches [x] which circumscribed it, could not contain less than twenty-three acres, and the principal entrance was from Ber street [y] through the Barbican [z] over a bridge cross the outward vallum [a], which was at the South end of what is now called the Golden Ball lane, which you enter at D. Plate XXIII. The outward vallum has been from time immemorial filled up. On the inside verge of this vallum stood the outward wall of the outer ballium or space between the middle and outer ditches [b]. The space between the

---

[x] Ditch, moat, fosse, vallum, a hollow space on the outside of walls or ramparts.

[y] Ber, Berg, Barg-street, i. e. the street leading to the castle.

[z] An advanced work placed at the front of the entrance of a castle, a watch-tower.

> " Within the Hollow a porter sat,
>
> " Day and night duly keeping watch and ward."
>
> Spenser's Fairie Queene.

For repairing the *Barbican* a tax called *Barbicanage* was levied on certain lands. Carta 17 Edward III. m. 6 n. 14.

[a] On the triangular space, see Plate XXIII. at F, on the right-hand as you enter the Barbican stood the church of St. Martin in *Balivo* or Bailiffwick of the castle, which was totally exempt from all episcopal and archidiaconal jurisdiction. It was taken down in the reign of Queen Elizabeth.

[b] See plate XXIII.

4   mid-

middle and inner ditch was called the inner ballium, and had a wall in the fame manner. Round the upper ballium was another wall, which circumfcribed the keep or caftle. " Thefe walls were commonly flanked with towers, and had a parapet, embattled, crenellated, or garetted; for the mounting of it there were flights of fteps at convenient diftances, and the parapet often had the merlons pierced with long chinks ending in round holes, called œillets (*c*)."

The middle vallum has been more recently levelled, and veftiges of it may yet be feen in a South-eaft direction from the keep, towards Beaumont's hill, and towards London-lane and the back of the inns to the North-weft, where there are private yards of 18 or 20 feet defcent in fome parts. Some few points of the outer vallum may alfo be traced : on the North fide (fee plate XXIII. at A.), is an entrance to Pottergate-ftreet from the London-lane. A few years fince the defcent was fo fudden at this point, that the communication from one ftreet to the other was by means of fteps only, and the paffage is ftill called St. Andrew's fteps, from their being within that parifh. This agrees exactly with the proper fite of the wall of the outer ballium. Another point is at B on the Weft fide, where Blomefield fays, the outer vallum extended as far as the *Magna Croft*, or the Great Croft of the caftle, now the market-place [*d*]. Another point is alfo given at G, where he fays [*e*] that on the Eaft the ditch ex-

[*c*] Grof's Preface on ancient caftles, p. 6. The walls to the city of Norwich, which were built in 1294, were conftructed in this way. Plate XXII.

[*d*] Blomefield's Norwich, p. 046. " The market-place was the *Magna Croffa*, or Great Croft, belonging to the caftle, to the outward ditch of which it adjoined, and at firft was open from St. Stephen's church to the Hill, now called Dove lane." The part is yet called St. Peter of Mancroft.

[*e*] Blomefield, p. 525.

tended

tended almoft to the Conisford-ftreet; and, indeed, I remember fome veftiges of it, which were levelled in the caftle meadow within the laft twenty years. There were bridges over each of thefe vallums, and the foundations [f] of the bridge over the middle vallum may yet be traced in a line from the Barbican to the prefent paffage over the inner vallum.

The bridge over the inner vallum to the keep of the caftle is ftill remaining, and is probably the fame which was originally built by the Saxons [g]. The arch which fupports it is a *cima* of forty feet three inches in diameter, and the largeft arch of Saxon workmanfhip in the kingdom. The foffit of the arch is conftructed with bricks, which have induced fome to pronounce it of Roman workmanfhip; but we have fufficient evidences of bricks made and ufed in Saxon edifices [h], although the ufe of them was foon after the Norman Conqueft laid afide; befides, the bricks of which I am now fpeaking are fo very unlike the Roman tiles in fcantling, that we may without conjecture determine the work not to be Roman; and the abutments on which the arch refts have the fame fimple kind of impoft molding in ftone fo generally ufed by the Saxons, and afterwards by the Norman architects [i]   The height of the impofts on which the arch refts is three feet and a half, and the radius of the arch is twenty feet one inch and a half; fo

[f] Workmen were employed fome years fince to deftroy thefe foundations. Their progrefs was fo flow, from the materials being fo ftrongly cemented together, that their employers defifted from the undertaking, and they ftill appear, in fome places, a few inches above the furface of the ground.

[g] "The bridge leading to it is indeed unqueftionably one of the moft perfect Saxon arches now extant." Mr. King's Obfervations, Archæol. vol. IV. p. 377. See Plate XLIV. p. 175, 176.

[h] See Mr. Effex's Remarks on brick and ftone buildings. Archæologia, vol. IV.

[i] See profiles of thefe mouldings, fig. 4, &c. Plate XXXV.

that

that its height is twenty-three feet seven inches and a half; of course it was formerly much more, from the fosse having been at various times the receptacle for filth and rubbish.

At the termination of the bridge upon the upper ballium are the remains of two circular towers (Plate XXIII. marked a a), fourteen feet in diameter. I imagine these were connected together, and formed the original portal, joining the wall which circumscribed the upper ballium [*t*]. Plate XXIII. is a plan of these fortifications, which it cannot be said are formed in conjecture. The keep, the upper ballium, the inner vallum, the bridge over it, and the portal foundations, are even now existing; the form of the adjacent streets, and of the ground on which many houses are now erected on the North and West sides corresponding with both the external and internal lines of the middle vallum, with other circumstances before mentioned, which an observer may very easily trace, are sufficient evidences of the site of the middle vallum. As to the outer vallum, we cannot doubt that the extent was equal to the plan here shewn, though from the site being mostly covered with buildings, &c. it cannot be traced so as to mark out its form with the same precision as the inner and middle vallums, yet from what has been advanced, and from some of its points being given, it may fairly be presumed the plan cannot be very erroneous. Mr. Blomefield [*f*], whom I have often quoted on this occasion, says,

[*t*] " The entrance into the ballium was commonly through a strong machicolated and embattled gate, between two towers secured by a herse," (Grose's Preface, p. 7.) or portcullis, *je as clude,* q. d. a port clofe, a machine like a harrow, which slided through grooves of stone in the jambs of the gateway, and hung before the gates.

[*f*] See Hist. of Norwich, p. 573.

" At

" At the North end of the Golden ball lane [*m*] was the gate
of the caſtle entering the outward vallum or trench, and was
the principal entrance into the Barbican." In this I have differed from him; for that plan would bring the ſite of the
outer ballium into the middle ditch; I have therefore placed
the entrance into the Barbican at the South end of the lane [*n*]:
for it appears clear to me, that the lane was the actual road
through the Barbican. I cannot conceive there could be
any reaſon for making this ſudden turn from the wide road in
Berg-ſtreet to approach the caſtle. Had the entrance into the
Barbican been at C, the road would doubtleſs have pointed
from Berg-ſtreet to C, whereas it goes by the corner at D,
which was the entrance into the outwork; beſides the form of
the ſtreet from D to E, called Beaumont's hill, agrees exactly with the half plan of ſuch walls as were generally uſed
for defending the Barbican.

Such were the exterior fortifications as practiſed by the
Anglo-Saxons, which, although different from the Romans,
are, notwithſtanding, probably of as great antiquity [*o*]: for
it agrees with the mode cited by Joſephus from Beroſus,

[*m*] See plan, Plate XXIII. at C.

[*n*] See plan, Plate XXIII. at D.

[*o*] " I cannot help obſerving, that the reſemblance which the devices, and
the mode of fortification, both in this (Norwich) Saxon caſtle, and in that
at Colcheſter, have to thoſe built in the more improved Norman times, ſeem to
indicate that the general plan was taken from ſtructures of a ſtill earlier date in us
either, eſpecially as the deſcription given by Joſephus of the tower of Antonia at
Jeruſalem may lead us to ſuſpect this mode of building to have been very ancient indeed, and to have been known and introduced even before the age in
which he lived." Mr. King's Obſervations on Ancient Caſtles. Archæologia,
vol. IV. p. 398.

" That

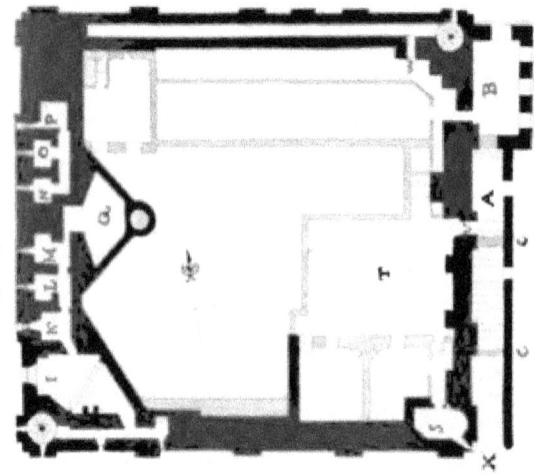

·FIG·2·

PLAN·OF·THE·FIRST·FLOOR·

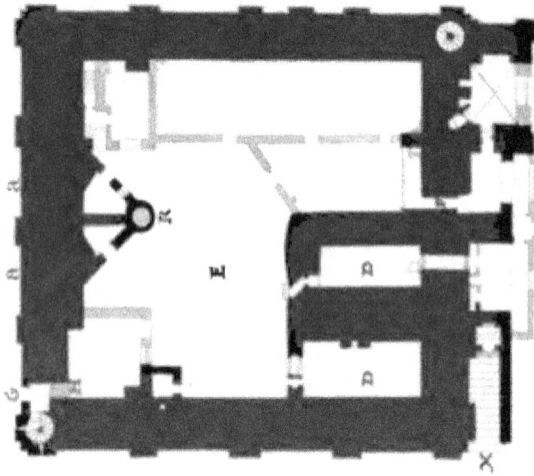

·FIG·1·

PLAN·OF·THE·BASEMENT·FLOOR·

·NORWICH·CASTLE·

" That Nebuchadonofor fortified Babylon with a *triple en-clofure of brick walls* of a furprizing ftrength and height [*p*]."

Polybius fpeaking of Syrinx the capital of Hyrcania, which Antiochus befieged, fays " That city was furrounded with *three foffes*, each forty-five feet broad, and twenty-two feet deep ; upon each fide there was a double entrenchment, and behind all a wall [*q*]. " The city of Jerufalem," fays Jofephus [*r*], " was furrounded by a *triple wall*, except on the fide of the valleys, where there was but one, becaufe they were inacceffible. The whole was flanked with towers of extrordinary folidity, and built with wonderful art."

The keep [*s*], which was the laft refort of the befiegers, is here placed, as they generally were, in the upper ballium, or center of the other works [*t*]. Its extent from Eaft to Weft, including a fmall tower, through which was the principal entrance, 110 feet 3 inches, and from North to South 92 feet 10 inches, and its height to the top of the merlons of the battlements 69 feet 6 inches ; the height of the bafement-floor is about 24 feet, the outfide of which is faced with flints, and has no external ornament except two arches on the Weft fide (fee Plate XXIV. at *a a* of the bafement plan, fig. 1.) : Thefe arches, Mr. King obferves [*u*], were originally intended as a deception to an enemy, giving an idea of weaknefs externally, where in fact was the greateft ftrength and fecurity ; for the wall is not only of thirteen feet in thicknefs in this place, but within,

[*p*] Rollin on Ancient Fortifications, vol. II. p. 46.
[*q*] X. c. 28. p. 138.
[*r*] Bell. Jud. VI. c. 6.
[*s*] The contrivances of thefe buildings are defcribed by Mr. King. Archæol. vol. IV. and VI.
[*t*] The keep of Cambridge caftle was in the exterior works.
[*u*] Obfervations on Norwich caftle. Archæol. vol. IV. p. 401.

it

it was additionally barricadoed with two oblique walls, which have been recently taken down. See the plans at A and K. The approach to the keep was at the stair-cafe by X, at the South-eaft corner facing the bridge, which paffed through two portals (at C C fig. 2.) to the landing A, where Mr. King conjectures was a draw-bridge [x], and from thence up a few more fteps at B into Bigod's tower, which is now enclofed, and its height divided into two rooms. This was an open portal or veftibule to the grand entrance of the caftle, with three arches facing the Eaft, which commanded a moft beautiful and very extenfive view down the river for feveral miles, and one arch facing the North. From this veftibule is ftill remaining a fmall entrance at V, and the only one into the caftle at that time, excepting the paffage F fig. 1, which appears unqueftionably to have been the old fally-port under the arched landing, and is the only paffage from the bafement floor to the upper ballium. A few only of the original apartments of the firft floor are now remaining. The door-way at W is now bricked up, which communicated to the fmall ftaircafe at the North-eaft corner, and a long narrow paffage, which moft probably led to the fmall rooms on the Weft fide of the caftle. The infide of the caftle has been fo much altered from having been long ufed as a county gaol [y], that little can be faid, or even conjectured, of the original plan, and the various ufes of the rooms. What remains in the bafe-

[x] Archæol. vol. IV. p. 398. This has, however, been fince taken down, when I found the landing was ftrongly fupported by very ftrong arched work of apparent antiquity with the original building.

[y] It appears from the record called *Rotus de Novo* that felons were imprifoned here fo early as king Henry the Firft's time.

ment-

ment-floor ferves for little more than to excite our wonder at
the thicknefs and ftrength of the walls, and horror for the
wretches who were confined in thefe darkfome dungeons, deprived of light and of a free circulation of air, as they muft
neceffarily have been in thofe vaults, D D, whofe arches appear to have been, and moft undoubtedly were, covered over
with floors for the apartments of ftate for the chieftain, and
others for his foldiers, his vaffals, and alfo war machines,
which at that time were large and occupied much room. In the
South-weft corner is another winding ftair-cafe, that has now
no other approach but at G. fig. 1. plate XXIV. but this door
is of recent workmanfhip ; the way was formerly at H in the
prefent chapel [a]. This ftair-cafe is now the only communication to the rooms on the firft floor I, K, L, M (fee fig. 2.
Plate XXIV.). The room I has an arch croffing it diagonally,
as fhewn by the double lines, and beyond thefe are other apartments over the folid wall of the bafement floor, marked N, O, P,
which were probably bricked up when the building Q was de-
molifhed, where, from the apertures now ftopped up, appears
to have been the principal accefs to all thofe rooms in the
Weft fide of the caftle ; and I am led to conjecture, that Q
alfo communicated with the ftate apartments as well as with
apartments for the foldiery ftill higher ; for in a gallery over
thefe rooms the arched work is vaulted to a confiderable
height, and a fpacious paffage is formed towards Q, giving
room, apparently, to raife the war engines in ufe at that
time [a], as well as for the convenience of getting water from
the

[a] The chapel is now taken away to give room to new alterations.

[a] Catapultæ, Efpringolds, Arblafters, &c. &c. In 1342 the gates and
towers of the city were furnifhed by Richard Spynk, citizen, with 30 efpring-olds

the well at R, fig. 1 [*b*], for it was usual to have their wells
so contrived, that, in case of a close siege, the garrison could
be supplied with water by a pipe in the wall, communicating
with every floor, and also with the leads of the castle. In the
South-east corner of the building, room S from the upper
gaol-yard T, was probably an oratory, or oriel, lighted
from the East, having some rude sculpture in one of the
walls, which I caused to be cleared of the white-wash which
hid it. See Plate XXV. fig. 8. The first figure appears to be the
Virgin Mary crowned with the child Jesus in her arms, and by
him an angel ; the second St. Catharine ; the third St. Christopher ; below is St. George, or St. Michael the archangel
and the Devil ; and the next is a mutilated figure holding a
large sword.

It is not possible at this time to conjecture, of what rooms
the remaining large space consisted. In a building of this magnitude they were, probably, very spacious and elegant, as it
was sometimes usual to ornament the walls of the principal
apartments with paintings, as those of " the hall of Tamworth
castle in Warwickshire, where is an old rude painting on the
wall of Sir Launcelot du Lake, and Sir Tarquin, drawn in
gigantic size, and tilting together [*c*] ; and at the Duke's

to cast great stones with, and to every espringold one hundred gogions, or balls
locked up in a box, with ropes and other accoutrements belonging to them, also
four great arbalisters, or cross-bows, and to each of them one hundred gogions, or
balls, and two pair of grapples to draw up the bows with, besides other armour.
Lib. Inrroit. civium I. pp. 3, 5.

[*b*] This is now entirely built over, but the well has been partly filled up in
the memory of persons still living.

Fig. 3. is a capital in the same room.

Fig. 4 is a capital on the great stair-case near the portal.

[*c*] Warton's Observations on *Spenser's Fairie Queen*, vol. I. p. 43.

castle

·NORWICH·CASTLE·

FIG 4

FIG 3

FIG·2·

FIG·1·

·BIGODS·TOWER·   ·NORWICH·CASTLE·

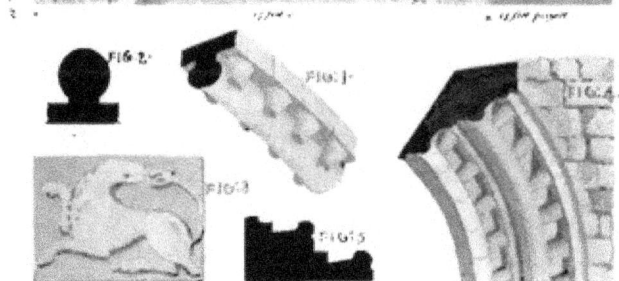

FIG 6

FIG 2

FIG 1

FIG 3

FIG 4

FIG 5

caftle at Hefden in Artois, wherein was *craftyly and curyoufly depeynted the Conjurfte of the Golden Fleece* [d]."

Since the foregoing Effay was written, the caftle has undergone a very material alteration. The Eaft front, in which was the grand entrance, is grofsly mutilated and entirely hidden by an additional building, that appears to have no kind of connection with it, and though in all former repairs and changes the original elevation of the ftructure had been conftantly attended to, yet this unfortunate addition has totally deftroyed its fymmetry. Every eye is fenfible of the incongruity which this novel kind of prifon architecture has occafioned; and we have now only to lament, that the original ftyle and purity of the building has been fo palpably violated by this heavy excrefcence, which, inftead of affimilating wi h the character of the edifice, ferves only to hide fo much of its original ftructure. This venerable pile of antiquity has been the feat and caftle of defence to Britifh, Saxon, and Norman kings, and powerful baron chieftains; it has been the boaft and pride of the province for ages paft; it was not lefs the admiration of the ftranger than the antiquary, and this admirable fabric was alfo one of the few remaining models of Antonia at Jerufalem [e]; yet by a recent change it is now bereaved of its ancient beauty, under pretence of giving more internal convenience for the accommodation of its miferable tenants; but furely, whatever additions were neceffary, might have preferved externally the fame character and apparent date of architecture with the mutilated parts of this ftately pile. The interior has been gutted alfo, and equally as ill

[d] Warton's Obfervations on Spenfer's Faiy Queen, vol. I. p 171, from Caxton's Prologue.

[e] See Mr. King's Account of Ancient Caftles in Archæologi .

X 2   managed;

managed; fmall courts furrounded by lofty buildings, which almoft, I may fay totally, exclude every cheering ray of the fun from its wretched inhabitants. The felon, the prifoner untried, the debtor, and the gaoler, the guilty, and the innocent, fhare in the calamity. Perhaps, no place on earth accords better with Milton's defcription:

> " Dungeon horrible, on all fides round
> . . . .
> " No light, but rather darknefs vifible
> " Served only to difcover fights of woe,
> " Regions of forrow! doleful fhades! where peace
> " And reft can never dwell."
>
> Paradife Loft, B. I. l. 61.

Of the Architecture of NORWICH Castle.

THIS country, although fubject to Rome, the miftrefs of the world, in an enlightened age, partook but in a very fmall degree of its elegance and luxuries, if we may judge from the architectural Roman remains exifting at this time. After the departure of Conftantine, a ftyle was adopted in which were united ftrength and grandeur; but it differed fo much from the ancient architecture of Greece and Rome, that, although it is faid by fome authors [f] to be a corruption of the Roman, from fome of its refemblances, yet an architectural eye may immediately difcover the difference; indeed, it is now

[f] Bentham's Ely, p. 18. and Warton on Spenfer, vol. II. p. 186.

better

better and more generally known by the title of *Saxon*, from its being practised by the Saxons prior to the Norman Conquest. In the eleventh century some alterations in the Saxon style of architecture took place. They were introduced by the Normans, and were executed in a very rough massive way at first; but in a short time they became more expert workmen, and there were many stately buildings remaining to bear testimony of the profuse ornaments they afterwards adopted, especially the principal entrances and choirs of ecclesiastical buildings. We find them improving in their workmanship until the middle of the twelfth century, in almost every province in the kingdom, particularly at Rochester under the superintendance of bishop Gundulph, whose skill and expertness in masonry caused it there to be styled GUNDULPH's ARCHITECTURE. Ernulph [g], a native of France, soon after the death of Gundulph, was promoted to the Abbacy of Peterborough. He also became proficient in this style of building, and various specimens of his taste are still to be seen at Rochester, Canterbury, Peterborough, &c. Notwithstanding the semi-circular arch and the frequent repetition of ornament in some of the detailed finishings of the mouldings may, at first sight, give these works an appearance of similarity to Roman architecture, yet it is altogether widely different. Authors are not agreed as to the origin of Saxon architecture; and it is equally difficult to trace the origin of the Gothic style, which immediately succeeded it, and continued in use for upwards of four hundred years after.

Some writers are of opinion, that the Saxons or Normans had it from Persia, where there are still ancient remains of

[g] Gundulph died 1107. } Thorpe's Antiquities of Kent, p. 153.
Ernulph died 1125.

buildings

buildings bearing some of the massive features characteristic of this style, particularly that of Tauk Kessera [*h*]; and that of some of the buildings in India described by the pencil of the ingenious Mr. Hodges has also some resemblances.

The Rev. Mr. Ledwich, in his Observations on ancient churches, has given copies of arches [*i*] surrounded with the Zig-zag ornament from a Syrian MS. written A. D. 586, which agrees with the arches of many buildings to be seen here, though the capitals, columns, and bases, are not characteristic of the style in question.

There is also a door-way to the grand apartment of a very magnificent house [*k*] at Grand Cairo, said to have been built by *Sultan Nasir Ibn Calaboun*, who was the seventh king of Egypt of the Mamalukes called Bacharites, and lived about the year 1279 [*l*].

The

[*h*] " The East face of *Tauk Kessera*, near the river Tygris, is 300 feet in length, the breadth of the arch 85 feet, and height 106 feet; the front on each side the arch is full of niches like our cathedrals; the length of the arched roof from East to West 150 feet. One of our Turkish servants, who spoke a little of the Portuguese language, told my man, that the general opinion of the country was, that *Tauk Kessera* was not built by a *Persian, Parthian, Turk*, or any other *Asiatic*, but by an *European* prince, who came into this part of the world with a large army and subdued it. As we had not yet met with any edifice in *Asia* carrying with it so great a resemblance of the ancient *European* architecture as this, it struck me that *Tauk Kessera* might have been constructed, soon after the conquest of this part of the world, by Alexander the Great, or one of his captains *."

Mr. Ives's Route from Bassora to Latiches, p. 293.

[*i*] Archæologia, vol. VIII. p. 170. Pl. XIII.

[*k*] Dr. Pocock's Description of the East, vol. I. p. 33. Pl. XIII.

[*l*] This must have been more than a hundred years after the Norman taste was dropped in England, and the new style generally adopted, when pointed

* Ctesiphon, &c.

arches

The Saxons fupported their arches which feparated the ailes by a fingle column, or rather pier, which was circular, octangular, or hexangular, in the plan; whereas the Norman architects fupported theirs in general with extremely maffive piers, ornamented on their fides and angles with upright fmall columns, and fometimes they intermixed them with round piers like the Saxons [m], as may be feen in Ely, Norwich, Peterborough, and other cathedrals. They differed widely, however, from the Roman proportions, and the Normans encreafed the difference, as is fhewn by the following comparifon.

Saxon proportions.

		Diameters		Heigh		
		ft.	inc.	ft.	inc.	diam.
Piers to the chancel at Orford in Suffolk		3	3	13 = 0		4
Width of the arches	3 diameters					
Piers to the conventual church at Ely		2	4	14 = 6		2
Width of the arches	3 diameters					

Norman proportions.

Piers in Norwich cathedral	——	7	3	14	6 = 1
Width of the arches	2 diameters				

The fame proportions may be obferved in Ely, Peterborough, and other Norman buildings.

arches † and prominent buttreffes made their appearance; although this is fubfequent to the origin of what is called Gothic, yet it fhews that the former ftyle was ftill continued in fome degree in thofe countries.

[m] Gundulph's tower in Rochefter caftle appears divided by all round piers. See the beautiful view by Mr. Hearne in Bowyer's elegant Hiftory of England, Nº 10.

† The firft appearance of the pointed arch in this country was probably towards the latter end of the reign of Henry the firft, in the church of Frendfbury, built by Paulinus the Sacrift, between the years 1125 and 1133.

Biblioth. Topograph. Brit. Nº VI. part 1. p. 118.

The

The semi-circular and interfected arches, the *Zig-zag* [n] ornament, the *Billet moulding* [o], *Hatched-work* [p], and various other species of ornament, were still continued : and though architecture cannot be said to have improved on the Saxon manner, either in lightness or in execution, yet in magnitude of design the Normans far exceeded their predeceffors. The buttrefs of this ftyle varies extremely from the Gothic which fucceeded it ; they are broad and flat on the furface, without ornament, unlefs a *torus* on the angles, which is fometimes to be met with, may be called fuch. The buttrefs, even in large buildings, feldom projects more than feventeen or eighteen inches : and thofe of Norwich caftle, which are nearly fix feet in width, do not project fo much [q]. One of the characteriftics of the ftyle called Gothic, which fucceeded, is the very prominent buttrefs, which moftly terminated in turrets or fpires, enriched with *crockets* of foliage formed of *trefoil, quatrefoil,* or *cinquefoil,* as thofe of King's chapel, Cambridge, and almoft every other Gothic building.

The only mouldings ufed, both by the Saxon and Norman architects, were the *torus,* the *fcotia* or *reverfed torus,* the *cavetto* or *hollow moulding,* and a kind of *chamfered fafcia,* which latter was generally ufed for *imposts* or *abacufes* to their capitals. Thefe mouldings were combined, more or lefs, for the various purpofes of forming *arches, imposts, cornices, bafes, &c.* The *cima recta,* the *cima reverfa,* the *ovolo* or *quarter round,* the *planiere,* and other regular Grecian *mouldings, cornices, friezes,* &c. which compofe the *entablature,* are never

[n] [o] [p] Thefe terms are ufed by Mr. Warton in his Obfervations on Spenfer's Fairy Queen; Mr. Bentham, in his Hiftory of Ely ; Capt. Grofe, in his Preface to the Hiftory of England, and other writers.

[q] fee A A, Plate XXV.

to

to be met with in the Saxon or Norman fabrics [r]. Yet their builders were more fond of variety; for it may be frequently observed in a range of columns there are as many different capitals [s]. In this respect they may be said to have copied from the Egyptians, where, in an ancient temple in the middle of Esnay, formerly Latopolis, it is said, " one capital of a column does not resemble another; though the proportion is the same, the ornaments are different [t];" and in most of our regular Saxon buildings, as that of the conventual church at Ely, and the churches of Orford and Dunwich in Suffolk, not only the capitals, but the columns and piers also differ materially. The piers at Ely are some of them circular in the plan, some octangular, some with one side of the octagon, and others with the angle of the octagon towards the choir; and at Orford every pair is differently designed.

The external ornaments of Norwich castle are in this style of architecture. From the basement floor upwards, the whole building is faced with stone, and is subdivided into three stories, flanked with *small projecting* buttresses, enriched between with semicircular arches, supported by small columns in *alto relievo* [u], and between some of the upper arches is faced with, what was called by the Romans, *reticulatum* or *net-work*; from the stones being laid diagonally, the joints represented the meshes of a net; and, to give the work a richer appear-

[r] As at Canterbury, Grimbald's cript at Oxford, conventual church at Ely, chancel at Orford, Dunwich, Norwich castle, &c. built by the Saxons, and all the cathedrals of Norman workmanship.

[s] Fig. 13 and 20, plate XXXIV.

[t] Norden's Travels in Egypt and Nubia, vol. II. p. 88.

[u] Fig 2, plate XXV. a specimen of the exterior decoration, taken from the West side; A A are the upper parts of two buttresses with the arched work between them.

unce, each stone was subdivided (by two crofs lines pretty deeply chafed) into four equal parts, the upper point receding fo as to receive a fhadow from the work above [x], giving it the appearance of *Mofaic*. This kind of work was ufed for ornament only; for the workmen, knowing its want of folidity, never applied it where strength was required.

On the Eaft fide of the caftle is a tower projecting fourteen feet by twenty-feven feet in breadth, of a richer ftyle of architecture, which I have ventured to call BIGOD's TOWER [y]. It is decidedly of the tafte in general ufe fubfequent to the Conqueft, and continued through great part of king Stephen's reign; and it was, moft probably, repaired and finished in its prefent ftyle by Hugh Bigod, who fucceeded his brother William in the conftablefhip of the caftle early in the twelfth century.

It is an extraordinary circumftance that the arms of a king and two barons, who have held this caftle, fhould fo nearly coincide as to caufe a contention between hiftorians refpecting the æra in which this caftle was built, from a lion which is roughly fculptured on two of the impoft ftones [z] of the bafement arch of this tower.

The animals alluded to by Camden [a], Gurdon [b], Blome-

[x] Plate XXV. fig. 1.

[y] See the upper part of the tower, fig. 6, plate XXVI. fhewing the open veftibule to the entrance of the caftle.

[z] See Plate XXVI. fig. 3.

[a] " The reafon why I fancy Bigod repaired the caftle is, becaufe I obferved *Lions faliant* cut in the ftone, in the fame manner as the Bigods formerly ufed them in their feals; of whom though there was one who made ufe of a crofs."

Gibfon's Camden, p. 187.

[b] See note a page 145.

field,

field [c], and Mr. King [d], who have given them to king Canute, Bigod, and Thomas de Brotherton, were executed

[c] And it seems by his (Thomas de Brotherton) arms still remaining, carved in stone on the walls, that it was he that fitted up the castle as it now stands, for I think by his * coat, twice cut on the pilasters of the arch of the stair-case, that he built that stair-case, made that arch, and added the battlements which were on the top, and left the building much as we see it now. "

Blomefield's Norwich, p. 56.

[d] " There is indeed a trace of its having been built in its present form by Roger Bigod, about the time of William Rufus, and of its having been finally completed by Thomas de Brotherton, even so late as the time of Edward II, but I cannot help suspecting all this to be a mistake; for, though it may be true, with regard to the outworks, and the many great buildings enclosed within the limits and outward walls of this castle, which were formerly very extensive and numerous, that a great part of them were built and completed by those two powerful lords, yet, as to the keep, or master tower (the only considerable part now remaining), the style of its architecture is, in many respects, so different from that of the towers erected in the reigns of William Rufus and Henry I. and II., and the ornaments are so different from those which were in use in the reign of Edward II. (when pointed arches had been long introduced, and were esteemed the most elegant of any), that I cannot but think the building of much greater antiquity, and completely Saxon, though it is possible the stair-case might be repaired, or even rebuilt, by Thomas de Brotherton, whose arms are to be seen on a part of the wall. In short, as to the main body of the building, I take it to be the very tower which was erected about the time of king Canute, who, though himself a Dane, yet undoubtedly made use of many Saxon archi-tects, as the far greater number of his subjects were Saxons. And I am rather induced to form this conclusion, because I can find no authentic account whatever of the destruction of the castle built in Canute's time, either by war or by acci-dent; or of its being taken down in order to erect the present structure, as is supposed by some." Observations on Ancient Castles. Archæologia, vol. IV. p. 356 7.

* The author of the essay, fol. 36, quite mistakes the lions, by calling them either to Canute or Bigod, they being plainly the arms of Thomas de Brotherton, second son to King Edward I, by his second wife, and so half brother to Edward II, who bore the arms of England with a label of three Argent; or, if there never was any label, he put them there in honour of his brother, under whom he held the castle.

in

in times when the art of carving figures in particular was
at a very low ebb, and might probably be intended for the
arms of one of those persons, yet the style of the architecture
alone is sufficient, and is indeed an indisputable proof of the
æra in which this addition to the keep was repaired or built.

Brotherton, Mr. King suggests, " might probably repair
or rebuild the great stair-cale [*e*] leading to this tower, which
being uncovered and exposed would require more frequent
repairs ;" but even this probability ought not to be admitted,
as the whole of the architecture is of the style antecedent to
the Gothic, which was the taste prevalent in the time when
Brotherton lived.

The lower part of Bigod's tower was formerly open to
the upper ballium of the castle. The cieling is groined with
intersecting arches of stone, and its angles are decorated with
a very singular kind of *hanging billet moulding*, projecting ten
inches from the cieling [*f*]. The first floor of Bigod's
tower [*g*] is a landing from the great stair-case, and forms a
kind of open portico to the entrance of the building ; and a
superb entrance it must have been at that time ! The piers
are enriched with groupes of small columns supporting arches
ornamented with *architvolts* of mouldings enriched with *bil-
letting* [*h*].

[*e*] This stair-case has been taken down to make room for the recent alterations, and although a great part of it was always open to the weather, the hard-
ness of the cement was astonishing ; a number of labourers were employed
many weeks in demolishing it.

[*f*] Plate XXVI. fig. 1. and the geometrical section fig. 2. of the moulding.

[*g*] Plate XXVI. fig. 6.

[*h*] Fig. 4. The arched mouldings to Bigod's tower.

Fig. 5. Geometrical section of the mouldings.

Having

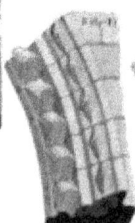

Having now finiſhed my obſervations on Norwich caſtle, I ſhall proceed to explain the detailed ſpecimens of Saxon and Norman architecture, which I have been able to collect from various buildings. I have added the geometrical plans and the ſectional forms of the mouldings; but in many they are perſpectively applied, to give a better idea of the forms they are intended to repreſent, by which means the curious may with eaſe determine (if there be no other data) the Saxon and Norman ſtyle from the Roman, the Gothic, or the Saracenic, which latter indeed never occurs in this country [*i*].

Plate XXVII. fig. 1. is the capital of an octagon pier in the ruins of the old conventual church at Ely, built in the time of the Heptarchy, A. D. 673 [*k*], and repaired in king Edgar's reign, A. D. 970 [*l*]. The piers are about two feet four inches in diameter; but as they now form the fronts of ſome of the prebendal houſes, and are walled and plaſtered between ſo as to bury five ſides of the octagon, the plate ſhews the remaining three ſides only, which the plan applied perſpectively ſerves to explain.

Fig 2. The capital of another octagon pier of the ſame building. This deviates from the laſt alſo in having one of its angles next the choir, as is ſhewn by the plan. The capitals are fifteen inches and a half in depth, excluſive of the necking, ſeven inches of which are occupied by the abacus or impoſt.

[*i*] See Swinborne's Travels in Spain.

[*k*] Bentham's Ely.

[*l*] Benedict is ſaid to be the firſt who brought maſons, painting, and glaſing, into this realme to the Saxons, and to have flouriſhed Anno Domini 658.

Stowe's Chronicle, p. 74.

Fig–

Fig. 3 and 4. Two capitals of round piers of two feet four inches diameter. I before observed, that the space between the piers is now enclosed; the segments of the plans are therefore only shewn, as the dark shadow at the bottom of the capital will explain.

Fig. 5, 6, 7, 8, 9, and 10. other capitals to octangular and circular piers in the same choir. Notwithstanding the same proportions prevail throughout the building, yet the capitals are various, as shewn in plate XXVII.

Fig. 11 and 12, the mouldings and other ornaments to the arches are still more various than the columns: but as a great part of them is also hidden by walls recently built, a small piece of the arches, one of nine inches, and the other of eleven inches in breadth and five inches projection, the sections are perspectively applied.

Fig. 13, 14, and 15, three small capitals to columns of five inches in diameter, whose depth with four inches of abacus is ten inches. They are taken from the ruins of a Saxon church at Dunwich in Suffolk [m], which consists of three divisions, like that at Ely, " not much unlike the primitive Eastern churches, consisting of the sanctuary, the temple, and ante-temple [n].

The whole building is one hundred and seven feet seven inches in length. The nave is 60 feet ten inches in length within, by twenty-four feet six inches in breadth, and was divided from the chancel by an arch. The chancel is twenty-one feet ten inches in length by twenty feet nine inches in breadth, and the sides are ornamented with small intersecting arches of twenty two inches *radius*, which is peculiar to Saxon and

[m] Gardiner's History of Dunwich, p. 63.
[n] Plate XXVII*. the plan of the church at Dunwich.

Norman

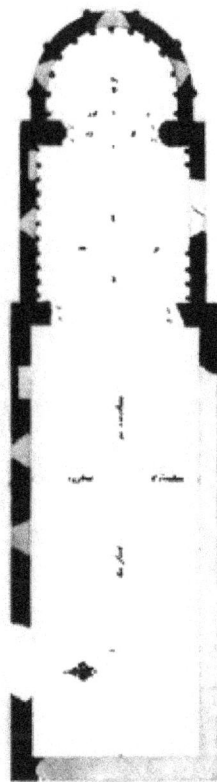

Vol. XII. Pl. XXXVII. p. 226.

DVNWICH· IN· SVFFOLK·

·PLAN·OF·THE·SAXON·CHVRCH·OF·THE·HOSPITAL·
·OF·SAINT·IAMES·THE·APOSTLE·

Pl. XII P. XXVIII p. 8

MOVLDINGS·TO·THE·ARCHES·IN·THE·OLD·CONVENTVAL·CHVRCH·

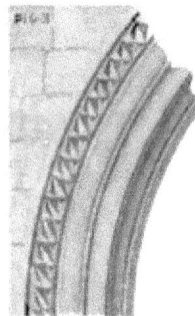

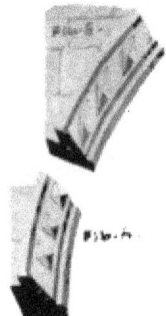

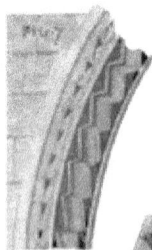

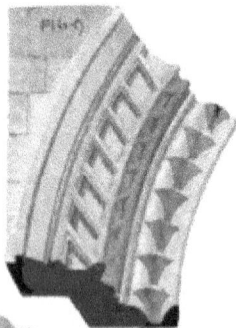

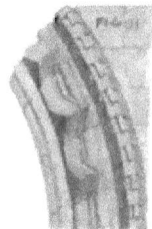

·SAXON·ARCHITECTVRE·AT·ELY·

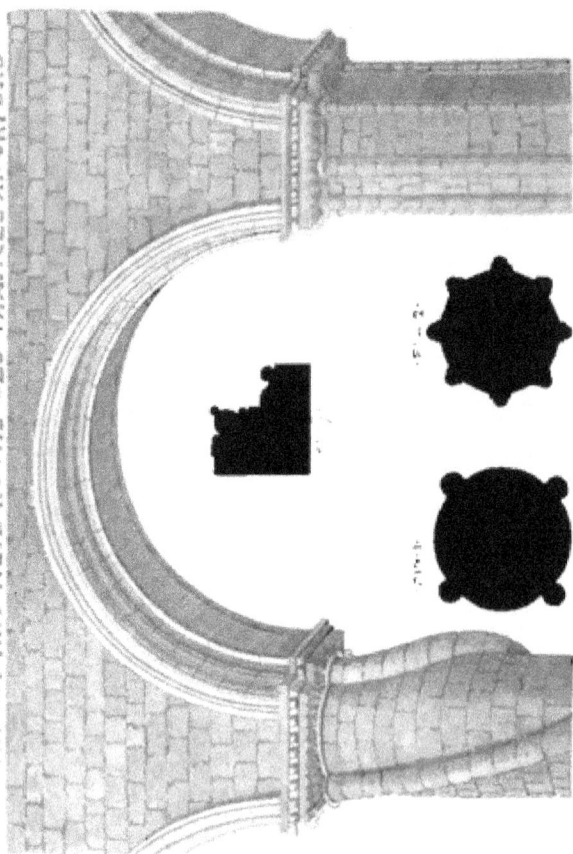

ARCHES AND PIERS IN THE OLD CHANCEL AT ORFORD

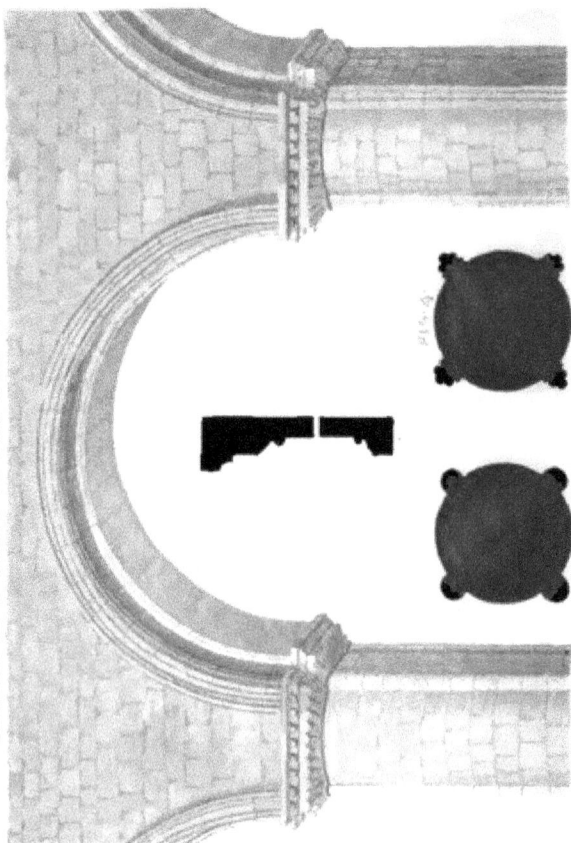

ARCHES AND PIERS IN THE OLD CHANCEL AT OBBORNE

Norman architecture. The altar is divided from the chancel by an arch of thirteen feet and a half span, and the plan forms something more than a semi-circle of eighteen feet two inches in diameter. The walls are also ornamented with small arches of two feet six inches in width; but they are not interfecting like those in the chancel part. The capitals fig. 13, 14, and 15, are copied from the altar walls. The historian of Dunwich says, " The hospital to which this church did formerly belong was undoubtedly of great antiquity; for neither history nor ancient records give any light whereby may be discovered either the founder or time of its foundation [o]."

Plate XXVIII. Arches at Ely: fig. 1, the design of one side of one the arches in the conventual church; fig. 2 is the geometrical section, or profile; fig. 3 and 4, another arch with the profile.

Fig. 5 and 6, another ornament on two other arches

Fig. 7, part of an arch with the profile, fig. 8.

Fig. 9, part of an arch with the profile, fig. 10.

Fig. 11, one side of a smaller arch which divided the nave from the chancel, with the section, fig. 12.

Fig. 13, the surrounding ornament to a larger scale.

Fig. 14, the soffit of one of the larger arches.

Plates XXIX. and XXX. represent the RUINED CHAPEL at ORFORD in SUFFOLK.

The arches and piers in this chapel appear to have been built on a similar plan with the church at Ely, and probably about the same date. The mouldings of the arches are alike, although the capitals have some small difference; the forms

[o] Rivett's Collections.

of

of the piers however are extremely different, yet their proportion is the same.

Fig. 1, 2, 3. and 4, are the plans of the piers they are next to, and are three feet three inches diameter, and thirteen feet in height. Fig. 5. is the section of the capitals, fig. 6 the base moulding of the piers, and fig. 7 the profile of the mouldings which form the arches.

Plate XXXI. Specimens of NORMAN architecture.

Fig. 1. An arched entrance to the North aile of the nave of Peterborough cathedral, with the plan applied perspectively.

Fig. 2. A geometrical plan of the jamb and arch mouldings.

Fig. 3. A section of the capitals.

Fig. 4. Capitals in Orford castle in Suffolk, with a perspective plan.

Fig. 5. Profile of capitals.

Plate XXXII. Specimens of Norman architecture of the 11th century.

Fig. 1. Half the design of a range of curious interfected arches over the West entrance of the church at Castle Rifing in Norfolk.

Fig. 2, 3, and 4, are some of the capitals on a larger scale; the columns are five and six inches in diameter.

Fig. 5. Capital on the North side of the nave of Norwich cathedral; the columns are six inches in diameter.

Fig. 6. An horizontal blocking in St. Luke's chapel of the same building.

Fig. 7. Part of a string course in Magdalen chapel near Norwich.

Fig. 8. Another within the tower of Attleburgh church, Norfolk.

Fig.

NORTH ENTRANCE TO
PETERBOROUGH CATHEDRAL

FIG·3

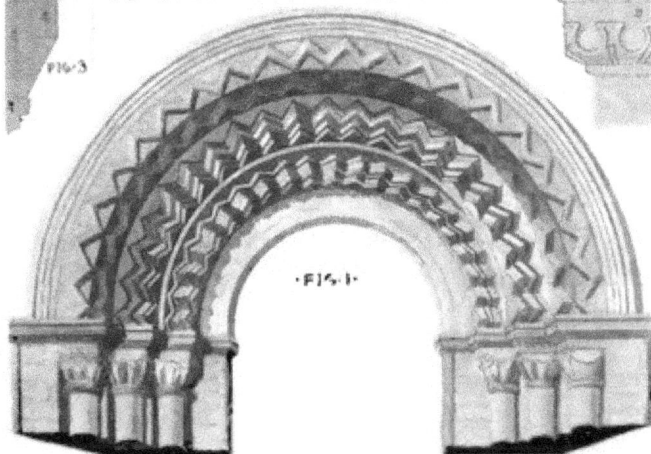

·FIG·1·

·FIG·2

FIG·4·

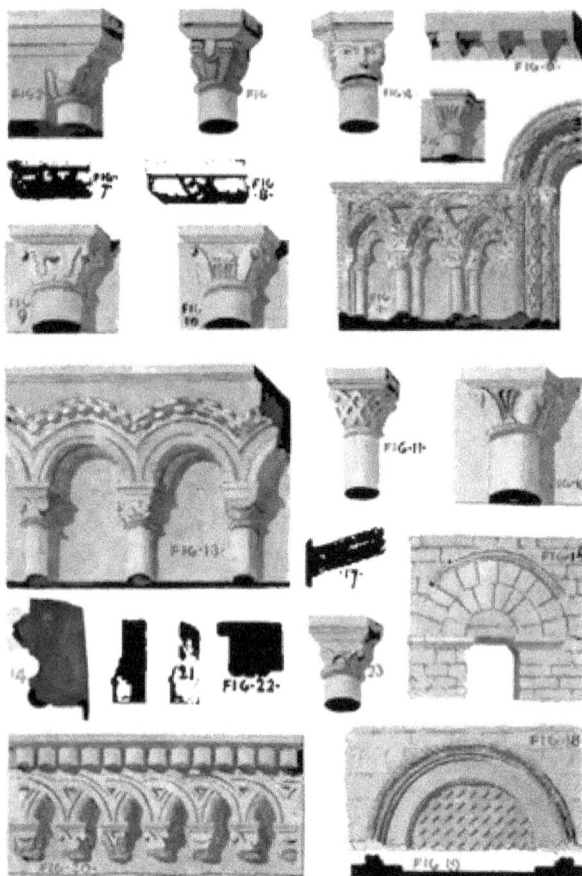

· NORMAN · ARCHITECTVRE ·

Fig. 9, 10, and 12, Capitals in the nave of Norwich cathedral; columns six inches diameter.

Fig. 11. Another ditto of nine inches diameter.

Fig. 13. Arches in the transept of Norwich cathedral: columns six inches diameter.

Fig. 14. Profile of the arch moulding to ditto, on a larger scale.

Fig. 15. Section of the base mouldings to the same columns.

Fig. 16. An arched entrance on the South side of Nettleton church in Lincolnshire, and the enriched moulding on a larger scale, fig. 17.

Fig. 18. An arch over a door in the transept of Norwich cathedral; the archivolt circumscribes divisions of *reticulata*, where the upper point of every other square recedes from the face of the work. The extent of the arch is nearly five feet, and is encompassed with an ornamented moulding, something like that shewn in N° 16. An arch like this may be seen in the transept of Peterborough cathedral.

Fig. 19. A section of the arch.

Fig. 20. Interfecting arches peculiar to this style of architecture from St. Luke's chapel in Norwich cathedral. They are within an arch of seven feet one inch diameter. Over them is a cornice composed of *dentated cableing* formed with pieces of *torus* placed upright. The capitals are seven inches and a half deep. The shafts of the columns, which are now gone, were four feet in height from the base. This is another instance of varying the capitals in the same range; the proportions are, notwithstanding, the same.

Fig. 21. The profile of the base 27½ inches deep.

Fig. 22. The section of the arch mouldings.

Vol. XII.   Z   Fig.

Fig. 13. Capital to a column, nine inches diameter, in the tower of Attlebury church in Norfolk.

Plate XXXIII. Specimens of Norman architecture.

Fig. 1. An arch to the entrance of St. Botulph's priory [*p*] at Colchester; the mouldings are worked in stone, and are in good preservation; the angles, which are stained red, are formed with Roman tiles, with which a great part of this curious edifice is built. These tiles are supposed to have been taken from the ruins of some Roman fabric near. The entrance is six feet eight inches in width.

Fig. 2. Geometrical plan, or profile of the mouldings.

Fig. 3. A piece of the *zig-zag* ornament in a larger scale.

Fig. 4. One of the capitals which supports the arch, twelve inches deep.

Fig. 5. A capital to the entrance of Colchester castle, twelve inches deep.

Fig. 6. A leaf of the capital on a larger scale.

Fig. 7. Another capital to the same entrance.

Fig. 8. Part of the arch to ditto.

Fig. 9. Profile of the moulding.

Fig. 10. The enriched part of the arch to a larger scale, and the profile perspectively applied.

Fig. 11. Arch to the North entrance of Speckfall church in Suffolk, two feet nine inches diameter; impost three inches deep; arch six inches broad.

Fig. 12. One of the lozenge shaped sinkings, and its profile, on a larger scale.

[*p*] This priory was founded in the beginning of the 12th century.

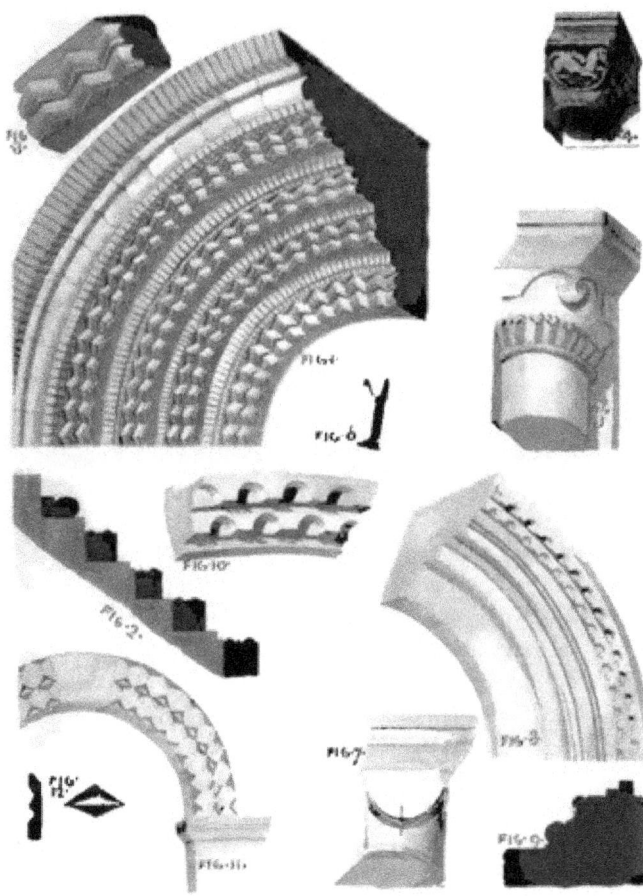

FIG·3·

FIG·1·

FIG·4·

FIG·5·

FIG·6·

FIG·10·

FIG·2·

FIG·8·

FIG·5·

FIG·7·

FIG·9·

FIG·11·

·NORMAN·ARCHITECTVRE·

FIG·1·

FIG·2·

FIG·5

FIG·4·

FIG·7·

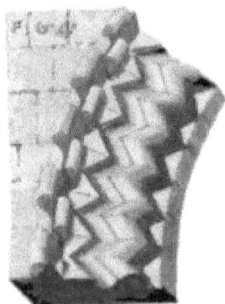

FIG·11·

FIG·9·

FIG·6·

FIG·12·

FIG·13·

FIG·10·

FIG·8·

·NORMAN·ARCHITECTVRE·

Plate XXXIV. Specimens of Norman architecture.

Fig. 1. Arched mouldings from the ruins of Binham priory, built by Peter lord Valoins, nephew to William the Conqueror [q].

Fig. 2. Profile of the moulding eight inches wide, with *billet moulding* lying in *cavetto*.

Fig. 3. An arch of eight feet diameter, enriched with *diagonal* or *crossed torus's* of seven inches in length, much like an arch in the ruin at Ely. See Plate XXVIII. fig. 9.

Fig. 4. An arch in the ruins of the transept of the same building, very neatly executed, and surrounded with *zig-zag* of *torus* and *cavetto*, a *billet moulding* encompassing the whole.

Fig. 5. The profile of the moulding, fifteen inches wide, and seven inches and a half projection.

Fig. 6. An ornament to three small arches in the tower of Westall church in Suffolk.

Fig. 7. The profile, four inches wide, and three inches deep.

Fig. 8. Ornament to the arch of the North entrance of Cookley church in Suffolk.

Fig. 9. The section, six inches wide and five inches deep.

Fig. 10. Ornament round the South entrance of Walpole church in Suffolk.

Fig. 11. Section 4 inches wide, and 2 inches and a half deep.

Fig. 12. Capital to the North entrance of Mettingham church in Suffolk, ten inches deep, column six inches diameter.

Fig. 13. Ornament round the arch of the same entrance.

[q] Blomefield, vol. V. p. 787.

Z 2   Plate

Plate XXXV. Specimens of Norman architecture.

Fig. 1, Figure of a bishop with his pastoral staff, over the entrance into the transept of Norwich cathedral. This, it is supposed, is intended for bishop Herbert de Losinga, the founder of the church. It is remarked as a specimen of sculpture of the early Normans [r]. The niche is four feet eleven inches high, and one foot three inches in width ; the wreathed columns are four feet six inches high, and six inches in diameter.

Fig. 2 and 3, *Mosaic jambs* to arches in the tower of Westal church in Suffolk ; the dark part shews the plan.

Fig. 4, 5, 6, and 7. There is very little variety in the sections of the mouldings for horizontal purposes in this style of architecture. These four figures may be said to comprehend almost all of them. They are used for *imposts* to arches, cornices, *abacus's*, and *bases*, generally plain, but when they are enriched it is after the manner shewn in fig. 8, 9, 10, 11, and 12, which are impost mouldings to be met with in Herringfleet, Gisleham, and some few other churches in Suffolk.

Fig. 13, A string course on the North side of Binham priory in Norfolk, of ten inches in depth, and to every space of eight inches are the circular projection of four inches and a half in diameter.

Fig. 14, is the profile.

Fig. 15, A horizontal string course to be found in most of our cathedrals and other buildings of early Norman workmanship. It is what is called *hatched* moulding, from appearing as if cut with one stroke of an axe.

[r] Bentham's History of Ely.

4

Fig.

NORMAN·ARCHITECTVRE

FIG. 1.

FIG. 2.

FIG. 3.

FIG. 14.

FIG. 13.

4 5 6 7

FIG. 15.

FIG. 12.

FIG. 8.

FIG. 9.

FIG. 11.

FIG. 17.

FIG. 10.

FIG. 16.

18.

SAXON·AND·NORMAN·ARCHITECTVRE·

Fig 16, Another string course formed with *reverfed* zig-zag, from the ruins of Wangford priory in Suffolk. This is the only specimen of this kind I ever met with.

Fig. 17. An ornamented *fascia* under the parapet of the North and South sides of Binham priory. When this building was repaired, and the Weft end newly built, they were fo partial to the new Gothic tafte, that although they added to the nave of the church alfo, they neither continued this *fascia* or the original circular headed form of the windows, but made a motly range by adding pointed arches. Indeed the fame may be obferved in moft of our cathedral and conventual buildings.

Fig. 18, Profile of the *fascia* about twelve inches deep.

Fig. 19. Part of the South entrance to Wimboltfham church in Norfolk. The columns feven inches diameter.

Plate XXXVI. Specimens of Saxon and Norman architecture.

Fig. 1. Arch to the entrance of Magdalen chapel, a ruin converted to a barn, in the village of Sprowfton near Norwich, built by bifhop Herbert in the eleventh century.

Fig. 2, Section of the arch one foot fix inches deep, and nine inches projection.

Fig. 3. An arch round another door of the fame building.

Fig. 4. Profile of the arch moulding, nine inches and a half deep.

Fig. 5, Work on the chamfered face between the billeting to a larger fcale.

Fig. 6, A column of *hatched work* in the upper walk of the North tranfept of Norwich cathedral. The plan is octagonal, and nine inches in diameter.

Fig. 7, Another column near it of nine inches diameter.

Fig.

Fig. 8, Capital to one of the entrances to Magdalen chapel.

Fig. 9, An arch, formerly an entrance, on the South side of St. Julian's church in Norwich, probably executed before the Conquest, as the church was founded before that time [r]. It is four feet six inches diameter within.

Fig. 10. Section of the arch mouldings, sixteen inches three-eighths wide, and thirteen inches projection.

Fig. 11 and 12. Two enrichments of the arch on a larger scale.

Fig. 13. One of the arches, in perspective, in the upper walk of the nave of Norwich castle. The window is pointed, consequently of modern date.

The arch of the Newport gate at Lincoln might at first sight be mistaken for *Saxon* or *Norman*, being evidently much older than the pointed *Gothic*; but its date is decidedly Roman, as appears by the fragment of an impost moulding, which is a *cima recta*; for it is remarkable, as I have before observed in page 160, that neither in the Saxon or the Norman architecture an instance occurs of the following mouldings,

Cima recta;   Cima reversa;   Ovolo.

It is well known that the dates of ancient MSS. may frequently be ascertained by the form of the letters only, without any reference to the subjects; as if Providence had, doubtless, for wife purposes, been pleased to mark the lapse of ages in peculiar characters. Thus, it seems likewise, that the respective dates of architecture are distinguishable by peculiar characters also; since it is not only by the great contour of the building, the shape of the arch, or the proportion of columns and piers that their dates are ascertainable, but each little fragment of a moulding or vestige of enrichment marks the æra of the structure, and assists the curious investigator in his researches into antiquity.

[r] Blomefield, vol. II p. 54.

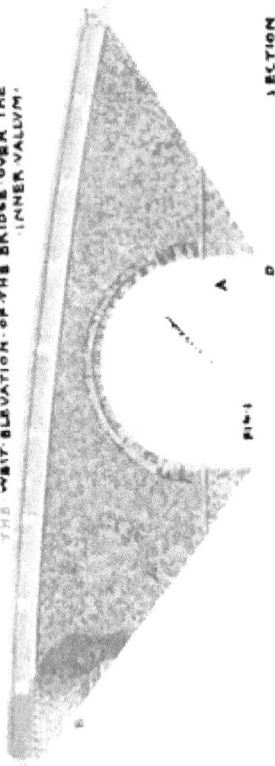

NORWICH · CASTLE ·

THE · WEST · ELEVATION · OF · THE · BRIDGE · OVER · THE · INNER · VALLVM ·

FIG · 1

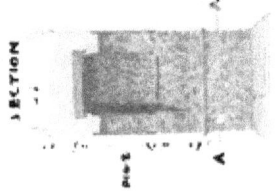

SECTION

FIG · 2 ·

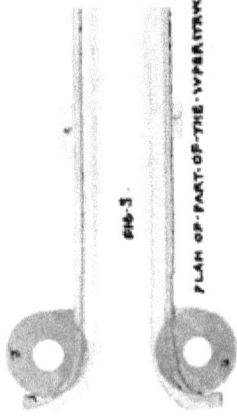

FIG · 3 ·

PLAN · OF · PART · OF · THE · VPPER STAYRWAY ·

————————

To the Rev. Mr. BRAND, *Somerset Place, London.*

SIR,   *Norwich, October* 1, 1795.

IN compliance with the request of the Council of the Society of Antiquaries, transmitted by your polite letter of the
29th of June last, I have taken the earliest opportunity my
avocations would permit, of making the architectural Drawings of the Bridge, and the four elevations of the Keep of
Norwich Castle, for the further embellishing the memoir
Sir Joseph Banks has done me the honour of submitting to
the Society; to which I have added a few more observations
that occurred in the course of taking the necessary measures, and which I hope will not be thought irrelative to the
subject.

I remain, Sir,

most respectfully,

Your obedient

humble Servant,

WILLIAM WILKINS.

Plate XXXVII. The bridge over the nearer vallum is
nearly one hundred and fifty feet in extent, and rises from the
inner to the upper ballium sixteen feet. The basement is
built with free stone up to the impost moulding, which is also
                                                of

of stone. The arch is likewise formed with two ribs of the same stone of four feet three inches each in thickness, upon which rests the internal soffit of brick work, which is explained by the section fig. 2, where the brick work is shaded darker. The present carriage-way is over this bridge, and is sixteen feet eight inches in width bounded by a parapet on each side of modern construction [a].

The elevation (fig. 1.) of the bridge is at present faced with squared flints, which is of modern execution, and in a dilapidated state. It was most probably originally of the same kind with the basement of the Keep, but wet and frost have subjected it to the necessity of frequent repairs. The dotted lines A A A, fig 1 and 2, shew the line of the fosse in its present state, which has been constantly accumulating, and very much of late, from the rubbish deposited in erecting the addition to the gaol. I therefore caused the earth to be cleared away at D more than ten feet in depth, that I might with accuracy ascertain the height from the base to the impost moulding [b], which is nine feet, where I discovered seven projections which are of faced stone, as are shewn in fig. 1. and fig. 2. and others most probably continue to a much greater depth; but the labour caused by the looseness of the earth, which was incessantly tumbling in as we increased our digging, prevented my further investigation that way. At the North end of the bridge are the remains of two towers

(B B B

[a] Upon the crown of the arch stood an arch of *Gothic* workmanship, as is shewn, I believe, in Buck's views; but, as this was no part of the original building, I shall make no observation upon it.

[b] In my former letter, p. 148, I observed, that the section of the impost moulding was alone sufficient to decide that this bridge was of Saxon or Norman, and not of Roman architecture, and by a similar observation in passing through the city

Pl. XLI. *Pl. XXXVII. p. 258*

NORWICH CASTLE.

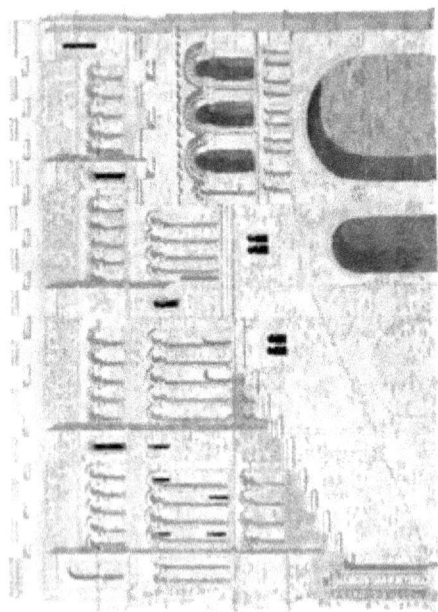

·EAST· ELEVATION·
·OF·THE· KEEP·

0   10   20   30   40   50   60   70   80   90   100.

(B B B fig. 1. and fig. 3.), which, as I before obferved, were probably united by a portal [c] to the upper ballium.

The projections to the plan at C C fig. 3. are the fite of two buttreffes which have been added as lateral fupports to the bridge, as the walls have been fpreading for a long time, and, indeed, the whole is rapidly perifhing.

When I underftood that the magiftrates of Norfolk had determined on a plan which propofed the taking down the ftaircafe afcending the keep, I made drawings from the Eaft elevation, by which I am able to detail the particulars which are now deftroyed ; and by means of a dotted line in Plate XXXVIII. have explained the fection of the ftair-cafe and the draw-bridge at the entrance of Bigod's portal, which an elevation in the ufual way would have concealed. Nearly oppofite to the North end, and at a few paces diftant from the bridge, the ftair-cafe took place, and afcended along the Eaft front over a draw-bridge to the tower, under which is ftill the door from the loweft apartment, which Mr. King fuggefts to have been the fally port. The Eaft elevation exhibits the front richly ornamented with arches as in its former ftate, yet the uppermoft row, which is continued through the South, the Weft, and the North elevations, is omitted in this ; indeed the third row of arches in this front is fo much higher than in the others, as not to leave the fame fpace for ornament.

of Lincoln four years fince, I accidentally, and without any previous information, determined the gate through which the prefent turnpike road paffes towards Spital to be of Roman workmanfhip, from which I made a drawing, and prefented it to Sir Jofeph Banks. I have added another drawing to this collection, as the fection of the impoft moulding ferves alfo to elucidate the prefent fubject. See Plate XLII.

[c] As there is no appearance of a portcullis to the outlet of the keep, might there not have been one to this portal ? or was the portcullis of fubfequent invention ?

The South elevation (Plate XXXIX.) shews the beginning or front of the stair-case at E; the basement of the whole building is constructed with coarse flint work [d], between the

[d] Flints, which are one of the abundant productions of this county, have not been overlooked by our predecessors in building. We find the substance of all old walls, in this part of the kingdom composed of that material, and with strong-made mortar, which was well incorporated with a large quantity of sand, we find them so cemented as to become one solid mass of stone. The Romans availed themselves of this material; and we find their works in as good, and generally in better, preservation here than in most parts of the kingdom. They not only made the interior substance with coarse flints, but afterwards they faced their work with alternate courses of squared flints, as at Burgh castle (*Garianonum*). This kind of facing after their time became neglected; for the basement of the keep of Norwich castle, although made with flints, and some of them faced, nevertheless they were not squared or laid in regular courses. No material whatever can excel the durability of flints; for we do not find any where an instance of their perishing by frosty or wet weather; and, when squared or laid with care, they are extremely beautiful; in building they have, notwithstanding, but little bond, and depend much upon the mortar cement they are fixed with; for, if wet by any means get behind them, the frost soon levels the work. Many, indeed most, of our churches and public buildings in this county are built almost wholly with this material; but, the most remarkable I have observed, in which flints faced and squared are laid in small regular courses, is the convent gate to Norwich cathedral, which was built in the reign of Edward the First, where the walls to the East and the South have a tracery work formed with free-stone, and the intervals are filled with square flints; and some, about Erpingham's gate, built in penance for Lolardism in the reign of Richard the Second. The chapel of the Virgin Mary on the South side of St. Michael's Coslany church, which is indeed a master-piece (where the stone tracery is so beautifully filled with black flints as to resemble such old cabinets as we sometimes see inlaid with ivory), was built about the year 1500; and a building in St. Andrew's parish, which is recorded as a very rare and beautiful piece of flint work, built in 1403 by William Appleyard, who was the first mayor, and served the office in this house, which was afterwards sold to the corporation, and is the present bridewell. Many country churches have been also built in this way, as at Cromer, &c. in Norfolk, and many in Suffolk and Essex. The art of squaring the flints

4

NORWICH·CASTLE·

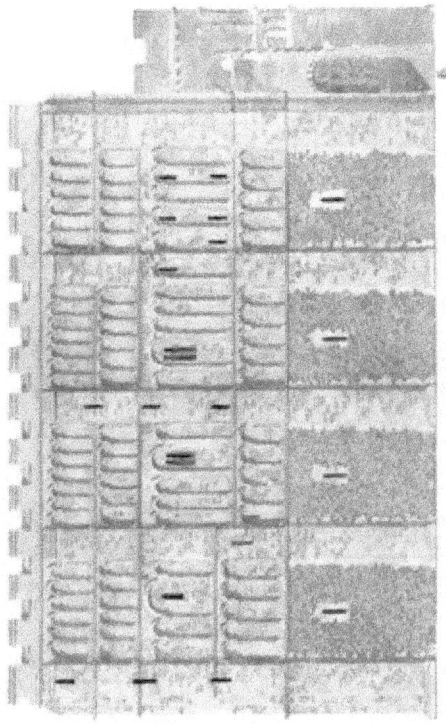

···SOUTH·ELEVATION·
OF·THE·KEEP·

0 10 20 30 40 50 60 70 80 90 100

SECTION·of·THE·HOUSE·
TWAN·HEADS·

·NORWICH· CASTLE·

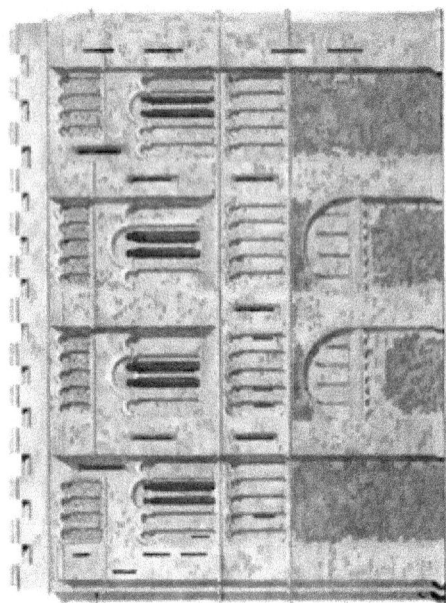

·WEST· ELEVATION· ·OF·THE·KEEP·

·SECTION·OF·THE· ·WEST·WALL·

·NORWICH CASTLE·

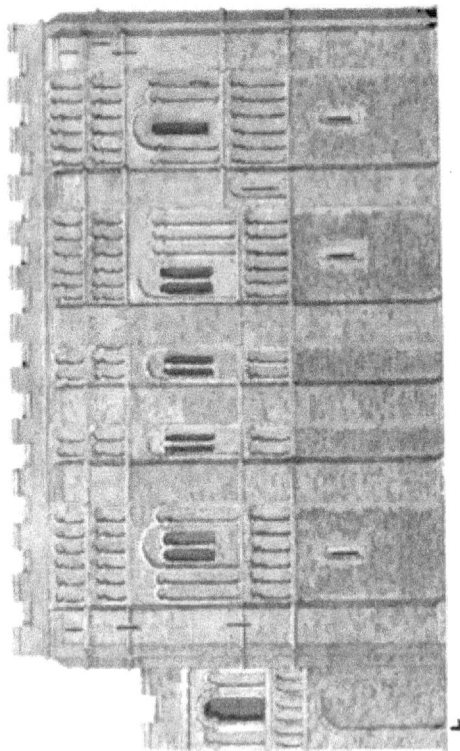

·NORTH·ELEVATION·
·OF·THE·KEEP·

THE NEWPORT GATE AT LINCOLN

FIG 2

the buttreffes and the appearance of fmall chinked windows, which were intended for ornament, or deception, for they never could be of real ufe. Fig. 2. is the fection of the South wall, which, for upwards of twenty-five feet in height is eleven feet in thicknefs; the aperture at F fhews a paffage communicating with rooms on the firft floor, that are now deftroyed.

The Weft elevation (Plate XL.) of the keep is flanked with five buttreffes, and fhews the two arches, which appear like an original entrance ftopped up. Thefe, it was before obferved, were probably intended as a deception to an ene-my, giving an idea of weaknefs where the wall is of an ex-traordinary thicknefs, as is fhewn by the fection fig. 2, where the apertures G, H, and I, were fmall rooms and paffages to the ftair-cafes. A door is fhewn in the bafement plan at K, but, as it was not originally made there, I have omitted it in this elevation.

The North elevation (Plate XLI.), againft which the fhire-houfe abuts, is flanked with fix buttreffes. L is the North end of Bigod's tower; the embattled termination of the keep is of recent workmanfhip.

The Newport gate at Lincoln (Plate XLII.) was the North gate of the ancient *Lindum* of the Romans, through which a Roman military way is ftill obvious for upwards of twelve miles. This, like fome of the gates of Rome, confifted of three cima arches. Only two of them are remaining (fig. 1.) built with hard, reddifh, fquared ftones. Thofe which form the

in this curious manner is now almoft totally neglected, though I am convinced it might very foon be brought to perfection again, from the facility I obferved the workmen acquire by a little practice in repairing under my fuperintendance in Bifhop Bagot's time a tower belonging to the palace.

arches

arches are wedged, and are of various scantling, two feet in
depth, and some of them sixteen inches in width, diminishing towards the centre; and three feet seven inches in length,
which forms the breadth of the soffite. The great arch is fifteen feet; and the remaining small one seven feet in diameter. The center arch is still the passage of the great road,
which has been necessarily widened (for the convenience of
carriages and passengers), from the great accumulation of
the earth, which is within four feet of the chord line of the
arch. In a field adjoining to the East is yet remaining a
large specimen of Roman wall, which from its direction has
been evidently continued from the gate. There does not at
this time appear to have been any kind of ornament about
this edifice, excepting an impost moulding, a small piece of
which only remains at M on the South side, sufficient however to determine (if there were any doubts) its being a Roman structure (section fig. 2.); the upper part has been
broken off, and might probably be something like the dotted
line, but the lower part still retains the perfect profile of the
cima-recta moulding, which was never used by the Saxon or
Norman builders.

XVI.

XVI. *A short Account of several Gardens near* London, *with remarks on some particulars wherein they excel, or are deficient, upon a View of them in* December 1691. *Communicated to the Society by the Reverend Dr.* Hamilton, *Vice President, from an original Manuscript in his possession.*

Read July 3, 1794.

1. HAMPTON COURT Garden is a large plat, environed with an iron palisade round about next the park, laid all in walks, grass plats, and borders. Next to the house, some flat and broad beds are set with narrow rows of dwarf box, in figures like lace-patterns. In one of the lesser gardens is a large green house divided into several rooms, and all of them with stoves under them, and fire to keep a continual heat. In these there are no orange or lemon trees, or myrtles, or any greens, but such tender foreign ones that need continual warmth.

2. *Kensington* Gardens are not great nor abounding with fine plants. The orange, lemon, myrtles, and what other trees they had there in summer, were all removed to Mr. London's and Mr Wise's greenhouse at Brompton Park, a little mile from them. But the walks and grass laid very fine, and they

were

were digging up a flat of four or five acres to enlarge their garden.

3. *The Queen Dowager's* Garden, at *Hammersmith*, has a good greenhouse, with a high erected front to the South, whence the roof falls backward. The house is well stored with greens of common kinds; but the Queen not being for curious plants or flowers, they want of the most curious sorts of greens, and in the garden there is little of value but wall trees; though the gardener there, Monsieur Hermon Van Guine, is a man of great skill and industry, having raised great numbers of orange and lemon trees by inoculation, with myrtles, Roman bayes, and other greens of pretty shapes, which he has to dispose of.

4. *Beddington* Garden, at present in the hands of the duke of Norfolk, but belonging to the family of Carew, has in it the best orangery in England. The orange and lemon trees there grow in the ground, and have done so near one hundred years, as the gardener, an aged man, said he believed. There are a great number of them, the house wherein they are being above two hundred feet long; they are most of them thirteen feet high, and very full of fruit, the gardener not having taken off so many flowers this last summer as usually others do. He said, he gathered off them at least ten thousand oranges this last year. The heir of the family being but about five years of age, the trustees take care of the orangery, and this year they built a new house over them. There are some myrtles growing among them, but they look not well for want of trimming. The rest of the garden is all out of order, the orangery being the gardener's chief care; but it is capable of being made one of the best gardens in England,

England, the soil being very agreeable, and a clear silver stream running through it.

5. *Chelsea Physick* Garden has great variety of plants, both in and out of greenhouses. Their perennial green hedges and rows of different coloured herbs are very pretty, and so are their banks set with shades of herbs in the Irish stitchway, but many plants of the garden were not in so good order as might be expected, and as would have been answerable to other things in it. After I had been there, I heard that Mr. Watts, the keeper of it, was blamed for his neglect, and that he would be removed.

6. My Lord *Ranelagh's* Garden being but lately made, the plants are but small, but the plats, borders, and walks, are curiously kept, and elegantly designed, having the advantage of opening into Chelsea college walks. The kitchen garden there lies very fine, with walks and seats, one of which, being large and covered, was then under the hands of a curious painter. The house there is very fine within, all the rooms being wainscoted with Norway oak, and all the chimneys adorned with carving, as in the council-chamber in Chelsea college.

7. *Arlington* Garden, being now in the hands of my lord of Devonshire, is a fair plat, with good walks, both airy and shady. There are six of the greatest earthen pots that are any where else, being at least two feet over within the edge ; but they stand abroad, and have nothing in them but the tree holy-oke, an indifferent plant, which grows well enough in the ground. Their greenhouse is very well, and their greenyard excels ; but their greens were not so bright and clean as farther off in the country, as if they suffered something from the smutty air of the town.

8. My

8 My Lord *Faucenbergh's* Garden, at *Sutton Court,* has several pleasant walks and apartments in it; but the upper garden next the house is too irregular, and the bowling green too little to be commended. The greenhouse is very well made, but ill set. It is divided into three rooms, and very well furnished with good greens; but it is so placed, that the sun shines not on the plants in winter, where they most need its beams, the dwelling-house standing betwixt the sun and it. The maze or wilderness there is very pretty, being set all with greens, with a cyprefs arbour in the middle, supported with a well-wrought timber frame; of late it grows thin at the bottom, by their letting the fir trees grow without their reach unclipped. The enclofure wired-in for white pheafants and partridges is a fine apartment, efpecially in fummer, when the bones of Italian bayes are fet out, and the timber walk with vines on the fide is very fine when the blew pots are on the pedeftals on the top of it, and fo is the fifh-pond with th greens at the head of it.

9. Sir *William Temple,* being lately gone to live at his houfe in Farnham, his garden and greenhoufe at *Weft Sheene,* where he has lived of late years, are not fo well kept as they have been, many of his orange trees, and other greens, being given to Sir John Temple, his brother, at Eaft Sheene, and other gentlemen; but his greens that are remaining (being as good a ftock as moft greenhoufes have) are very fresh and thriving, the room they ftand in fuiting well with them and being well contrived, if it be no defect in it that the floor is a foot at leaft within the ground, as is alfo the floor of the dwelling houfe. He had attempted to have orange trees to grow in the ground (as at Beddington), and for that purpofe had enclofed a fquare of ten feet wide, with a low brick wall,

and

and sheltered them with wood, but they would not do. His orange trees in summer stand not in any particular square or enclosure, under some shelter, as most others do, but are disposed on pedestals of Portland stone, at equal distance, on a board over against a South wall, where is his best fruit, and fairest walk.

10. Sir *Henry Capell's* garden at *Kew* has its curious greens, and is as well kept as any about London. His two lentiscus trees (for which he paid forty pounds to Verfprit) are said to be the best in England, not only of their kind, but of greens. He has four white striped hollies, about four feet above their cases, kept round and regular, which cost him five pounds a tree this last year, and six laurustinufes he has, with large round equal heads, which are very flowery and make a fine shew. His orange trees and other choicer greens stand out in summer in two walks about fourteen feet wide, enclosed with a timber frame about seven feet high, and set with silver firs hedge-wise, which are as high as the frame, and this to secure them from wind and tempest, and sometimes from the scorching sun. His terrace walk, bare in the middle, and grass on either side, with a hedge of rue on one side next a low wall, and a row of dwarf trees on the other, shews very fine, and so do from thence his yew hedges with trees of the fame at equal distance, kept in pretty shapes with tonsure. His flowers and fruits are of the best, for the advantage of which two parallel walls, about fourteen feet high, were now raised and almost finished. If the ground were not a little irregular, it would excel in other points, as well as in furniture.

11. Sir *Stephen Fox's* garden at *Chifwick* being but of five years standing, is brought to great perfection for the time.

It excells for a fair gravel walk betwixt two yew hedges, with rounds and spires of the same, all under smooth tonsure. At the far end of this garden are two myrtle hedges that cross the garden; they are about three feet high, and covered in winter with painted board cases. The other gardens are full of flowers and talleting, and the walls well clad. The greenhouse is well built, well set, and well furnished.

12. Sir *Thomas Cooke's* garden at *Hackney* is very large, and not so fine at present, because of his intending to be at three thousand pounds charge with it this next summer, as his gardener said. There are two greenhouses in it, but the greens are not extraordinary, for one of the roofs being made a receptacle for water, overcharged with weight, fell down last year upon the greens, and made a great destruction among the trees and pots. In one part of it is a warren, containing about two acres, very full of coneys, though there was but a couple put in a few years since. There is a pond or a mote round about them, and on the outside of that a brick wall four feet high, both which I think will not keep them within their compass. There is a large fish-pond lying on the South to a brick wall, which is finely clad with philaria. Water brought from far in pipes furnishes his several ponds as they want it.

13. Sir *Josiah Child's* plantations of walnut and other trees at *Wansted* are much more worth seeing than his gardens, which are but indifferent. Besides, the great number of fruit trees he has planted in his enclosures with great regularity, he has vast number of elms, ashes, limes, &c. planted in rows on Epping forest. Before his outgate, which is above twelve score distance from his house, are two large fish-ponds on the forest, in the way from his house, with trees
on

on either side lying betwixt them; in the middle of either
pond is an island betwixt twenty and thirty yards over, and
in the middle of each a house, the one like the other.   They
are said to be well stocked with fish, and so they had need to
be if they cost him five thousand pounds, as it is said they
did; as also that his plantations cost twice as much.

14. Sir *Robert Clayton* has great plantations at *Marden* in
Surrey, in a soil not very benign to plants, but with great
charge he forces Nature to obey him.   His gardens are big
enough, but strangely irregular, his chief walk not being level,
but rising in the middle and falling much more at one end
than the other; neither is the wall carried by a line either on
the top or sides, but runs like an ordinary park wall, built as
the ground goes.   He built a good greenhouse, but set it so
that the hills in winter keep the sun from it, so that they
place their greens in a house on higher ground not built for
that purpose.   His dwelling house stands very low, surrounded
with great hills; and yet they have no water but what is
forced from a deep well into a waterhouse, whence they are
furnished by pipes at pleasure.

15. The Archbishop of *Canterbury's* garden at *Lambeth*
has little in it but walks, the late archbishop not delighting
in one, but they are now making them better; and they have
already made a greenhouse, one of the finest and costliest
about the town.   It is of three rooms, the middle having a
stove under it; the foresides of the rooms are almost all glass,
the roof covered with lead, the whole part (to adorn the
building) rising gavel-wise higher than the rest; but it is
placed so near Lambeth church, that the sun shines most on
it in winter after eleven o'clock; a fault owned by the gardener, but not thought on by the contrivers.   Most of the

greens

greens are oranges and lemons, which have very large ripe fruit on them.

16. Dr. *Uvedale* of *Enfield* is a great lover of plants, and having an extraordinary art in managing them, is become master of the greatest and choicest collection of exotic greens that is perhaps any where in this land. His greens take up six or seven houses or roomsteads. His orange trees and largest myrtles fill up his biggest house, and another house is filled with myrtles of a less size, and these more nice and curious plants, that need closer keeping are in warmer rooms, and some of them stoved when he thinks fit. His flowers are choice, his stock numerous, and his culture of them very methodical and curious ; but, to speak of the garden in the whole, it does not lie fine to please the eye, his delight and care lying more in the ordering particular plants, than in the pleasing view and form of his garden.

17. Dr. *Tillotson's* garden near *Endfield* is a pleasureable place for walks, and some good walls there are too ; but the tall aspin trees, and the many ponds in the heart of it, are not so agreeable. He has two houses for greens, but had few in them, all the best being removed to Lambeth. The house is moated about.

18. Mr. *Evelyn* has a pleasant villa at *Deptford*, a fine garden for walks and hedges (especially his holly one, which he writes of in his Sylva), and a pretty little greenhouse, with an indifferent stock in it. In his garden he has four large round philareas, smooth clipped, raised on a single stalk from the ground, a fashion now much used. Part of his garden is very woody and shady for walking ; but his garden, not being walled, has little of the best fruits.

6

19.

19. Mr. *Watts's* house and garden made near *Endfield* are new; but the garden for the time is very fine, and large and regularly laid out, with a fair fish-pond in the middle. He built a greenhouse this summer with three rooms (somewhat like the archbishop of Canterbury's) the middle with a stove under it, and a sky-light above, and both of them of glass on the foreside, with shutters within, and the roof finely covered with Irish flate. But this fine house is under the same great fault with three before (Numbers 8, 14, 15.): they built it in summer, and thought not of winter; the dwelling house on the South side interposing betwixt the sun and it now when its beams should refresh plants.

20. *Brompton Park* garden, belonging to Mr. *London* and Mr. *Wife*, has a large long greenhouse, the front all glass and board, the North side brick. Here the King's greens, which were in summer at Kensington, are placed, but they take but little room in comparison of their own. Their garden is chiefly a nursery for all sorts of plants, of which they are very full.

21. Mr. *Rowston's* garden at *Endfield* is observable for nothing but his greenhouse, which he has had for many years. His orange, lemon, and myrtle trees, are as full and furnished as any in cases. He has a myrtle cut in shape of a chaire, that is at least six feet high from the cole, but the lower part is thin of leaves. The rest of the garden is very ordinary, and on the outside of his garden he has a warren, which makes the ground about his seat lye rudely, and sometimes the coneys work under the wall into the garden.

22. Mr. *Richardson* at *East Barnet* has a pretty garden, with fine walks and good flowers; but the garden not being walled about they have less summer fruit, yet are, therefore, the

the more induftrious in managing the peach and apricot dwarf ftandards, which, they fay, fupply them plentifully with very good fruit. There is a good fifh-pond in the middle of it, from which a broad gravel walk leads to the highway, where a fair pair of broad gates, with a narrower on either fide, open at the top to look through fmall bars, well wrought and well painted, are a great ornament to the garden. They have orange and lemon trees; but the wife and fon being the managers of the garden (the hufband being gouty and not minding it), they cannot prevail for a houfe for them other than a barn end.

23. Captain *Fofter's* garden at *Lambeth* has many curiofities in it. His greenhoufe is full of frefh and flourifhing plants, and before it is the finest ftriped holly hedge that perhaps is in England. He has many myrtles, not the greateft, but of the moft fanciful fhapes that are any where elfe. He has a framed walk of timber covered with vines, which, with others, running on moft of his walls without prejudice to his lower trees, yield him a deal of wine. Of flowers he has good choice, and his Virginia and other birds in a great variety, with his glafs hive, add much to the pleafure of his garden.

24. Monfieur *Anthony Vefprit* has a little garden of very choice things. His greenhoufe has no very great number of plants, but what he has are of the beft fort, and very well ordered. His oranges and lemons (fruit and tree) are extraordinary fair, and for lentifcus's and Roman bayes he has choice above others.

25. *Ricketts*, at *Hoxton*, has a large ground, and abundantly ftocked with all manner of flowers, fruit-trees, and
other

other garden plants, with lime trees, which are now much
planted ; and, for a fale garden, he has a very good greenhoufe, and well filled with frefh greens, befides which he has
another room very full of greens in pots. He has a greater
ftock of Affyrian thyme than any body elfe ; for, befides
many pots of it, he has beds abroad, with plenty of roots,
which they cover with mats and ftraw in winter. He fells
his things with the deareft, and, not taking due care to have
his plants prove well, he is fuppofed to have loft much of his
cuftom.

26. *Pearfon* has not near fo large a ground as Rickets (on
whom he almoft joins), and therefore he has not fo many
trees, but of flowers he has great choice, and of anemonies
he avers he has the beft about London, and fells them only
to gentlemen. He has no greenhoufe, yet has abundance of
myrtles and ftriped philareas, with oranges and other greens,
which he keeps fafe enough under fheds, funk a foot within
ground, and covered with ftraw. He has abundance of cy-
preffes, which, at three feet high, he fells for four pence
apiece to thofe that take any number. He is moderate in his
prices, and accounted very honeft in his dealing, which gets
him much chapmanry.

27. *Darby*, at *Hoxton*, has but a little garden, but is mafter
of feveral curious greens that other fale-gardeners want, and
which he faves from cold and winter weather in greenhoufes
of his own making. His Fritalaria Craffa (a green) had a
flower on it of the breadth of a half crown, like an embroidered
ftar, of feveral colours; I faw not the like any where, no,
not at Dr. Uvedale's, though he has the fame plant. He
raifes many ftriped hollies by inoculation, though Captain
Fofter grafts them as we do apple tres. He is very curious
in.

in propagating greens, but is dear with them. He has a folio paper book in which he has pasted the leaves and flowers of almost all manner of plants, which make a pretty shew, and are more instructive than any cuts in herbals.

28. *Clements*, at *Mile-end*, has no bigger a garden than Darby, but has more greens, yet not of such curious sorts. He keeps them in a greenhouse made with a light charge. He has vines in many places about old trees, which they wind about. He made wine this year of his white Muscadine, and white Frontinac, better I thought than any French white wine. He keeps a shop of seeds in plants in pots next the street.

Jan. 26, 1691.   J. GIBSON.

XVII.

XVII. *An Inscription in the Tower of* London. *Communicated by* George Nayler, *Esq.* York *Herald,* F. A. S. *In a Letter to the Secretary.*

Read November 5, 1795.

College of Arms, London, June 24, 1795.

REV. SIR,

I Will thank you to prefent to theSociety of Antiquaries a drawing and explanation of a marble monument or tablet fixed in a wall on the North-weft fide of the Tower of London, and in the apartments of the Deputy Lieutenant, called the *Council Chamber.* It was erected, as appears from the infcription, by Sir William Wade, knight, Lieutenant of the Tower in the year 1608, evidently with a view of perpetuating the infamy of the confpirators concerned in the Gunpowder plot. It is compofed of marbles of feveral colours: fee the annexed plate *, in which the different infcriptions are flightly fketched, and referred to by the letters A. B. C. D. E. and figures 1. 2. 3. 4. in the following pages.

It is fituated near the fire-place, about four feet from the floor, and is inclofed by a pair of folding doors that cover

* Plate XLIV.

the whole completely, to which it is probable we may attribute the good prefervation in which we find it, notwithstanding the lapfe of one hundred and eighty-feven years. This circumftance, perhaps, is rendered fomewhat dubious by a remark of that venerable Antiquary *Stow*, who, in his Survey of London *, fays, " In an upper chamber in the " Lieutenant's lodgings is an ingenious device to defcribe " the Gunpowder Treafon Plot, fet up about that time by " Sir William Wade, Lieutenant of the Tower ; the mo- " nument confifteth of feveral pieces of marble, in fafhion " round, inlaid with infcriptions on them ; in the middle " whereof is a larger ftone, on the extremities feveral coats " of arms of the chief nobility, as of Howard, Cecil, &c. " It is *fcarcely legible*, the defcription being almoft worn out." But notwithftanding this, after a very clofe examination, I have not been able to difcover the leaft appearance of its having been retouched or repaired. As the drawing and infcription fufficiently explain every circumftance relative to this fingular monument, I fhall not trouble you farther than to obferve, that of the nine coats of arms ranged in a line on the upper part of the tablet, eight belong to knights of the garter, whofe names are feverally fpecified in the defcription annexed, and who were the commiffioners appointed to try the confpirators. The ninth and laft is the coat of the lord chief juftice Sir John Popham, knight.

I remain, Reverend Sir,

Your moft obedient humble Servant,

Rev. Mr. Brand,   G E O R G E   N A Y L E R.
Somerfet Place.

* Stow's Survey of London. Edit. 1720, vol. I. p. 75.

A.

A.

Jacobus magnus Magnæ Britanniæ Rex, pietate, justicia, prudentia, doctrina, fortitudine, clementia, ceterisq. virtutibus regiis clariss' ; Christianæ fidei, falutis publicæ, pacis univerfalis propugnator, fantor, auctor acerrimus, augustiss', auspicatiss'. Anna Regina, Frederici 2. Danorum regis invictiss' filia serenifs'. Henricus Princeps, naturæ ornamentis, doctrinæ præsidiis, gratiæ muneribus instructiss' ; nobis & natus, & a Deo datus. Carolus Dux Eboracensis divina ad omnem virtutem indole. Elizabetha utriusq. foror germana, utroque parente digniffima. Ilos, velut pupillam oculi tenellam providus muni, procul impiorum impetu alarum tuarum intrepidos conde fub umbra.

———

B.

Robertus Cicill comes Salisburiensis, sūmus & Regis Secretarius & Angliæ Thefaurarius, clariss. patris & de repub. meritiffimi filius, in paterna munera fucceffor longe digniffimus. Henricus comes Northamptoniæ, quinq. portū præfectus, & privati figilli custos, difertorum litteratiffimus, litteratorum difertiffimus. Carolus comes Nottingamiæ, magnus Angliæ admirallius victoriofus. Thomas Suffolciæ comes, regis camerarius fplendidiffimus, tres viri nobiliffimi ex antiqua Howardorū familia ducumq. Norfolciæ profapia.   Edwardus

C c 2   wardus

wardus Somerfetus comes Wigorniæ, equis regiis præfectus
ornatiffimus. Carolus Blunt comes Devoniæ, Hyberniæ
prorex & pacificator. Joannes Arefkinus illuftris Marriæ
comes, præcipuarum in Scotia arcium prefectus, Georgius
Humius Dumbari comes, Scotiæ thefaurarius prudentiffim'.
Omnes illuftriff' Ordinis Garterii milites. Joannes Popham, miles, Jufticiarius Angliæ capitalis, juris & jufticiæ
confultiffimus.

C.

Deo Opt. Max. Triuno Sofpitatori, et tantæ, tam atrocis
tamque incredibilis in Regem clementiff', in Reginam fe-
reniff', in divinæ indolis & optimæ fpei Principem, exte-
ramq; progeniam regiam, & in omnem omnium ordinum,
& nobilitatis antiquæ & fortitudinis avitæ & pietatis caftif-
fimæ & Juftitiæ fanctiffimæ florem præcipuum, conjurationis
exequendæ nitrofi pulveris fubjecti inflammatione, Chrif-
tianæ veræq; religionis extinguendæ furiofa libidine & regni
ftirpitus evertendi nefaria cupiditate, a Jefuitis Romanenfibus,
perfidiæ Catholicæ et impietatis viperinæ autoribus et affertori-
bus, aliifq; ejufdem amentiæ fcelerifq; patratoribus et fociis fuf-
ceptæ, et in ipfo peftis derepente inferendæ articulo (Salutis
anno 1605, menfis Novembris die quinto) tam præter fpem,
quam fupra fidem mirifice et divinitus detectæ, averrunco, et
vindici, grates quantas animi capere poffent maximas et im-
mortales a nobis omnibus, et pofteris noftris haberi et agi Gu-
lielmus

lielmus Waade, miles, Turri a Domino Rege præfectus, pofito perpetuo hoc Monumento voluit. Die nono menfis Octob. Anno Regni Jacobi prime * fexto, Anno D'ni 1608.

(The Cypher of William Wade.)

D.

Conjuratorum nomina, ad perpetuam ipforum infamiam et tantæ diritatis deteftationem fempiternam.

Monachi falutare Jefu nomen ementiti.	Henry Garnet	Thomas Winter	Thomas Percy
	John Gerrard	Robert Winter	Robert Catefby
	Ofwald Tefond	John Winter	John Wright
	Edward Hall	Guy Fawkes	Chriftopher Wright
	Hamō	Thomas Bates	Francis Trefham
	Baldwī	Everard Digby, K'	Tho'as Abbington
		Am. Rookewood	Edmo'd Baineham, K'
		John Graunt	Wil' Stanley, K'
		Robert Keyes	Hughe Owen
		Henry Morgā.	

מְגַלֶּה עֲמֻקוֹת מִנִּי־חֹשֶׁךְ וַיֹּצֵא לָאוֹר צַלְמָוֶת׃

Pandit, et in lucem profert de nocte profunda
Terra immerfa alte et fati caligine cæca.

E.

Hi omnes illuftriff" viri, quorum nomina ad fempiternam eorum memoriam pofteritati confecrandam proxime fupra ad lineam pofita funt, ut Regi a confiliis, ita ab eo delegati

* Sic.

quæ-

quæfitores, reis fingulis incredibili diligentia ac cura fæpius
appellatis, nec minore folertia & dexteritate pertentatis
eorum animis, eos, fuis ipforum inter fe collatis refponfi-
onibus convictos, ad voluntariam confeffionem adegerunt &
latentem nefariæ conjurationis feriem, remq. omnem, ut hac-
tenus gefta, & porro per eos gerenda effet, fumma fide eru-
tam, æterna cum laude fua, in lucem produxerunt, adeo ut
divina fingulari providentiâ effectum fit, ut tam præfens,
tamq. fœda tempeftas a Regia Majeftate, liberifq. regiis &
omni regno depulfa, in ipfos autores eorumq, focios re-
dundarit.

---

1. Inclite Rex tu es Vinclum per quod Refp. cohæret ;
   Tu fpiritus Vitalis quem tot millia trahunt.
   Nihil ipfa per fe futura, nifi onus et preda,
   Si mens illa Imperii fubtrahatur.

2. Rex, Regina, pius Princeps regni, omnis & ordo
   Deftinata truci præda voranda rogo.
   Vipereo a genere & graviter fpirantib' hydris
   Virus Jefuadum de feritate lupæ.
   Spemq; fidemq; fupra eripitur divinitus, Ergo
   Ordo habeat grates omnis agatque Deo.

3. In nos, fancte Parens, quot vigilantiæ
   Et quam mira tuæ pignora fupperunt ?
   Que nec mens acie cernere languida
   Poffit, nec numero lingua retexere.

                                          4. Cuf-

6

4. Cuſtodis Cuſtos ſum, Carcer Carceris, Arcis
   Arx, atque Argu' Argus ; ſum Speculæ Specula,
   Sum Vinclum * inclis, Compes cum compede Clavū
   Firmo hærens teneo tentus habens habeor.
   Dum Regi Regnoque ſalus ſtet firma quieta
   Splendida ſim Compes Compedis uſque licet.

On the Cornice of the Tablet are the Arms of

1 Robert Cecil, Earl of Saliſbury,
2 Henry Howard, Earl of Northampton,
3 Charles Howard, Earl of Nottingham,
4 Thomas Howard, Earl of Suffolk,   } Knights of the
5 Edward Somerſet, Earl of Worceſter,   Moſt Noble Order
6 Charles Blunt, Earl of Devon,   of the Garter.
7 John Areſkin or Ereſkin, Earl of Marr,
8 George Hume, Earl of Dunbar,

9 Sir John Popham, Knight, Lord Chief Juſtice.
10 Sir Edward Coke, Knight, then Attorney-General.
11 Sir William Wade, Knight, Lieutenant of the Tower.
12 Ditto, quartering : 1. Gules, a chevron between three
   boars heads couped, Argent ; 3. Gules, three garbs, Or ;
   4. Or, two bars Azure in chief three water bugetts, Gules.

* Sic, pro vinclis.

C c 4   Copy

Copy of the Letter to the Lord Mounteagle, which occasioned
the Discovery of the Gunpowder plot; with an engraved
Fac Simile *.

Read June 2, 1796.

" My lord, out of the love I beare to some of youere frends,
i have a caer of your preservation. Therfor I would advyse
yowe, as yowe tender youer lyf, to devyse some exscufe to
shift off youer attendance at this parleament, for God and
man hathe concurred to punishe the wickednes of this tyme,
and thinke not slightelye of this advertisment, but retyere
youre selfe into youre contri, where yowe maye expect the
event in safti, for thowghe theare be no apparance of anni
stir yet i saye they shall receyve a teribel blowe this parleament, and yet they shall not fei who hurts them. This cown-
cel is not to be contemned, because it maye do yowe good,
and can do yowe no harme, for the dangere is passed as soon
as yowe have burnt the letter, and i hope God will give yowe
the grace to mak good use of it. To whose holy proteccion
i comend yowe."

Inscribed on the back,

" To the ryght honorable
The lord Mow'teagle."

King James, in his speech to the parliament, November 9,
1605 (printed in the Journals of the House of Lords, vol. II.
p. 358.), gives the following account of the discovery of the
gunpowder plot, *viz.*

" The discovery hereof is not a little wonderful, which
would be thought the more miraculous by you all, if you

* Communicated by John Topham, esq.

were

my lord out of the loue i beare ~~to~~ to some of youere frendz
i haue a caer of youer preseruacion therfor i would...
aduyse yowe as yowe tender youer lyf to deuys~ some
exscuse to shift of youer attendance at this parleament
for god and man hathe concurred to punishe the wickednes
of this tyme and thinke not slightlye of this aduertisment
but retyere youre self into youre contri wheare yowe~
maye expect the event in safti for thowghe theare be no
apparance of ami stir yet i saye they shall receyue a terrible
blowe this parleament and yet they shall not seie who
hurts them this councel is not to be contemned becaus
it maye do yowe good and can do yowe no harme for the
daugere is passed as soon as yowe haue burnt the letter
and i hope god will giue yowe the grace to mak good
use of it to whose holy proteccion i comend yowe

To the right honorable
the lord mounteagle

The Letter to Lord Mounteagle which occasioned the discovery of the Gunpowder plot.

were as well acquainted with my natural difpofition as thofe are who be near about me. For, as I ever did hold fufpicion to be the ficknefs of a tyrant, fo was I fo far upon the other extremity, as I rather contemned all advertifements or apprehenfions of practices ; and yet now at this time I was fo far contrary to myfelf, as when the letter was fhewed to me by my fecretary, wherein a general obfcure advertifement was given of fome dangerous blow at this time, I did upon the inftant interpret and apprehend fome dark phrafes therein, contrary to the ordinary grammar conftruction of them (and in another fort than, I am fure, any divine or lawyer in any univerfity would have taken them) to be meant by this horrible form of blowing us up all by powder : and thereupon ordered that fearch to be made, whereby the matter was difcovered, and the man apprehended ; whereas, if I had apprehended or interpreted it to any other fort of danger, no worldly provifion or prevention could have made us efcape our utter deftruction.

"And in that alfo there was a wonderful providence of God, that when the party himfelf was taken, he was but new come out of his houfe from working, having his fire-work for kindling ready in his pocket, wherewith, as he confeffeth, if he had been taken but immediately before, when he was in the houfe, he was refolved to have blown himfelf up with his takers."

Rela.

Relation of the Difcovery of the Gunpowder under the
Parliament Houfe.

This Relation is preferved in his Majefty's Paper Office, and
is corrected in the Hand Writing of the Earl of Salifbury,
then Secretary of State.

Read June 2, 1796.

" Before the King's Ma" comming from Royfton, there was
a letter delivered to the lo: Mounteagle's footman, as he
paffed in the ftreete towards night, directed to his lord, by a
partye unknowne, written in a hand *disguifed*, w"out date or
name; whereof thefe were the contents:

" My lord, out of the love I beare to fome of yo' friends,
&c."

As foone as he had read it, and obferved the fame, he refolved in his Ma" abfence, to impart it to fome of his M"
Privy Councell, not fo much in refpect of any great credit
his l'p gave to the letter, as becaufe he tooke himfelf bound
in duty to make all thinges any way concerning the King's
perfon or ftate, in honor or fafety, knowne to his M', either
by himfelf immediately, or by fome of thofe to whom the
confideration thereof did more properly belong; for which
purpofe he repaired to Whitehall to the earle of Salifbury,
his Ma" principal fecretary, whom he fownd in the company
of the lo: admirall, the erle of Suffolke, erle of Worcefter,
and erle of Northampton, ready to go to fupper, and there
drewe

drewe the erle of Salifb. afyde into another chamber, and imparted to him the letter, and in what manner he received it, ufing onely thefe woords, that although he would not take upon him to urge the importance of this advertifement, more or leffe, but rather leave the judgement to his Ma⁹. and thofe with whom he did ufe to communicate his affairs ; yet he would do himfelf fo much right as to proteft, that he had no other intention of fhewing this l're wrytten in fuch a fafhon, but onely to manifeft his love and duty to his Ma⁹ʳ perfon and ftate, more deare to him than his lyfe, and wherein (howfoever others may go before him in power) yett in true faith and zeale he would never be found fecond to any. As foone as the erle had read the letter, he made him anfwere that he had done like a difcreete nobleman, not to conceale a matter of fuch nature, whatfoever the confequences might prove ; becaufe oftentimes fuch loofe advertifements have growndes unfitt to be neglected, thoughe the qualitie of the informer, or yᵉ fudden apprehenfion of great and terrible things, may make them be delivered in fuch a ftile, or fuch a manner, as may blemifh the creditt of the overture : adding thus much further, that in refpect he had always found his l'p full of duty and love to his Mᵗⁱᵉ and the eftate, he would confeffe thus much unto him, as an argument yᵉ fome practife might be doubted yᵗ he had any time thefe three moneths acquainted the K. and fome of his Maⁱᵉ inward councellers that the priefts, and lay men abroad and at home, were full of the papifts of this kingdome, feeking ftill to lay fome plott, for procuring at this parlement exercife of their religion ; for which they had it in confultation, under colour of delivering a petition to his Maⁱᵉ, to appear in fome fuch generall combination, as the K. and ftate fhould be loath to denye their

over-

overtures. And fo the erle concluded, that the matter was worthy confideration, and that he would communicate this prefently with fome of my lords (his Ma" being not come to London), to which the lord Mounteagle willingly aflen'ed ; intreating him alfo fo to ufe it, as he for his extraordinary affection might not be taxed of humor or levity for his dif-covery, howfoever the matter fhould prove hereafter.

Whererunto the earle of Salifbury replied, that he would therein be his warrant : and fo immediately the erle of Salif-bury firft intreated the erle of Suffolke to come into an inner room, there they three only perufed the l're againe, and ob-ferving ftill that the woords prefaged fome defperite and fod-daine practife againft the K. and the whole ftate, and that the party was fo carefull to procure the lo: Mounteagle to be abfent from the Parlement Houfe, they apprehended, that forafmuch as could be collected by the woords, no other fenfe could be gathered, then of fome refolution to attempt upon the K. and all that were in the Parlement Houfe. Where-upon the lord chamberlane, who hath the care of all the places where his Ma" is to come or remaine, either in pub-lique or private forme, inftantly remembered, that there were diverfe houfes and roomes near adjoyning to the Chamber of Parlement in which he had never beene, and therefore agreed that he would take fome particular care of that point. And fo prefently after the lord Mounteagle was gone, the Lo: Ad-mirall, earles of Worcefter and Northampton, were all made privy to the letter, and the manner of delivery, who fell all upon the fame confideration and refolution, that the lo: chamberlane fhould take care to vifit all thofe places, but not before the feffion, both becaufe it mighte appeare whether any other nobleman fhould receyve the like advertifement,

a   which

which would make the matter of more regard ; and becaufe
any fuch as had fuch practife in hand might not be fcarred
before they had let the matter runne on to a full ripeneffe for
difcovery, confidering how apt the world is now a dayes to
think all Providence and intelligences to be but practifes.

Some three dayes after his Ma[ty] returned from Royfton
(being the 31ft of October), to whom the erle of Salifbury
firft fhewed the letter privately, the Lord Chamberlane being
hard by in the gallery. Whereupon the K. called him to it,
at which time no one of them delivered any opinion to the
King, as of a matter likely to prove materiall, but onely attended to heare his Ma[ty] owne conceyte, whom they find in
all fuch occafions not only endued with the moft admirable
guifts of piercing conceipt, and a folide judgement that ever
was heard of in any age ; but accompanyed alfo with a kind
of divine power in judging of the nature and confequence of
fuch advertifements, wherein his own great experience and
fucceffe have appeared in matters of higheft importance.

When his Ma[ty] had redd the letter (although nothing is fo
contrary to his nature, as to apprehend idle jealoufies, or
vayne tayles, but ftill to relye upon thofe inward and judiciall
growndes, from which all his refolutions and directions do
proceed), he onely made this fhort replye, that although the
incertainty of the writer, and generality of the advertifement,
befides the fmall likelyhood of any fuch confpiracy to be attempted upon the generall body of any realme compounded
of fuch a nobility, gentry, and commonalty, as this was,
gave him the leffe caufe to apprehend it as a thing certaine to
be putt in execution, confidering that all confpiracies commonly diftinguifh of men and perfons; yet, feeing the words
did rather feeme (as far as they were to be regarded) to pre-

sage danger to the whole Court of Parlement, over whom his care was greater than over his owne lyfe, and becaufe the woords difcribed fuch a forme of doing as could be no otherwife interpreted then by fome ftratageme of fire and powder, he wifhed that there might be efpecial confideration hadd of the nature of all places yielding commodity for thofe kynds of attempts ; and there, as he fhould be informed of all particulars, he would deliver his further pleafure and direction how the matter fhould be carried ; in the mean time, he faid, the lord Mounteagle had not deceyved his expectation, in yielding him this tryall of his love and duty towards himfelf and his countrey.

His Ma`ty` further directed, that fome good obfervation fhould be made of all fuch as fhoulde without apparent neceffitie feeke libertie to be abfent from the Parlement ; becaufe it was improbable, that among all the nobilitie this warning fhould be onely given to one ; and fo the matter being left for that tyme, it was agreed by all, that the Lo: Chamberlane fhould take occafion to repaire to the Parlement Houfe the day before, to fee the roomes according to the accuftomed fafhion, and fo under fome other color furvey all places under thofe chambers.

The next day, being Munday, about 3 o'clock, the L. Chamberlane, accompanied onely with the Lo: Mounteagle (who was very defirous to go thither himfelf), went accordingly to the Parlement Houfe, and, after fome tyme fpent above in the place where the King and both houfes fhould affemble, he tooke an occafion by reafon of fome ftuffe of the Kinge's, which lay in part of a cellar under thofe rooms in the keeping of one Wynnyard (an honeft and auncient fervant of the late Queene of happy memory), to go downe

into

into fome lower roomes, and thereby finding that Wynnyard had lett out fome part of a roome directly under the Parlement Chamber to one that ufed it for a cellar, he onely looked into it fleightley, and obferving ftore of cole, billets, and faggots piled up, he afked to whom it belonged ; whereunto, when anfwere was made by him that had the key, that the wood belonged to Mr. Thomas Percy, one of his Ma^{ts}. penfioners, his Lo^p, as it were by chance, inquired further where he was, and how long he had kept houfe there ; to which it was anfwered, that he had taken that houfe a yeare and a half fynce, but had deferred his lying there, in refpect of fome other occafions which had forced him to be abfent.

As foone as the Lord Chamberlane heard that, and his name, remembring what Percy was in religion and converfation, and obferving the commodity which that place might yield for a divelifh practife, he began to apprehend the more neceffitie ftill to looke into the matter, though no other materialls were vifible in the place then were ordinary to be beftowed in fuch roomes ; but yet forbare in any fort to give order for it, untill he had returned to the King, without fhewing any fufpicion there, or curiofity. To which it is not amiffe to add this circumftance, that the lord Mountegle's mynd fo much mifgave him, upon hearing him named, as he very earneftly told the Lo: Chamberlane, that the more he obferved the words of the letter, which conteyned a friendly warning, the more jealous he was of the matter, and of this place, becaufe there had beene indeed long acquaintance and familiaritie betwixt Mr. Percy and him, and alfo becaufe he had never fo much as any inkling that he lay there ; and fo, to be fhort, the Lo: Chamberlane returned to the court to inform his Matie what he had fownd. This was now betwixt

C c 8 fyve

fyve and sixe a clock at night; and then his Ma" hearing all
these circumstances, persisting still in his former opinion,
that it could be no other kynd of attempt but with powder
(reciting the woords that carried the sense), his Ma" calling
unto him some other of the lords that were in the gallery
(where also the Lo: Tresorer was present,) he collected
again the circumstances remarqueable, and resolved of a
searche to be made to the bottome of that vault, declaring,
that in such a case as this, he ever held one maxime, which
was either to do nothing, or else to do that which might
make all sure; to this his Ma" further added, that he would
have this search made in such a fashion, as the yll affected
might not disperse any malitious bruits of vaine jealousies,
when no extraordinary matter should appeare; and therefore,
for avoyding of that, this way was found, that a report
should be raised, that some stuffe and hangings in the keeping of Wynnyard afore-mentioned were stolen, and in that
respect a privy search should be made, not onely in that
vaulte, but in some other houses there-adioyning; and so accordingly choise was made of Sir Thomas Knevett, a gentleman of his Ma" privy chamber, of great fidelity and good
discretion, who suddaynely and secretely repayring to the
place about 11 a cluck, where fynding the same party
with whom the Lo: Chamberlane before and the lord Mountegle had spoken, newly come out of the vault, made stay of
him, and so going into the said vault, after a diligent and
careful removing of all the materialls, he found the whole
masse of powder, which was laid in for execution of this most
tragicall and divelish woorke intended; whereupon the cay-
tiff being surely seized, he made no difficulty to confesse,
that the same should have been executed on the morowe.

Where-

Whereupon Sir Thomas Knevett bynding him hand and foote, leaving a good gard upon him, and upon the place, immediately returned to the court, to the erle of Salilbury's lodging, about one a clock at night, to whom as foon as he had imparted the matter, Sir Tho: Knevett went to the Lo: Chamberlane, and from thence fent woord to the Lo: Admiral, erles of Worcefter and Northampton, formerly acquainted, who fent to all the lords of the councell lodged in the houfe to repaire to the King's bed chamber, where, after order given to the L. of Dirlton to make all doors faft, they repaired to the K. and caufed Sir Thomas Knevett to deliver all he had fownd.

As foon as his Ma'' heard it (as is his manner on all fuch occafions), he rendered a religious thankfgiving to Almightie God for his gracious goodnefle in this difcovery, no lefle in refpect of his deare and worthy fubjects, who fhould all have perifhed with him, then for him himfelf, and fo, with no manner of alteration, reforted ftraight to direct his councell how to procede in all things depending upon fuch an accydent; firft, to command the Lo: Maior to fett a gard of honeft citizens, for prevention of fuch, or fpoile of them, yf upon this difcoverie the parties guilty fhould feeke to ftirre any tumults; next, to preferve the prifoner from killing himfelf; with diverfe other directions, whereof you have feen the happy effects.

Upon the firft apprehenfion, the wretch gave himfelf the name of John Johnfen, which fynce he hath confefled to be falfe, and his true name to be Guy Fawkes (a gentleman borne near Spofforth in Yorkfhire); he carried himfelf with great obftinacy, ftanding ftill for a day or two upon thefe grounds, that he fhould have been the actor himfelf, and the

C c 9   in-

instrument to have given fire as aforesaid ; that he would reveale none of his complices ; that he held it a meritorious act ; that although much particular innocent blood should have been shedd, yet in such cases, for the generall good, such private respects must be passed over ; that he was sorie it was not done, and for himself despised desire of life, deriding all torture or violence that could be offered to drawe it from him : yet (all this bravery notwithstanding), by the good directions of his Ma⁰ⁿ, and by the wisdome of his councell (of whose care for the preservation of this estate the whole world may take notice), as also by the particular labors and discretion of such part of his Ma⁰ⁿ councell as have been used as commissioners in this cause, viz. the Lo: Admirall, the erle of Suffolke, Lo: Chamberlane, the erles of Devonshire, Northampton, Salisbury, and Marre, and the Lo: Chiefe Justice, attended by the Attorney Generall, who privately dealt with him in the Tower of London, the whole particular plott is clearly confessed by him, as yo⁰ shall now heare redd, though being prest to name the rest, besides Thomas Percy, whom he called his Mr ; he standeth nicely upon the points to name men himself, although, when he is shewed his owne vanitie herein, seeing their own flights have discovered themselves, he returned this answer, " That it is superfluous for him to name them, seeing by the circumstance they named themselves."

A letter from the earl of Salisbury to Sir Charles Cornwallis, Ambassador to the Court of Madrid, dated 9th of November, 1605, contains an account of this transaction, nearly similar to the above. That letter is printed in Sir Ralph Winwood's Memorials of Affairs of State, vol. II. p. 170 : from the Cottonian Library, Vespasian, C. IX.

The

The lord Mounteagle had a grant of £.200. a year in land, and a pension of £.500. *per annum* for life, as a reward for discovering the letter which gave the first hint of the conspiracy.

Read June 9, 1796.

In the examination of Guy Fawkes, Wynter, Rookwood, and Keyes, four of the conspirators, taken on the 30th of November, 1605, before the Lords of the Privy Council, is this passage:

" They (the conspirators) wished that certain of the nobility might be preserved, that is to say, the lord viscount Mountague, the lord Mordaunt, the lord Stourton, and others. And Percy named the earl of Northumberland and the lord Mounteagle. It was agreed amongst them, the *noblemen should be warned.*"

A passage in the narrative, " That the lord Monteagle's mind so much misgave him upon hearing (Percy) named, as he very earnestly told the Lord Chamberlain, though the more he observed the words of the letter which contained a friendly warning, the more jealous he was of the matter, and of the place, because there had been indeed long acquaintance and familiarity betwixt Mr. Percy and him."

These circumstances render it extremely probable, that the letter of warning to lord Mounteagle was sent by Percy; it is evidently written in a disguised hand.

C c 10   XVIII.

XVIII. *Obfervations on a Calendar in the Poffeffion of* Francis Douce, F. S. A. *In a Letter from him to the Secretary.*

Read November 12, 1795.

DEAR SIR,

I Have to beg of you to communicate to the Society the memoir herewith fent upon the firft vacant occafion. The original is to be exhibited with the copy, which, if worth keeping, I intreat you to depofit in the Society's collection.

I am, dear Sir,

Yours, very fincerely,

June 1, 1795. F. D O U C E.

THE drawing * which I have the honour of prefenting to the Society is a copy of an illumination prefixed to an ancient book of Prayers in my poffeffion, which is therewith exhibited. The name of Thomas Becket in the Calendar, and the method of blazoning the royal arms of England upon the fhield, furcoat, and pennon of the right hand figure in the drawing, fix the date of this manufcript to a period between the reigns of Henry II. and Edward III; and it is therefore to be examined by what perfons the arms as here reprefented, *viz.* the arms of England on a label of five points charged with fleurs de lis, were at that time borne.

* Plate XLV.

6   The

Illumination prefixt to a Missal.

The first person whom I have been able to trace as using them, is Edmund Crouchback earl of Lancaster, second son of Henry III. and brother of Edward I. upon whose seal they may be seen in Sandford's Genealogical history of our kings. It is to be observed, that upon the seal there appear to be three fleurs de lis on each point of the label, whereas on those in the drawing there is but one. This difference may be accounted for from the circumstance of the artist not having had room to paint more than one fleur de lis so as to be well distinguished, a conjecture which derives support from what Sandford tells us, that " he sometimes used the label of three points, and sometimes that of five points, as his seals and other places would most conveniently receive them [*a*]."

The same arms were borne by the earl's two sons, Thomas and Henry ; and this affords ample proof that the label was not used at this time as a distinction for eldest sons, as insinuated by most writers in the science of heraldry. Edward I. before he was king, appears to have borne the royal arms on a label of five points, but without the fleurs de lis ; and Sandford notices this as the first distinction of the royal family that he had seen. Afterwards the eldest sons of our kings appear to have uniformly taken these arms.

Edmondson says, that labels of three points each, charged with a fleur de lis, are borne as distinctions of the royal family [*b*], and yet we see that this is by no means a general rule, as none of the eldest sons of our monarchs appear to have taken the fleurs de lis. It should rather seem that the labels charged with fleurs de lis, or other bearings, were the

[*a*] Genealogical History of the Kings of England. p. 103. Edit. 1677.
[*b*] Edmondson's Complete Body of Heraldry, vol. II. in the Glossary.

diftinguifhing marks of the younger branches of the royal family, inftances of which occur on the feals of John of Gaunt,
Edmund and Richard dukes of York, and others.

With refpect to the other figures in the drawing, it is
worthy of remark, that among the knights depicted on the
monument of Edmund in Weftminfter abbey, there is one
that bears a ftrong refemblance to it, but from the decayed
ftate of the painting on that monument, it is hardly poffible
to decide whether thefe figures reprefent the fame perfonage
or not. The above paintings have been engraved in Mr.
Carter's Specimens of antient Sculpture and Painting [c],
and are there defcribed by an ingenious member of this Society, who has conjectured that the knight above alluded
to might be Edmund himfelf, from an opinion held by fome,
that he affumed the name of Crouchback on account of his
wearing a large crofs. Our learned Director, in his noble
work upon the Sepulchral Monuments of Great Britain, with
great reafon fuppofes the crofs upon the monumental figure
to be an armorial bearing, and not a badge, fince all the
other knights are reprefented with arms [d]. In the figure
here exhibited the diaper field on the fhield and furcoat feems
to indicate that the crofs is in this inftance a badge, and not
an armorial bearing; for heralds are agreed, that thefe di-
apered fields are the mere fancy of the painter, and not regular paternal bearings. Should it be objected, that in the
drawing the crofs appears in front only, it is to be remarked,
that it was cuftomary to wear badges as well as arms both on
the breaft and back; of this many inftances may be adduced
if neceffary.

[c] Vol. I. p. 21.   [d] Vol. I. p. 24.

It

It has been a subject of much doubt whence the name of Crouchback was derived, that is to say, whether from a real deformity in the person of Edmund, or from the circumstance already mentioned of his wearing a crofs. Hardyng vindicates him from the abovementioned aspersion in the following words—

> By all his lyfe grete manhode toke on honde,
> In batail did as wele as any knyght,
> It is not trewe that *crouge bak* fhuld be hight [*e*] —

and adds, that falfe chronicles feigned him to be " broken bakked or howge bakked [*f*]." Vincent thinks the matter fufpicious, from his being always ftyled *gibbofus* in Latin records [*g*]; but Mr. Gough has well obferved, that we may juftly doubt the use of nick-names in public records [*b*]; and it is further to be confidered, that the original word fignifying both *crooked* and *bearing a crofs on the back*, it would be much eafier to find a Latin word for the one term than for the other.

From the foregoing obfervations a conjecture may be hazarded, that the artift has thought fit to give a fecond reprefentation of Edmund in his character of a crufader, which, if it be well founded, amounts to a confirmation that he actually bore fuch a diftinction as might very properly give occafion to the epithet of *crouch* or *crofs backed*. But inafmuch

[*e*] MS. Chronicle, penes F. D., or, as the printed copy has it :
It is no true that *crole barkd* he hight,
For valiaunt he was in all his doynges,
And perfonable withal to every man's fight.
[*f*] *Bode barkd* and *hes bark d*. Printed copy.
[*g*] Difcovery of Errors in Brooke. Tit. Lancafter.
[*b*] Sepulchral Monuments, vol. I. p. 69.

as the explanation of the last mentioned figure in the drawing may be deemed liable to many objections, and is by no means satisfactory to myself, I shall beg leave to submit another to the consideration of this learned Society.

It is well known to have been the practice in former times to adorn the manuscript hours, psalters, missals, breviaries, and other services of the books of the church of Rome, with the portraits of those eminent persons for whom they were executed, and that these were not consequently accompanied by their *patron saints*. Of this many instances occur in the fifteenth and sixteenth centuries, and the like representations are found upon portable and other altar pieces. If this drawing was intended to exhibit such a subject, it is perhaps one of the earliest specimens of the kind. The red cross upon the surcoat and pennon is what is usually called a saint *George's cross*; and, the earl of Lancaster being of the royal blood, it is very natural that he should adopt that saint as his patron.

It is to be examined in the next place, whether Saint George was represented with this device at such an early period. We learn from Polydore Virgil, that when Edward III. founded the order of the garter, he chose Saint George for his patron, and represented him with a silver shield, whereon was a red cross; that he cloathed his soldiers in white coats with red crosses on both sides [1], " parallel," adds Ashmole, " to the arms *anciently* assigned to Saint George, as also to the kingdom of England placed under his patronage, which arms the kings of England have ever since advanced on their

[1] Pol. Virgil Hist. Angl. lib. I.

standards

standards both by land and sea [k]." Legh also says, that it
pleased king Edward III. to take Saint George for his patron,
and to bear his cross on a shield [l]. Dr. Pegge, in his
very learned memoir on the History of Saint George [m], has
produced numerous authorities to shew, that the name of
this saint was well known in England during the Saxon times,
and that he was regarded as the patron of this country before
the time of Edward III. There is every reason to suppose,
that Richard I. introduced him here in that character, from
having observed, during the crusades, the great military
estimation in which he was held in the East. Matthew Paris
relates, that long before this, *viz.* in the year 1098, at the
battle of Antioch, Saint George, Saint Demetrius, and Saint
Mercury, appeared in a miraculous manner, and were immediately known by their standards [n]. And Jacobus de
Voragine, who wrote his Golden Legend at the end of the
thirteenth century, during the reign of Edward I. citing
some history of Antioch, says, " and when it so was that
they had assyeged Jherusalem, and durst not mount ne go
upon the walles for the quarrelles and defence of the Sara-
syns; they saw appertly Saint George, which had *whyte armes
with a reed crosse*, that went up before them on the wall, and
they folowed hym, and so was Jherusalem taken by his
helpe [o]".

It has been suggested to me by the Abbé de la Rue, an
honorary member of this Society, that many churches in

[k] Order of the Garter, p. 246.
[l] Accedence of Armory, fol. 27. Edit. 1591.
[m] Archæologia, vol. V.
[o] M. Paris, p. 43. Edit. 1640.
[o] Golden Legende, fol. cxii, verso. Edit. 1527.

Nor-

Normandy were dedicated to Saint George before the Conquest, and that the Normans might have introduced this faint as a military patron. Yet it is certain, that his name was not invoked by the Normans at the battle of Haftings, nor is there any evidence that I have been able to difcover, of its having been ufed as a war cry before the reign of Edward III.

XIX.

XIX. *Description of the Reliefs on the Font at* Thorpe Salvin *in* Yorkshire. *In a Letter from Mr.* Holden *to his Grace the Duke of* Leeds.

Read November 26, 1794.

My Lord Duke,

I HAVE taken the liberty of inclosing to your Grace a flight drawing *, which is a tolerably accurate reprefentation of a curious antique font in the church in Thorpe Salvin, near Kiveton.

Your Grace's condefcenfion in receiving the fketch I formerly fent you, has induced me to hope you will not think me impertinent when I beg your acceptance of this ; as I have reafon to think you have no drawing of it, and, perhaps, your Grace may never have been informed that you have fuch a curiofity fo near your own houfe.

This font has attracted the notice of feveral Antiquaries, who have fpoken of it as a very extraordinary thing of the kind, though I have not heard that any one has ventured to give an explanation of it ; and, indeed, the fculptor himfelf had no other idea than a few devices purely fymbolical. Many of thefe antient fonts have been charged with reprefentations of fome marvellous actions of legendary faints or bifhops, and others feem to have had nothing in view but to remind the fpectators of fome circumftance in the life of our bleffed Saviour, or fome ceremony in the Chriftian church. Of the

* Plate XLVI.

latter.

latter fort I take this font to be ; the two firft compartments being evidently a reprefentation of the baptifm of a child, in which a monk is preparing to immerfe it in a font, whilft four fponfors are ftretching out their hands in token of their vow. In the next is a man tying up fheaves of corn with a fickle under his girdle. The fourth compartment prefents a perfon on horfeback, riding over a bridge, and holding in his hand a cenfer, out of which feems to iffue fomething like flames. The next is a man with a helmet on his head, and a bafket hung by a belt acrofs his fhoulder, out of which he appears to be fowing feed ; and next him is a perfon who feems about to feat himfelf in a chair, or rather a tub, which, from the appearance of the top, feems to bear fome allufion to the Papal dignity.

Here the fculptor's invention was exhaufted, or his ftory was told ; for the remainder is filled up with an odd unintelligible thing by way of ornament, and fome beautiful pillars with capitals and arches interwoven.

All thefe figures are cut in ftone in alto relievo, and as far as one may judge from the circular arches and the mouldings, which are beautifully cut, are of Saxon origin, and probably contemporary with the church itfelf.

I fhall be extremely proud if your Grace looks on this drawing as the fmalleft acquifition, and will give it a place in your collection. The fubject at leaft is curious, and may make up in fome meafure for the badnefs of the performance. and I remain, My Lord Duke,

Your Grace's moft obedient

and moft humble Servant,

Fotherham,
Auguft 8, 1795.   RICHARD HOLDEN.

XX.

3

XX. *Illustration of the Reliefs on the Font at* Thorpe Salvin. *By* Francis Douce, *Esq. In a Letter to the Secretary.*

Gower Street, December 15, 1795.

DEAR SIR,

WILL you allow me to submit to you some explanation of the drawing of the font at Thorpe Salvin, Yorkshire, which, by the condescension of his Grace the Duke of Leeds, has been lately communicated to the Society.

I conceive that four of the compartments represent the seasons of the year. Winter is figured by an old man warming himself before a fire in a chimney. Spring, by one riding out a hawking, as would probably appear from an attentive inspection of the original. Summer, by a man reaping corn and bundling it up into sheaves ; and Autumn, by a husbandman sowing seed. The other compartments exhibit the ceremony of Baptism, with the parents and sponsors.

I think the sculptor's design was to intimate, that the baptismal rite might be performed at all times of the year ; in contradistinction to that of marriage, which was not allowed but at particular seasons. Among our Saxon ancestors, baptism was required to be administered within nine, or sometimes within thirty, days, under a certain penalty. Among other nations, during the early periods of Christianity, baptism was not permitted but at Easter and Whitsuntide, a practice that continued in

VOL. XII.   E e   France

France until after the year 1200, as appears from several councils. I think this a presumption in favour of the antiquity of the font in question, which is probably Saxon. The figures of the seasons are borrowed from the representations of particular months, as we find them in very ancient calendars. Should you perceive no objection to these conjectures, you may, perhaps, do me the honour of laying them before our Society.

I remain,

Dear Sir,

Yours, very faithfully,

FRANCIS DOUCE.

XXI.

XXI. *Account of the Hospital of St.* Margaret, *at* Pilton *in* Devonshire. *By* Benjamin Incledon, *Esq. In a Letter to* John Wilmot, *Esq.* F. A. S.

Read December 24, 1795.

DEAR SIR,   *Pilton House,* 1794.

THERE is a charity at Pilton in Devonshire, distinguished by the name of St. *Margaret's* Hospital.

This hospital, or house, as it was sometimes called, was formerly appropriated for the reception of lepers of both sexes [a].

[a] " Adam Teache dedit tenementum in Pilton fratribus et sororibus Lep'for " hosp. beate Margarete de Pilton." Dat. 24 Edw. III. [A. D. 1350.] Hospital Deed.

E e 2   It

It was situated in Pilton-street, near the chapel [b] of St. Margaret, in honour of whom, perhaps, it was originally founded. But I have not met with any record which declares by whom, or when, it was founded.

Although the time of its foundation cannot be ascertained, the old writings in the hospital chest (many of which are in high preservation) discover strong proofs of its antiquity. It appears, that the benefactions to it were numerous, consisting of small tenements, gardens, and rents annually issuing out of other lands.

The following extracts from some [c] of the writings will not, I flatter myself, be uninteresting to the subject.

I. " Om'ibz Xri fidelibz &c [d]. H. di grā Exon. eps salūi in deo,
" &c. h est transactio sta corā nob anno confectonis ūre sexto in octav'
" Sti Laurencii iot' ecel de Pilton de co..hsu Rad tunc ejusd loci pri-
" oris [e] & monachorū ibm duo iviernia' & Lepfos de Pilton, sopitis
" hinc in om'ibz q'rel & exsecūta vidl* qd dti Lepsi reddent anno-
" atim eccle de Pilton in die Sta Margarete duas libras cere & si due
" libre cere cariores fūint sex denariis reddent sex denar' cū duabz lib
" cere; reddent & annuatim in die pasche eid eccle de Pilton' duodecim
" denar'. P'dictis autem Lepsis omēs obvectōns capll: Saint Margarete
" cū integritate remanebit in ppetuum. Quicūq autem prior fuit de
" Pilton nichil exiget ab eisdm Lepsis, neqz in introitu dom' neq; in
" ultimo articlo mortis ñ sjd ipi dte eccle de Pilton glis confte voluint
" sicut parochieni. Monachi aūt dte eccle in die pasche intuitu divino in
" die pasche & die venis in paraskeven & die Sta Margarete d'tis Legin
" celebratūem divinos' plenarie ministrabit. Onus qui ē de seudo Pilton

' [b] Now a dwelling house, and part of the hospital possessions.

[c] The originals, and seal, are sent up for your inspection.

[d] Henry Marshall, consecrated bishop of Exeter, A. D. 1191. Heylin.

[e] Pilton priory was a cell to Malmesbury abbey, and filled with black monks. Dugdale.

" ipis

" ipis Lepsis sub p̄sata pensione ī ꝑpetuū remanebit.   Et ut h̄ transactō
" rata &c. eam tam scr̄pti q̄m sigilli ūi testimonio corroborrwim'.   Hiis
" Test'. W. de Svind canonicō Exon' R. de Winkel Offic Bardestapl. Ma-
" grō I I. de Wilton, Magrō G. de Sutton'.   G. decano de Okemt.   Henr.
" de Eling, Gilcō & Bad clicis Sris.   Steph elico.   Reg' Beanpeh.   Ric'
" de Porta, & multis aliis.

[*The Seals are torn off.*]

II. " Omnibz Xī fidelibz ad quos p̄sens scriptum ꝑvenit Ric. fil Ric.
" fil Walli, noverit universitas īra me &c. dedisse &c.   Lepsis de
" Pilton sex denar' quos recipiant, annuatim de burgagio in villa de
" Barnastapl, &c. huic scripto sigillum meum apposui. Hiis Testibz ; Ro-
" gō Cole canonico Exon' ʄ) Hen' de Merton, Rogero filio Symoon, Johe
" p' de Esse.   Willo p' de Chiriton, Galfrido p' de Bochland, et
" multis aliis.

[*Here the Seal.*]

III. " Sciant p̄sentes, &c.   Ego Phillipp' p̄sbeyn de Barnastaple di-
" vine caritatis intuitu &c. dedi &c. pro aīabz patris, &c. . . . Sᵗ
" Margarete de Pilton & Lepsis ibidem deo servientibus, &c. sex denarios
" de reddit cujusdam oni int' porta' septentrionalem Barnastapolie, &c.
" Eam p̄senti scripto & sigilli mei appositione confirmavi. Hiis testibus ;
" Dño Willo de Raleg' [g] Dño Phillippo de Bello monte, Willo Panel,
" &c. et multis aliis.

[*The Seal is torn off.*]

At the dissolution of the monasteries, this hospital, I suppose too insignificant to be separately rated in the estimate of
the ecclesiastical lands, was disposed of as an appendage to
the priory of Pilton ; and, after having had various possessors
(who to their honour kept it on a charitable foot), it is
now become a part of the poor lands of the parish.

[ʄ] Roger Cole, canon of Exeter, was a justice itinerant in Devon, in the
3d year of king Henry III. A. D. 1218.   From an old deed of Bremridge, penes me.
[g] Sir William de Ralegh, knight, was a witness to an old deed of Combmartin,
in the 48th year of king Henry III. A. D. 1264. penes me.

4

The

The feoffees of those lands, as patrons, prefent, when vacancies happen, fome poor inhabitant of the Church of England to the place of PRIOR, BROTHER, or SISTER, of the HOSPITAL of St. MARGARET, who hold this charity for life, grant leafes of their little poffeffions under their common feal, and receive the fines and conventionary rents, amounting to about three pounds a year, to their own ufe.

The common feal, perhaps not lefs curious than the old writings, feems to be made of tin, or fome metal like it, and to have been caft in a mould before the armorial bearing and the infcription paffed through the hand of the engraver. It is fomewhat fingular, that the infcription meant for SIGILL. LEPROSORV' BEAT. MARGARET. DE PYLTON, is perfectly legible in the face of the feal, but not fo on the impreffion. Many feals of the kind you may poffibly have met with in your extenfive refearches into antiquity, but this is the only one of the kind that has ever occurred to me in my confined walk.

If the above account of the hofpital, or its feal, affords you any amufement, it will give great pleafure to one of its patrons, who is

Dear Sir,

Your moft obedient

humble Servant,

BENJAMIN INCLEDON.

XXII.

XXII. *Observations on certain Ornaments of Female Dress. By* Francis Douce, *Esq.* F. A. S.

Read January 14, 1796.

THE female ornaments of dress which Mr. Douce has the honour of laying before the Society * were prefented to him by an old lady, in whofe family they had always remained. They confift of a purfe, a pin-cufhion, and *a pair of knives*, the latter of which cannot be better illuftrated than by the following extract from a note on a paffage in Romeo and Juliet, by our worthy member George Steevens, Efq.

" Knife lie thou there." It appears from feveral paffages in our old plays, that knives were formerly part of the accoutrements of a bride; and every thing behoveful for Juliet's ftate had been juft left with her. So in Decker's Match me in London, 1631.

    " See at my girdle hang my *wedding knives*."
Again, in King Edward III, 1599.

      " Here by my fide do hang my *wedding knives*:
      " Take thou the one, and with it kill thy queen,
      " And with the other I'll difpatch my love."

To the above curious note it may be added, that the practice of wearing knives and purfes at the girdle appears to have been pretty general among the European women at the end of the fixteenth century, as may be collected from feveral contemporary prints. There feems therefore to be no other

    * Plate XLVII.

way

way to account for the term of *wedding knives*, than by supposing
that at the time of marriage ladies were presented, amongst
other articles of a domestic nature, with the ornaments in queftion, but of a particular and more splendid kind than ordinary.
No other representation of this fashion of wearing knives &c,
at the girdle in our own country, has yet occurred to the writer
of this article, than the small print of an English woman upon
Speed's Map of Europe ; the attention, therefore, of the pof-
feffors of ancient English portraits to this circumstance might
be the means of hereafter affording some more satisfactory
illustration.

It is proper to observe, that the date 1610 occurs upon
both the handles, and to suggest to the recollection of this
Society, that the use of forks found its way from Italy into
this country much about that period, though they were not
generally adopted till a confiderable time after.   It may not
be altogether useless to add, that they were known in Italy
much earlier, as appears from a book intituled, " Il Trin-
ciante di M. Vincenzo Cervio.   Venetia, 1581," in which
cuts of double pronged forks are to be found, as well as three
pronged ones for eating fruit.

The materials of these articles confist of purple velvet embroidered with gold.   The handle of one of the knives is of
amber ; that of the other, of a reddish coloured glass.   They
were all suspended together at the girdle.

XXIII.

XXIII. *Extracts from a MS. intituled " The Life of Mr. Phineas Pette, one of the Master Shipwrights to King James the First, drawn up by himself." Communicated by the Reverend* Samuel Denne, F. A. S.

Read December 10, 1795, and February 4, 1796.

I Phineas Pette, being son of Mr. Peter Pette, of Deptford Strond in in the county of Kent, one of his majesty's ship-wrights, was born in my father's dwelling-house in the same town on All Saints day in the morning, being the first day of November, in the year of our Lord 1570.

At nine years of age I was put to a free-school at Rochester, in Kent, to one Mr. Webb, with whom I boarded about one year; and afterwards lay at Chatham Hill in my father's lodgings at the Queen's house, from whence I went every day to school to Rochester, and came home at night for three years space; afterwards, by reason of my small profiting at this school, my father removed me from thence to Greenwich, to a private school kept by one Mr. Adams, where I so well pro-fited, that in three years time I was fit for Cambridge.

In the year 1586, at Shrove-tide, against Bachelors' com-mencement, I was sent to the university of Cambridge, and by the means of Mr. Howel, a minister in Essex, was placed in Emanuel college, with a reverend tutor, president of the houfe, called Mr. Charles Chadwick, where I was allowed 20 *£. per ann.* during my father's life, befides books, apparel, and other necessaries.

In the year 1589, about the 6th of September, it pleafed God to call to his mercy my reverend loving father, whofe lofs proved afterwards my utter undoing almoft, had not God been more merciful to me; for, leaving all things to my mother's direction, her fatal matching with a moft wicked hufband, one Mr. Thomas Num, a minifter, brought a general ruin to herfelf and family.

By reafon of my mother's crofs matching, my means of maintenance being wholly taken from me, and having no hopes of exhibition from my friends, I was forced, after four years continuance at Cambridge, my graces for Bachelor of Arts being paffed both in houfe and town, to abandon the univerfity prefently after Chriftmas 1590.

At Candlemas after, I, by the inftant perfuafion of my mother, was contented to put myfelf to be an apprentice to become a fhipwright (my father's profeffion), and was bound a covenant fervant to one Mr. Richard Chapman of Deptford Strond, one of her majefty's mafter fhipwrights, and one whom my father had bred up of a child to that profeffion; my allowance from him, to find myfelf tools and apparel, being bare but 46*s.* 8*d. per ann.* This man I ferved almoft two years altogether, at Chatham in the queen majefty's works (and then he died), where I fpent all that time, God he knows, to very little purpofe.

After my aforefaid mafter his death, I laboured to have ferved Mr. Matthew Baker, one of her majefty's mafter fhipwrights alfo, but, by the working of one Mr. Peter Buck, then clerk of the cheque at Chatham, and fome other back friends,

friends, I was crossed in my service, and so put to my shifts, and left to the wide world without either comfort or friend, but only God.

At this time my eldest brother by my father's side, Mr. Joseph Pette, succeeded in my father's place one of her majesty's master shipwrights, which preferment, no doubt, God brought him to, the better to enable him to give his help to us; but we found it clear contrary; and I was constrained to ship myself to sea upon a desperate voyage in a man of war, not greatly caring what became of me.

I was shipped on this voyage a little before Christmas 1592, in a ship called the Gallion, Constance, of London, of the burden of 200 tons, or thereabouts, belonging to a gentleman of Suffolk, one captain Edward Glenham, for the carpenter's mate, the master carpenter being one Edward Goodhall, born in Deptford.

To my setting out to sea I found none of my kindred so kind as to help me with either money or clothes, or any other comfort, only another brother I had by my father's side, Peter Pette, then dwelling at Wapping, that vouchsafed me lodging, meat, and drink, till the ship was ready to sail; one William King, a yeoman in Essex, and a stranger to me, lent me £. 3. in ready money, to help to furnish my necessaries, which afterwards I repaid him again.

In this voyage I endured much misery for want of victuals and apparel, and, after twenty months spent in the Levant seas, coasts of Barbary and Spain, with many hazards both of loss of life and time, without taking any purchase of any value, we extreme poorly returned for Ireland into the river of Cork, and there taking leave both of ship and voyage, I travelled to Diveling to visit my uncle, captain Thornton,

F f 2   and

and my brother Noah, being then master with him in the Popenjay of the queen's majesty, and presently after bent my course for England, taking my passage at the town of Waterford.

With some difficulty I got to London some three days before Christmas 1594, having neither money nor apparel, and took up my lodging at my brother Peter's house in Wapping, who, although I returned very poor, yet vouchsafed me kind entertainment. The next day I presented myself to my brother Joseph, who received me very coldly, and out of his bounty lent me forty shillings to apparel myself, which I bestowed as frugally as I could, in Borthen-street in London, contenting myself as well as I could with mean attire, till such time as it should please God to provide better for me. At that time it so fell out, that there were certain of her majesty's ships to be made ready for the voyage of Sir Francis Drake and Sir John Hawkins, among which the Defiance was to be brought into Woolwich dock to be sheathed; which work being commended to my brother Joseph's charge, he was contented to admit me, amongst many others, to be one, where I was contented to take any pains to get something to apparel myself, which by God's blessing I performed before Easter next after, and that in very good fashion, always endeavouring to keep company with men of good rank, far better than myself.

About Bartholomew tide in 1595, the Triumph of her majesty was had into Woolwich dock to be new built by Mr. Matt. Baker, under whom I was entertained as an ordinary workman, and had allowed me a boy, which was Thomas Wood, being the first servant that I ever kept. But presently after Mr. Baker was appointed to go in hand with the building of a great new ship at Deptford, called the Repulse, and

6   was

was admiral of my lord Essex's squadron in the Cadiz journey. The Triumph was appointed to my brother Joseph's charge, with whom I a while continued, but finding him unwilling to preserve me in his work, as next under him, with some passage of discontent betwixt us, I left him, and had ready entertainment by Mr. Baker in his new business at Deptford, yet no otherwise than an ordinary workman, with whom I continued from the beginning of the aforesaid ship till she was wholly finished, launched, and set sail on her voyage from Woolwich, which was about the latter end of April 1596. All that winter, in the evenings, commonly I spent my time to good purposes, as in cyphering, drawing, and practising to attain the knowledge of my profession, and then found Mr. Baker some time forward to give me instructions, from whose help I must acknowledge I received my greatest lights. At this time the lord admiral lay most of the winter at his house; I got some acquaintance amongst his men, and was much importuned to have attended his lordship in that voyage, which no doubt would have proved very much both profitable and beneficial unto me; besides it would have brought me into acquaintance and favour with the lord admiral; but some other reasons restrained me from all these likelihoods, and kept me at home, to my no small hindrance as it fell out.

After I was discharged from the Repulse, my brother Joseph entertained me at Woolwich upon the Triumph, upon which I wrought till her launching, and the discharge of men from her; and afterwards was employed at my brother's at Limehouse, upon a small model for the lord Treasurer's house, called Theobald's. About this time I was desirous, by the instigation of some friends of mine, to have been a

follower

follower of the lord Effex, and was three feveral times brought purpofely to have been prefented unto his lordfhip, but was every time delayed by reafon of his great eftate affairs, and the Lord of Heaven having otherwife in his fecret wifdom determined to difpofe of me.

In the beginning of 1597, my dear and loving mother departed at Wefton in Suffolk, not far from Bury. In the latter end of March, or beginning of April, 1597, by the means of one Mrs. Gilbert Wood, one of the lord admiral's chamber, an efpecial good friend of mine, I was prefented to the Lord High Admiral of England at his manor at Chelfea, where his lordfhip was not only pleafed to accept me as his fervant, but openly fhewed fuch extraordinary refpect to me, that I had much caufe to give God thanks, who no doubt had ftirred his honourable heart to regard me, but a fimple and mean fellow, even far beyond my expectation or defert; and this was the very firft beginning of my rifing.

About Midfummer, 1598, was the Elizabeth Jonas launched out of Woolwich dock, and fudden preparations made to have received her majefty on board the fhip riding afloat, but for fome unknown reafon her majefty came not at all. For even at that inftant had one Mr. Wigs procured a commiffion for examination of certain abufes in the navy, which was purfued with a great deal of malice againft divers particular men, but with very little profit to her majefty's fervice.

From Midfummer all the enfuing year to Chriftmas I lay ftill and idle without any manner of employment or comings-in but what my fervants got with working now and then abroad, which was very little, and hardly able to buy me

5   food.

food. About Christmas my honourable lord and master the Lord High Admiral commended me to an employment in Suffolk and Norfolk, for the finishing of a purveyance of plank and timber, formerly undertaken by one Child of Sole, who dealt in Norfolk, and, dying, left the business in much disorder; and one Robert Ungle, who dealt in Suffolk, and for divers abuses by him there committed fled the country, and all the service in great disorder and spoile; for the rectifying of which abuses, saving of her majesty's provisions, and discharging of the country, it pleased my lord to make a choice of me to undertake the same, and to take order to send in all the said provisions of timber and plank; which accordingly I did, using all care and diligence in the performance of the same, for the benefit of her majesty's service, the content of my Lord Admiral, and his officers of the navy, and satisfaction of the countries where I had to do. Notwithstanding, through the malicious design of old Matthew Baker, Bright Adye, and others, all my doings and accounts were truly sifted (but thanks be to God), nothing could be found against me, so I had all my bills posted quietly, but by reason of Mr. Fulk Grevil being then Treasurer of the Navy did not greatly affect me, because of some particular spleen between him and Mr. John Trevor, then newly made surveyor, who was my especial and worshipful friend, he laid a rub in my way, cutting me off wrongfully 20£. in my accounts, after all my bills were past, and signed by the hands of the principal officers, according to the custom of the navy. All this year, 1599, I spent wholly in this service, in which time these occurrences happened.

In December, 1599, I began a small model, which being perfected, and exquisitely set out and rigged, I presented to

my

my good friend Mr. John Trevor, who very kindly accepted the same of me.

In the beginning of the year 1600, I, having no employment, determined with myself to have bought some part of a castle carvel, and to have gone in her myself, whereby I thought, by God's blessing, to have got an honest and convenient maintenance; and to that end I began to follow one John Goodwin, of London, professor of the mathematics, with whom I spent three days in a week in practice, and so was purposed to have continued the whole year to the spring; but God, who in his secret counsel had otherwise decreed of me, altered all my determinations; for, upon the 28th of June, I was sent for to the court, lying then at Greenwich, by my honourable lord and master the Lord High Admiral, who, after some speeches expressing both his love and honourable care of me, his lordship concluded to send me down to Chatham, where I was to succeed in the place of one John Holding, a shipwright, that was keeper of the plank-yard, timber, and other provisions (upon some displeasure turned out of all). The means whereof being but small, *viz.* 18*d. per diem*, and £. 6. *per annum* fee, for myself, and allowance for one servant at 16*d. per diem*, I was very unwilling to undertake so mean a place, by which I was neither sure of competent maintenance, nor of any reputation; but that I was encouraged by the persuasion of my ever honoured lord, who comforted me with promise of better preferment to the utmost of his power, whereupon being contented to accept his lordship's offer, I was the 29th of June placed at Chatham by Sir Henry Palmer, the comptroller, Mr. John Trevor, surveyor, and Mr. Peter Buck, clerk of the ships.—Upon this occasion of my being placed at Chatham

ham, my brother Joseph and I were reconciled, and ever after lived together as loving brethren. It also happened that Sir Fulk Grevil, then treasurer, continued his spleen against me, and for Mr. Trevor's sake opposed me all he could, which after turned me to much trouble.

In March 1601, I was made assistant to the master shipwright at Chatham, in the room of Mr. Thomas Badman. In this year the first business I undertook was the repairing of the Lion's Whelp, haled up at the storehouse and at Chatham. In the year 1602, I also new-built the Mone, haled up in the same place, enlarging her both in length and breadth.

In November 1601, Mr. Grevil, having undertaken the preparation of a fleet with her majesty, to be fitted to sea by a set time, was contented (upon my promise to him to procure the said fleet to be fitted in six weeks) to receive me to his favour ; which promise I accordingly (by God's gracious assistance) fully accomplished, by which means I gained his love, favour, and good opinion, had there not happened a sudden alteration, by the death of her majesty, which presently followed.

In 1603, I divers times solicited my brother to be joined packate * with him, but his remissness caused me to overslip the opportunity so long, that one Mr. Stephens of Limehouse, this year, by means of some great friends about my Lord High Admiral, got a general reversion of all the master shipwrights places, cutting me off from all hopes of any timely preferment, to my great discouragement, considering what pains I took at Chatham to further his majesty's service. When I

* Sic Orig.

was most dejected with the conceit of this enemy as I took it, it pleased God of his great mercy to me, when I least expected any such thing, to raise me up a means of some hope of preferment after this manner; for, about 15th of January, a letter was sent post to Chatham from my honourable Lord Admiral, commanding me with all possible speed to build a little vessel for the young prince Henry to disport himself in about London bridge, and acquaint his grace with shipping, and the manner of that element; setting me down the proportions, and the manner of her garnishing, which was to be like the work of the Ark Royal, battlementwise. This little ship was in length by the keel 28 feet, and in breadth 12 feet, garnished with painting and carving, both within board and without, very curiously, according to his lordship's directions. I laid her keel the 19th of January, wrought upon her by day as well as by night, by torch and candle light, under a great awning made with sails for that purpose. The sixth day of March after, I launched this ship, being upon a Tuesday, with a noise of trumpets, drums, and such like ceremonies, at such time used. I set sail with her on Friday after, being the third day. Between the Nore Head and the East end of Tilbury we had a very great storm, so that it was Sunday before we could get Gravesend, and on Monday we anchored at Blackwall. Mr. George Wilson, boatswain of the Lion, was master with me, and myself captain: I was manned with almost all boatswains of the navy, and other choice men.

On Wednesday the 14th, by my Lord Admiral's command, we weighed from Limehouse, and anchored right against the Tower, before the king's lodgings, his majesty then being there before his riding through London. There the young Prince,

ac-

accompanied with the Lord Admiral, and divers of the Lords, came and took great pleasure in beholding the ship, being furnithed at all points with ensigns and pendants. Friday the 16th, we unrigged, and shot the bridge; and the 17th we rigged again, and received both ordnance and powder from the Tower. On Tuesday afternoon, being the 18th day, fitted, with a noise of trumpets, drums, and fifes, we weighed and turned up with the wind at South-west as high as Lambeth, with multitude of boats and people attending upon us. As we passed by Whitehall, saluted the court with a volley of small shot and our great ordnance; and upon the ebb turning down again we did the like, and then taking in our sails we came to an anchor against the Privy Stairs. On Monday the 19th his majesty went by barge to the parliament. We shot our great and small ordnance off both at his taking barge and landing. All Tuesday and Wednesday we rode still, without doing any thing but giving entertainment to gentlemen, the king, and prince's servants, that hourly came on board us. On Thursday morning I received commands from the Lord High Admiral to prepare the ship, and all things fitted to receive the young prince aboard in the afternoon, who accordingly presently after dinner came on board us in his barge, accompanied with the Lord High Admiral, earl of Worcester, and divers others of the nobility. We presently weighed, and fell down as far as Paul's wharf, under both our topsails and foresails, and there came to an anchor; and then his grace, according to the manner in such cases used, with a great bowl of wine christened the ship, and called her by the name of Disdain. His Grace then withdrawing himself with the lords into the great cabin, there my honourable lord (and till then master), with his own hands presented

G g 2

me

me to his grace, using many favourable words (far beyond my desert) in my commendations, with this addition, that I was a servant worthy the acceptance of the greatest prince in the world. From his hands it pleased his grace very thankfully to receive me as his servant, with many promises of his princely favour to me. The next day, being Friday, it pleased my Lord Admiral to entreat my worthy friend, Sir Thomas Trevor, to accompany me to the lord Thomas Howard, then Lord Chamberlain, from whom receiving a ticket, I was sent to St. James's, the prince's house, where, by Mr. Alexander and Mr. Abington, then gentlemen ushers, I was sworn his grace's servant, and by them presented to the prince before he went to dinner, with as much favour and respect as I could desire.

During my attendance at the court as his grace's captain of his ship, it pleased my honourable Lord Admiral to give orders to Sir Thomas Winebank *, and one of the clerks of the signet, to draw me a bill for the reversion of Mr. Baker or my brother Joseph Pette's place, which should first happen to be void, notwithstanding the Letters Patent formerly granted to Mr. Stephens, which accordingly was with all expedition performed, and the 11th of April following was presented to his majesty and signed, and shortly after passed the great seal; for the whole charge whereof I gave Sir Thomas Winbank £.17. About the same time Sir Robert Mansell had his patent passed for the Treasurer of his majesty's navy.

My eldest brother, Joseph Pette, died November 15, 1605, and was buried on the 11th of November in Stepney church-

---

* Q. Winderbank.

yard;

yard; my good friends Sir Robert Manfell, Sir Henry Palmer, Sir John Trevor, the principal officers of the navy, and many other good friends and neighbours, accompanied, who, after the funeral, returned to my brother's house, where they were all welcomed with a very great dinner and feast.

Presently after my brother's decease, it pleased my very good lord, the Lord High Admiral, to grant his warrant for my entrance into my brother's place to the effect of my letters patent, notwithstanding the claim made unto it by one Edward Stevens of Limehouse, who had formerly procured a general reversion of all the master shipwrights' places; but, by reason the fee was mistaken, wherein his majesty was abused, and charged with an innovation, he could not prevail in his claim, albeit he often petitioned the Lords of the Council, and made great friends against me; yet it pleased God, by the noble favours of the prince my master, and the Lord High Admiral's countenance, I enjoyed my place with a general approbation both of the state and officers, and so finished the year 1605.

The 17th of July, 1606, his majesty the noble king of Denmark arrived in England, against whose coming, being but only supposed two months before, I received private directions from the Lord High Admiral, and some of the principal officers, to have all the ships put into a comely readiness, which accordingly was performed in as decent and warlike a manner as if they had been prepared for sea. But, upon news of his arrival, they were all rigged and furnished with their ordnance, and great preparation made on board the Elizabeth Jonas, and the Bear, for entertaining the kings, queen, prince, and all the other states and troops. Wherein, I confess, I strove extraordinarily to express my service for the

3   honour

honour of the kingdom; but, by reason the time limited was short, and the business great, we laboured night and day to effect it, which accordingly was done, to the great honour of our sovereign king and master, and the no less admiration of all strangers that were eye-witnesses to the same. The solemnity of the entertainment was performed the 16th of August, being Sunday; at this time Sir Oliver Cromwell, and other gentlemen, my very good friends, lodged at my house.

About the 15th of April, I received a warrant for going in hand with the ships at Woolwich; whereupon I removed thither with my houshold presently after, and began to work upon the ark with a small company till provisions could be brought in to put on more workmen, which was not till the beginning of August, at which time I began to victual all the workmen.

The 25th I was elected and sworn master of the company of Shipwrights, and kept a feast with a great number of our friends, well stored with venison, at the King's Head in New Fish-street.

After my settling at Woolwich, I began a curious model for the prince my master, most part whereof I wrought with my own hands, which, being most fairly garnished with carving and painting, and placed in a frame, arched, covered, and curtained with crimson taffety, was, November 10, 1607, presented to the Lord High Admiral, at his lodgings at Whitehall, his lordship well approving of it. After I supped with his honour that night, he gave me commandment to carry the same to Richmond, where the prince my master then lay, which was accordingly performed the next day after, being Tuesday the 11th. On Wednesday morning, having acquainted Sir David Murray with my business, and

he

he delivering the fame to his highnefs, order was given to
have the model brought and placed in a private room in the
long gallery, where his highnefs determined to fee it in the
afternoon. But my ever honoured old lord and mafter, unknown to me, ftudying by all means to do me good, had
acquainted his majefly with this thing; and, the fame day,
unlooked for of any, had procured his majefty to make a pur-
pofed journey from Whitehall to Richmond to fee the model,
where he came in the afternoon, accompanied only with the
prince, the lord admiral, and one or two attendants. His
majefty was exceedingly delighted with the fight of the model,
and paffed fome time in queftioning the divers material things
concerning the fame, and demanded whether I could build the
great fhip in all parts like the fame; for I will, fays his majefty,
compare them together when fhe fhall be finifhed. Then the
Lord Admiral commanded me to tell his majefty the ftory of
the Three Ravens I had feen at Lifbon, in St. Vincent's church;
which I did as well as I could, with my beft expreffions, though
fomewhat daunted at firft at his majefty's prefence, having
never before fpoken before any king. It pleafed his majefty
to accept all things in good part, and to ufe me very gracioufly, and fo returned to Whitehall the fame night.

The fucceeding year (1608) brought with it many great
troubles; for the lord of Northampton having, by the infli-
gation of fome that were not great friends to the Lord Admiral, and fome of the principal officers of his majefty's navy
in efpecial favour with his lordfhip, procured a great and
large commiffion from his majefty, for enquiring into all the
abufes and mifdemeanors committed by all officers in their
feveral places, under colour of reformation, and faving great
fums to his majefty, which he expended yearly in the maintenance of his fhips; which inquifition was profecuted with
fuch

such extremity of malice, as not only many were brought into great question, and tossed to and fro before the commissioners at Westminster, to their no small charge and vexation; but the government itself of that royal office was so shaken and disjoined as brought almost ruin upon the whole navy, and a far greater charge to his majesty in his yearly expence than ever was known before. In this great inquisition it pleased God, for the punishment of my sins, to suffer me to be grievously prosecuted, and publicly arraigned, as shall in its proper place be more at large described.

The 20th of October, 1608, being Thursday, by God's help, I laid the keel of the new great ship upon the stocks in the dock, and the 25th I raised her, and presently after the stem, and so proceeded in order with the floor as fast as I could, notwithstanding the many practices underhand attempted to have diverted the whole course of the building. During the time that I proceeded with the new frame, the inquisition against the navy growing then to the height, was prosecuted with extremity of malice against Sir Thomas Trevor, Sir Robert Mansell, and some others, among whom myself held not the least place.

About the 5th of March, 609, there was discovered unto me (by Mr. Sebastian Vicars, carver to the ships, my ever true and faithful friend) a secret combination against me, concerning the building of the great ship, suggested first by the practice of my fellows, old Mr. Matt. Baker, and Mr. William Bright, old adversaries to my name and family, assisted by Edward Stevens, a master shipwright, who laid great claim to my place by a former patent to him granted under the broad seal of England, with some other shipwrights also joined with them, by the especial warrant from
the

the great lord of Northampton, my moſt implacable enemy, my fellows bearing me no ſmall grudge, becauſe by the prince's highneſs means, my maſter, I was preferred to that great buſineſs before them, and Mr. Stephens malicing me, becauſe he could not prevail againſt me to recover my place from me. They had alſo won to their party by much importunity, and by means of a particular letter from the lord Northampton to him to that very purpoſe, a great braggaducio, a vain and idle fellow, ſome time a mariner and maſter, called by the name of captain George Weymouth, who, having much acquaintance abroad amongſt gentlemen, was to diſperſe the inſufficiency of my buſineſs, reporting that I was no artiſt, and altogether inſufficient to perform ſuch a ſervice; of no experience, and that the king was cozened, and all charges loſt, and the frame of her was unfit for any other uſe but a dungboat, with many other ſuch falſe opprobrious defamations, wherein he was better practiſed than in any other profeſſion.

Theſe rumours being thus divulged, the report thereof coming to Mr. Sebaſtian Vicars's ears, was the cauſe that he, out of his great love and honeſty to me, wrote to me what he had already heard abroad, willing me to keep a careful watch over myſelf, for that they would bend all their powers, practices, and friends, to the diſgracing of the building, and ruining me. But I, being very confident of the goodneſs of my cauſe (though I received that admonition as from a dear friend, with much acknowledgment of his love and care to me), little regarded what their malicious practices could bring forth, made ſmall reckoning after their plottings, till ſuch time as the good honeſt man, underſtanding from ſome of their own mouths what was intended againſt me, made a

pur-

purposed journey to me to Woolwich (though he was scarce able to travel by reason of a tedious sickness), and there thoroughly possessed me of the certainty of what he before by his writing had truly informed me.

I now perceiving it was no idle flim-flam, as I before supposed, considered that the goodness of my cause might by my secure neglect either suffer hazard, or be overborn by greatness, and began to call my wits about me, and to advise what was to be done in the business; at which time, to make good the supposition, I received a message by word of mouth from a worthy gentleman, a good friend of mine, Mr. William Burrell, principal master-workman to the East India Company, of all their projects, which were discovered to him, particularly by that captain Weymouth, being at that instant time between drunk and sober.

The 13th of April, this Weymouth was by consent of the rest sent to Woolwich to survey my work, and thereupon to deliver his opinion; and I in the mean time was appointed to be at Rotherhithe, at a meeting at a court held for the incorporation of shipwrights, whereof I was the master, that in my absence he might have the better opportunity to perform his malicious instructions, as he was directed by his great master; of the which his purpose I receiving certain intelligence, leaving my intended journey to Rotherhithe, I waited his coming, and received him after a courteous manner; after some discourse and ordinary compliments, he returned back to his confederates, frustrate of his great purpose.

Within a few days after, I wrote something to this purpose to my very good friends Sir Robert Mansell, and Sir John Trevor, being then the treasurer and surveyor of the navy, desiring them, for that it was a business highly concerning the

the honour of our honoured lord, the Lord High Admiral, and
their own particular reputation, that they would be pleased
to take the pains to make a sudden journey to Woolwich,
there truly to inform themselves not only concerning the state
of the work, but of divers other material businesses wherewith
I was to acquaint them at their coming thither. According
to my request, they both came the next day; where being thoroughly possessed of all the passages and occurrences concerning the project of our adversaries, after they had also carefully surveyed the works, with all other things necessary to be
advised of, leaving me with good deliberation and instructions how to proceed in my defence, they departed again to.
Westminster the same afternoon.

Presently after the departure of these gentlemen, desiring
the Lord first to guide and direct my pen, so as might best
tend to his glory, and the discharge of my duty, I betook
myself to my study. In the briefest manner I could, I certified
the Lord Admiral of the truth of all the whole project, plotted
against me, with the names of the principal actors therein,
and the reasons inducing them unto it; withal earnestly be-
seeching his lordship to be pleased, since the matter so nearly
concerned his majesty's profit, the honour of the state, his
lordship's own safety, and the reputation of his office, to
leave all respect of my particular good, and to procure such
evidence to be presently made of the work, by judicious and
impartial persons, as his majesty might receive no loss, the
strength of the kingdom no prejudice, his honour no im-
peachment, and the officers of the navy no just calumniation
nor blame.

It pleased his lordship, then lying at Whitehall, presently
after the receipt of my letter, wherewith he was not a little

troubled to obferve their malicious practices, to fend for me
to wait upon him, that by conference with me his lordfhip
might be the better informed of each particular paffage in
this fo dangerous information and conspiracy ; and after his
lordfhip had received from me fuch fatisfaction as he defired,
comforting me with many noble encouragements, as being
(as he faid) fufficiently perfuaded both of my fkill, experience, and honefty, wifhing me to take a good heart, and
never a whit to diftruft the goodnefs of my caufe, albeit I had
ftrong adverfaries, but that God in his mercy would never permit
fuch a malicious practice to prevail againft thofe that rely upon
him, with many other fatherly inftructions; and fo being fomewhat late for that night, his lordfhip was pleafed to difmifs
me, giving me commandment to attend his farther pleafure
the next morning ; and this was the 20th of April. It was
no fooner day the next morrow, but his lordfhip, very careful of doing fomething in this weighty bufinefs, made himfelf
ready by four o'clock, taking my letter in his hand, fpeeds
himfelf to his majefty's chamber, lying then at Whitehall,
and fending in word that his lordfhip was there to acquaint
his majefty with fome bufinefs of great confequence, was prefently admitted to his majefty's bed chamber, and having in
a few words given his majefty a tafte of his errand, delivered
him my letter, and befought him to be pleafed thoroughly to
perufe the fame. The letter his majefty read twice over, and,
perceiving how malice was the original of all this ftir, feemed
greatly to pity the wrong and injury done unto me, ufing
this gracious fpeech in my behalf, that whatfoever my act
was he knew not, but I deferved great commendation for my
honeft plainnefs delivered in my letter, and that it was great
reafon I fhould be juftly proceed withal. To the end therefore

fore that I might not be wrongfully oppressed, and the works
disgraced without just cause, his majesty took present order
with the Lord High Admiral, that he should join unto him
the right honourable lords the earls of Worcester, then master
of his majesty's horse, and of Suffolk, then lord high chamberlain, and repairing to Woolwich should there upon their
oaths, honours, and faithful allegiance to his majesty, without
respect of any particular person, call before them my ac-
cusers, and as well by examination of them, as trial of the
work itself, both in point of sufficiency as well as of matter, as
manner, should truly inform themselves, whether their main
accusation so much concerning his majesty's honour were
justly commenced or no, which charge by his majesty being
performed, they should return the true report thereof with
all speed to his majesty, as they should answer it upon their
allegiance.

Whilst these things were ordering thus, my malicious adversaries were not idle, but plotting as fast against me, and
had so far prevailed with the lord Northampton, that there
should be a private warrant directed to the chief of them, viz.
to Mr. Baker, Bright, and Stevens, and to some others whom
they should associate with them; which warrant should have
been signed with the king's own hand, to authorize them to
repair to Woolwich, and there strictly to make a survey of
the work, which being done, upon return of the insufficiency
of the same under their hands, and confirmation by oath, it
was resolved amongst them I should be turned out, and for
ever disgraced, the work utterly defaced, and I never to
come to any personal answer; and one of them, who could
make his party strongest, would undertake the business, about
which

which they were in great contention amongst themselves who
should be preferred to it.   But it pleased my good God (who
never leaves his servants destitute of his help when all other
means fail them) so mightily to work for me, by means of
my letter sent to my lord Admiral, and, as is shewed before,
delivered to his majesty, so far to prevent their purposes, that
upon that very day when they had determined to have
displaced and disgraced me, that they were, unawares to
them, warned by one of his majesty's messengers to appear
before the three lords before named, to answer them at that
very place and time wherein they made their account to triumph over me.   This was the Lord's doing, and it is marvellous in our eyes ; and this day was appointed to be on
Tuesday the 28th of April, which time was accordingly kept,
and the lords were come to Woolwich by nine o'clock the
same morning.

The first thing they did was to take a diligent survey of the
work ; first, touching the form and manner of the same, and
then concerning the goodness of the materials, which having
very carefully perused, they repaired into the house, and sat
at a little table in the middle of my dining-room.   Their lordships being sat, first Mr. Baker was called, and demanded,
for the good of his majesty's service, to deliver plainly what
he could justly except against the ship, either by point of
art, or insufficiency of the materials, and leading him from
point to point concerning her proportion of length, breadth,
depth, draught of water, height of jack, rake afore and abaft,
breadth of the floor, scantling of the timber, and other circumstances ; after a deal of frivolous arguings to no purpose,
their lordships found, by his examination, nothing worthy of
observing, and directly finding him to be more led out of an

6   envious

envious malicious humour againſt me, than upon any certain ground of error in the mould, or probability of inſufficiency of any of the materials uſed in the frame, whereupon he was diſmiſſed. After him was Bright called, and then Stevens, who were ſo tript in their ſeveral examinations, as their lordſhips found them in their anſwers clear contrary one to the other, almoſt in every queſtion, by which their lordſhips concluded, as they did of Mr. Baker, that all this queſtion and infamous report of the buſineſs was plotted by them out of ſome malicious reſpects to diſgrace me and my work, and not of any care or conſcionable regard for the good of his majeſty's ſervice, and ſo they were diſmiſſed. Then was great Kilcow Weymouth called, who being examined as the others before him were, was able to ſay nothing to any purpoſe, but held their lordſhips with a long tedious diſcourſe of proportions, meaſures, lines, and an infinite rabble of idle and unprofitable ſpeeches, clean from the matter, wherewith their lordſhips were ſo much tired, that he was commanded ſilence.

Then every man being diſmiſſed the room, they conſulted in private about half an hour, and then we were all called in again, where their lordſhips, addreſſing their ſpeech to me, delivered, that by all this time of inquiry they in their judgment could find no juſt cauſe of exception againſt the buſineſs, and this accuſation grew, for aught they could perceive, out of envy and malice, and therefore I had no cauſe to be diſcouraged in my ſervice, but to go on both comfortably and cheerfully, aſſuring me they would ſo effectually return the account of the particulars of their day's work to his majeſty, as ſhould not only give his majeſty ſatisfaction, but alſo ſecure and defend me from all the oppoſition any of my adverſaries could practiſe againſt me, with many other noble ſpeeches of encouragement ;

ragement; and fo about four o'clock in the evening, taking their coaches, they returned to court at Whitehall. The fame night, after their coming to the court, their lordfhips repairing to his majefty, they there delivered the account of their journey, together with all particular paffages in the fame, there offering to prove upon their honours, allegiances, and lives, the ground of that confpiracy to fpring from no other reafon but inveterate malice to me, and that they found the bufinefs in every part and point fo excellent as befitted the fervice of fo royal a king, with which his majefty refted marvellous well fatisfied.

My adverfaries, whofe malicious practices nothing could daunt, hunting after nothing fo much as my ruin and utter difgrace, were fo fired with this prevention, that redoubling their fury, they went altogether the next morning to their great patron and abettor, the lord Northampton, who being vehemently incenfed before, to have fuch an affront to the proceeding of his commiffion, as he termed our courfes to have wrought, was willing to entertain any thing that carried but likelyhod to give him means to be revenged on me for it. Therefore, after thefe caterpillars had difcourfed to his lordfhip all the circumftances of the hearing before the lords, complaining very grievoufly, as they termed it, of their partiality to me, and bitternefs to them, and that they were not fuffered to fpeak, nor could be heard in any thing they could inform againft me, they offering upon their lives to make good all their informations againft me to be true, fo that they might but gain an equal hearing, his lordfhip promifed to move his majefty in the granting of a fecond hearing, where he doubted not, as he faid unto them, but they fhould have amends made unto them for their former injuries, and

obtain

obtain their purpose against me in despight of all my friends
and upholders. His lordship upon this immediately repaired
to his majesty, and there made a grievous complaint against
the partiality of the three lords, which they shewed in the examination of the business there in that behalf of the plaintiff, tendering to his majesty, that they did offer upon their
lives to prove all their informations true ; and besought his
majesty very earnestly, there might be a second examination
committed to his lordship's care, whereby all partiality
should be prevented, and his majesty receive better confirma-
tions of their good service than what the lords had before
upon their superficial survey, and partial examination, exhibited to his majesty. His majesty answered, that upon his
lordship's first complaint, he had made special choice of
three principal peers of the realm, of whose fidelity he was
so well assured, that he could not but give credit to that account their lordships had returned upon their serious examination of that weighty business ; notwithstanding, seeing his
lordship urged so earnestly a review and second examination,
since it was a business of such main consequence, for his better satisfaction and clearing all doubts and scruples, his majesty resolved to take the pains in his own person to have the
hearing of the cause indifferently between all parties, ap-
pointing Monday the 8th of May following to be the time for
the said hearing at Woolwich, in the yard where the ship was
building, giving orders to the Lord High Admiral to provide
for the same, and to command all such persons as were any
ways interested in the business to give their personal attendance upon his majesty at that time and place. This resolution of his majesty made known, there was preparation of
both sides to be provided, both of information and defence,

to give his majesty satisfaction. But the contrary parties, doubting their malicious practices would now be plainly discovered, never dreaming of such a course, still laboured to bring disgraces upon me, informing, in the interim of ten days, if I might be suffered to continue the workmen on the frame, I would so handle the matter, that all things should be reformed that had by them been formerly found defective both in point of materials and proportions, and therefore were earnest suitors to have all the workmen presently discharged, and the work to stand.

His majesty, upon the advice of some of the lords, whereof the then lord treasurer, Sir Rober Cecil, and earl of Salisbury, being chief, would not consent to any conditions to have the workmen discharged ; but that orders should be taken that the work should cease; and the men be continued at his majesty's charge, till the hearing should be past, and his majesty to determine what was after to be done ; whereupon his majesty commanded a letter to be written to me to the same effect, charging me upon my allegiance to follow the directions therein contained, which I accordingly very carefully observed. In the mean time, no day almost passed wherein Mr. Baker, Bright, Stevens, Clay, Graines, captain Weymouth, with their malicious associates, did not meet at Woolwich, to take all the dimensions of the ship, to deface the works by striking aside the shores, and condemning the materials, aggravating continual disgrace upon me, and railing despitefully to my face, which I was forced to endure with patience, and put up with silence, flying to God, on whose mercy I wholly depended in these extremities.

The good Lord Admiral was not idle in this interim to provide for and to give his majesty full satisfaction in all

things

things that could be objected by the informers, and to that
purpose carefully advising with Sir Robert Mansell and Sir
John Trevor, principal officers of his majesty's navy, together with myself whom it did most concern, what course was
to be held to meet with all objections, that could by any
means be produced against me; for that the adverse party
had made choice of a certain number of masters and builders
in the river of Thames to strengthen their proceedings, it was
held fit and resolved the like course should be taken by us
for our better defence; whereupon sundry experienced men,
known to be honest and impartial of both sides, were nominated and appointed, by the Lord Admiral's warrant, to attend
this service; some inhabiting about the river of Thames, and
others of remote places; with whom divers consultations were
held, as well to inform them of the truth of every particular,
as also to satisfy their doubts in any thing wherein it was fit
they should be thoroughly resolved. I, for my own part,
confident of my own integrity, commending my cause to God,
provided myself to be able to answer all objections whatsoever
that could be alleged against me, either in point of art, experience, or care, in this so weighty service of trust and consequence. I must not here forget the princely favour of my
royal then master, prince Henry of ever famous memory,
who, in his noble care of me, in the interim of the time appointed by his majesty for my hearing, did almost every day
send me a comfortable encouragement by some one of his
princely gentlemen, to hearten me and to put life in me,
lest I should any way be disheartened with the apprehension of the power of my great and potent adversaries, and,
when the time drew near for my trial, sent me a commandment to wait on his grace the Sunday preceding the day at

Saint James's, which accordingly I performed; where his highness vouchsafed to lead me in his hand, through the park to Whitehall, in the public view and hearing of many people there attending to see him pass to the king his father; and in such loving manner counsel me with such comfortable, wise, and grave advice, touching my carriage and resolution in my trial, as was no little testimony of his principal care of me, to my great comfort, and joy of all those who were both eye and ear witnesses of it. Besides, casting the worse that might be, if I had been overthrown by the censures of his majesty, his highness had graciously determined to have received me into a place in his house, and resolved to provide for me while I lived.

The time drawing near, there were sent from London, at the appointment of the Lord Admiral, hangings to furnish the room where his majesty was to sit, and the next room to it where he was to withdraw, the one being the common dining-room of the workmen, the other my own dining-room, both which I caused to be hanged and trimmed up with such furniture as was befitting such a presence, with all conveniency the place could any way afford.

On Monday morning, being the 8th day of May, the Lord Admiral came betimes to Woolwich, attended by Sir Robert Mansell, Sir John Trevor, and others, where his lordship was met by all those persons who were formerly warned to be there on our part, and his lordship took those rooms which were fitted for his majesty. Presently after came the lord Northampton, attended with all the spiteful crew of his informers, and he took Hugh Lyddiard's house, being clerk of the cheque, which was fitted for him, and was there attended with all his rabble. Before his majesty's coming, Weymouth

6   and

and his affociates pried up and down the yard, belching out
nothing but difgraces and deceitful fpeeches, and bafe opprobrious terms, being fo confident of their wicked ends, as they
before had given out that I fhould be hanged, and the work
defaced at the leaft, which was likely enough to have proved
fo, had not God put a hook in their noftrils, and, by the juftice of the king, caufed themfelves to fall into the pit they
defigned for another. The noble admiral fpent the time till his
majefty's coming very quietly and privately, confulting ad-
vifedly with thofe appointed for the bufinefs, never fo much
as taking notice of the bafe ufage of them on the other fide.

All things being in readinefs, about eight o'clock his majefty came in his coach, attended with prince Henry, and the
principal lords of his majefty's counfel. The lord Northampton met him before he came to the ordinary gate of the yard,
and ufed all the means he could to have led his majefty
through Lyddiard's garden by a back way into his houfe ; but
his majefty told his lordfhip, that the Lord Admiral, whom
he efpied waiting with his train at the ordinary gate of the
yard, would juftly take exceptions at his fo doing, for that it
belonged properly there to his lordfhip to receive and entertain him ; fo alighting, the Lord Admiral, after his duty
performed, guided his majefty in the room provided purpofely for the bufinefs, whom I ufhered as belonging to my
place.—After his majefty had a little repofed, he defired the
Lord Admiral to bring him to the fight of the work then in
hand ; which being done, directing his majefty to a brow or
ftage, made at the ftem of the fhip, where he might take a
perfect view of the whole ground-work of the frame, being
then about half fet up, and planked as high as the wrong-
heads, no foot wailing as yet begun.

                                                    After

After his majesty had satisfied himself sufficiently, he returned back to the place again, and there seated himself in the chair under the state, at a little table standing right before him; the prince and lords taking their stands on his majesty's right hand, with the Lord Admiral and all those warned on our part, and the lord Northampton on the left hand of his majesty, with all his crew of informers, and others appointed to assist him on his part, of sea-masters and shipwrights of the Thames. These things thus ordered, his majesty (silence being commanded by his gentleman usher) began a very worthy speech; first, to signify the cause of his coming to that place, and how much it imported the royal care of a king to take to his personal examination a business of such consequence, as so much concerned the strength and honour of the kingdom and state, besides the expence of his treasure; then he addressed his speech to the actors on both sides, to those who were informers, and to those that were defendants, the substance of his royal speech tending to religious exhortation, that none on both sides should either accuse for malice or other pretence, or excuse for love, favour, or other particular respects; for that his majesty, in the seat of justice representing God's person, would not be deluded nor led by any coloured pretences from understanding the very plain truth of that business which was to be handled; and therefore wished such on both sides, whose conscience accused them either of malicious proceedings, private ends, or partial favour, to give over, and depart before they took the oaths to be administered to them, threatening severe punishment to those who should be found offenders herein, declaring what danger it was to be perjured before the majesty

of

of God and the King. His majesty's speech so effectually delivered to the purpose of the matter in hand to the admiration of the hearers, commandment was given to call the names of those to be sworn on both sides.

The names were then specified—the persons were in number,

On the lord Northampton's side	On the other side
14 seamen, 8 shipwrights,	14 seamen, and
and 2 other informers.	13 shipwrights.

These several persons called and appearing, the form of the oath was read unto them by the earl of Salisbury, lord treasurer, who personated the clerk of the session, and the book was presented to them by the right honourable Charles Howard earl of Nottingham, Lord High Admiral; this and these ceremonies performed, his majesty willed the lord Northampton to begin his accusation, and then I was called personally to answer, and kneeled right before his majesty near the side of the table, the Lord High Admiral standing on my right hand, Sir Robert Mansell and Sir John Trevor standing both right behind me. The accusation against me was exhibited by lord Northampton in writing, containing sundry articles in point of my sufficiency, art, and experience, and in point of my care and honesty in discharge of my duty, in unserviceable materials, to the great detriment of his majesty's service. His majesty perceiving the articles to be many, and very intricate to answer each particular, very judiciously contracted the business to three principal heads,—the point of art —the point of sufficiency of materials—and the point of charge —and to those heads I was commanded to make my answers, and they their accusations. I must confess, that at the first I was so daunted at the majesty of the king, the power of my enemies, and the confused urging of the objections, that I

2   was

was confounded in myself, till it pleased God, by the help of the lord treasurer, and his discreet directions, I was recollected, and recovered my spirits, and so orderly answered to each objection, his majesty still holding us on both sides to the proportions. Much time was spent in dispute of proportions, comparing my present frame with former precedents, and dimensions for the best ships for length, breadth, depth, floor, and other circumstances, in all which they could not fasten any thing upon me, but reflected to their disgrace and apparent breach of oath, and plain demonstration and expression of combined practice. Our point of proportion was mainly insisted upon, and with much violence and eagerness urged on both sides, which was the square of the ship's flat in the midships, they offering constantly upon their oaths it was full 13 feet, we as constantly insisting that it was 11 feet 8 inches. But, because this difference was long, and could not be tried upon the small plats, his majesty referred the trial to be made on the great platform, which was purposely framed of planks to the full scale of the ship, where all the lines of the midship bend were drawn, and the square of the flat only described, with their centres, perpendiculars, and sweeps; which trial, because it much concerned the truth or falsity of all the rest, his majesty would not give trust to any of those who by oath were interested in the same; but made choice of the noble and worthy knight, Sir Thomas Chaloner, the governor of the prince his highness houshold, and of the learned reverend Mr. Briggs, reader of geometry lecture in Gresham college in London, and master of arts, student in St. John's college, Cambridge, who were to decide the controversy. This thus concluded, we came to the point of charge,

to

to which was anfwered, that the charge of building this fhip fhould not exceed other fhips that had been built in her majefty's time, I mean queen Elizabeth of famous and happy memory, allowing proportion for proportion, the garnifhing not exceeding theirs. This gave full fatisfaction to the point of charge, being the fecond head propounded.

It being then almoft one o'clock, his majefty called for his dinner, referring the other points to be handled in the fhip after dinner. All this time I fat on my knees, baited by the great lord and his bandogs, fometimes by Baker, fometimes by Stevens, Bright, Clay, gaping Weymouth, and fometimes confufed by all ; and, which was worft, his majefty's countenance ftill bent upon me ; fo that I was almoft difheartened and out of breath, albeit the prince's highnefs ftanding near me from time to time encouraged me as far as he might without offence to his father, labouring to have me eafed by ftanding up, but his majefty would not permit it. So foon as his majefty and the lords had dined, the king rofe and went into the body of the frame of the fhip, to make trial of the goodnefs of the materials ; all the lower futtocks were placed, and many upper futtocks alfo. The adverfe party had chalked with a mark almoft half the lower futtocks for red wood, crofs-grained, and merely unferviceable, all which timber his majefty caufed to be dubbed by workmen ready with their tools for that purpofe ; and, being tried, they were all approved very found and ferviceable ; and, touching the crofs-grained timber, his majefty faid very earneftly " the crofs-grain was in the men, and not in the timber." His majefty fpent much time in the furvey of thefe things, ftill opening way to what objections the adverfe party

could allege, and what answer I could make for my defence.
This business performed within board, his majesty well satisfied in every particular, he openly delivered, that the ship
would be too strong, if one third part of the timber were left
out, and then began to give me a princely countenance and
encouragement, protesting oftentimes, that all this grievous
accusation proceeded of nothing but malice. Then his majesty came without board, and curiously surveyed the planks,
the treenails, and workmanship, all which gave such satisfaction as still confirmed his opinion of their malicious proceedings. All the while his majesty was intent upon this
search, the gentlemen forenamed, who were appointed for
the trial of the point of the true flat of the floor, were busied
in taking the measures from the ship, and bringing them to
the platform ; and when they found by due trial all lines to
be truly set off, they acquainted his majesty that all things
were in readiness. His majesty, having then received satisfaction of all things about the frame, repaired to the platform,
attended with the prince, lords, and many thousand spectators
besides. His majesty caused the gentlemen to measure each
dimension of breadth and depth for his own satisfaction, and
then coming to the point of the square of the floor, whether
it were answering their assertion of thirteen feet, or agreeable
to ours of eleven feet eight inches. The square of thirteen
feet was tried from the true centre, and perpendicular, which
being applied to the swaps of the mould did differ about sixteen inches ; at the wronghead the like trial made by our true
centre and perpendicular fell as just in our lines as could be
possible ; which done, his majesty with a loud voice commanded the measurers to declare publickly the very truth ;
                                                    which

which when they had delivered clearly on our fide, all the whole multitude heaved up their hats, and gave a great and loud fhout and acclamation. And then the prince his highnefs called with a high voice in thefe words; " Where be now thefe perjured fellows, that dare thus abufe his majefty with thefe falfe informations? Do they not worthily deferve hanging?"

By that time all thefe things were performed, and his majefty wonderfully fatisfied, and it growing fomething late, his majefty returned again into the hall where he formerly fat, and being placed, and the room filled as full as it could be packed, his majefty began a moft worthy and learned fpeech for conclufion of the bufinefs, wherein he exprefled, with many effectual fpeeches, what content he received in beftowing his pains that day to fo good a purpofe. Next, his majefty addrefled himfelf to the lord Northampton for his great care and diligence for fearching out fuch errors in the office of the admiralty, wherein his majefty and the ftate were abufed, with encouragement for him to go forward with profecuting his commiffion, notwithftanding his lordfhip had been mifinformed by being drawn to queftion this bufinefs. Next directed his fpeech to Mr. Baker, Bright, Stevens, and the reft of the informers, very bitterly reprehending their malicious practices, more to bring to effect their own private ends, than out of any confcionable care of the good of his majefty's fervice, or benefit of the ftate, repining at the preferment I had, and the countenance of his fon the prince, combining together to difgrace and ruin me ; though otherwife they envied one another, and were at controverfy who fhould be preferred to my bufinefs, with many good exhortations to will them to beware how they did abufe the majefty of God, and himself his substitute, with malicious informations, in which he could do no less than think them perjured, as in the prosecuting of this whole business was too apparent to himself and all the world, whereby they deserved to be punished severely, if he should censure them as they worthily merited.

His majesty then began to shew me a very pleasing countenance, and turned his speech to me, willing me not to be discountenanced with those proceedings against me, since he was now sufficiently persuaded of my honesty, integrity, and ability to perform what I had undertaken ; advising me not to refuse counsel of my fellow servants, since it was his service, wherein we ought to join together for his good, and the honour of the state, with many other princely expressions of his good opinion of me, and readiness not only to give me countenance, but assurance of future favour toward me ; and, lastly, he cleared all imputations and aspersions unjustly cast upon the Lord Admiral, with recital of all his honourable service performed to the honour of the state, and his perpetual fame ; commending his great wisdom and impartial carriage of himself in this day's trial, wherein he was never observed to give impediment to his majesty's proceedings, but all furtherance possible, as was both evidently manifest to his majesty by the great pains he had endured that day, and the noble patience he had given public testimony of to all present, who were eye-witnesses, with many other gracious speeches to put new life and power into him, to go on as he had begun, to the perpetual remitting his name and honour.   Then giving general thanks to those who had taken pains in that day's business, with protestations of his princely care in all matters of such

con-

confequence, for the fafety and honour of the ftate and kingdom, he concluded his fpeech.

Then the noble Admiral, as his majefty was rifing, humbly
befought his majefty to licenfe him to fpeak a few words, as
well to declare his own innocency concerning thefe unjuft
accufations, as to clear me in the point of my infufficiency,
and care and honefty to perform the fervice intrufted to me;
to which his honour's requeft (though it grew now to be late)
his majefty moft willingly condefcended. The fum of his
lordfhip's fpeech tended to admire and extol his majefty's
juftice, great wifdom, and princely care of the good of the
commonwealth, in that he had refufed no pains (as this
day's work and honourable affembly could juftly witnefs) to
provide, to rectify, and to fet ftreight, to the wonder and
admiration of them all, a work of fo great confequence, and
of fuch a kind of intricacy, as his majefty had never been accuftomed to before, and yet fo clearly to examine and try in
fo fhort a fpace, as if he had been only bred and accuftomed
to fuch elements, with many other fpeeches tending to that
purpofe. His lordfhip then laying his hand upon my head,
ftanding next to him upon his right hand, did there freely
offer to pawn all his lands, his honour, and his life, in my
behalf, for the performance and finifhing of this royal work;
which being once perfected, if his majefty (by advice of the
beft experienced artifts and feamen of his kingdom) fhould
diflike, he would willingly, with the aid of his friends, take
off from his majefty's hands, at his and their proper charge,
without any damage to his majefty. To this fpeech his majefty replied briefly with a gracious acknowledgment of his
princely acceptance of his lordfhip's true and faithful fervice and zeal expreffed in that his worthy fpeech, of which
he

he had so great assurance as he confidently protested never king could be more happy than himself in the service of such an honourable subject, and therefore there was no need why he should any way engage either himself or his honour in that which his majesty had by the course of upright justice before the face of God and the world so apparently cleared. This said, his majesty arose.

In passing through the hall, the Lord Admiral going before, and leading me in his hand, the lord Thomas Howard, then lord chamberlain of the household, made a motion to his majesty to lay a charge upon me, that I should not make any quarrel against any person or persons that had that day given information against me, alleging, he knew my stomach to be such (as if I were not contained by his majesty's commandment), I would call them to account for their doings, whereupon blood might ensue. His majesty giving ear to what his lordship advised, gave him thanks for his worthy counsel, and calling me to him before the whole company, I *sitting upon my knees* [*], he gave me an especial charge upon my allegiance and life, that I should not quarrel or challenge any person or persons whatsoever, that had that day given information against me, alleging, I had honour sufficient to have been cleared of all questions and objections unjustly charged against me by the equity of my cause and his justice. This speech concluded, his majesty hasted to take his coach, which attended at the gate. The noble lord brought me in his hand to kiss his royal hand, and take my leave. His majesty gave me his hand to kiss with such an expression of his princely favour and encouragement to proceed cheerfully in

[*] Sic in MS.

my

my bufinefs, as did not only infufe new life into me, but alfo gave great comfort and content to all ftanders by. Then I prefented myfelf upon my knee to the moft noble prince, my then mafter, who, taking me from the ground, did fo affectionately exprefs his joy for my clearing, and the fatisfaction his father had received that day, that he protefted he would not only countenance and comfort me hereafter, but take care to provide for me and my pofterity whilft he lived. I received the like noble courtefy from all the lords, who declared their joy for the happy fuccefs God gave me in this great deliverance. The great lord Northampton, feeing the event of this bufinefs, and that all things forted out clear contrary to his expectation, railing bitterly againft his informing inftruments, took the back way to his coach, and would not fo much as take leave of his majefty, but pofted away with no little expreffion of great difcontentment, as did alfo the reft of their partakers.

The Lord Admiral attended his majefty, being never better content in all his life, and returned to Whitehall with the company, it being almoft eight o'clock before they went from Woolwich. Sir Robert Manfell, Sir *John* * Trevor, captain Button, and the reft of my good friends followed, amongft whom was the good old lady Mrs Manfell, and Mrs. Button, who had taken the pains to attend the hearing in an inner room all that day. This day, as it was a very tedious day to me by reafon I was to anfwer all objections, and kneel fo long together, fo was it a day of jubilee to me, a day never to be forgotten by me nor mine, wherein my good God fhewed me wonderful favour and mercy to enable me to en-

* Thomas in the MS.

duxe

dure the frowns of the king, and to strengthen my weak abilities to withstand the malice of such and so many powerful adversaries by the space of one whole long summer's day. For, albeit his majesty was sufficiently persuaded of their malice and my integrity, yet till he had cleared all doubts by the course of strict examination, and found me in his justice guiltless, he would shew me no countenance at all, but after their malice was discovered, and all those heads and points fully answered, and clearly resolved, his majesty then both in countenance, words, and all other princely expressions, declared his royal disposition towards me.

The next day, being the 9th of May, I began to work again, every man striving to express his willingness thereunto, by reason of the great encouragement his majesty had publicly and generously given them; and within two or three days after, the Lord Admiral, Sir Robert Manfell, Sir John * Trevor, advising together with me, we resolved to move the lords of the council, to have two principal men, who were shipwrights, to be by their order appointed to repair twice at least in the week to Woolwich, to survey the provisions, and to foresee that no unserviceable materials should be wrought upon the ship, which we did to clear all suspicion of any ends of our own. This accordingly was consented to of the lords, and Mr. Matthew Baker and Henry Reynolds were appointed to be overseers, who, for fashion's sake, some three or four times came to Woolwich; but finding our care to be more to perform honestly, than theirs could be to prevent with their best endeavours, they gave over the trust recommended to them, and left me to myself.

* Thomas in the MS.

The

The 7th of June, the Red Lion, which was newly built by Mr. Baker of Deptford, was launched, where were present the king's majesty and the prince; I attending then near the place at the great ftorehoufe end, where his majesty had his ftanding, he was pleafed very gracioufly to confer with me, and to ufe me with extraordinary expreffions of his princely favour.

The 8th of June, being the Thurfday in Whitfun week, his majesty began to hear the great and general caufe of the navy, in his prefence chamber at Greenwich, wherein three whole days were fpent in feveral examinations of the truth and circumftances of the informations delivered by the lord Northampton and his agents, againft Sir Robert Manfel, Sir John Trevor, and Captain Button, Sir Thomas Bluther, Mr. Legatt, and many others, together with myfelf. Firft day the lord Northampton made the very entrance into the bufinefs, a great complaint of the difhonour he reaped by the hearing at Woolwich, infifting very malicioufly in incenfing his majesty againft me and others, who, as he faid, traduced him in every tavern and alebench, to his great difhonour; and therefore humbly befought his majesty that bufinefs might be again called in queftion, alledging the confidence of the informers, who were ready to maintain the truth of the former information with their lives. His majesty, taking it ill that my lord fhould dare to queftion his juft proceedings which he had taken fuch pains perfonally to hear determined, took him fhort with a fharp reprehenfion, and willed him no further to infift upon that whereof his majesty and the whole world were fo fufficiently fatisfied.

In the beginning of January, 1610, there were two new fhips, built at Deptford for the Eaft India merchants, to be launched, whereat his majesty, with the prince, and divers lords, were present, and feasted with a banquet of sweetmeats on board the great ship in the dock, which was called The Trade's Increase, the other was called The Pepper Corn, the names being given by his majesty. I did there attend, and receive gracious public usage from his majesty, the prince, and the lords. The tide was so bad that the great ship could not be launched out of the dock; and the smaller, which was built upon the wharf, was so ill struck upon the launching ways, that she could by no means be put off, which did somewhat discontent his majesty. The last day of January, the prince's highness came to Woolwich to see what forwardness the ship was in, where I gave him and his followers entertainment. The 7th of January, by commandment from the prince's highness, I attended at the great feast made by him at St. James's to the king, queen, duke of York, lady Elizabeth, and lords of the council, and all the knights who were actors at the barriers. The supper was not ended till ten at night; whence they all went to the play, and, that ended, returned again to a set banquet in the gallery, where the supper was, the table being 120 feet long, and it was three o'clock in the morning before it was all finished. The 25th of April, the prince's highness came to Woolwich, and dined there with all his train in my dining-room. The second of May, the lady Elizabeth, with her train, came to see the great ship at Woolwich, and was entertained by my wife, I being in London. The 18th of June, the prince's highness came to Woolwich to see the ship, which was now in great forwardness, and almost ready; and the next day he came thither again, in company with the king his father, and a great train attending on them. In the afternoon his

majesty

majesty spent almost two hours in great content, in surveying
the ship, both within and without, protesting it did not re-
pent him to have taken such great pains in examination of the
business of the work, since the fruit thereof yielded him such
content. His majesty then did me the honour to come into
my house, where my wife had prepared a banquet of sweetmeats and such fruits as were then to be had, whereof he was
pleased to taste plentifully, and did very graciously accept of
his homely entertainment, giving me special commandment
not to launch the ship till his progress was ended.

Between Easter and Michaelmas that the ship began to be
garnished, it is incredible what numbers of people continually
resorted to Woolwich, of all sorts, both nobles, gentry, and
citizens, and from all parts of the country round about, which
was no small charge to me, in giving daily entertainment to
all comers, which could not possibly be avoided in that place
at such a time. The 9th of September, being Sunday, about
six o'clock in the morning, divers London maids coming to
see the ship, brought in their company a little boy of twelve
years old, the only child of his mother, a widow woman
dwelling in Tower-street, who carelessly going up and down
upon the main orlop, fell down into the hold of the ship,
and was thereby so bruised and broken, that he died before
midnight, being the first mischance that had happened in the
whole time of the ship's building. About the middle of this
month, being ready to have the ship strucken down upon her
ways, I caused twelve of the choice master carpenters of his
majesty's navy to be sent for from Chatham, to be assisting in
her striking and launching; and, upon the 18th day, being
Tuesday, she was safely set upon her ways; and this day
Sir Robert Mansell dined with me at my lodgings. The

20th of this month the French ambassador came to Woolwich to see the ship, whom I entertained in the best manner I could ; and in the time of his being with me, the prince, my royal master, sent me a wonderful fat buck, which he killed with his own hand.

Now began we on all sides for the preparations to launch the ship, and for that purpose there was provided a rich standard of taffety very fairly gilded with gold, with his majesty's arms to be placed on the poop, and a very large ensign of crimson rich taffety, with a canton of the prince's crest to be placed upon the quarter deck, and all other ornaments were carefully provided befitting that purpose. There was a standing set up in the most convenient place of the yard for his majesty, the queen, and the royal children, and places fitted for the ladies and council (all railed in and boarded). All the rooms, both in my own lodgings and at Mr. Lydiard's, were prepared, and very handsomely hanged and furnished with a cloth of state, chairs, stools, and other necessaries. Nothing was omitted that could be imagined any ways necessary both for ease and entertainment. Upon Sunday in the afternoon, being the 23d, Sir Robert Mansel, Sir John Trevor, and Sir Henry Palmer, came to Woolwich to see how every thing was ordered ; and finding all things prepared and fitted to their liking, about three o'clock they returned all to Deptford, where they lodged that night with Sir Robert Mansel. This evening, very late, there came a messenger to me from them, bringing a letter, which was sent to them from court at Theobalds, to give me orders to be very careful to search the ship's hold, for fear some persons disaffected might have bored some holes privily in the ship to sink her, after the

should

should be launched; but my care had prevented their fears beforehand, so far as could be searched or discovered.

On Monday morning, assisted by the help of my brother, Pimonson, and sundry others of my friends, we opened the dock gates, and made all things ready against the tide; but the wind blowing very hard at South-west kept out the flood, so that it proved a very bad tide, little better than a neap, which put us afterwards to great trouble and hazard. The king's majesty came from Theobalds, though he had been very little at ease with a scouring, taken with surfeiting by eating grapes, and landed here about eleven o'clock, prince Henry attending him, and most of the lords of the council. The Lord Admiral, attended by the principal officers of the navy, together with myself, received him on land out of his barge, and conducted him to the place provided for him in Mr. Lydiard's house. His dinner was dressed in our great kitchen. After dinner came the queen's majesty, accompanied with the duke of York, lady Elizabeth, and divers great lords and ladies in her train, the drums and trumpets placed on the poop and forecastle, and the wind instruments by them, so that nothing was wanting to so great a royalty that could be desired. When it grew towards high-water, and all things ready, and a great close lighter made fast to the ship's stem, and the queen's majesty with her train placed; the Lord Admiral gave me commandment to heave taught the crabs and screws, though I had little hope to launch by reason the wind over blew the tide: yet the ship started, and had launched, but that the dock gates pent her in so straight, that she stuck fast between them, by reason the ship was nothing lifted by the tide, as we expected she would; and the great lighter, by unadvised counsel, being cut off the stem, the ship settled

so

so hard upon the ground, that there was no possibility of launching that tide; besides which, there was such a multitude of people got into the ship, that one could scarce stir by another.

The noble prince himself, accompanied with the Lord Admiral and other great lords, were on the poop, where the standing great gilt cup was ready filled with wine, to name the ship so soon as she had been afloat, according to ancient custom and ceremony performed at such times, by drinking part of the wine, giving the ship her name, and heaving the standing cup overboard. The king's majesty was much grieved at the frustrate of his expectation, coming on purpose, though very ill at ease, to have done me honour. But God saw it not so good for me, and therefore sent this cross upon me, both to humble me and to make me know, that, howsoever we purposed, he would dispose all things as he pleased; so that about five o'clock his majesty, with the queen and all her train, departed away to Greenwich, where the houshold were removed. Prince Henry staid a good while after his majesty was gone, conferring with the lord admiral, principal officers, and myself, what was to be done, and leaving the Lord Admiral to stay here to see all things performed that were resolved on. He took horse, and rode after the king to Greenwich, with promise to return presently after midnight.

So soon as the multitude were gone and all things quiet, we went presently in hand to make way with the sides of the gates, and having great store of scavel men and other labourers, we had made all things ready before any flood came; which performed, every man applied himself to get victuals and to take rest. The Lord Admiral sat up all night in a chair in his chamber till the tide was come about the ship; and

Sir

Sir Robert Manſel, Sir John Trevor, and Sir Henry Palmer, and the reſt, made a ſhift in my lodging to reſt themſelves. The beginning of the night was very fair, and bright moon-ſhine, the moon being a little paſt full ; but after midnight the weather was ſore overcaſt, and a very ſore guſt of rain, thunder, and lightning, which made me doubt that there were ſome indirect working among our enemies to daſh our launching. Theſe guſts laſted about half an hour with great extremity, the wind being at South-weſt. In the midſt of this great guſt prince Henry and all his were taken upon the top of Blackheath in their coming to Woolwich ; but his in-vincible ſpirit, daunted with nothing, made little account of it, but came through, and was no ſooner alighted in the yard, but calling for the Lord Admiral and myſelf, and Sir Robert Manſel, went all preſently on board the ſhip, being about two o'clock, almoſt an hour before high water, and was no ſooner entered but the word being given to ſet all taught, the ſhip went away without any ſtraining of ſcrews or tackles till ſhe came clear afloat in the middle of the channel, to the great joy and comfort of the prince's highneſs, the lord ad-miral, and all the reſt of my noble friends ; which mercy of God to me I pray I may never forget. His highneſs then ſtanding upon the poop with a ſelected company only, be-ſides the trumpeters, with a great deal of expreſſion of princely joy, and with the ceremony of drinking in the ſtand-ing cup, threw all the wine forwards towards the half deck, and ſolemnly calling her by the name of the Prince Royal, the trumpets ſounding all the while, with many gracious words to me, gave the ſtanding cup into my own hands, and would not go from the ſhip till he ſaw her faſt at her moor-

a   ings.

ings. In heaving down to the moorings, we found that all the hawsers that were laid athore for landfalls were treacherously cut to put the ship to hazards of running athore, if God had not blessed us better. In the interim of warping to her moorings, his highness went down to the platform of the cook-room, where the ship's beer stood for the ordinary company; and there finding an old can without a lid, went and drew it full of beer himself, and drank it off to the Lord Admiral, and caused him, with the rest of his attendants, to do the like. At nine the same morning, being very rainy, he took his barge, accompanied with the Lord Admiral, and the rest of his train, and giving us a princely gracious farewell, rode against the tide to Greenwich, where he made relation of all the business, and the circumstances thereof, to the king his father. We then came ashore to refresh ourselves with victuals, and to take some rest, having toiled all the night before; and amongst the rest Sir Henry Palmer was pleased to stay dinner, where we drank Prince Henry's health round, to handsel the standing cup given at the launching.

The 25th of September, 1612, the new charter for incorporating the shipwrights of England, granted by king James, in which, by the same charter, I was ordained first master, I was sworn in my place of master, the dinner being kept at the king's head in Fish Street, Mr. Dr. Pay making the sermon at the next church adjoining. About this time my picture was begun to be drawn by a Dutchman, working then with Mr Rock at Rochester.

Mr. Pette mentions the sickness and death of Prince Henry, at which time, he adds, began my ensuing misfortunes, and

found

the utter downfall of all my forlorn hopes, to the ruin of all my poor posterity, being now exposed to the malicious practices of my old enemies. Upon my going to St. James's, I found a house turned to a *mapp* * of true forrow, every man with the character of grief written in his dejected countenance. About six at night, November 6, the most renowned prince of the world, our royal and most loving master, departed this life, not only to the loss and utter undoing of his poor fervants, but the general loss of all Chriftendom of the Proteftant religion. The beginning of December I had warning to attend at St. James's upon the preparation of the funeral of our mafter, and had black cloth delivered to me according to the place I was ranked in above ftairs, which was of gentleman of the privy chamber extraordinary; and the fixth day, being Sunday, all his highnefs's fervants at St. James's waited upon his herfe then ftanding in the chapel, to whom Dr. Price, then one of his highnefs's chaplains, directed an excellent fermon. His text was 2 Sam. ch. iii. v. 31. *Rent your clothes, put on fackcloth, and mourn for Abner.* There were very few at the fermon who mourned not bitterly, and fhed abundance of tears.

The 6th of January, 1612, I received a letter from the Lord High Admiral, together with a lift of thofe fhips that were appointed to be made ready to tranfport the lady Elizabeth, with warrant to be grained and fitted accordingly.

January 1612. The 11th day I was fent for from Chatham by a meffenger to attend the Lord Admiral, lying then at Chelfea, which accordingly I prefently performed, and rode to London, where I ftayed full three days, the Lord Admiral

* Mapp in MS.

fitting

fitting every of thofe in council, attended by the principal officers of the navy, the mafters and mafter fhipwright, to refolve not only for the preparation of the fleet to attend the tranfportation, but alfo for preparing many veffels to be built upon long-boats and barges for fhips and gallies for a fea-fight, to be prefented before Whitehall againft the marriage of the lady Elizabeth; the manner whereof concluded and or-dered in writing, I was licenfed to go to Chatham to take order for the Difdain, and fending up of as many long-boats and fear-barges as could be fpared from the navy; which ha-ving ordered, I returned again prefently to London, and did there attend daily in overfeeing thofe bufineffes, which were put out by the great to divers yard-keepers by reafon of the fhortnefs of time limited for making them ready againft the marriage. By reafon of this my continual attendance, not only upon that fervice, but alfo upon the Admiral and Sir Robert Manfel (principally entrufted to the ordering of the whole fervice) I firft took lodging at Weftminfter, near Sir Robert's houfe, in St. Stephen's alley, where I continued many years after. Amongft other veffels fitted for this piece of fer-vice was an old pinnace of the king's, called the Spy, of the burden of fixty tons, having nine pieces of brafs ordnance ap-pointed to ferve as an argoffey, whereof I was fomewhat againft my will (by the Lord Admiral's perfuafion) made to ferve as captain, in which jefting bufinefs I ran more danger than if it had been a fea-fervice in good earneft. After the fea-fervice was performed, I was intreated by divers gentlemen of the inns of bufinefs, whereof Sir Francis Bacon was chief, to attend the bringing of a mafk by water in the night from St. Mary Over's to Whitehall in fome of the gallies; but the tide falling out very contrary, and the company attending
the

the maskers very unruly, the project could not be performed so exactly as was purposed and expected. But yet they were safely landed at the plying stairs at Whitehall, for which my pains the gentlemen gave me a fair recompence.

The marriage consummated, and the royalties ended, the Lord Admiral gave me a present difpatch to poft to Chatham, and get the fleet ready, the Prince being appointed to go admiral, to tranfport the lady Elizabeth and the Palfgrave's perfon, and the lord admiral to command her. On the 27th of February I launched the fmall ship I had begun the fummer before, which the Lord Admiral was pleafed to call the Phœnix, and was alfo appointed one of the fleet, under the command of Sir Allen Apfley, then victualler of the navy. About the 14th of March, the Lord Admiral, very careful to have all things ordered as befitting the royalty of fuch a fervice, came down to Chatham in perfon, and ftayed two days to direct all things to his liking, wherein I gave his lordfhip much fatisfaction, and by the end of the month I had by my diligence fitted the whole fleet to fail to Gillingham. The firft of April, being Monday, the prince failed over the chain, captain John King being mafter; the Lord Admiral being newly come to Chatham, came aboard of us, as we were under fail, and went down in her to Gillingham. On Eafterday, the 4th of April, the Lord Admiral, with his retinue, received the holy facrament. Dr. Pay, chaplain to the lord William Howard, baron of Effingham, and vice admiral in the Ann Royal, preached and delivered the facrament. On Eafter Tuefday, the lord admiral with all his retinue, removed from Chatham, and came aboard to their feveral charges at St. Mary Creek at Gillingham, and lay on-board in his own cabin this night. So foon as prayers were done this evening,

and

and the tables covered, the Lord Admiral, out of his noble favour to me, called me, and there ordered me to take my place at his table all the voyage, and would not commonly have grace said till his lordship had seen me fit down, except I was upon earnest business, and gave his officers charge to let me at all times have what I would of his own provisions. The 7th we set sail from Gillingham, wind South-west, a pretty fresh gale. The ship wrought exceeding well, and was so yare of conduct that a foot of helm would steer her. We came to an anchor at Queenborough, and there lay all night. He then mentions, how by the inattention of the master, and from other circumstances, the prince was put aground, and could not be got off till the next tide ; and adds, that this unfortunate accident not only discouraged the Lord Admiral, but also gave advantage to the ship's enemies, of whom the lord of Northampton was chief, to persuade the lady Elizabeth not to venture her person in such a vessel that had so ill a beginning, but rather to embark herself in some other ship, and to return home. He observes, that with the ship's company, and the Lord Admiral's retinue, the number of persons on-board could not be less than eight hundred.

The 15th we came to an anchor in Margate road ; the next day the Lord Admiral went ashore at Margate, and lay there three days, at Mr. Roger Morris's, one of the four masters of his majesty's navy, and then returned aboard. The 21st, the lady Elizabeth, his grace the Palsgrave, and all their train, came to Margate, and were embarked in barges and the ships boats, and were received on-board the admiral, and lay there all night. The 22d the wind getting Easterly, and likely to be foul weather, her highness and the Palsgrave, and most part of her train, were carried ashore to Margate. The 25th
they

they were all brought on-board again; prefently we fet fail, and that night anchored without the Foreland. He then proceeds in his account of the voyage, and obferves, that whilft the prince lay at Flufhing there were fuch a multitude of people, men, women, and children, that came from all parts of Holland to fee the fhip, that thofe belonging to it could fcarce have room to go up and down till night, and that the confluence lafted from the time they anchored till they weighed from Flufhing.

The 19th we weighed upon the flood, and turning up to Flufhing fome mile fhort of the town, her highnefs, with the Palatine, and moft part of the train, were embarked in the barges and boats, being very fair weather, and was faluted with all the ordnance of the whole fleet, and landed at Flufhing, where they were received with all royalty, and faluted with all the ordnance of the town and caftles, and guarded with the foldiers and garrifon of the town; our fhips anchored a little above the Rammapeers; this afternoon I went on fhore to attend the Lord Admiral, and lay in Flufhing, our charges being defrayed by the town. The 30th day, being Friday, the Count Palatine took leave of her highnefs, and went poft to the Palatinate.

May 1613. This forenoon, being Monday, divers of our retinue took a coach and rode to Camphire to fee the ifland; this afternoon her highnefs and her train were received into Middleburgh with all royalty. The fecond day, being Sunday, the burghers feafted her highnefs at the town-houfe; this evening the Lord Admiral brought me to take leave of her highnefs, and to kifs her hand; the next day her highnefs took leave of the Lord Admiral and his train, having attended her to the place where fhe was embarked; which done, the Lord

Admiral

Admiral returned from Middleburgh in her barge on-board the Prince, where he found such a multitude of people, men, women and children, that came from all places in Holland to fee the ship, that we could fcarce have room to go up and down till very night, which confluence of people lafted from the time we anchored at Flushing till we weighed thence. The 4th day the Lord Admiral gave order we should weigh from Flushing to avoid the number of people, which accordingly was done, and we fell down to Caffant Hogut, where we anchored all that day and next night.

The 7th day, the wind continuing Eafterly, we weighed and fet fail, and by twelve o'clock we came to anchor at Gillingham, from whence I attended the Lord Admiral in his barge to Chatham, where he lay that night at Mr. Legatt's houfe. I found my wife and family in health, and gave God thanks for his prefervation of us in our journey and fafe return home, to our mutual comforts.

June 1613. At Whitfuntide Sir Robert Manfel was committed to the Marfhalfea upon fome difpleafure his majefty took againft him, by the inftigation of the lord Northampton, where he was detained prifoner till the 13th of June following, when he was releafed at Greenwich.

The 22 of June, 1613, the king of Denmark came fuddenly to Somerfet-houfe unexpected. The firft of Auguft my gracious mafter, king James, with the king of Denmark, prince of Wales, and many other lords, came to Woolwich, and went on-board the Mer Honeur, then lying in the dry dock, and almoft finifhed, which fhip liked them wondrous well. Here our king took leave of his majefty of Denmark, returning to Whitehall. From thence the king of Denmark took barge to Gravefend, accompanied with the Prince and

Lord

Lord Admiral ; Sir Robert Manfel and myfelf were commanded to attend them. The 2d, the king of Denmark was entertained on-board the Prince, riding at her moorings in the river of Chatham, the Prince of Wales and the Lord Admiral accompanying, Sir Robert Manfel and myfelf attending. The fhip was completely rigged, and all her fails at the yards, richly adorned with enfigns and pendents all of filk, which gave a very great contentment to the king of Denmark, yet it was a very rainy foul day. From thence they returned to Gravefend, where the king of Denmark took leave, and embarked in his own fhip.

The 25th of July, 1614, the archbifhop of Canterbury lay at Rochefter, and went aboard the Prince, where he was entertained with a banquet of fweetmeats by Sir Robert Manfel, myfelf attending.

About the 27th of March, 1615, I bargained with Sir Walter Raleigh to build him a fhip of five hundred tons, which I procured leave from the Lord Admiral to build in the Galley Dock at Woolwich, towards which I prefently received £. 500. to begin with, and the 8th of April following I fet my men to work on her. In July, Sir Henry Manwaring caufed me to build a fmall pinnace of forty tons for the lord Zouch, then lord warden of the Cinque Ports—towards the whole of the hull and rigging I received only £.100. from my lord Zouch ; the reft Sir Henry Manwaring cunningly received in my behalf, without my knowledge, which I could never get from him but by piece-meal, fo that by the bargain I loft at leaft £. 100. The 16th of December I launched the great fhip of Sir Walter Raleigh's, called the Deftiny, and had much ado to get her into the water, but I delivered her to him afloat in good order, by which bufinefs I loft £. 100. and
could

could never get any recompence for it, Sir Walter going to
sea, and leaving me unsatisfied.

The 19th of July, 1616, the great duke of Buckingham,
lately made Lord High Admiral of England, came to visit
the navy then riding at Chatham, accompanied with divers
lords, and Sir Robert Mansel, who, on his being here, used me
with such extraordinary respect that wrought me much prejudice in the opinion of the commissioners, who ever after
plotted my ruin, and to bring me out of favour with the Admiral and the king himself. The 20th of November, attending at Theobalds to deliver his majesty a petition, his majesty
in his princely care of me, by means of the honourable Lord
Admiral, had before my coming bestowed on me for the sup-
ply of my present relief the making of a knight baronet, which
I afterwards passed under the broad seal of England for one
Francis Ratcliff of Northumberland, a great recusant, for
which I was to have £.700; but, by reason Sir Arnold Herbert
(who brought him to me) played not fair play with me, I
lost some £.30. of my bargain.

In the beginning of 1622, before I was two months out of
England in a voyage against the Algier pirates, by the malice
of Mr. Burrell, and some of the rest of the commissioners of
the navy, divers master shipwrights of the Thames, and
masters of the Trinity house, were ordered to Chatham to
survey the state of the Prince; amongst which commissioners
were, besides old Burrell and his son, my fellow Stevens,
Granes, Dearsley, Barnes, Thomas Brumneting of Woodbridge, and one Chanler, a creature of Burrell's, and divers
other mariners, who maliciously certified the ship to be unserviceable, and not fit to continue; that what charges should
be bestowed upon her would be lost, which they certified under
                                                        their

their hands. But the 24th of February, by especial command of his majesty, who well understood their malicious proceedings, the self same surveyors were again sent to Chatham, who gave under their hands, that the ship might be made serviceable for a voyage to Spain for £. 300. bestowed upon her hull and masts; which certificate was returned under their hands, and given to his majesty; whereupon present warrant was granted to have the ship docked and fitted for a Spanish voyage, which was accordingly done, and brought into dock the 8th of March, 1623, and was launched the 24th of the same at Chatham. About the 17th of February I attended at Theobalds, the very morning the Prince and the Duke of Buckingham took leave of his majesty, to take their journey into Spain, being carried so privately that few knew of it. At their taking horse I kissed both their hands, and they only gave me an item that I should shortly go to sea in the Prince. After the Prince and the rest of the fleet were all fitted and prepared to set sail from the moorings, the St. George and the Antelope fell down to Gillingham, being both appointed to go before to St. Andrew's with the jewels and other provisions ; the other noble gentleman, my honoured friend Sir Francis Steward, commanding in her, whom my eldest son John attended as one of his own retinue. Captain Thomas Lane commanded the Antelope. The 2d of May the Prince removed from her moorings to St. Mary Creek ; thither came down from London many commissioners of the navy, with Sir Thomas Smith and the Lord Brook, who plotted to hinder me going the voyage which the king had commanded me, but their malicious practices were prevented. The 17th I took leave of his majesty at Greenwich Park, and kissed his hand, with expressions of his favour,

which was not very pleasant to Sir John Cook, then present.
The first of July came to anchor in Stoke's Bay, by Portsmouth.
The 29th of August, his majesty, then lying in the New Forest
at Beauly house, came on-board the Prince, with the marquis
of Hamilton, the lord Chamberlain, Holdernefs, Kelly, Car-
lisle, Montgomery, and divers other attendants, and dined
on-board our admiral, the earl of Rutland being at London.
His majesty was very pleased, and after dinner lay hovering in
his barge till all the ships had discharged their ordnance, and
then landed at Calshot castle. An account of the voyage to
Spain is given by Mr. Pette. On the return he landed at
Dover, October 16.

The 23th of May, 1624, being sent for to St. James's, I
received a gold chain from Robert Carr, by his highness's
order, valued at £.104. as a reward for my attendance this
voyage, which I was commanded to wear one day, and to
attend his highness to parliament, from whom I received very
gracious respects. About the end of December the Prince
was docked to be fitted for sea; meanwhile the duke of
Brunswick came to Chatham, with divers of the prince's servants, and came on-board the ship in the dock. The 29th
of January she was launched, and soon after her masts set,
and divers other ships *graved* * and made ready for a voyage
to sea. The 28th of March, 1625, certain news was brought
to Chatham of king James's death; and the next day his majesty was proclaimed among us in the navy at the Hill-house,
the masters, boatswains, pursers, and gunners, belonging to
the navy, being present.

All April and May I attended at Chatham, to repair the
fleet then bound to fetch over the queen. In the latter end of

* Graved in Ms.

May

May his majesty came to Rochester, where I presented myself to him in the Dean's yard, and kissed his hand, and had speech with him till he came into the house where he dined. I attended all the dinner while, and waited his majesty's coming by towards Canterbury : he alighted at my house, and staid there awhile, and gave me leave to drink his health, and returned to his coach, ordering me to follow him, and hasten on board the Prince then in the Downs, which I presently did, and lay at Sandwich that night. Next day I was on-board the Vanguard, captain Pennington commander, bound for France, where I met Sir Thomas Button, captain Edward Gyles, and other good company, where I dined, and then was set on-board the Prince. The 4th of June his majesty came on-board the Prince, riding then in Dover road, where he dined, and was safely landed again, yet this evening we let slip from the Downs in very bad weather. The 5th we anchored in Bulloign road ; the 10th we had a storm, the wind North-west, all our ships drove ; we broke our bell bower, and were forced to let go our sheet anchor, which put us to great danger of losing both men and boats. Sunday the 12th of June, all things prepared, and the storm allayed, about eleven o'clock we received our young queen ; and, having a fair leading gale fit to entertain a queen, we sailed from Bulloign at one o'clock, and landed her at Dover before eight.

In 1627, I received warrant from the lord duke of Buckingham to go to Portsmouth, there to hasten the fleet out, which I did accordingly, taking my journey from Lambeth, August 1. During my stay at Portsmouth I saw many passages, and the disaster which happened to the lord duke.

In the same year his majesty gave me a blank for making a baronet, which was signed by his own hand. About the

beginning

beginning of June, 1629, by captain Pennington's procurement, I passed the baronet formerly given me by the king, for which the captain received for me £. 200. which he sent to Woolwich.

In 1630, towards the middle of February, there was a resolution, by his majesty and the lords of the Admiralty, to make an addition of assistants to the principal officers of the navy; Mr. William Burrell was one, and myself, by his majesty's appointment, the other, not without strong opposition, which not prevailing, there was a letter under his majesty's signet to the officers and ourselves to sit with them, to authorize us to proceed together in all business concerning his majesty's service, which was twice read at the public meeting in Mincing-lane. The 8th of March we took our places at the board, when it was concluded first to begin a general survey of the whole navy at Chatham, and all the stores within and without doors, and to put out by the great, as we should think fit, the repair of all the ships that were deficient; which was wholly recommended to Mr. Burrell and myself, and effectually performed by us, the work being put to Mr. Goddard, one of the master shipwrights, to be done by contract.

The 4th of August there was a great commission sent to Portsmouth for viewing the harbour and river running up to Fareham, for removing his majesty's navy to a more safe road; all the principal officers of the navy, with his majesty's masters of the navy, and six of the chief masters of the Trinity-house. There was much dispute and contrariety about the business, but at last a fair agreement was concluded. About the 23d of November I was sent to Portsmouth to enquire after the worm, which was reported to eat the ships in the harbour. Several master shipwrights being joined with me, me, we found upon oath that it was only a rumour to hinder the keeping of any of his majesty's ships in that harbour. At the end of December his majesty signed my patent for the place of a principal officer and commissioner of the navy, and January 19 following I had my letters patent read publicly at the navy-office in Mincing-lane, and accordingly took my place among them. The 26th they were publicly read before the whole navy men at Chatham.

The 21st of April, 1631, his majesty, with divers of the lords, viz. Treasurer, Chamberlain, marquis of Hamilton, Holland, and others, came to Woolwich to see the Vanguard launched, which was performed to his majesty's great content. I entertained them in my lodgings with cakes, wine, and other things, that were well accepted. His majesty commanded me into his barge with him, designing to see the St. Dennis at Deptford, in the dry dock, but, the rain preventing him, I was put into a pair of oars. On Friday morning the Victory, lying above the Vanguard, was launched out of the same dock.

In the beginning of the year 1632, I was commanded to assist my son Peter in building a new ship of eight hundred tons at Woolwich, which was begun in February, most part of her frame being made in the forest of Shutover and Stowkwood, Oxfordshire. My son had the oversight of the work. About the 8th of June his majesty came to Woolwich to see the work ; I entertained him in my lodgings, and attended his majesty to Deptford, where he landed to see the new ship built by Mr. Goddard.

The 30th of January, 1633, the new ship at Woolwich was launched, his majesty being present, and stood in my lodgings. It was fair weather, and a good tide, so the ship

was

was put into the water without straining the tackle, which much pleased his majesty, who soon after took his barge for Whitehall. The ship's name was Charles, after his own name. The next day Mr. Goddard's ship was launched; the king and queen were present, and was called after the queen's name, the Henrietta Maria.

1634. The Leopard, built at Woolwich by his son Peter Pette.

The 22d of June, a little ship completely rigged, gilded, and finished, was placed on a carriage, whose wheels resembled the sea, being enclosed in a great box, was sent in the Fortune pink to London, and carried in a wherry to Scotland-yard, and thence to St. James's, where it was placed in the long gallery, where it was presented to the prince, who entertained it with great joy, being purposely made to disport himself withal. The 26th his majesty came to Woolwich in his barge to see the frame of the Leopard, then half built; and, being in the ship's hold, he called me aside privately, and told me his resolution of building a great new ship, which he would have me undertake; and said, you have made many requests to me, and now I will make it my request to you, to build the ship; commanding me to attend his coming to Wanstead, where he would farther confer about it. October 29th, the model of this great ship being finished, was carried to Hampton Court, and placed in the gallery, and then carried back to Whitehall, till his majesty's return thither.

March the 11th, 1635, his majesty came to Woolwich to see the new ship, built by my son, launched. I caused her masts to be set in the dock, and completely rigged her, having on-board ten pieces of ordnance, with the sails at the

yards.

yards. The ship being launched betimes, she was, at his command, named the Leopard by Sir Robert Manfel. After she was clear out of the dock, his majesty came and stayed almost an hour on-board. We hoped to have failed her with his majesty on-board, but the wind came against us. The middle of April his majesty was pleased to renew my privy feal for my pension of £.40. *per ann.* payable in the Exchequer, with orders for all my arrears due on it; and May 8, my son Peter received the same arrears, being £.100.

May 14, I took leave of his majesty at Greenwich, with his command to hasten into the North to provide and prepare the frame, timber, plank, and treenails, for the new ship to be built at Woolwich; and having dispached all warrants and letters concerning the business, and some imprefs of moneys for travelling charges, I left Woolwich, and got to Chatham. I left my sons to see the moulds and other neceffaries shipped in a Newcastle ship, hired on purpose to transport our provisons and workmen to Newcastle, and to fend the ship and take us in at Queenborough. Mr. Pette gives a circumstantial detail of this voyage, of the occurrences he met with in the North, and of his return home. At Stockton we found mean entertainment, though lodged in the maior's house, which was a mean thatched cottage. Lodged at the Post-house in Durham, with homely entertainment.—Attended the bithop of Durham with my commifions and instructions, whom I found wonderfully ready to assist us, with other knights, gentlemen, and justices of the county, who took care to order prefent carriage, so that in a short time there was enough of the frame ready to lade a large collier, which was landed at Woolwich, and as fast as provisions could be got ready, they were shipped off from Chapley-wood

at

at Newcastle, and that at Branspeth Park from Sunderland. The 30th of July we dined at Huntingdon, where I met my old acquaintance and noble friend Sir Oliver Cromwell. I lodged at the Falcon in Cambridge, and visited Emanuel college, where I was formerly a scholar. I passed the Ferry at Gravesend, August 4, on my return home.

November 2, my son Peter met me at Woolwich, where we gave orders for our proceedings. The 21st of December we laid the ship's keel in the dock, most part of her frame coming safe, was landed at Woolwich. The 16th of January, 1636, his majesty, with divers lords, came to Woolwich to see part of the frame and floor laid, and that time he gave orders to myself and my son to build two small pinnaces out of the great ship's waste. The 28th his majesty came again to Woolwich with the Palsgrave, his brother, duke Robert, and divers other lords, to see the pinnaces launched, which were named the Greyhound and Roebuck. About the 10th of April his majesty's ship the Ann Royal, bound Admiral for the narrow seas, anchoring in Tilbury Hope, being unmoored, and shifting upon the flood, came foul on her own anchor, which pulled out a great deal of her keel abaft the mast, and in sinking suddenly was overthrown. Some of her company were drowned, and among them the master's wife and another woman. Myself, among others, was commanded by his majesty to assist the weighing her, which cost much trouble, great charge, and no small danger to those that were employed in it, which afterwards was objected to them as a fault, and they received a check from the lords. The ship was weighed, and carried into the East India dock at Blackwall, about the 10th of August.

The

The 3d of February, 1637, his majesty, the prince Elector,
and divers lords, came to Woolwich by water, and after
viewing the work without board, they did the same within
board, both aloft and in the hold, being well satisfied. Then
retiring to my lodgings, they staid till the flood, and then returned in his majesty's barge to Whitehall.

Tuesday the 29th of August proved very rainy, yet the shipwrights of the river, who were called to help to strike the
ship on her ways, being come, we struck her by eleven o'clock.
The 25th of September was the day peremptorily appointed
by his majesty to launch the ship, so every thing was prepared
to be in readiness. His majesty, accompanied with the queen,
and all the lords and ladies their attendants, landed at Woolwich dock stairs about twelve o'clock, and went directly on-
board the ship, where staying about an hour, they retired
into our room, furnished for their entertainment. About
two o'clock the tackles were heaved taught, and the ship
startled till the tackles failed, and the water pinched, being
a very bad tide. Then we shored the ship, and their majesties
returned to Whitehall, very sorry she could not be launched.
After attempting two or three tides, we concluded to stay till
the next spring, the ship being so easy she could receive no
damage. After our resolution of letting the ship remain
till the next spring, which was about the 12th of October, in
the interim many reports were raised to disable the ship, and
bring as much disgrace on me as malice could possibly in-
vent; all proceeding from the masters of the Trinity-house,
and other rough hewn seamen, with whom Mr. Cook, one of
four masters of his majesty's navy, anxiously adhering, to please
Mr. Secretary Cooke, and Mr. Eddisbury the Surveyor of the
Navy, all professed enemies to the building, and more to me,

joined together to caſt what aſperſions, as far as they durſt,
for fear of the king's diſpleaſure.   But the ſpring coming on,
Sir Robert Manſel called a meeting at Woolwich of ſuch Trinity maſters as were employed in the buſineſs, with all the
officers of the navy, to reſolve on the time of launching,
which was generally concluded to be the Sunday following,
being October 14, and that I ſhould not attempt to ſtir her
before.   But the Saturday night, the wind chopping fair
Weſterly, promiſing a great tide, I cauſed the two maſters of
the navy to be ready, commanding all the hands we could
on ſudden to attend us, contrary to the mind of Mr. Cooke,
who was unwilling to meddle with the ſhip in the night.   But
Mr. Auſten, being the moſt reſolute man, was for taking
the firſt opportunity.   The tide came on ſo faſt that the ſhip
was afloat by three quarters flood ; ſo I ordered to heave her
out, which done, and the ſhip brought into the channel by
ſeveral warps, ſhe was got to her moorings, lights being
made all along the ſhore with reeds till the moorings were
made faſt to the bits ; which done, I ſent a meſſenger to Sir
Robert Manſel at Greenwich, who came aboard with all
ſpeed, and, according to his majeſty's order, called her *The
Sovereign of the Seas* *.   The next morning the Trinity maſters and others came to give their attendance, but finding the
ſhip at her moorings, they were much diſcontented, which
they expreſſed as much as they could.   This morning Sir
Robert Manſel rode poſt to his majeſty then at Hampton-
court, and acquainted him with our proceedings, with which
he was well pleaſed.   The week following we reared our

* See *The Royal Sovereign*, as ſtyled by Mr. Wilſon in Memoir of Britiſh Naval
Architecture, Archæol. vol. XI. p. 164.   And in the Liſts of the Navy, given at
p. 172. 174. there is, as I ſuſpect, another ſhip mis-named, viz. *Mer Honor*, becauſe in the Liſt of Peter he mentioned *M. Honor*, i. e. as I imagine, *The Sea's Glory*.

ſheers

sheers to set our masts, which were all done in fourteen days; and as soon as the rigging was fixed, and the sails at the yards, we removed from Woolwich to Erith for depth of water. His majesty had been on-board before she removed thence. The 6th of June following, his majesty, with the queen, the duchess of Sheverees, duke and duchess of Lenox, and divers other lords and ladies, came on-board the ship at Greenhithe, where they dined. At their going away we gave them seventeen guns. About the 11th of June the Sovereign weighed from Greenhithe, and anchored below Gravesend, where she rode till his majesty came on-board, which was July 21. Whilst his majesty was on-board, he observed the condition of the ship, how she rode ready to sail, the draught of water, distance of the lower tire of ports from the water, number of guns, and other circumstances, to her complete furnishing, with which he was mightily pleased. I had placed my then wife, Byland, Daughter Fenn, and many other gentlewomen, my special friends, in the great cabin, to kiss his majesty's hand; and prevailing with his majesty to go aft into the cabin, he most graciously gave each his hand to kiss. Then he took barge, and we saluted him with seventy-two guns.

Thursday morning, September 27, I took leave of my family at Chatham and rode to Gravesend, there took boat to Woolwich, where I stayed one night, and with my son Peter went by water to Kingston, where we lay in a private house, the inns being full. The next day we went by water to Hampton-court, where we presented ourselves to his majesty, who used us very graciously, where we spent all the day; at night returning to our lodgings at Kingston. The next morning we rode to Sion-house, to wait on the Lord Admiral, who presently commanded us to hasten to Chatham,

to

to prepare barges and boats to be sent to Dover to receive the Queen Mother expected there.

The Life of Mr. Phineas Pette is in the British Museum, among the Harleian MSS. vol 6279; but it was from a copy that the preceding extracts were made, and I am not apprized whether the transcript I had contained the whole of the original MS. Supposing the memoirs not to be brought down to a later period than the year 1637, there are, as I apprehend, ten years of the life of the writer that are unnoticed, because I am apt to believe, that he may be the person who is thus entered in the register belonging to the parish of Chatham.

Phineas Pette, esq. and captain, was buried 21st August, 1647.

At page 282 of these extracts a note is inserted respecting a ship called *Mer Honneur*. In the underwritten passages in the life of Mr. Pette this ship is thus mentioned.

The latter end of July, 1612, I received orders to take charge of the building of the Defiance, then in the dry dock at Woolwich, old Mr. Baker having the charge of re-building the *Mer Honneur*, at the same time, in the same dock. About the middle of August Mr. Baker sickened, and perceived it would be his death, and was determined to recommend me to the finishing of the *Mer Honneur*, and to this end importuned me to ride to Windsor to the Lord Admiral, to signify his earnest suit to his lordship first, which I willingly consented to, and had his lordship's warrant at the same time for it, he dying the last of the month. The 25th of March, 1613, it pleased God to preserve my life aboard *Honneur*, being only going from deck to deck, narrowly escaped falling into the

the hold, which would certainly have dafhed me to pieces.
The 14th of June, my honourable and implacable enemy,
lord Northampton, died at his houfe at Charing-crofs. The
1ft of Auguft, my gracious mafter king James, with the king
of Denmark, came to Woolwich, and went aboard the *Mer
Honeur*, that lying in the dry dock, and almoft finifhed;
which fhip pleafed them wonderfully. In the end of November, all the workmen that wrought on the *Mer Honeur*
were difcharged; the 6th the *Mer Honeur* and the Defiance
were both launched in one tide; and the 25th of April following both failed from Woolwich, and the next day came
to their moorings at Chatham.

" I am informed, writes Fuller, in his Worthies of England, under article Kent, that the myftery of fhipwrights
for fome defcents hath been preferved fucceffively in families,
of which the Pettes about Chatham are of fingular regard."

From Memoir on Britifh Naval Architecture, by Ralph
Willett, efq. Archæologia, vol. XI. article XVIII, p. 176.
Extract from Heywood the Hiftorian's defcription of the
Sovereign.

" The prime workman is captain Phineas Pette, overfeer
of the work, whofe anceftors, father, grandfather, and great
grandfather, for the fpace of two hundred years and upwards, have cont'nued in the fame name, officers and architects in the Royal Navy." As this fhip, obferves Mr. Willet,
was built in 1637, the account would carry fomething like a
regular eftablifhment as far back as 1437, the reign of king
Henry the Sixth. However, it is a remarkable account of this
family,

family, especially as I can farther add, that the same family made a distinguished figure in the same line, and the same office, in the king's yard to the end of William the Third. But to return to Heywood. "The master builder is young Mr. Pett, who, before he was twenty-five years of age, made the model, and perfected the work: the master carvers are John and Matthew Christmas, &c."

Quære. Was not Peter the fifth son of Phineas Pette, the young Mr. Pette alluded to by Mr. Heywood?

Of this son there is this notice in the MS Life of Mr. Pette. "1630, August 6, my wife was delivered of her fifth son."

See other notices of Peter in these extracts.

Copy of Passages in the Life of Mr. Phineas Pette, in which he has mentioned his relations.

I Phineas Pette, being the son of Mr. Peter Pette, of Deptford Strond, in the county of Kent, one of her majesty's shipwrights, was born in my father's dwelling-house in the same town, November 1, 1570.

In the year 1589, about the 6th of December, it pleased God to call to his mercy my revered loving father, whose loss proved afterwards my utter undoing almost, had not God been more merciful to me, for, leaving all things to my mother's directions, her fatal matching with a most wicked husband, one Mr. Thomas Nun, a minister, brought a general ruin to herself and family.

At Candlemas, 1599 (after leaving Emanuel college in Cambridge), I was contented, by the instant persuasion of my mother, to put myself to be an apprentice to become a shipwright, my father's profession, and was bound a covenant servant to one Mr. Richard Chapman of Deptford, one

of

of her majesty's master shipwrights, and one whom my father had bred of a child to that profession.

My eldest brother by my father's side, Mr. Joseph Pette, succeeded in my father's place, one of her majesty's master shipwrights; which preferment God brought him to, the better to have enabled him to have given his help to us, but we found clear contrary.

To my setting out to sea, in 1592, I found none of my kindred so kind as to help me with either money or cloaths, or any other comfort, only another brother I had by my father's side, Peter Pette, then dwelling at Wapping, that vouchsafed me lodging, meat, and drink, till the ship was ready to sail.

We, extreme poor, returned for Ireland into the river of Cork, and taking leave of both ship and voyage, I travelled to Diveling, to visit my uncle Thornton, and my brother Noah, being then master with him in the Popinjay of the queen's majesty, and presently after bent my course to England.

With some difficulty, I got to London three days before Christmas, 1594, having neither money nor apparel, and took up my lodging at my brother Peter Pette's house in Wapping, who, although I was returned very poor, yet vouchsafed me kind entertainment. The next day I presented myself to my brother Joseph, who received me very coldly, yet of his bounty sent me forty shillings to apparel myself. About 1594, it so fell out, that there were certain of his majesty's ships appointed to be made ready for the voyage of Sir Francis Drake and Sir John Hawkins, amongst which the Defiance was to be brought into Woolwich dock to be sheathed, which being committed to my brother Joseph's
care,

care, he was content to admit me, amongst many others, to
be one, where I was contented to take any pains to get something to apparel myself.

In 1593, the new building of the Triumph was appointed
to my brother Joseph's charge, with whom I a while continued, but finding him unwilling to prefer me in his work, as
next under him, with some passage of discontent betwixt us,
I left him.

After I was discharged from the Repulse, my brother Joseph entertained me at Woolwich upon the Triumph, which
ship I wrought till her launching, and the discharge of men
from her, and afterwards was employed at my brother's at
Linehouse, upon a small model for my Lord Treasurer's
house at Theobalds.

In the beginning of the year 1597, my dear and loving
mother deceased, at Wilton in Suffolk.

About Bartholomew next following, the Elizabeth Jonas
was brought into her majesty's dock at Woolwich, and there
was the first preferment my brother Joseph helped me to,
making me principal overseer of that business under him.
During all the time of this work, we both lodged and dined
at old Mr. Lydiard's in the yard.

I was married to my now wife Ann, the daughter of Richard Nichols, of Highwood Hill, in the parish of Hendon
in Middlesex, a man of good report, and honest stock, the
15th of May, 1598, at Stepney church.

Mr. Pette, under the year 1599, relates the very ill treat-
ment which his three sisters received after the death of their
mother from their father-in-law, Mr. Thomas Num, who,
for a very slight offence, furiously fell upon Abigail the eldest,
beating her so cruelly with a pair of tongs and a fire-brand,
that

that she died within three days after the beating. He mentions, that, upon complaint to a justice, the body, which had been privately buried, was taken up, and so, by the coroner's inquest which passed upon her, and miraculous tokens of the dead corpse, as fresh bleeding, sensibly opening one of her eyes, and other things, he was found guilty of her death, and so committed and bound over to answer the matter at the next general assizes to be held at Bury, which was in the Lent after. In his arraignment, Sir John Popham, then lord chief justice of England, and chief judge of that circuit, shewed such true justice, (notwithstanding great interest was made for him, not only by his friends, but by the clergy of that county), that all his cruelty and wicked proceedings were laid open, and he convicted of man-slaughter by the jury; was committed to sue for the king's pardon, from whence being shortly freed, by God's just revenging hand, he lived but a short time after.

Upon the occasion of my being placed at Chatham, in 1600, my brother Joseph and I were reconciled, and ever after lived together as loving brethren. By means of his encouragement, I took a lease of the mansion-house at Chatham for twenty-one years, paying £.25. income, which lease was sealed to me October 17. The 24th, having bestowed all my poor stock upon the lease of my house, and furnishing the same in some convenient manner, I shipped the same in a hoy of Raynam, and so moved to Chatham, myself going down in the hoy, where I missed a great danger, for, at the west end of the Nore, about three o'clock in the morning, about the 28th day, we were were likely to be surprized by a Dunkirk piccaroon full of men, who being at our passing by (although it was very dark) at an anchor, suddenly weighed and gave chase, and had boarded had not God prevented him

by our bearing up, the wind being at East, and running oor-
selves ashore within the Swatch, [quere, the Swale?]

1601, March 23, my wife was delivered of her first-born
son, John; died in 1628.

1603, March 18, my wife was delivered of her second son,
Henry; died September 22, 1612.

This year happened the great plague throughout England,
but especially at London. The sickness being very hot at
Chatham, upon the persuasion of some of my friends, I removed (August 16) my wife and children from thence to
my wife's father's, in Middlesex. They remained at Highwood Hill till the 3d of October.

I divers times solicited my brother to be joint-patentee
with him; but his remissness caused me to slip the opportunity.

1604, during my attendance at court as his grace's (the
prince of Wales's) captain of his ship, it pleased my honourable
Lord Admiral to give orders to Sir Thomas Windbank, one
of the clerks of the signet, to draw me a bill for the reversion
of Mr. Baker's, or my brother Joseph Pette's place, which
should first happen.

1605, my eldest brother, Joseph Pette, died November 19.
Presently after my brother's decease, it pleased my very good
lord, the Lord High Admiral, to grant his warrant for my
entrance into my brother's place, to the effect of my letters
patent.

1606, my third son, Richard Pette, born June 21.

1608, my fourth son, Joseph, born April 27.

1610, August 6, my wife was delivered of her fifth son;
[Quere, Peter?]

1611, My eldest and first daughter was born October 15.
[Quere, Anne?]

1614, October 9th, my wife delivered of a fon, Phineas; died October 18, 1617.

1617, April 15, my wife was fafely delivered of twins—daughters, Mary and Martha. Mary died November 21, 1617.

1618, January 24, my wife was delivered of a fon, Phineas.

1620, May 14, my wife was delivered of her eleventh child, the laft fhe had, a fon, Chriftopher.

1623, After the Prince and the reft of the fleet were all fitted and prepared for the voyage to Spain, the St. George and Antelope fell down to Gillingham, being both appointed to go before to St. Andrew, with the jewels and other provifions, the noble gentleman, my honourable friend, commanding her, whom my eldeft fon, John, attended as one of his retinue.

1625, July 14, my eldeft fon, John, was married to Katharine, the daughter of Mr. Robert Yardley, deceafed.

1627, February 14, being Wednefday, and Valentine's day, my dear wife Anne died in the morning, and was buried the Friday following in Chatham church, leaving behind her a difconfolate hufband, and fad family.

This fummer my fon was made captain of a merchant fhip, and ferved under Sir Sackville Trevor at taking the French fhip called the St. Efprit.

1627, in July, I was contracted to my fecond wife, Mrs. Sufan Yardley, Mr. Robert Yardley's widow; the 16th we were married at St. Margaret's, by Mr. Franklyn.

1622, July, my fon John was made captain of the Six Whelp, built by my coufin Peter Pette, making choice, by the Duke's leave, of any one of the ten fmall fhips built for the enterprize of Rochelle, with one deck and quarter only, to row as well as fail; I took that for my fon, fuppofing fhe would prove beft, but it fell out the contrary.

I re-

I received warrant from my lord duke *to go* to Portfmouth, there to haften the fleet out; which I did accordingly, taking my journey from Lambeth, August 1, having my fon Richard, &c. The 4th of September my fon John took leave of me in the evening, and went on-board his fhip, whom I never faw afterwards, he being unfortunately caft away in the return from Rochelle; both fhip and men perifhed in the fea, as was fuppofed foundered in the ftorm, which was a great affliction to myfelf, and his wife, left big with child. She was delivered of a fon, Phineas.

1629, November 27, my fon Richard died at Woolwich, and was buried in the church chancel the next day. He was my eldeft fon living, a very hopeful young man, and for his years an excellent artift, being bred up by me to my trade.

1633, April 11, my fon Peter made his firft vifit to Mr. Cole's eldeft daughter, of Woodbridge in Suffolk, whom he married. About the middle of Auguft my fon Peter had orders to prepare moulds for the frame of a new fhip of one hundred tons, to be built by him at Woolwich, and was ordered his timber out of the ftore of Shotover, Oxon.

1634, The Leopard built at Woolwich by his fon.

1634, in the month of February, the James, built by nephew Peter Pette, was launched at Deptford, his majefty being prefent, where I attended all the while.

1635, March 11, his majefty came to Woolwich to fee the new fhip built by my fon launched. She was named the Leopard.

1635, November 2, My fon Peter met me at Woolwich, where we gave orders for our proceedings in building the new great fhip (The Sovereign of the Seas).

1636, April 15, My daughter Martha was married at Chatham church to John, fome time my fervant, accompanied with the better fort of my neighbours, who were entertained

3   .   in

in the garden under a tent set up on purpose, where we dined and supped.

On the 21st of July, I brought my wife from Woolwich to Chatham, having been ill some weeks, but was then, to our thinking, very cheerful; but on Monday morning she fell into a sweet sleep, and so died, and was buried the next Wednesday. Mr.   preached her funeral sermon.

The 8th of September his wife sickened with a fever, being big with child, and the 19th she died. Her Christian name was Mildred, there being this entry concerning her in the parish register; " Mildred, wife of Phineas Pette, esq. was buried the 20th of September, 1638."

After the death of his dear wife Anne, Mr. Pette did not remain quite half a year a disconsolate widow; nor could many months have passed between his wife Susan's falling into a sweet sleep, and his marrying Mildred, whose surname and connections are omitted in the MS.

Sir Phineas Pette, who was resident commissioner of the navy at Chatham in the reign of Charles II *, was probably the son of Phineas Pette, mentioned by his father to have been born January 24, 1618. Sir Phineas was commissioner in 1667, the year in which the Dutch fleet sailed up the Medway and destroyed several ships. In the ensuing year he was impeached in the House of Commons, on a charge of inattention to the security of this harbour; but the Parliamentary prosecution was soon dropped, it being well known, that the culpable neglect was not in him, but in the king, who

* Dr. Wallis, in his letter, April 7, 1662, to Sir Robert Moray, prefixed to Consequences, or the Shipwright's Circular Wedge, mentions, that the solids and lines, made by the sections thereof, were proposed to his consideration by Mr. Pette, one of his majesty's commissioners for the navy, and an excellent shipwright.

had

had idly squandered the large sums of money granted for the national defence.

Peter Pette, the nephew, mentioned by his uncle Phineas as the builder of the James at Deptford in 1634 (Extracts, p. 292), was probably son of the kind brother, Peter Pette of Wapping, with whom the Memorialist occasionally boarded and lodged (Extracts, p. 210); and I am apt to believe the nephew, Peter, might be the father of Peter Pette, who was educated at St. Paul's school, and became afterwards a member of Sidney college in Cambridge, and of Pembroke and All Souls colleges in Oxford. He was also a student of the common law at Gray's Inn; and, being appointed advocate-general to king Charles the Second in Ireland, was chosen a member of the House of Commons in that kingdom, and at length received the honour of knighthood from James duke of Ormond, the Lord Lieutenant. In the account given of him by Mr. Knight in the Life of Dean Colet, p. 407, he is thus described:

" Peter Pette, son, grandson, and great grandson, of Peter Pette (which last, who was grandson of Peter Pette. of Cumberland, had been master-builder in the Navy Royal to queen Mary, and afterwards to queen Elizabeth), was born at Deptford in Kent, &c. &c.

Mr. Willett (see before, p. 285), from what Heywood, the historian, had advanced concerning the Pettes, has inferred, that of the family there were persons in a regular line of descent, who were shipbuilders of eminence in the service of the crown from the reign of Henry VI. to the end of the reign of William the Third. But, as I conceive, the passage just cited from Knight's Life of Dean Colet will not warrant the ascending to so early a period by near a century. For, if I rightly understand the parenthesis, it implies, that Peter Pette,

father

father of Joseph and of Phineas, as well as of Peter Pette, was master-builder to queens Mary and Elizabeth; and what is farther mentioned of Peter Pette the father is, that he was grandson of Peter Pette of Cumberland, without noticing what was the occupation of the grandfather. But, supposing the grandfather to have been a shipwright, is there any evidence of there being in the reign of Henry VI. or in the 15th century, any dock yard in Cumberland, in which he could have held the office of a principal naval architect to the king?

Extracts, p. 247. "I was called personally to answer, and *kneeled* right before his majesty, near the side of the table."

Page 249. "All this time I sat on my *knees*, baited by the great lord and his bandogs; albeit the prince's highness laboured to have me eased by standing up, but his majesty would not permit it."

"Page 255. "This day, as it was a very tedious day to me, by reason I was to answer all objections, and *kneel* so long together, &c."

To kneel, so as to rest the muscular part of the body on the heels, is a ceremony used in the East, as expressive of the greatest humiliation, and therefore suitable for a devout worshiper in a solemn act of devotion to his Creator. The propriety of this submissive and servile homage from man to his fellow-creature may, however, be thought very questionable, especially when, from the long continuance of it, it must be productive of much fatigue and pain, as was the case in this instance. But James was in his disposition and conduct more like a despotic Eastern potentate than the sovereign of a free people. To dispute what a king might do in the height of his power, as he told his parliament, was as seditious as it was blasphemous to dispute with God. And, though only presiding

siding on the trial of a shipbuilder on a charge of insufficiency, he could not forbear reminding his auditors, that he was in the seat of God, as his representative and substitute. Of the kind of homage he imposed upon the presumed delinquent, a contemporary monarch judged very differently, this anecdote being related of Gustavus Adolphus: "When the town of Landshut in Bavaria surrendered to him at discretion, the principal inhabitants fell down upon their knees before him on presenting to him the keys of their town. "Rise, rise," said he, "it is your duty to fall upon your knees to God, and not to so "frail and feeble a mortal as I am *.""

Page 163. "After midnight the weather was very sore o'er-cast, and a very sore gust of rain, thunder, and lightning, which made me doubt there were some *indirect practices among our enemies to dash our launching*."

Mr. Pette seems to have suspected, that his implacable adversaries might have invoked the wayward sisters, "with whom fair is foul, and foul is fair," to exercise their spells and charms in harassing him; nor ought his credulity to be a matter of surprize, as the influence of witchcraft was at that time a prevailing notion; and king James himself, who was by his courtiers termed the Solomon of the age, had contributed to strengthen a belief of this superstitious opinion, by his learned elaborate system of Dæmonologie.

In a person who has the honour of being F. S. A. it may be deemed somewhat invidious to observe, it was not a mark of the supereminent wisdom of this prince, that he had so unfavourable an opinion of Antiquaries as to suppress their original Society soon after his accession to the throne †.

SAMUEL DENNE.

* European Magazine, July, 1794. p. 35.
† Archæol. vol. I. Introduction, p. xiv.

XXIV. *A Letter to Sir* Joseph Banks, K. B. *Bart. President of the Royal Society, Fellow of the Society of Antiquaries,* &c. *concerning the Lives and Writings of various* Anglo-Norman *Poets of the* 12th *Century. By the* Abbé de la Rue.

Read February 4, 1796.

SIR,

I Have already intimated, in my Diſſertation upon the Works of Robert Wace, that the French are indebted to England, and its monarchs, for the moſt eminent poets that we know of in their language. It will be the purpoſe of that which I have now the honour to preſent you with, to expatiate more at large upon this fact ; not that I undertake to decide upon a queſtion oftentimes diſcuſſed, but never yet reſolved, concerning the original founders of the French Parnaſſus. I ſhall not diſpute with the natives of Picardy the honour which has been conferred on them by Monſieur Fontenelle [a] ; nor attempt to deprive the Troubadours of the palm which the Abbé Millet has adjudged to them [b] ; and, though myſelf a Norman, I ſhall not unite with Monſieur de la Ravallière in demonſtrating, that my coun-

[a] Fontenelle, Hiſt. du Theatre Français, vol. III. p. 11. edit. of 1758.
[b] Millet, Hiſt. des Troubadours.

Q q trymen

trymen have been the fathers of French poetry [*r*]. It little
becomes me to lay down a positive opinion upon so important a subject. With respect to Monsieur de Fontenelle, I
shall only remark, that it was not sufficient to advance opinions without proof or foundation, as he has done. Before
he could expect the public to adopt them, he ought to have
maintained their accuracy, either by monuments left by the
poets of Picardy, and anterior to those of the poets of other
provinces, or at least by some kind of historical evidence.

To the Abbé Millot I shall readily acknowledge, that his
Troubadours are indeed of great antiquity; but then they
wrote in a language which never was that of the French nation; and therefore his great learning, and generous efforts in favour of the Provençals, can never operate in di-
minution of the merit or antiquity of the Norman and Anglo-
Norman Poets.

And, lastly, I shall beg leave to observe to M. de la Ra-
valliere, that although the evidence of history, and the remains of Norman and Anglo-Norman poetry, equally valuable and numerous, attest to us, that even in very antient
times those people had penetrated into the sanctuary of the
Muses, yet these proofs in their favour amount, after all, but
to strong probabilities; to which I shall add, that in order to
judge decisively in this case, it becomes necessary above all
things to shew, that the other provinces of France, where
their language was used, had not likewise *their* particular
poets, and that time has not deprived us of their works and
of those of such historians as might have noticed them: in
a word, that without this certainty the celebrated question,

[r] Poësies du Roi de Navarre, vol I. pp. 166, 196, 261, & 262.

con-

concerning the original cultivators of the French Muse, can never be determined.

But, as in the present instance even mere probabilities contribute greatly to the honour of a nation, which, in those obscure ages, produced men in whose compositions the Muses were by no means neglected, I have thought it incumbent upon me, Sir, to present you with the fruits of my researches relating to several of the Anglo-Norman poets of the 12th century.

The Normans imported with them from the North a peculiar taste for poetry; and, from the moment in which Neustria was ceded to them by Charles the Simple, they began to familiarize themselves with the language of the country, and to transplant it into their songs. Of this it is easy to find proofs in almost all the ages which followed this event; for, although these ancient monuments of French literature are no more, history has very carefully preserved their remembrance.

A long time before the Conquest, Thibaut de Vernon, canon of Rouen, translated into French verse the lives of Wandril, and many other saints held in reverence by the Normans [d]. The minstrel Taillefer, at the head of the Norman army, announced the moment of the celebrated battle of Hastings, by chanting the song of Charlemagne and Roland; and, repeating this composition, the troops marched on to victory [e]. After the combat, again did the Normans express by songs their love for their victorious leader; and in this manner celebrated his triumphs [f]. When the conqueror divided with his followers the fruits of his victory, a

[d] Acta ord. St Bened. vol. III. p. 379.
[e] Polychron. Ranulph. Higden, lib. III.
[f] Gul. Pictae. Hist. apud. Duchesne, p. 193.

minstrel

minstrel named Berdic, and attached to the court, was rewarded with the gift of three parishes in Gloucestershire [g].

Under the reign of William Rufus we only find *Sirventes*, or *Serventois*, a sort of satyrical songs, made by the Normans against Arnold of Caen, then chaplain to Robert Courthose, and afterwards patriarch of Jerusalem [h].

Under Henry I. the poets were rewarded, by his queen Matilda, with the most splendid presents, according to the testimony of William of Malmsbury [i]. At the same period, according to Robert Wace, the Norman poets sang the atchievements of their antient dukes ; and the same author has related many historic facts which he had collected from them in his infancy [k].

Under this prince also these minstrels, as we are informed by Ordericus Vitalis, recited the life of St. William ; and, as they had changed many facts in it by virtue of a poetical licence, the historian declares, that he had corrected and restored them after a manuscript of Antony of Winchester [l]. About the year 1112, when the Chevalier de Bechadie de Lastour in Limousin was desirous of writing in French verse his poem on the taking of Jerusalem, he consulted above all men Gaubert the Norman, both with respect to his style and the vulgar tongue, which he had made choice of for the purpose of presenting his work to the public ; a proof that Normandy was then in possession of men celebrated for this employment [m].

[g] Domesday book, Glouces.   [h] Gesta Dei per Francos, p. 180.
[i] Will. Malmsb. Hist. lib. i.
[k] Wace, Roman de Guillaume Longue espée.
[l] Ord. Vital. Hist. p. 598.
[m] L'Aubé, Nova Bibl. vol. II. p. 296.

And,

And, laſtly, the Chevalier Luc de la Barre had the boldneſs to write a ſatire againſt Henry I. for which the enraged prince cauſed his eyes to be put out; a dreadful puniſhment, but which ſerves to ſhew either an exceſſive fear of ridicule in the monarch, or the dangerous conſequences that might reſult from ſatire amongſt a people who delighted ſo much in poetry [*n*].

It is to be lamented, that time has deprived us of the works of theſe authors during the firſt age of French poetry; it has even obliterated almoſt all their names; and it is only during the early part of the 12th century, that we begin to diſcover any of the monuments left by the Anglo-Norman poets. According to the beſt of our ability, we ſhall detail theſe in chronological order.

PHILIPPE de THAN.

Philippe de Than, or, as the name was then written, *Philip de Thaun,* or *de Thaon,* is the moſt ancient Anglo-Norman poet whoſe works have reached us. We believe this author to have been of the ancient family of the lords of Than, proprietors of the eſtate of that name, three leagues from Caen, in the dioceſe of Bayeux.

The firſt work of this poet is intituled *Liber de Creaturis;* it is a treatiſe of practical chronology in French verſe. The author treats of days, of weeks, of ſolar and lunar months, of the phaſes of the moon, of eclipſes, of the ſigns of the Zodiac, and in general of all that is neceſſary for the intelligence of eccleſiaſtical computations. He explains, with tole-

[*n*] Order. Vital. Hiſt. p. 180.

rable precifion, the various calculations of the Jews, the
Greeks, and the Romans, the history of the calendar of
Numa Pompilius, and that of its reform by Julius Cæfar ; he
often cites Pliny, Ovid, Macrobius, St. Augustine, St. Gregory, venerable Bede, &c. ; he relates the various opinions
of thofe authors, who, like himfelf, had laboured at ecclefiaftical computations, but whofe works have not come down
to us, or have remained in libraries, fuch as Johannes de
Garlandia, Turkill, Hilperic, Nembroch, &c.

Philippe de Than compofed this work for the ufe of the
clergy, and dedicated it to Humphry de Than his uncle,
chaplain to Hugh, fenefchal to the king. This Hugh could
only have been Hugh Bigod, fenefchal to Henry I. and afterwards earl of Norfolk. His father, Roger Bigod, came to
England with the Conqueror, and had been fenefchal to that
monarch, as well as to his fon Henry [*o*] : but, as he died in
1107, and his fon Hugh immediately fucceeded him in that
office [*p*], we are of opinion, that the work of Philippe de
Than muft be placed after that period ; and the rather, becaufe he does not beftow the title of earl upon Hugh Bigod ;
an honour, which he did not acquire until a long time afterwards, but only that of fenefchal. Humphry de Than is
called his chaplain ; and it is well known, that from that
period it was the cuftom of the Englifh barons to have chaplains, who were particularly attached to them [*q*].

The fecond work of Philippe de Than is intituled *Beftiarius.*
It is a treatife in French verfe upon beafts, birds, and precious ftones. It is dedicated to queen Adelaide of Louvain,

[*o*] Wace, Roman de Guill. I.   [*p*] Order. Vital. Hift. p. 833.
[*q*] Kennet's Parochial Antiquities and Gloffary, v. *Capellanus.*

4   whom

whom Henry I. married in 1121; so that this work is to be placed after that period. The Benedictines fix it about the year 1125; but in the course of its perusal we have perceived nothing which contributes to ascertain this date with precision. Without any hazard of contradiction therefore, a date, either anterior or posterior to that presumed by the Benedictines, may be assigned to it.

Philippe de Than, with respect to a great part of this work, performs only the office of a translator. He allows that he had extracted his ideas from a treatise called *le Bestiare*, written first in Latin, and of which a manuscript copy in that language is to be found in the library of Mr. Douce, a member of the Society of Antiquaries.

In translating this work into French verse, the poet seems to have had no other motive than the instruction of mankind, and the correction of their morals. After having described the particular character of each beast and bird, he deduces from every description a moral, which is always adapted to excite his readers to the practice of civil and religious virtues. In a word, throughout all his designs, he endeavours at once to instruct and improve mankind, whilst he developes the most interesting particulars of natural history.

With respect to the kind of poetry which Philippe de Than has used, we believe it would be difficult to find any authors who have adopted it. His method does not consist in making one line rhime with another, but one half with the other half; or what may be called two hemistichs, as in the following verses of his first work;

" Al busuin est truved, lami é epruved,
Unches ne sud ami, qui al busuign failli.

Pur.

Por cel di ne targez, racs ma raifon oiez ;
Prei vos del ciculter, e puis del amender."

Or in thefe verfes of his fecond work, in which he deferibes the addrefs of the hedgehog in carrying off the grapes from the vine :

" El tens de vendenger, lores munte alpalmer,
La u la grappe veit, la plus meure feit,
Sin abat le raifin, mult li eft mal veifin,
Puis del palmer defcent, fur les raifins feftent,
Puis defus fe volupe, ruunt cume pelote,
Quant eft tres ben charget, les raifins enbrocet,
Eifli pofte pulture, a fes fiz **par nature.**"

It appears that our poet had borrowed his tafte from the Latin verfifiers of his time, who, for the moft part, wrote in this bad ftyle. Of this we may be eafily convinced by reading the poem of Marbodius bifhop of Rennes upon St. Mary the Egyptian ; his verfes on Odo bifhop of Bayeux, &c. [r] ; or the elegy of Serlon Paris, canon of Bayeux, addreffed to the fame Odo upon his quitting the prifon in which he had been five years confined by the Conqueror ; his fatire againft Gilbert abbot of Caen ; his poem on the fiege of Bayeux in 1106 [s] ; or, laftly, in going through all thefe epitaphs compofed by the Norman and Anglo-Norman poets of the 11th and 12th centuries, which are to be found in Dumouftier, Sandford, and Ducarel [t].

Both the works of Philippe de Than are to be found in the Britifh Mufeum among the Cotton MSS. Nero A.V. That relating to ecclefiaftical **computation** is, with refpect to **a**

[r] Edit. Cotton. Vitell. A. XII.　　　　[s] Ibid.

[t] Neuftria pia, paffim. Gervaf. Hift. of the Kings of England, paffim. Anglo-Norman Ant. 3 p. &c.

large

large part of it, at the beginning and end of a MS belonging to the library of the duke of Norfolk in that of the Royal Society, N° 230.

The Benedictines have taken upon them to criticife this author without having even read him, or known any thing relating to him, but from the notice of his works in the catalogue of the Cotton MSS, fol. 48. Hence very much uncertainty, and even miftakes, in their opinion of this writer. At firft, not comprehending the word *Thaonenfis*, they conceived it fhould be read *Toarcenfis*; they have confequently intitled Philippe de Than, *Philippe de Thouars*; and, inftead of a Norman, have made him a Poitevin [1].

Upon farther reflection, however, and perceiving at the fame time their correction of the Cotton manufcript was too hafly, and founded upon a mere conjecture, which could not be fupported by any kind of proof, they have admitted that the addition of *Than*, which had only appeared extraordinary to them from being mifunderftood, ought to remain; but having difcovered a charter of the 12th century, in which Thomas de Than was named as a witnefs, with feveral other noblemen [2], they concluded that this Thomas was either the fon or grandfon of our poet; and, as the charter which he had fo witneffed related to the eftate of Combourg in Bretagne, upon the confines of Normandy, they have declared, that there was reafon to believe Philippe de Than was a Breton [3].

From what has been faid then, it will be perceived that many conjectures have been fhewn to be ill-founded; but,

[1] Hiâ. Litter. de la France, vol. IX. pp. 173, 190.
[2] Martene Thefaur. Anecd. vol. I. p. 624.
[3] Hift. Litter. de la France, vol. X. p. LXII.

with a very trifling knowledge of the ancient French poets,
one may discover in every page, that the Benedictines were
entirely ignorant of this branch of our literature, and that
their criticisms upon most of the other poets are equally superficial with those upon Philippe de Than.

SAMSON de NANTEUIL.

This poet translated the Proverbs of Solomon into French
verse, with a metrical gloss far more ample than the text.
He appears, in his prologue, to have been a man well versed
in the knowledge of authors of the purest Latinity, and delighting above all things in the works of morality left us by
the ancients. He consequently often cites Horace, Cicero,
Juvenal, &c. as authors very familiar to him.

He composed this translation of the Proverbs at the instance of Adelaide de Condé, whom he calls his *lady*, and for
whom he professes as much attachment as he does respect
for her virtues. She was the wife of Osbert de Condé, and was
the owner of Horncastle in Lincolnshire [*u*]. She lived under
Henry I. and Stephen, and, as well as her son Roger de
Condé [*w*], gave many benefactions to the priory of St. Mary
at Rufford in 1148. Her castle was rased at the end of the
reign of Stephen [*x*]; and in the first year of Henry II.
Horncastle fell into the hands of the king, who gave it to
Gerbaud de l'Escaut, a Flemish knight [*y*]; so that the pe-

[*u*] Mon. Angl. vol. II. p. 645. Camden's Britannia, by Gough, vol. II.
p. 229.   [*w*] Thoroton's Nottingham, p. 330.
      [*x*] Camden, loco citato.   [*y*] Rot. Fin. 6 Hen III.

riod

riod in which Samfon de Nanteuil compofed his works muft be placed under the reign of Stephen.

This writer ufed only verfes of eight fyllables ; and, as his mind was wrapped up in works of morality, his ftyle is almoft always fententious. This may be feen by the beginning of his prologue ;

> " A tort fe lait murir de faim,
> Ki afez at è blé et pain ;
> Turner li pot lum a perefce
> Se ne fen paift u a feblefce ;
> Sil fameillet è ne fe paiffe,
> E par defileing murir fe laiffe,
> De cels eft dunc, fi cum jeo crei.
> Ki al mulin muerent de fei.
> Pur nent irreit conquere en France,
> Ki fuffraite at en habundance, &c."

This work is in the Britifh Mufeum among the Harleian MSS, N° 4388.

GEOFFROI GAIMAR.

This poet is known only by a hiftory of the Anglo-Saxon kings written in French verfe, and continued to the reign of William Rufus. In my differtation upon the Life and Writings of Robert Wace, I had afferted after Mr. Tyrwhiet [a], that this poet had had a continuator of his Brut in Geoffrey Gaimar ; and, confequently, that the latter wrote after the

[a] Canterbury Tales, vol. IV. p. 62.

former.

former. But, in examining myself the history of the Anglo-Saxon kings by Gaimar, I discovered that this work is anterior by several years to the history of the British Kings by Wace.

In the first place, Gaimar assures us, that in order to compose his Anglo-Saxon history, he had been obliged to collect materials for it during a considerable time; to resort for them to Latin, French, and English, manuscripts; and that he had found much difficulty in procuring them : he even confesses, that he should have never succeeded unless Constance Fitz-Gilbert had assisted him in his researches. He informs us, that this lady sent to Hamlake, in Yorkshire, to a then celebrated baron named *Walter Espee*, for the purpose of engaging him to borrow from Robert of Caen earl of Gloucester, the history of the British Kings, which he had caused to be translated from the books of the Welch. This work the earl lent to Walter, and he to Ralph Fitz-Gilbert, who put it into the hands of Constance his wife [*a*].

We find then, that Geoffrey Gaimar composed his work chiefly from others translated from Welch manuscripts. But as Walter Espee died in 1153 [*b*], Robert earl of Gloucester, in 1147, or, according to others, in 1146 [*c*], and Wace did not write his Brut till 1155, we are to look upon the work of Gaimar as anterior to that of Wace, and with reason to conclude, that the former author cannot be considered as the continuator of the latter.

In short, what serves completely to demonstrate the truth of this opinion is, that Geoffrey Gaimar speaks of queen Ade-

[*a*] Gaimar, at the end of his Anglo-Saxon History, Bibl. Reg. 13 A. XXI.

[*b*] Dugdale's Baronage, vol. I. p. 590.

[*c*] Bishop Lloyd's Letter on Geoffrey of Monmouth, p. 72.

laide

laide of Louvain as then living; and we know from the chronicle of Thomas Wikes, that she died in 1151 [d]. Besides, the poet assures us at the end of his Anglo-Saxon history, that he had been more than a year in composing it from the various manuscripts which he had borrowed, and therefore it is more than probable, that his work should have at least preceded one year the death of the earl of Gloucester.

It must not be concealed, however, that in the only manuscript of the works of Gaimar that we know of, and which is preserved in the British Museum, Bibl. Reg. 13 A. xxi. Wace's Brut is placed at the beginning, and followed by Gaimar's Anglo-Saxon history. But the history of the British Kings ought naturally to precede that of the Anglo Saxon; and accordingly this arrangement is properly adopted by the transcriber of the manuscript, and there is no reason to infer upon this account that Gaimar wrote after Wace. An exact copyist, without attending to the ages of the authors, would in the first instance transcribe into his manuscript the work of Wace, which deduced the history of England from its beginning, and then insert that of Gaimar, which was a necessary and indispensable addition.

Again, if we minutely examine in the manuscript before cited, the part belonging to Gaimar, it will be impossible not to perceive more and more that he could never have been regarded as a continuator of Wace. Indeed, he formally declares at the end of his work, that he had begun it with the Conquest of the Golden Fleece by Jason; and, as in what remains he only begins with the reign of the first Anglo-Saxon king, we may conclude that he had translated the history of the British kings into French verse, as well as that of the.

[d] Tanner, Notitia Monast. p. 557.

Anglo-

Anglo-Saxons; and that we do not poſſeſs a complete copy of his work.

Another reaſon, no leſs ſtrong in itſelf, will ſerve to eſtabliſh this fact. The poet aſſures us that the Brut of Walter archdeacon of Oxford, tranſlated into Latin by Geoffrey of Monmouth, had been much *amended*; this is his expreſſion in his own work; that he had corrected it by two manuſcripts which he cites, and of which we know nothing more, that is to ſay, a hiſtory of Wincheſter, and a book written in Engliſh, called *The Book of Waſſinburc* [e]. Now, to have thus corrected the archdeacon of Oxford's Brut, Gaimar muſt neceſſarily have written concerning the hiſtory of the Britiſh Kings: for, to ſay that an author's work has been corrected, is as much as to declare, that either new facts have been inſerted, or thoſe rectified which were before inaccurate; and to add, that in correcting it, a tranſlation has been made into French verſe, amounts to a poſitive aſſertion, that the ſame work has not merely been uſed, but a new one made.

In ſhort, if the beginning of the hiſtory of the Anglo-Saxon kings by Gaimar be attentively examined, his opinion will appear to be, that it ought to be preceded by his hiſtory of the Britiſh Kings; of which he reſumes the laſt recitals, in order to connect them with the new details which he is about to give; he recalls them to his reader's attention, to appriſe him of the affinity between the two hiſtories; but unfortunately the alluſion to the firſt part of his work is the only remembrance of it that has been preſerved. The tranſcriber of the manuſcript in the royal library, for ſome reaſon that is not apparent, preferred copying the Brut of Wace to that of

[e] Waſſingburgh, in Lincolnſhire.

Gaimar;

Gaimar; and, as the former had only tranflated the hiftory of the Britifh Kings, the copyift completed the work by adding the Anglo-Saxon hiftory of the latter.

Amongft the fources reforted to by Gaimar for compofing his two hiftories, we have already mentioned the Brut, the Hiftory of Winchefter, and the Englifh Book of Wafhinburgh. He alfo cites Bede and Gildas, and mentions John of Beverley; but we are ftill ignorant of the French and Welch books, of which he only fpeaks generally, and in which he tells us he had found many hiftorical facts.

As the fecond part of his work extends only to the reign of William Rufus, he announces, that it had been his intention to add the hiftory of Henry I. his fucceffor; but that the materials being very ample, he defigned to write it feparately, and upon a much more extenfive fcale than had already been done by other hiftorians. We are not informed whether the poet performed his promifed tafk; but no feparate hiftory of Henry I. in French verfe is now remaining that we know of.

Amongft the things worthy of remark which have been related by Geoffry Gaimar, it is incumbent on us to notice, as particularly connected with the Norman poets, the ideas he has furnifhed us with concerning the profeffion of the minftrels in William the Conqueror's army. The office of Taillefer was not alone confined to the finging of the fong of Charlemagne and Roland at the head of the Norman army; the poet informs us, that advancing on horfeback towards that of the Englifh, the minftrel three times caft on high his lance in the air, and received it as often by the point; that the fourth time he threw it againft his enemies, one of whom he wounded; that afterwards, he drew his fword, and, darting it

6   2s.

as before three times in the air, he caught it again with such address, that his adversaries could not help regarding these flights of hand as miraculous, and the effect of enchantment; that at length, after these manœuvres, he galloped full-speed towards the army of the enemy, and, precipitating himself amidst the ranks, he laid on furiously upon each side of him, thereby giving to the Normans the signal of battle.

The verses made use of by this writer are in lines of eight syllables. His style is much more clear than that of preceding poets, and his diction simple and fluent, as in the following verses, wherein he describes the dexterity of the minstrel Taillefer in throwing and catching his lance and sword.

" Armes aveit et bon cheval,
Si est hardiz e noble vassal,
Devant les altres cil se mist,
Devant Engleis merveilles fist;
Sa lance prist par le tuet,
Com si co fust un bastunet,
Encontre mont halt la geta,
Et par le fer receue la
Trais fez iffi geta fa lance,
La quarte feiz mult pres favance;
Entre les Engleis la lanea,
Parmi le cors un en naffra.
Puis treist s'espee, arere vint,
Geta s'espee kil tint,
Encountre mont puis la receit,
Lun dit al altre ki co veit
Ke co esteit enchantement,
Ke cil fefait devant la gent,
Quant treiz faiz out gete l'espee," &c.

DAVID.

D A V I D,

A poet contemporary with the former, and who lived, like him, under Stephen; but his writings have not come down to us. We know him only from the very honourable mention made of him by Geoffrey Gaimar at the end of his history of the Anglo-Saxon kings. According to this author's testimony, David composed an abridgment of the Life of Henry I. in French verse, which appears to have been undertaken by the desire of Adelaide of Louvain, the second wife of that king. Gaimar informs us, that he had seen some of the poet's verses set to music.

Although David was an excellent *trouveur*, according to Gaimar; although his poems were dispersed every where, read with delight by queen Adelaide, and held in such repute, that Constance Fitz-Gilbert had been obliged to pay a mark of silver, *ars et pese* [*f*], to have them transcribed; nevertheless Gaimar reproaches him for having forgotten many things, the remembrance of which would have done great honour to the king's memory.

He also admonishes him to revise his work, and tells him, that, should he decline it, he will himself take up his pen, and publish a more ample life of Henry, whom he styles the best of kings, whose virtues, nobleness of mind, magnificence, and a thousand other actions that would immortalize him, he wishes to see detailed with more splendor than they ever had been.

[*f*] *i. e.* Tried by fire as to the alloy, and weighed. T.

We know not whether David yielded to the preſſing ſolicitations of Gaimar, or if the latter, upon his refuſal, celebrated more at large the actions and deſerts of Henry Beauclerk ; at leaſt, except the work cited by Gaimar, we are not acquainted with any French poetry upon this ſovereign which has fallen from the pen of either of theſe writers.

B E N O I T.

He lived under Henry II. This king, according to the teſtimony of Robert Wace, had injoined him to tranſlate into French verſe the hiſtory of the dukes of Normandy. A taſk ſo flattering leads us to imagine, that he was already known by other works, in which he had diſplayed a diſtinguiſhed talent for poetry. Wace, emulous to deprive him of the glory of the undertaking, haſtily compoſed his ſeveral Romances of the dukes of Normandy, which he had already brought down to duke Richard II. and completed the hiſtory of the dukes of that province a long time after Benoît had finiſhed his. But the latter, far from giving up a race wherein his rival had already got the ſtart of him, redoubled his ardour, and fulfilled the wiſhes of the monarch.

His work begins with the irruption of the firſt Normans under the conduct of Haſting and Bier, ſurnamed *Ironſide*. The author paſſes on to Rollo firſt duke of Normandy, and to his ſon Longſword, and connects their hiſtory. That of duke Richard I. forms a ſeparate work ; thoſe of duke Richard II. Richard III. Robert, and William the Baſtard, likewiſe conſtitute particular works ; and, laſtly, thoſe of the three children of William are united in one.

6   The

The collection which forms thefe various hiftories confifts of nearly 23,000 lines of eight fyllables. The author often prefents us with certain turns and images which are truly poetical. Of this an idea may be formed by his defcription of Spring, at the beginning of which Rollo quitted England for Neuftria.

> " Quant li ivers fu trepaffez,
> Vint li duls tens e li eftez,
> Venta l'aure fuevè e quoie,
> Chanta li merles e la treie ;
> Bois reverdirent e prael,
> E gent florirent li ramel,
> Parut la rofe buen olanz,
> E altres flors de maint femblanz."

Benoît frequently obferves, in the courfe of his work, that he had no other object for its publication than the pleafure of Henry II. He celebrates the love which this prince had for the Belles Lettres, and his elegant and refined tafte in judging of the merits of the writers of his age ; and concludes his account of the firft irruption of the Normans with the following lines :

> " Avantage ai en ceft labur,
> Que al foverain e al meillur,
> Elefit, tranflat, truis e rimei,
> Qui el mund fei de nule lei ;
> Qui meux connift oevre bien dite,
> E bienfeant e bien efcrite,
> Deus mi dont faire fon plaifir,
> Kar ceft la riens que plus defir."

It

It is eafy to afcertain the time in which this poet compofed his hiftories of the dukes of Normandy, by means of Robert Wace, who fpeaks of him as his contemporary. Both thefe writers mention the tranflation of the body of duke Richard II, which Henry II. caufed to be made to the abbey of Fef-camp in 1161 [g]; fo that each muft have written after that period. Wace, in another place, mentions, that he had feen the young prince Henry, fon of Henry II, crowned king; which event not having taken place before 1170 [b], it muft have been fubfequent to that year that Benoit finifhed his hiftories of the dukes of Normandy.

Mr. Warton has afferted, that this work abounds with fa-bulous and romantic events [i]; but it was incumbent upon him to have brought fome proofs in fupport of an opinion, which, without them, appears to us to be entirely given at random. Indeed, if this author be compared with the hif-torians who have preceded him, fuch as Dudo of St. Quintin, William of Jumieges, William of Poitiers, Ordericus Vitalis, &c. we fhall find, throughout his work, the moft exact con-formity with thofe writers, both in his narrations, and the connection of his facts. Wace himfelf, although a rival, coincides with him in hiftorical details. It is true, that he has the advantage of him in a clearer and concifer diction; but, on the other hand, we find in Benoit information as curious as it is extenfive concerning the manners and cuf-toms of the Normans; the court of their dukes; their cof-tume, and the ornaments of their palaces; their public and domeftic life; and, in fhort, upon an infinite variety of other

[g] Chron. Norm. apud Duchefne, p. 598.
[b] Rog. Hoveden Annal. ad an. 1170. Edit. Savile.
[i] Warton's Hiftory of English Poetry, vol. II. p. 235.

fub-subjects, of which not the slightest knowledge can be collected from any other source.

It must be owned that we have not ourselves been able to discover in Benoit's work more fables than are usually met with in the writers of that age. He has put into French verse what had been written in Latin before his time, and even in the age he lived in. When he departs from other historians, it is solely for the purpose of describing more fully the manners and character of the Norman nation, and its leaders; and even upon this occasion his work becomes more interesting. It is impossible, for instance, to read without the most lively emotions the recital of the loves of duke Robert and Harlotta, the mother of the Conqueror. Of their first interview Benoit has left us a detail so much the more impressive, as it describes the extreme simplicity of the manners of that age. In a word, this poet is the *only* writer who has preserved these valuable memorials of the birth of William the Bastard; and we are persuaded, that Mr. Warton has pronounced his opinion of this author in a manner which at least induces a supposition, that he has not understood him.

Benoit's history of the dukes of Normandy is among the Harleian manuscripts, N° 1717. It has remained unknown to all the French writers who have treated of the ancient poets. At the end of this manuscript there is a song, or rather canticle, set to music, upon the advantages of the crusade. It is an invitation to the barons to take up the cross. There is no indication for what Crusade it was composed, but the style proves it to be of the time of Benoit, that is, near the end of the reign of Henry II, or the beginning of that of Richard Cœur de Lion. As it is found at the end of the works of our poet, it may readily be ascribed to him; nor do we think, that

in

in adopting this opinion we incur any rifque of deviating
from the truth.   Befides, it is certainly the moft ancient fpecimen of this fort of poetry that has been tranfmitted to us
by the Anglo-Normans.   This canticle is compofed of feven
ftanzas, and each ftanza of feven mafculine verfes of ten feet ;
the four firft verfes of every couplet confift of mixed rhimes ;
but the rhime is always the fame in each couplet.   It is a
piece that has efcaped the refearches of the learned Dr. Burney, in his Hiftory of Englifh Mufic.   Mr. de la Borde, in his
Effays upon Ancient and Modern Mufic, has not exhibited
any thing of this kind in the French language of equal antiquity.   If Mr. Warton had been acquainted with this canticle, as well as with the fongs in the Royal Library, 16 E. viii.
in the Harleian manufcripts, N° 3775, &c. he would not have
afferted fo pofitively, that all the works of the Anglo-Norman *Trouveurs* perifhed with the ancient caftles of thofe barons for whofe pleafure they were compofed.

The fong upon the crufade, which we imagine to have
been compofed by Benoit, contains fome ftanzas which indicate a rich and brilliant imagination, that could upon occafion affume even a fublime ftyle, although the author had but
a harfh and almoft barbarous language, wherein to convey his ideas.   Of this an opinion may be formed from the
following ftanza :

> " Cunte ne duc, ne li rois corune,
> Ne fe poent de la mort deftolir,
> Kar quant il unt grant trefor amaffe,
> Plus lur convient a grant dolor guerpir,
> Miels lur venift en bon vis departir,
> Kar quant il unt en la terre bute,
> Ne lur valt puis ne chatel ne cite."

We

We cannot prevail on ourselves to agree with the learned Mr. Tyrwhitt, that amongst the works of Benoit is to be reckoned a Life of Thomas Becket, Archbishop of Canterbury, in French verse, still remaining among the Harleian manuscripts, N° 3775. The author of this piece appears to have been an English monk, likewise named Benoit. The style and form of it oblige us to place it as low as the reign of Edward III [*k*].

Still, however, as we have before remarked, in order to have induced Henry II. to invest Benoit with the glorious task of composing, in French verse, the History of the Dukes of Normandy, it became necessary that the poet should have been previously recommended by distinguished talents, and, of course, by such works as would have intitled him to be classed amongst men of letters. A life of Thomas Becket would not, most assuredly, have recommended him to the monarch; and the poem upon the Crusade, of which we have just spoken, does not appear to us a sufficient claim whereon to found a literary reputation; a song could but at best give a very slight idea of a man's talents; and Benoit would necessarily have begun with works of more importance to induce the king to honour him with the office of the French Historian of the dukes of Normandy.

Under this persuasion, we do not hesitate to consider him as the author of the History of the wars of Troy in French verse. It is true, however, that, in the beginning of this work, the author styles himself Benoit de Sainte More.

" Ceste hystoire n'est pas usee,
    Ne en gaires de lieu trouvee,

> Ja retraite ne fuſt encore,
> Mais Beneois de Sainte More ;
> La comencie et faite et dite
> Et a ſes mains la toute eſcrite."

But the ſurname of St. More does not invalidate our opinion. It is clear, that there was a family of this name in England under the reign of Henry II. The chronicle mentioned by Leland cites Hugh, William, and Jocelin de St. More [*l*]. Beſides, the poet ſimply calls himſelf Benoit in the body of the work which we aſcribe to him, as well as in his Hiſtory of the Dukes of Normandy.

> " Des or porreis oir hui mes,
> La treſime bataille apres,
> Beneois qui l'eſtoire a dite,
> Oies coment il la deſcrite."

Neither this poet, or his writings, were known to Fauchet. Mr. Galland, in ſpeaking of this hiſtory of the Wars of Troy, places it after the Brut of England, by Wace ; and we believe this chronology to be ſufficiently exact. He cites two paſſages from this poem, but with extreme inaccuracy, as will appear from a compariſon with thoſe we have tranſcribed [*m*]. Mr. Warton has copied Mr. Galland's quotations, but without correcting them after the manuſcript in the Britiſh Muſeum, which we may therefore preſume could not have been known to him [*n*].

The Hiſtory of the Wars of Troy, by Benoit, is to be found amongſt the Harleian manuſcripts, N° 4482. It is in verſes of

[*l*] Lelandi Collect. vol. I. p. 187. 2d Edit.
[*m*] Mem. de l'Acad. des Inſcript. vol. II. p. 729.
[*n*] Warton's Hiſtory of Engliſh Poetry.

eight

eight syllables, and contains near twenty thousand lines. The author professes to have translated from the Latin; and, to raise the merit of the original work, he begins with depreciating that of Homer upon the same subject: he says, that this writer is not faithful, inasmuch as he was not an eye-witness of the events which he describes, and did not live till a hundred years after the taking of Troy; that when he came to Athens to read his work, the citizens would have condemned him for having imagined his fabulous combat of the Gods with men; that his poem was considered as the production of a madman, and at length rejected; but, adds Benoit, Homer possessed so many talents, that he afterwards succeeded in persuading the Athenians to receive his work, and it became of authority amongst them.

To substitute in the room of Homer an author of greater veracity, Benoit has invented other fables: he informs us, that one Dares, a native of Troy, who had very much distinguished himself during the siege of that city, wrote a journal of the famous war of ten years; that this work was for a long time lost, but that Cornelius, the nephew of Sallust the historian, having recovered it at Athens, translated it out of Greek into Latin. From this Latin translation it is that Benoit professes to have given his French version. He adds, that he had also made great use of the work of Dictys, who, fighting in the army of the Greeks, had written the history of their battles, in like manner as Dares had the atchievements of his Trojans.

Whatever be the opinions of the critics upon the history of the siege of Troy by these apocryphal writers, as they all agree, that their works existed in the 12th century, and that they were again enlarged in the 13th by Guido of Co-

lonna.

lonna, a civilian of Meſſina, we are more and more convinced that the tranſlation of them into French verſe, is the
work of our Anglo-Norman poet.   Beſides, the frequent al-
luſions which he employs, when, to give additional luſtre to
his Norman Dukes, he compares them with his Greek and
Trojan heroes, leave us no room to doubt, that he had celebrated the exploits of all of them.   Thus, when Harlotta la-
ments her diſtreſs upon quitting her relations to go to the
caſtle of Falaiſe, the poet commiſerates her becauſe ſhe was
unable to anticipate the greatneſs of the hero to whom ſhe
was about to give birth, and who was to equal that of
Hector ; and, to raiſe the glory of the Conqueror, who in
one day, and by a ſingle battle, obtained the crown of England, the poet recalls to mind the uſeleſs efforts of the kings
of Greece combined for the ſpace of ten years againſt a ſingle
city.

There are likewiſe to be found in this poem paſſages which
exhibit a rich and fertile imagination, together with the moſt
lively and animated deſcriptions that indicate a truly poetical
genius.   Nothing can be more cheerful than the deſcription
of the ſpring in which Jaſon embarks for the conqueſt of the
Golden Fleece.

> " Quant vint el tens qu'ivers deviſe,
> Que Jerbe vers point en la riſe,
> Lorſque floriſſent li ramel,
> Et doucement chantent oiſel,
> Merle, mauvis et loriol,
> Et Eſtornel et Roſſignol ;
> La blanche flors pent en leſpine,
> Et reverdoie la gaudine,

Quant

Quant li tens eft dout et fouez,
Lor partirent del port les nez, &c."

GUERNES.

This poet was an ecclefiastic of Pont St. Maxence in Picardy. His work is a Life of Thomas Becket, archbishop of
Canterbury, in French verse. It appears that he began it in
France; and he candidly acknowledges, that, for want of
proper information, he has filled it with untrue fabrications.
Desirous, however, of becoming better acquainted with the
truth, that he might infert nothing elfe in his work, he went
to Canterbury in 1172. There he fought after all thofe perfons who had known St. Thomas in private life, even thofe
who had ferved him in his infancy, and likewife the eye-wit-
neffes of his public life, both as chancellor and primate of
England; and upon their testimony he began compofing his
work. This was very much advanced when his fecretary
ftole his manufcript, and difappeared with it. The poet was
lefs chagrined at this lofs than at the idea of putting forth a
work which he had not completed, and which befides, as he
himfelf confeffes, was not rigoroufly faithful as to facts. He
was alfo much concerned at the probability that his name
might cover untruths, and that even the rich might purchafe at
a very dear rate a work which was not either fufficiently po-
lifhed or refined for the public tafte. Nevertheless, fo far
from being difcouraged by this unlucky robbery, the poet re-
fumed his work, and, redoubling his zeal for collecting hiftorical facts, completed it in 1177.

Guernes

Guernes himself has furnished us with these details in the prologue to his work. He also informs us, that he had several times publicly read it at the tomb of the archbishop. This proves, that at that time the Romance tongue was understood in England, even by the common people. The taste for works in that language appears to have been so general, that, according to the testimony of the same author, laymen as well as clerks, monks, and even women, composed in it lives of the archbishop; but he at the same time assures us, that the greater number of these histories were not conformable to truth. It appears also, that he thought them ill written; yet, as to his own work, he adds, that although it was composed in England, its style was pure, and its language correct, the author being born in France.

The work of Guernes of Pont St. Maxence is in the British Museum among the Harleian manuscripts, N° 270. This volume is the more valuable as it contains a work corrected by its author, and is also most probably the only copy existing. The sort of poetry used by this writer appears to be peculiar to him. His work, which consists of more than 6000 lines, is divided into stanzas of five Alexandrines, all in the same rhyme. It is uncertain whether Guernes adopted this method in order that his verses might be the more easily chanted; though this opinion seems to be very probable. To give an idea of the form and groundwork of his poetry, we shall transcribe two of his stanzas. He begins with that which follows:

"Tuit li physicien ne font ades bon mire,
Tuit clerc ne sevent pas bien chanter ne bien lire;
Asquanz des Troveurs faillent tort a bien dire,

Tel

> Tel choifift le mialz qui le mielz quide eflire,
> E tel quide eftre mieldre des altres eft li pire.''

When he fpeaks of other works which have been written on the fame fubject as his own, he thus delivers his opinion of them :

> '' Tut cil autre romanz qunnt fait del martyr
> Clere u lai muine u dame mult les oi mentir,
> Ne le veir ne le plain ne les i oi furnir,
> Mais ci purrez le veir e tut le plain oir,
> N' iflerai de verite pur perdre ne pur murir.''

With refpect to the manufcript which was ftolen from our author, we have difcovered in the Cotton library, Domitian, A. XI. feveral fragments, which appear to have been copied from it in the 13th century. Amidft thefe fhapelefs remains one really perceives the firft effays of our poet, whom the tranfcriber calls *Gerveis* inftead of *Guernes*. Several of the ftanzas are abfolutely the fame as thofe in the Harleian manufcript ; others again are either more correct, or differently given ; at the fame time, upon comparing the two manufcripts, one is foon convinced that the plan of the firft work is differently arranged from that of the fecond.

Such, Sir, are the fruits of a part of my refearches concerning the Anglo-Norman poets. But this letter having already attained to a great length, I think it right to put an end to it in this place. The fubject, however, being extremely ample, and at the fame time very honourable to the Englifh nation, I pledge myfelf to continue its difcuffion in other differtations. It is much to be lamented, that the domeftic avocations of Mr. Moyfant, an honorary member of the Society of Antiquaries of London, have prevented him from affifting me

in

in the hiftory of French poetry amongft the Englifh. His information upon this fubject would have been of great fervice to me; but I fhall not on that account perfevere with lefs zeal in endeavouring to prove that England formerly had its *Trouveurs* as well as Provence its *Troubadours*.

I remain, Sir,

with the greateft Refpect,

your very humble and obedient Servant,

D E   L A   R U E.

London,
June 10, 1795

Profeffor Royal of Hiftory at Caen.

XXV.

XXV. *Difcoveries in a Barrow in* Derbyfhire. *In a Letter from* Hayman Rooke, *Efq. to Mr.* Gough.

Read February 11, 1796.

Mansfield Woodhoufe, February 1, 1796.

DEAR SIR,

I Have ventured to fend you a little account of fome re..... lately found in a barrow in the Peak of Derbyfhire.

About the latter end of laft winter, Mr. Robert Needham, jun. of Afhford, a very refpectable farmer, who rents an eftate of the duke of Devonfhire, was induced to deftroy a large barrow for the fake of procuring a great quantity of lime-ftones, of which it was chiefly formed.

Having been informed that this barrow contained fome curious remains of antiquity, I fent to defire Mr. Needham would preferve the relics, and not proceed to a farther fearch in the barrow (which I was told had not been entirely cleared), till I came to examine it; and he very obligingly affured me, that he had already taken care of the antiquities, which he would referve for my acceptance, and that the barrow fhould not be touched. It is but juftice to the politenefs of Mr. Needham to mention this inftance of his readinefs to affift the Antiquary in his refearches.

6

I went

I went twice last summer to examine the barrow, which is situated on the summit of a hill that has a gradual rise from the South-east, and at about two miles North-west from Ashford. This hill is called *Fin Cop*. These are evidently British names, with but little variation from their radicals *Fyn* and *Coppa* : the former in the ancient Cornith and British language signifies an end, or a boundary, which this hill has on every side, and *Coppa* the top or summit.

At about seventy-two yards South-east of the barrow is a work thrown up, with a ditch on the inside of the vallum, which surrounds the top of the hill except on the North-west side, where there is a precipice fourteen yards from the barrow ; at the distance of one hundred and sixty yards beyond this work is another ditch and vallum, where the ditch is on the outside.

Fig. (a) in Pl. XLVIII. is a plan of the barrow after I had cleared away more of the sides ; circumference one hundred and sixty-one feet. It had been raised to a considerable height, and formed with lime-stones of various sizes, mixed with a very fine dry mould. In the bottom at (b) and (c) are two kistvaens ; (b) is cut into the solid rock, which incloses three sides, on the other is a flat stone, and one of the same kind was placed on the top ; the kistvaen (c), which is rather smaller than the other, was formed in the natural soil, with flat stones fixed in the sides, and one in the bottom. See a perspective view of these at (d and e).

In the kistvaen (b), was a skeleton placed with its face downwards, and on the top of the scull was an oblong piece of dressed black Derbyshire marble, which plainly appeared to have been fixed to the scull by a strong cement, part of which now adheres to the stone and scull. Under the head were found two arrow-heads of flint, the size of the

2   draw-

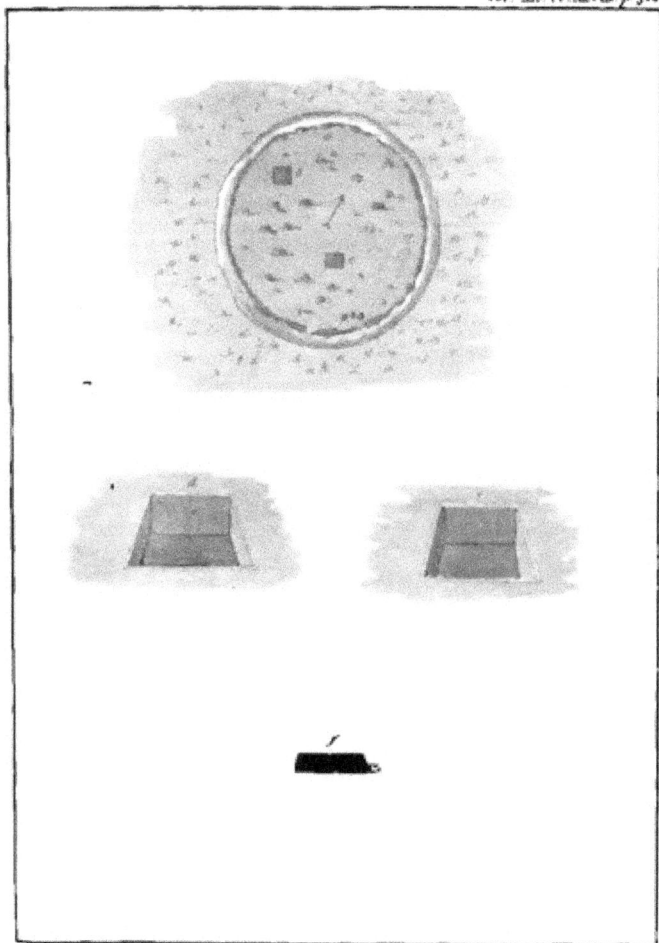

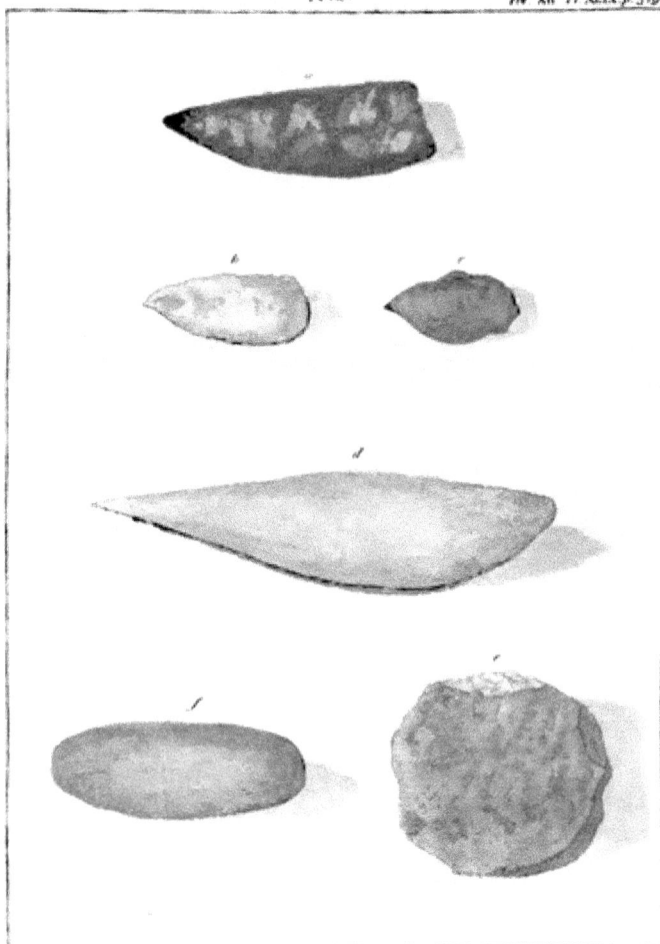

fig. (a) and (b) in Pl. XLIX. This kiftvaen was only two feet nine inches by two feet and one foot nine inches deep. The black ftone (f) in Pl. XLVIII. which was placed on the head, is two feet in length, nine inches broad, and fix inches thick.

At the South-eaft end of the barrow three urns, of very coarfe baked earth, were found nearly together, full of afhes and burnt bones, but fo much decayed that they fell to pieces in taking up. I meafured a fragment of the top rim of one, which did not appear to have been more than fix inches diameter, but, from another fragment of a rim, the urn muft have been much larger; on the top of one was a flint head of an arrow, the fize of (c) in Pl. XLIX.

At the Eaft end of the barrow two more fkeletons were depofited on the level ground. With thefe was picked up the fpear head (d), Pl. XLIX. which is fhaped out of a piece of lime-ftone, and made very fharp at the point.

The flat circular ftone (e), Pl. XLIX. was taken out of the kiftvaen (b), Pl. XLVIII. It has a thin body of ftucco on both fides; the top is of a yellowifh colour, and plainly appears to have been varnifhed. This poffibly might have been fome ornament to the drefs of thofe rude times in which this body was inhumed.

The fmooth ftone (f), Pl. XLIX. was found on the top of one of the urns. It differs only in fhape from the common boulder ftones, which, though ufually met with in fandy grounds, are not to be found in the Peak on a lime-ftone foil. It is therefore probable, that the fuperftitious Britons might have preferved thefe kind of ftones as fcarce and valuable amulets; and I am more inclined to be of that opinion from having,

fome years ago, met with two ftones fimilar to this depofited
with fome others on Stanton-moor.

The prefervation of the teeth, in the jaws of thefe fkeletons, which ftill retain their ivory, is very remarkable; the
bones alfo are but little decayed. This might probably be
owing to the very light dry earth with which they were covered.

The kiftvaen (c), Pl. XLVIII. was full of afhes and burnt
bones, and poffibly was the fpot where the bodies might have
been burnt.

The bones were thrown promifcuoufly in, and the principal care feems to have been in placing and fixing the piece
of marble to the fcull, nor, indeed, was there room for the
body to be depofited at full length. It is probable, therefore,
that the body might be burnt, and the bones collected and
placed in the kiftvaen; for, I fhould imagine, whilft there is
the leaft moifture left in the body the bones would not be damaged; but where we find the bones reduced to a very fine
powder in urns, we may conclude that they were burnt over
again by themfelves after the body was confumed: but I fhall
leave this to the learned Society, who will, moft probably,
form a more plaufible conjecture.

I am much inclined to think that this elevated fpot, thus
fecured by a double fence, may be the fite of a Britifh town
or fortrefs, and that the barrow was the fepulchre of the
chieftain and his relatives. There evidently appears to
have been more attention paid to the bones inhumed in the
kiftvaen (b), than to any of the reft, from this fingular inftance of a piece of black marble being fixed on the fcull.
As this kiftvaen is too fmall to admit of the body at full
length, may we not fuppofe that the body was firft burnt,
and the afhes depofited in the kiftvaen (c), which feems to
have

have been defigned for that purpofe, and the head and bones placed by themfelves, as above mentioned ?

It feldom happens, that interment and urn burial are to be met with in the fame barrow. The former is undoubtedly the moft ancient, and has been handed down to us by facred hiftory and authentic records. We find alfo, that the practice of burning the body was of great antiquity, and here the fame ancient weapons were found depofited with both ; I therefore think there is great reafon to fuppofe, that this barrow was of very remote antiquity.

The reverend Mr. James Douglas, in his learned and elegant Sepulchral Hiftory of Great Britain, fpeaking of thefe arrow-heads of flint, fays, " They are evidences of a people " not in the ufe of malleable metal ; and it therefore implies, " that, wherever thefe arms are found in barrows, they are " inconteftibly the relics of a primitive barbarous people, " and preceding the æra of thofe barrows in which brafs or " iron arms are found *."

If you think this little memoir will be acceptable to the Society, I muft beg you will do me the honor to prefent it to them.

I am,

    Dear Sir,

        your fincere

            and obliged humble Servant,

                H. R O O K E.

* Nænia Britannica, p. 154. note 3.

XXVI.

[332]

XXVI. *Description of a Tablet, from the* Arundelian *Collection. In a Letter to the Secretary.*

Read March 12, 1795.

SIR,

I Take the liberty of sending you the inclosed * for the inspection of the Society. I purchased it out of what was called the Arundel collection, which was sold at the conclusion of the sale of the dutchess of Portland's museum in the year 1786. From the letter which accompanied this little tablet (if it may be so called), it appears, that it was found in Essex, but unfortunately we are not informed in what part of the county. This, therefore, prevents the attaining any clue to discover who was the original owner, though I should conceive it highly probable that it belonged to some religious house. Though the letter contains no date, the names of lord Oxford and Mr. Wanley, which are mentioned in it, are so well known to the Society, that the period when it was found may well be conjectured.

On the outside of the tablet, which is of silver gilt, are represented various figures of saints, among which we may discover St. Christopher, St. John, St. Lawrence, St. Philip, St. James, St. Apollonia, St. Catharine, St. Margaret, St. Matthias, St. Anne and the Virgin, and St. George. The compartments on the inside, which are enamelled †, I imagine, represent The Annunciation, The Salutation, Joseph and Mary, The Na-

* See Plate L.   † The enamel on the outside is worn off.
6

tivity,

Size of the Originals.

(*An Antient Tablet.*)

tivity, The Angel appearing to the Shepherds, The Wife Men's Offering, The Circumcifion, or the prefentation in the Temple to old Simeon, The Flight into Egypt, Our Saviour's Dif-courfe with the Doctors, The Marriage in Cana, The Miracle of the Loaves and Fifhes, Our Saviour's Refurrection, His Afcenfion, The Defcent of the Holy Ghoft, God the Father, crowning the Virgin, and her Affumption.

This little tablet undoubtedly formed one of the appen-dages to an altar. As to its antiquity, from the dreffes of the female figures, and from the armour upon the figure of St. George, I conceive it to be about the time of Edward III.

I am, Sir,

your humble Servant,

Temple,
March 5, 1795.

P. H. LEATHES.

XXVII.

XXVII. *The Accompte of Sir* Edwarde Waldegrave *, *Knighte, oone of the Qwenes Highnefs Prevy Counceile, and Mr. of her Matie greate Warderobe. Afwell of all Receiptes of Monye, of Clothes, of Golde Velvatts, and other Sylkes owte of the Qwenes Maties Stoore. As alfo of all the Empc̓ons, Provifions, and Delivereis for the Buryall of the late famows Prince of Memory Kinge* Edwarde *the Syxte of that Name, who departed from this tranfitory Lyffe the Syxte Daye of* Julye, *in the 7th Yere of his Reigne, and was buryed the 8th Daye of* Augufte, *in the firfte Yere of the moofte profperos and victorius Reigne of owre moofte dradd Sovereigne Lady* Marye, *by the Grace of God Qwene of* Englnode, Fraunce, *and* Irelonde, *Defendor of the Faythe, and of the Churche of* Englonde *and* Irelonde, *in Earthe the Supreme Hedd. Communicated by* Craven Ord, *Efq. F. A. S. from the Original in the* Exchequer.

Read January 16, 1794.

FURSTE, received by the fayde Sr Edwarde Waldegrave, knighte, of Sr Edmonde Peckam, knighte, highe treaforer of the Qwenes Highnes Mynttes, by vertewe of oone warraunte. Dated in the Tower of London, the 14th daye of Julye, the furfte yere of her moofte gracios reigne, in prefte towerde the expenfes of the fayde buryall.   £. s. d.
1300 0 0

* Sir Edward Waldegrave married Frances daughter of Sir Edward Nevill, knight. He was made one of the knights of the carpet by the earl of Arundel after queen Mary's coronation, and held many valuable offices during her reign. Queen Elizabeth committed him to the Tower, where he died September 1, 1561, and was buried at Borley in Effex.

4

Clothes

Clothes of golde tifhewe, clothes of golde velvetts, and other fylkes received by the fayde S' Edwarde Waldegrave, knighte, for the ufe of the fayde buryall, of S' Rauffe Sadleir, knighte, of the Qwenes Highnes ftoore.

Clothe of golde and fylver tifhewed withe		
golde and fylver	—	20 yards qr. di.
Clothe of golde purple	——	51 yards di. di. qr.
Clothe of golde blacke withe woorkes		23 yards
Velvett blewe jeane	— —	3 yards 3 qrs.
Satten white at 11s.	——	4 yards
Damafke blewe	— —	2 yards qr.
Damafke Crimfin	——	2 yards qr.
Sarfcinett grene	——	3 yards 3 qrs.
Sarcinett whyte at 5s. 8d	——	3 yards qr.

The Charges of the Buriall of the late famos Prince of Memory Kinge Edwarde the Syxte, aswell of the Empc'on of Velvetts and Blacke Clothes, Cottons, as other Nc'c'yes, for the Ufe of the faide Buriall as fhall apere.

The hearffe withein the chapell at Whytehawle.

Thomas Stacye, for 32 yardes of blacke velvett jeane for to cover the hearfe rownde abowte above the majeftye clothe, and fowre pooftes of the faide hearfe of twoo bredeles of velvett at 11 yardes longe, to' 22 yardes; and for the fowre pooftes 10 yardes, to' 32 yardes; price the yard 15s.   £. s. d.

24 o o

Thomas

	£.	s.	d.

Thomas Stacye, for 14 yardes of blacke farfcinett for one majeftye clothe to hange in
the hearfe at Weftm', price the yarde 4s. 4d.   3   0   8

Laurence Ball, for 6lb. 11 ownces di. of
frendge of Venice golde for the faide majeftye, price the lb. £.4. 8s. price the ownce
7s. 4d.   50 12   4

Itm, for 4lb. one ownce di. of blacke fylke
frendge, for the fame caufe, price the lb.
£.1 4s. price the ownce 1s. 6d.   4 18   3

Thomas Stacye, for 12 yardes 3 qrs. of blewe
velvett do'ble jeane for the coveringe of the
coffyn wherin the co'pes laye, pryfe the
yarde 18s.   ————   —   11   9   0

John Grene, for coveringe the fame withe
the fame velvett, price ingrofs withe
nayles and workemanfhippe   1   0   0

Itm, for 2000 gylte nayles for the garnifhinge of fayde coffyn, price the 1000' 20s.   2   0   0

John Pincherdon, ferjeaunte plummer, for
leade fooder, workemanfhippe, and attendaunce geven for the coffyninge of o' Sovereigne Lorde Kinge Edwarde the Syxte to
him ordinarily dewe.   ————   10   0   0

Thomas Stacye, for 48 yardes of blacke velvett
do'ble jeane for one paw'e to laye upon the
coffyn ftandinge within the hearfe at the
Kinges Palaice of Whitehawle, within the
chappell there, of 6 yardes longe, and 8
breddes, price the yarde 16s.   ————   38   8   0

Black velvet jeane at 15s.   ————   32 y'ds.

Black farfenet at   4s. 4d.   ————   14 y'ds.

Yet

Yet for the said hearse.

	£.	s.	d.
Of the Qwenes ſtoore 3 yardes 1 qr. white farſcinett for parte of banners and ſtanderdes, price the yarde 5s. 8d.	0	18	5
Of the ſame ſtoore 3 yards 3 qrs of grene farſcinett, for the ſame cauſe		*fine precio.*	
Thomas Stacye, for 14 yardes qr. of blewe farſcinett for parte of ſix cooates of armes and banners, and ſtanderdes, price the yarde 4s. 4d.	5	5	1
Itm, of him, 31 yards di. of redd farſcinett, for the ſame cauſe, price the yard 4s. 4d.	6	16	6
Of the Qwene's ſtore 2 yards qr. of crimſon damaſk for one cooate of armes		*fine precio.*	
Itm, of the ſaide ſtoore 2 yardes qr. of blewe maſk for one cooate of armes		*fine precio.*	
ꝑ ſtauro	0	18	5

So'ma £. 138 8s. 9d. ꝑ nova

empc'oe   137 10 4

A clothe of eſtate of blewe velvet.

	£.	s.	d.
Thomas Stacye, for 35 yards of blacke velvett do'ble jeane for one clothe of eſtate of 4 breaddes and 7 yardes long, withe 7 yardes of velvett for the valaunce, parcel of the ſaide 35 yardes, price the yarde 18s.	31	10	0
Itm, of him, 6 yardes qr. of blewe velvett do'ble jeane for three qwiſh'ons, twoo of them of one yarde qr. long, and one qwiſhon of di. yard di. qr. longe, price the yard 18s.	5	11	6

VOL. XII.   X x   Yet

Yet in the faid cloth of eftate.

	£. s. d.
Item, 10 yardes qr. of blewe velvett do'ble jeane for coveringe part of two chayers for the faid clothe of eftate, price the yard 18s.	9 4 6
Of the Qwenes ftoore 3 yards 3 qrs. blewe velvett do'ble jean for covering the other parte of the fayde chayers	*fine precio.*
Laurence Ball, for 32 owuces of purple fylke frendge for frenginge the faid clothe of eftate, price every ownce thereof 2s.	3 4 0
Item, for 26 ownces di. of purple fylke frendge for the faide twoo chayers, price the ownce 2s.	2 13 0
Thomas Chappell, for making the faid clothe of eftate, price	0 16 8
Item, for blewe lyor for the faid clothe of eftate	0 3 0
Item for 18 yardes di. of blewe buckeram for lynynge the faid clothe of eftate, price therd 8d.	0 12 4
Item, for making of three qwifh'ons of velvett, price the pece makeinge 1s.	0 3 0
Item, for three yardes of white tyke for the faid 3 quifh'ons, price the yard 2s. 4d.	0 7 0
Item, for 18 lb. of fethers for the fylling of the faid 3 qwifh'ons, price the lb. 8d.	0 12 0
John Grene, for coveringe of the faid twoo chayres of tymbre withe velvett, for nayles, woorkemanfhippe, and other necc'yes to them, price	4 8 4

Som'a £.59. 6s. 4d. p nova empc'oe.

The

The cauapye of blewe velvett.

	£.	s.	d.

Thomas Stacye, for 17 yardes of blewe velvett do'ble jean for oone canapye to beare
over the corpes in the chariott from the
Kinges palace unto Westm' churche, of 4
breaddes and 3 yardes longe, the valaunce
of one qr. depe, conteigninge 5 yardes at
18*s.* —— —— 15 6 0

Thomas Chappell, for makinge the said canapye of blewe velvett, price — 0 10 0

Itm, for 21 yardes of satten of bruges for
lynynge the saide canapye, price therd
2*s.* 4*d.* —— —— 1 9 0

Lawrence Ball, for 2lb. 8 ownces di. of purple sylke frendge for the saide canapye, price
the lb. £.1 12*s.* price the ownce 2*s.* 4 0 12

Thomas Chappell, for lyor for the same, price 0 1 4
Som'a £.22 7*s.* 4*d.* ꝑ nova empc'oe.

Hatchementts and maunteletts.

Thomas Stacye, for one yarde di. of black velvett do'ble jean for the furniture of hatchementts for the Kinge, price the yard 18*s.* 1 7 0

Of the Qwene's stoore 4 yards blacke clothe
of golde for the saide hatchementts, man-
teletts, and sweardes, to hange over the
hearse —— —— *fine precio.*

Itm, of the saide stoore four yardes of white
satten for the same cause, price the yarde
11*s.* —— —— 2 4 0

Soma £3. 11*s.*   ꝑ stauro   £.2 4*s.*
          ꝑ nova empc'oe   £.1 7*s.*
The

The chariot covered with clothe of golde.

	£.	s.	d.
Of floore, 20 yardes qr. di. clothe of golde tishewed withe golde and fylver for to cover the chariott of tymbre that cariede the Kinge's corpes with the Kinge's pycture from White hawle to Weftm' churche	*fine precio.*		
Thomas Stacye, for 20 yardes di. of blewe velvett do'ble jeane for the nether parte of the fame charriott, price the yarde 18s.	18	9	0
Itm, for 10 yardes of blacke velvett jeane for coveringe the fhaftes of the litter and other neceffaries, price the yarde 15s.	7	10	6
Lawrence Ball, for 6lb. 2 ownces qr. of frendge of Venice gold twilted for the upper parte and nether parte of the faid chariott, price the lb. £.4 8s. price the ownce 7s 4d. — —	27	4	6

Yet the chariott cov'ed with clothe of golde, w' 7 horfes trapped withe black velvett.

	£.	s.	d.
Itm, for 50 yardes golde paffamente lace for garnifhing the pyllors of the chariott, weiynge 14 ownces di. price the ownce 9s.	6	10	6
Itm, for 28 ownces of black and purple peny breade ryb'an for garnifhing the chariott and fhaftes, price the ownce 1s 8d.	2	6	8
John Grene for woorkmanfhippe of the coveringe of the faide charyott withe the faide clothe of golde and velvett, price in greate — —	2	6	8
Itm, of him, for 2000 di. gylte nayle for the garnifhinge of the fame chariott, price the 1000 £.1. — —	2	10	0

Itm,

	£.	s.	d.
Itm, for one thoufande di. blacke garnifhinge nayles for the fame caufe, price the thowfande 5s.	0	7	6
Itm, for 11 bolion nayles gylte for the fame caufe, price the pece 5s. —	0	5	0
Anthony Silver, whelewrighte, for tymbre and workmanfhippe, withe wheles, withe all other n'cc'yes thereto belongeinge, price in greate —	8	4	0
Richard Pye, joiner, for 4 pillors to the fame chariott, withe the fame woorkmanfhippe of all neceffaries, withe wages and woorkemen abowte the fame, price ingrofs	2	0	6
John Keyme, fmith, for 40 focketts, 8 fqwiers, withe other neceffaries thereto ingrofs —	1	9	0
Thomas Cure, fadleyer, for 6 padde faddles for 6 chariotte horfes that leade the faid chariott, price the pere 6s. 8d. —	2	0	0
Itm, for cuttinge and makinge of 7 trappors of blacke velvett, withe buckeram, for 7 charyotte horles, price the pece 10s.	3	10	0
Itm, for 112 yardes buckeram for lyninge the fayde 7 trappers, price the yarde 8d.	3	14	8
Thomas Stacye, for 147 yardes blacke velvett do'ble jeane for the coveringe of the faid 7 trappors, price the yarde 16s. —	117	12	0
Itm, for 16 yardes of blacke velvett do'ble jeane for covering of harneffes for the faid chariott horfes, price every yarde thereof 16s. — —	12	16	0

6

Thomas

		£.	s.	d.
Thomas Cure for 7 payer of ſtirroppe lethers covered withe welvette, at 8*d.* —		0	4	8
Itm, for 7 payre of gyrthes, price the payer 10*d.*		0	5	10
Itm, for 7 payre of raynes coverde withe velvett, price the payer 1*s.* 4*d.* —		0	9	4
Itm, for 7 hedſtalls of black ledder withe there portemouthes, price the pece 1*s.*		0	7	0
Lawence Ball, for 7 owncs of blacke Spaniſhe ſylke frendge for taſſells, price the ownce 1*s.* 8*d.* — —		0	11	8
Itm, for 13 yardes of blacke Ingliſhe ryban to leade the chariott horſſes, price therde 1*s.*		0	13	0
John Baſeley, coller-maker for ledder Hungrye and black ledder do'ble ſtiched, withe traces and a lymmer ſaddle, withe all things apperteiginge to the ſame draughtes		4	0	0
Will'm Creſſente for 7 bytts withe boſſes price the pece 8*s.* 8*d.* —		3	0	8
Robarte Smithe, for 7 payer of ſtiropps, price every payer 2*s.* 4*d.* —		0	16	4
Thomas Cure, for 40 ſocketts to ſtaye the ſtanderdes withe ſtirroppe lethers, whereof 17 covered with velvett, and the other withe clothe, price the pece 1*s.* —		2	0	0
Itm, for 3 pyllions of buckeram ſtuffed withe flaxe, one for the lymmer ſadle, and the other twoo for the chariotte, price the pece 1*s.* 4*d.* — —		0	4	0
Itm, for cariage of all the ſtuffe to Weſtm', and for taylors to ſtitche on ſkochins upon horſes — —		0	9	0

Itm,

Itm, for canvas for patrons for to cutt the faide   £.   s.   d.
    trappers in the warderobe, price in greate   0   3   4
Frauncis Poope, for 17 yardes of blacke clothes
    for socketts and to laye within the charyott,
    price every yarde thereof 6s. 8d.   —   5   13   4
       Som'a   £.237 14s. 2d.

The trappor of clothe of golde for the horffe off eftate.
    Thomas Cure, for cuttinge and makinge of
      one trapper of clothe of golde for the hoorffe
      of eftate, lynede withe buckeram, price the
      makinge   —   —   —   0   10   0
    Itm, for one bolfter faddle covered withe blacke
      cotton for the fame horffe, price   —   0   10   0
    Of the floore in the greate warderobe, 11
      yardes of clothe of golde purple for the fayde
      trapper   —   —   —   *fine precio.*
    Thomas Cure, for 16 yardes of buckeram for
      lynynge the fayde trappor, price therde 8d.
    Laurence Ball, for 7 ownces di. frendge of   0   10   8
      Venice golde for the forefaide trapper,
      price thownce 7s. and fower pence   —   2   15   0
    Thomas Cure, for one payre of ftirroppe
      lethers covered withe velvett, price   0   1   0
    Itm, for a hedftall and the raignes coveredde
      withe clothe of golde, price   —   0   2   4
    Itm, a payer of longe gyrthes   —   0   1   0
    William Creffentte, for one bytte withe boffes
      withe antyke woorke do'ble gylte all over,
      price therof in greate   —   —   4   13   4
    Som'a £.9 3s. 4d. p nova empc'oe.

                                     The

The trappor of farfcinett for the manne of armes

	£.	s.	d.
Thomas Cure, for cuttinge and makinge of a trapper of redde and blewe farfcinett for the manne of armes there reprefented by twoo tables, price thereof —	0	6	8
Itm. for a ftele faddle and for the coveringe of the fame withe redde and blewe farfcinett, price — — —	1	6	8
Thomas Stacye, for 5 yardes of redde farfcinett for the faide trapper and faddle, at 4s. 4d. therd — — —	1	1	8
Itm, for 14 yardes of blacke farfcinett for a trapper for him, price the yard 4s. 4d.	3	0	8
Thomas Cure, for a hedftall and a payer of raynes coveredde withe farfcinett, price	0	2	4
Itm, for a payer ftirroppe lethers —	0	0	8
Will'm Creffente, for one greate bytte withe blacke boffes, price therof	0	10	0
Robarte Smithe, for one payer of ftirropps, price — —	0	3	4
Itm, for 5 yardes of blewe farfcinett for the fame caufe, price the yarde 4s. 4d.	1	1	8

Som'a £.7 13s. 8d.

A trappor of velvett for the chieffe mourner

	£.	s.	d.
Thomas Cure, for one faddle for the Lord Treaforer, Marques of Winchefter, cheffe mourner, price thereof —	0	6	8
Itm to him, for makinge of oone trapper of blacke velvett lynede withe buckeram, price	0	10	0
Thomas Stacye, for 21 yardes of blacke velvett do'ble jeane for a trapper for him, at 18s. — —	18	18	0

Itm,

Itm, for 16 yardes of buckeram for lynynge
of the faide trapper, price therde 8*d*.   0 10   8

Itm, for oone payer of ftirroppe lethers co-
vered withe velvett, price   —   0   0   8

Itm, for one payer of browne gyrtlies, price   0   0 10

Itm, for one payer of raynes coverde withe
blacke velvett, price   —   0   1   4

Itm, for oone hedftall of blacke ledder withe
portemouthes, price thereof   —   0   1   0

Will'm Creffente, bytt-maker, for one bytte
withe gylte boffes withe antyke woorke
do'ble gylte, price therof   —   4   3   4

Robarte Smithe, for one payre of ftirropps,
price   —   —   —   0   3   4

Lawrence Ball, for 2 rownde buttons of blacke
fylke for a payer of reignes, price the pece 1*s*.   0   2   0

Itm, for one ownce of blacke fylke frendge
for the fayde taffel, price the ownce   0   1   8

    Som'a £.14 19*s*. 6*d*. ,p nova empc'oe

The trappors of velvett for 9 henchmen.

Thomas Cure, for makinge of 9 trappers of
blacke velvett lynede withe buckeram for 9
of the kinges henchemen, price the pece 10*s*.   4 10   0

Thomas Stacye, for 84 yardes qr. blacke velvett do'ble jeane for coveringe of parte of
the faide 9 trappers, to every trapper 21
yardes, at 16*s*.   —   —   67   8   0

Itm, 60 yardes blacke velvett do'ble jeane for
the fame caufe, price the yarde 18*s*.   54   0   0

John Bridges, for 44 yds. 3 qrs. blacke velvett jeane for the fame caufe, price the
yarde 15*s*.   —   —   —   33 11   3

VOL. XII.   Y y   Tho-

Thomas Cure, for 144 yardes of buckeram for lynynge the fayde 9 trappors, price the yarde 8*d*.   —   —   4 16 0

Itm, for 9 payer of flirroppe lethers for them, at 8*d*,   —   —   0 6 0

Itm, for 9 payer of browne gyrtlies, at 10*d*. the pece   —   —   —   0 7 6

Itm, for 9 payer of raynes covered w^t^ blacke velvett, price the payer 1*s*. 4*d*.   —   0 12 0

Itm, for 9 hedftalls of blacke ledder withe portemouthes, price the pece 1*s*.   —   0 9 0

Will'm Creffente, for 9 greate byttes withe blacke boffes for 9 greate courfers, price the bytte 10*s*.   —   —   4 10 0

Robert Smithe, for 9 payer of blacke fliroppes, price the payer 2*s*. 4*d*.   —   1 1 0

Laurence Ball, for 4 grofs of blacke fylke ryban for trimmynge of all the trappors, price   1 14 0

Itm, for 9 owrces of fylke for 9 payer of raynes of velvett, price the payer 1*s*. 8*d*.   0 15 0

　　　Som'a £.173 19 9 ♕ nova empc'oe.

The hearfe in Weftm' churche.

Thomas Stacye, for 72 yardes of blacke velvett jeane for the coveringe and garnifhinge the hearfe and the poftes, price the yarde 16*s*.   —   —   57 12 0

John Warley, for 20 yardes of taffata for a ma^n^ clothe within the fayde hearfe, price the yarde 10*s*. 4*d*.   —   —   10 6 8

Thomas Stacye, for 8 yardes of blacke taffata for the fame caufe, price the yarde 10*s*.   4 0 0

　　　　　　　　　　　　　　　　Lau-

Laurence Hall, for 4lb. 10 ownces 3 qrs. of
frendge of Venice golde for the fayde ma.,
price the lb. £.4. 8s. and price the ownce
7s. 4d.   —   —   43 10 10

Itm, for 6lb 3 ownces of blacke fylke frendge
for the fame caufe, price the lb. £1. 4s. price
the ownce 1s. 6d.   —   —   7 8 6

Thomas Stacye, for oone yarde of crimfin
lukes velvett for the fayde hearfe, price   1 6 8

Som'a £.124 4s. 8d. p nova empt'oe.

Pawles of velvett and clothe of gold.

Thomas Stacye, for 48 yardes of blacke velvett
jeane for oone pawle to laye upon the coffyn
within the fayde churche at Weftm' price
the yarde 16s.   —   —   38 8 0

Nicholas Stayles, for 11 yardes of white
fatten for a croffe for the fame, price the
yarde 7s. 4d.   —   —   4 0 8

Thomas Laurence, 45 yardes of buckeram for
lynynge the fame pawle, price the yarde 7d.   1 6 3

Of the Qwenes floore 30 yards di. di. qr. of
purple clothe of golde for pawles to be offered by the Lorde Treaforer cheffe mowr-
ner, and other eftates mowrners there   *fine precio.*

Itm, of the fame floore, 19 yards of blacke
clothe of golde withe woorkes for the fame
caufe   —   —   *fine precio.*

Thomas Stacye, for 27 yards 3 qrs. blacke
velvett do'ble jeane, dd. to the Lorde Treaforer for the ufe of the fayde buriall, price
the yarde 16s.   —   —   22 4 0

Som'a £.65 18s. 11d.

Blacke

Blacke lynynges and blacke cottons for the
hanginge of White hawle.

Thomes Ackworthe for 1306 yards di. of
blacke narrowe cotton for the hanginge of
the Kinges paluice of Weftm', viz. The
chambre of prefence, the palliott chambre,
the hawle, the chappell, the hearfse, with em
the Chapell, price the y'de 8*d.*   43 11   0

Frauncis Poope, for 2282 yardes of blacke narrowe cotton for the fame caufe, price the
yarde 8*d.*   —   —   —   76   1   4

Thomas Ackworthe, for 344 yards of broade
cotton for the fame caufe, price the yarde
3*s.* 4*d.*   —   —   —   57   6   8

Frauncis Poope, for 281 yards qr. of broade
cottone for the fame caufe, price the yarde
3*s.* 4*d.*   —   —   —   46 17   6

John Goodwin for 21 yards qr. of broade clothe
for the fame caufe, price the yarde 2*s.* 4*d.*   2   9   7

The wages of taylors workinge abowte the fowinge and hanginge of the fayde cottons, etc.   4   8   2

Thomas White, for 7 boltes of blacke thred
for the fowinge of them, price the bolte
4*s.* 4*d.*   —   —   —   1 10   4

Som'a £.232 4*s.* 8*d.*

Blacke lynynges for the hanginge of Weftm' churche.

Thomas Ackworthe, for 809 yards di. of narrowe cotton for the hanginge of the hearfe
rownde abowte, and for the hanginge of the
fydes of the middell ile all alonge of the
churche of Weftm', price the yarde 8*s.*   26 19   8

4   Itm,

Itm, for 54 yards di. broade cotton for the
same cause, at 3s. 4d. —   —   9 1 8

Frauncis Poope, for a 1056 yardes of narrowe
cotton for the same cause, price the yarde 8d.   35 4 0

Thomas Mounte, for 22 yardes 3 qrs. blacke
clothe for the same cause, price the yarde
6s. 8d. —   —   7 11 8

Richarde Blackney, for 43 yards di. of broade
clothe for the same cause, price the yarde 3s.   6 10 6

Richarde Blackneye, for 22 yards di. blacke
clothe for the same cause, price the yarde
3s. 4d. —   —   3 13 0

Thomas White, for 48 yardes of blacke
clothe for the same cause, price the yarde
3s. 4d. —   —   —   8 0 0

John Hylles, for tenter hookes and arras
hookes to hange all the blacke lynynges in
in the churche and at White hall —   0 8 6

Thomas White, for taylors wages workinge
aboute the hanginge of the same churche   3 3 4

Itm, for boltes of blacke thred for sowinge
the same hanginges, price —   0 14 0

        Sem'a £.101 8s. 4d.

The PAYNTER's BOOKE assigned by the Lorde Treasorer.
The ma" clothe.

Inprimis, for the workmanshippe of a ma"
and vallence sett upp within the chapell at
White hawle —   —   3 0 0

Itm, for the workmanshippe of the ma" and
vallence sett upp within the churche at
Westm' —   —   —   5 0 0

        Itm,

Itm, for the workmanſhippe of a ma'' for the chareott — —   2 0 0

     10 0 0

Standerdes.

Itm, for the workmanſhippe of 3 Standerdes, the lyon, the dragon, and the greyhounde, price the pece £.6 beyng wroughte in fyne golde — — —   18 0 0

Banners.

Itm, for the workemanſhippe of 12 banners in fyne golde, price the pece £.2.   24 0 0

Itm, 6 lardge banners of damaſke wroughte in fyne golde, price the pece £.4 6s. 8d.   26 0 0

Itm, for 6 banners of farſcinett wroughte in fyne golde, at £.3 6s. 8d. the pece, beynge in depths oone yarde and a halffe —   20 0 0

     70 0 0

Bannerolls.

Itm, for 4 bannerolls of do'ble farſcinett in fyne golde, at £.2. — —   8 0 0

Itm, moore for 21 bannerolls of farſcinett in fyne golde, price the pece £.1 3s. 8d.   24 17 0

Itm, for 9 bannerolls of farſcinett for the pages of honor, price the pece 18s.   8 2 0

     40 19 0

The helmett and mauntells.

Itm for a large helme gylte all over —   4 0 0

Itm, for a crowne carved and gylte w' burniſhed golde — —   2 0 0

Itm, a lyon karved and gylte withe burniſhed golde — —   2 0 0

     Itm,

Itm, for an armynge fwearde, price —   1 0 0

Itm, for gylding the fame fwerde and for
the fhapinge of the fhethe, buckell, pen-
d'unte, and chape, price   —   0 10 0

Itm, for a targate of the Kinges armes within
the garter and the crowne over yt gylte   2 0 0

Itm, for the makinge of the mauntells of
clothe of golde lyned withe white fatten,
twoo knoppes of burnifhed golde withe
twoo taflells of fylke and golde   —   2 0 0

                                                        13 10 0

Penfells.

Itm for 21 dofen of pencells wroughte in fyne
golde and fylver upon do'ble farfcinett of
an elle longe, at 11. 4d.   —   —   16 16 0

Shafferons.

Itm, for 6 dofen of fhafferons, price the
pece 21.   —   —   —   7 4 0

Skochons.

Itm, 6 dofen fkochons of do'ble farfcinett
wroughte in fyne golde, price the pece 51.   18 0 0

Itm, for 3 dofen fkochons of buckeram
wroughte in fyne golde, price the pece, 51.   9 0 0

Itm, for 15 dofen of fkochons of buckeram in
partye golde, price the pece 3l. 4d.   30 0 0

Itm, for oone dofen fkochons of paper in fyne
golde, price the pece 41.   —   2 8 0

Itm, 58 dofen fkochons of paper in metall
partye golde, price the pece 21. 6d.   87 0 0

                                                              Itm,

Itm, for 68 dofen of fkochons on paper in
collore, at 1s. 4d.   —   54   8   0

                                   200 16   0

The crowne imperiall.

Itm, for a crowne imperiall of fyne golde to
be fett oon the hearfe at Weftm'   —   0 13   4

Itm, 7 yardes of blacke buckeram for the
greate majeftie, price the yard 10d.   0   5 10

Itm, for fhapinge and fowinge of the velvett
abowte the twoo hearfes, and for the
makinge of twoo pawles   —   1   0   0

                                       1 19   2

Banner ftaves.

Itm, for 3 ftanderde ftaves and payntinge the
fame, price the ftaffe, 4s.   —   0 12   0

Itm, 6 dofen blacke ftaves for the ban'ers
and ban'erolls, price the dofen 8s.   2   8   0

Itm, a blacke ftaffe for the embrawdered
banner   —   —   —   0   1   4

Itm, 21 dofen fpere ftickes, at 1s. 6d. the
dofen   —   —   —   1 11   6

Itm, 6 ftaves to beare the canapye all blewe,
the knoppes of them gylte with fyne golde,
at 3s. 4d. the ftaffe.   —   —   1   0   0

Itm, for 3 ftaves, oone to beare the cooate of
armes, oone for the helme, and the other
beare the targate   —   —   0   6   8

                                       5 19   6

Braces of iron.

Itm, for a brace of iron to fett uppe the
helmett, and four braces moore, as three
                                       for

for the ftanderdes, and oone for the greate
banner, price — — —   1   0   0

Itm, 36 brafes for the banners and banerolles   2   3   0

Itm, to the mafon for fettinge and foderinge
in the fayde brafes in places apoynted for
him and his men — — —   2   10   0

Itm, for 7 brafes of iron at 1s. the brafe   0   7   0

Itm, for a polle axe — —   1   0   0

Itm, for an armynge fwerde and a gurdle of
velvett — — —   0   16   0

Itm, a payer of gylte fpurres, price   0   16   0

                                            8   12   0

Itm, for bote hyer too and froo tranfportinge
of the preparementes of the fayde entier-
ment by water — —   0   12   0

Itm, for twoo hampers to truffe in the fayde
thinges — — —   0   4   0

                                            0   16   0

Itm, moore to the office of armes allowance
accordinge to the aunciente cuftome for
there attendaunce at the buriall aforefayde
of o' late fovereigne of mofte famows memory Kynge Edwarde the Syxte —   40   0   0

Som'a of the paynters booke £.434 11s. 8d.

Exfpenfes, neceffarys.

Thomas Whyte, for breade, drincke, and meate
for the officers of the warderobe and 4 other
honefte menne, fworne to be prayfers of
the blacke clothe boughte for the lyvereis
for the fayde Burialls, withe others there
attend'unte all the tyme of the provifion of

the fayde clothe, and other ncc'ies for
the fayde buriall appxrteynynge   —   8 5 6

Itm, payde for bote hyer from London to
Grenewiche at dyvers tymes   —   0 10 0

Itm, boote hyer from London to Weftm' at
fundry tymes   —   —   0 2 0

Itm, payde for boote hyer from London to
Richmonde at divers times   —   1 5 0

Itm, for paper and incke for theife premiffes   0 10 0

Som'a £.10 12s. 6d.

The wages of the prayfers and other attend'unts
all the tyme of the buriall.

John Bridges, attendinge by the fpace of 35
dayes upon the prayfinge of the blacke
clothe boughte for the fayde buriall, Thomas Ackworthe lykewife by the fpace of
35 dayes, John Bomarde 41 dayes, and
Frauncis Poope 35 dayes. Tota 146 dayes,
at 1s. 8d. the daye   —   —   12 3 4

Thomas White, porter, and Thomas Laurence, attendunte, upon the meafuringe of
the fame clothe, either of them by the fpace
of 41 dayes, at 1s. 8d. the daye   6 16 8

Rob'te Hubberde, lykewife attendunte there
for the fcaffe kepinge of the fame clothe by
the fpace of 20 dayes, Henry Wilcox 20
dayes, Rob'te Welton 20 dayes, and Walter Browne 10 dayes. Soma 70 dayes at 1s.
the daye   —   —   —   3 10 0

Som'a £.22 10s.

At £.1 the yarde   —   155 yards qr.   155 5 0

At £.1 2s. the yarde   —   30 yards   33 0 0

2   At

At 19s. the yarde	—	30 yards	28	10	0
At 18s. the yarde	—	116 yards qr.	104	12	6
At 17s. the yarde	—	65 yards qr.	55	9	3
At 16s. the yarde	—	93 yards 3 qrs.	75	0	0
At 15s. the yarde	—	130 yards	97	10	0
At 14s. the yarde	—	151 yards qr.	105	17	6
At 14s. 4d. the yarde	—	8 yards di.	6	1	10
At 13s. the yarde	—	97 yards di.	63	7	6
At 13s. 4d. the yarde	—	274 yardes	182	13	4
At 12s. the yarde	—	404 yards di.	242	14	0
At 12s. 8d. the yarde	—	12 yards di.	7	18	4
At 12s. the yarde	—	13 yards	7	16	0
At 12s. 4d. the yarde	—	24 yards di.	15	2	2
At 11s. the yarde	—	379 yardes	208	9	0
At 11s. 6d. the yarde	—	79 yards	45	8	6
At 11s. 4d. the yarde	—	18 yards	10	4	0
At 11s. 8 the yarde	—	71 yardes	41	8	4
At 10s. the yarde	—	658 yards qr.	329	2	6
At 10s. 4d. the yarde	—	69 yards	35	13	0
At 10s. 6d. the yarde	—	125 yards 3 qrs.	66	0	4½
At 9s. the yarde	—	511 yards	229	19	0
At 9s. 4d. the yarde	—	191 yards 3 qrs.	89	9	8
At 9s. 6d. the yarde	—	93 yards qr.	44	5	10½
At 9s. 8d. the yarde	—	58 yards di.	28	5	0
At 8s. the yarde	—	1237 yards di.	495	0	0
At 8s. 6d. the yarde	—	342 yards qr.	145	9	1½
At 8s. 4d. the yarde	—	218 yards 3 qrs.	91	2	11
At 8s. 8d. the yarde	—	84 yards qr.	36	10	2
At 7s. the yarde	—	639 yards di.	223	16	6
At 7s. 4d. the yarde	—	207 yards	75	18	0
At 7s. 6d. the yarde	—	395 yards 3 qrs.	148	8	11

Z z 2   At

At 7s. 8d. the yarde	—	213 yards 3 qrs.	81	18	9
At 6s. the yarde	—	550 yards di.	165	3	0
At 6s. 8d. the yarde	—	652 yards	217	6	8
At 6s. 4d. the yarde	—	507 yards qr.	160	12	7
At 6s. 6d. the yarde	—	22 yards di.	7	6	3
At 5s. the yarde	—	23 yards 3 qrs.	5	18	9
At 5s. 6d. the yarde	—	338 yards qr.	95	16	9
At 5s. 4d the yarde	—	68 yards qr.	18	4	0
At 4s. 4d. the yarde	—	14 yards di.	61	0	10

Som'a total yardes   9376 yards di.
Argent. £.4180 17s. 7d.

Sum' to' of all the pvic'ons and other
charges aforesaide   —   —   5946   9   9

The countinge howse.

			Servants.
John duke of Northumbelande, lorde great master	nil.		
Sir Thomas Cheyney, knighte, treasorer	10 yardes	8	24 yardes
Sir Rycharde Cotton, knighte, comptroller	10 yardes	8	24 yardes
Sir Thomas Weldon, coferer	10 yardes	{ 4 1 clarke	12 yardes 4 yardes
Myg'hell Wentewoorthe, Edwarde Shelley, and James Gage, masters of the howsholde, to every of them 9 yards	27 yardes	{ 12 6 clarkes	36 yardes 24 yardes James

		Servauntes	
James Sutton and John Dodge, to either of them 9 yardes	18 yardes	{ 8 { 4 clarks	24 yardes 16 yardes
Thomas Curſſon and Henry Byrkinhedde, clarkes comptrollers, to ether of them 9 yardes	18 yardes	{ 8 { 4 clarks	24 yardes 16 yardes
Henry Tepiple, yeoman uſher	4 yardes		
Henry Bloder, grome uſher	4 yardes		
The Bakehowſe.			
Anthonye Crane, ſjeaunte	7 yardes	2	6 yardes
Thomas Clarke, clarke	7 yardes	1	3 yardes
Hughe Gryſſythe, yeoman for the mowthe	4 yardes		
Arnolde Turner and Rauſſe Engliſhe, yeoman furnator, to ether of them 4 yardes	8 yardes		
Robarte Style, yeoman garnator	4 yardes		
Thomas Almner, grome for the mouthe	4 yardes		
Rycharde White, grome of the howſholde	4 yardes		
Thomas Fyſher, Benedict Roſkley, and John Venner, to everye of them 4 yardes	12 yardes		

Will'm

Servauntes

Will'm Williams, John
Dyer, Ellys Potter, Wil-
l'm Wrighte, Robarte
Wilfon, and James Bate,
conductes, to everye of
them 3 yardes　　　　　18 yardes

The Pantrye.

John Jofielyn, Cjeauntte　　7 yardes　2　　6 yardes
Nicholas Singleton and
Thomas Coxe, yeomen
for the mouthe, to ether
of them 4 yardes　　　　8 yardes
Will'm Coxe, yeoman　　4 yardes
Humfreye Dymmocke and
John Temple, yeomen,
for the howfholde, to
ether of them 4 yardes　　8 yardes
Robarte Lawrence, grome
Brewer　　　　　　　4 yardes
John Wallis and Anthonye
Tompfon, gromes for the
howfholde, to ether of
them 4 y'ds　　　　　8 yardes
Frauncis Cockes, Roger
Streate, and Henrye
Leeche, pages, to ev'y of
them 4 y'ds　　　　　12 yardes
Hughe Harper, breade
bearer　　　　　　　4 yardes

The

Servauntes

The celler.

Will'm Abbotte, ſjeaunte	9 yardes	2	6 yardes
Hughe Aſkewe and Robarte Gardener, yeomen for the mouthe, to ether of them 4 y'ds	8 yardes		
John Thorowgood and Jeffrey Perrens, yeomen brevers, at 4 yards the pece	8 yardes		
George Aſke and Thomas Hunttley, yeomen purveyors, to ether of them 4 yardes	8 yardes		
Richarde Mylner, grome grobber	4 yardes		
Thomas Apricharde, yeoman of the bottles	4 yardes		
Auſten Aſkewe and Richarde Guye, pages, to ether of them 4 yardes	8 yardes		

The Buttrye.

Edwarde Craſſewell, Thomas Walcotte, and Chriſtopher Buſte, to every of them 4 yards	12 yardes
Rycharde Hemmynge and Rycharde Smithe, to ether of them, beinge gromes, 4 y'ds.	8 yardes

Nicholas

Servauntes

Nicholas Tolley and John Wale, pages, to ether of them 4 yardes	8 yardes		
John Rowsley, yeoman pveior	4 yardes		
John Forman and Thomas Horsley, gromes purveyors, to ether of them 4 yardes	8 yardes		
The Picher howse.			
Will'm Lambertte and Edwarde Byrde, yeoman, to ether of them 4 yardes	8 yardes		
Will'm Bleke, John Davye, Henry Fryer, and John Danby, to every of them 4 yardes	16 yardes		
Peter Bygott, page	4 yardes		
The Spycerye.			
Rycharde Wade, cheffe clarke	9 yardes	3	9 yardes
Anthony Weldon, 2ᵈ clarke	9 yardes	2	6 yardes
Thomas Asbye 3ᵈ clarke	9 yardes	2	6 yardes
Thomas Garter, yeoman, powder beater	4 yardes		
The Chaundelorye.			
John Tymewell, sʰjeaunte	7 yardes	2	6 yardes
John Irelande and Thomas Sydwaye, yeomen, to ether of them 4 yardes	8 yardes		
John Harryson, Peter Lawarde, and Stephen Furnishe, gromes, every of them 4 yardes	12 yardes		

Henry

Servauntes

Henry Preston, page	4 yardes		
The confec'conarye.			
Thomas Alfoppe, ferjeaunte	7 yardes	2	6 yardes
John Bartelette and John Avon, yeomen, to ether of them 4 yards	8 yardes		
Thomas Dove, grome	4 yardes		
Thom's Hemmyngwaye, page	4 yardes		
The yewrye.			
Jeffrey Villers, ferjeaunte	7 yardes	2	6 yardes
Nicholas Celley and Allen Mathewe, gentilmen, to ether of them 7 yardes	14 yardes	4	11 yardes
Richarde Lewes, Rauffe Sherman, and Hughe Rogers, yeomen, to every of them 4 yardes	12 yardes		
Will'm Pulforde, Hugh Davye, gromes, to ether of them 4 y'ds	8 yardes		
Robarte Price, Hug. John Robertts, to ether of them 4 y'des	8 yardes		
The Lawndrye.			
Robarte Glaftowe, and Will'm Coke, yeomen, to ether of them 4 yardes	8 yardes		
John Jhones and Will'm Barland, gromes, to ether of them 4 yardes	8 yards		

VOL. XII.   A a a   John

Servauntes

John Meſſenger and Richarde Blage, pages	8 yardes		
The Waferye			
Adam Alee, yeoman	4 yardes		
John Gieffrey, grome	4 yards		
The Kechyn.			
George Stonehowſe, cheffe clarke	9 yardes	2 1 clarke 1	6 yardes 4 yardes 3 yardes
Robarte Beverley, 2ᵈ clarke	9 yards	1 clarke	4 yardes
Chriſtofer Skevington, thirde clarke	9 yardes	1 1 clarke	3 yardes 4 yardes
George Webſter, Mʳ. coke for the Kinges mouthe	9 yardes	3	9 yardes
Robarte Coole, Richarde Byſhoppe, and Philippe Yarrowe, yeomen for the mouthe, every one 4 y'ds	12 yardes		
Will'm Laurence, John Bodye, and John Houghton, gromes for the mouthe, to ev'y of them 4 y'ds.	12 yardes		
Myghell Haywarde, Thomas Mudde, Thomas Alderton, and Richarde Coo, children for the mouthe, to everye of them 3 y'des.	12 yardes		
Edwarde Wilkinſon, Mʳ Cooke for the hawle place	9 yardes	2	6 yardes
			Will'm

Will'm Moore, Henry Saxon,
and John Maye, yeomen for
the hawle place, at 4 yd's.
the pece   12 yardes

Thomas Thornebacke, Ro-
barte Longe, and Thomas
Clarke, gromes of the hawle
place, to every of them 4
yardes   12 yardes

Richarde Newton, Nicholas
Shelbye, Walter Freman,
and Gylbertte Copingey,
children of the hawle place,
to every of them 3 yardes   12 yardes

     The Larder.

John Brickett, sergeaunte	7 yardes	2	6 yardes
George Lovell, clarke	7 yardes	1	3 yardes

Thomas Inglifhe, Thomas
Durham, and Gylbertte
Hoope, yeomen, to ev'y of
them 4 yardes   12 yardes

Thomas Jolles, John Moyes,
Richarde Goodwin, gromes,
to every of them 4 yardes   12 yardes

Gregory Burton, Will'm Richardefon, and John Ma-
kender, pages, to every of
them 4 yardes   12 yardes

     The Boylinghowfe.

John White, yeoman   4 yardes

Serveauntes

Will'm Radley, John Bykeley,
  and   Will'm   Simpfon,
  gromes, to every of them 4
  yardes   12 yardes

    The Cateye.

John Hopkins, ferjeauntte	7 yardes	2	6 yardes
Stephen Darrell, clarke	7 yardes	1	3 yardes

Thomas Lucas, yeoman, pur-
  veyor of the fea fyfhe   4 yardes
Peter   Hunynges,   Edmonde
  Andros, yeomen, p'rveyors
  of freffie water fyfhe, to
  every of them 4 y'ds   8 yardes
Edwarde Mafter and Edwarde
  Ruffell, yeomen, purveyors
  of oxen and fhepe, to ether
  of them 4 yards   8 yardes
Will'm Byrde, Henry Good-
  win, yeomen, bowchers, to
  ether of them 4 yardes   8 yardes
Chriftopher   Harwoode   and
  RauffeSavage, gromes, bowchers, ether of them 4 yardes   8 yardes
Thomas Jury and John Wafte,
  yeomen,   purveyors   of
  caulves and hogges, to ether
  of them 4 y'ds   8 yardes
Rauffe Harris, yeoman, keper
  of the paftures   4 yardes

6   John

John Robbinſon and Richarde
Dawſon, gromes of the
herdes, to ether of them 4
yardes   8 yardes

George Hyll, yeoman, keper
of the ſtoore   4 yardes

     The Powltrye.

Davyd Sambroke, ſ'jeauntte   7 yardes 2   6 yardes

Edwarde Darrell, clarke   7 yardes 1   3 yardes

Will'm Gurley, yeoman for
the mouthe   4 yardes

Edmonde Hampſhere and Ed-
warde Albyn, yeomen, to
ether of them 4 yardes   8 yardes

John Dodge, yeoman, pur-
veior of lambes   4 yardes

James Mannynge, Thomas
Gorley, and John Pratte,
gromes, to every of them 4
yardes   12 yardes

    The Skaldeing Howſe.

Richarde Boughton, Robarte
Hyll, and John Hyde, yeo-
men, to every of them 4
yardes   12 yardes

Thomas Skirres and John
Taylor, gromes, to ether of
them 4 yardes   8 yardes

Connenaunte Robynſon, page 4 yardes

    The Paſtrye

Thomas Dover, ſerjeaunte   7 yardes 2   6 yardes
                                                James

		Servauntes	
James Woodfurde, clarke	7 yardes	1	3 yardes
Stephen Moone and Thomas Colley, yeomen for the mouthe, to ether of them 4 yardes	8 yardes		
Symon Dudley, John Campe, Geffrey Frenche, and Richard Typſhawe, gromes, to ether of them 4 yardes	16 yardes		
Richarde Perſon, John Mondaye, Rauſſe Battye, Roberte Dover, children, to everye of them 3 yardes	12 yardes		

The Sqwillarye.

John Worrall, ſerjeaunte	7 yardes	2	6 yardes
Alexander Horden, clarke	7 yardes	1	3 yardes
John Harvye, Edwarde Rowſley, and James Anyon, yeomen, to ev'ry of them 4 yards	12 yardes		
Thomas Cutler and Robarte Harryott, gromes, to every of them 4 yardes	8 yardes		
John White, Will'm Alate, Will'm Bartholomewe, Bryan Byrtte, pages, to every of them 4 yardes	16 yardes		
Thomas Auſten, Will'm Gilman, Will'm Crockforde, and Lewes Loyde, children, to every of them 3 yardes	12 yardes		

The

Servauntes

The Woodyarde.

John Brice, ferjeaunte	7 yardes	2	6 yardes
John Abington, clarke	7 yardes	1	3 yardes
John Skinner, Nicholas Wayneman, Henry Faierfelde, Frauncis Myghell, yeomen, to everye of them 4 yardes	16 yardes		
Will' Buke, Robarte Clotworthe, John Wells, Thomas Colman, gromes, to everye of them 4 y'ds	16 yardes		
George Writtington and Robarte Nevell, pages, to ether of them 4 yardes	8 yardes		

Surviors of the dreffor.

Will'm Ryther and John Danyell, furveiors of the dreffor for the Kinge, to ether of them 9 yardes	18 yardes	6	18 yardes

Marfhalls of the hawle.

Thomas Payne, Richarde Wheteley, Thomas Myles, John Apowell, John Fytzrichards, marfhalls, to ether of them 7 y'ds.	35 yardes	10	30 yardes

The Harbingers.

John Gylman, gentilman	9 yardes	2	6 yardes
Edwarde Wharton, Henry			

Man-

Servauntes

Mannynge, Edwarde Page, Richarde Darhye, yeomen, to every of them 4 yardes	16 yardes		
The Annorye.			
Doctor Coxe, amner	10 yardes	8	24 yardes
Will'm Todde, under amner	9 yardes	1	3 yardes
Doctor Standifhe, confeſſor of the howſholde	9 yardes	1	3 yardes
Thomas Boxeleye, Laurence Wetherhed, Bartholomewe Redhedde, yeomen, to everye of them 4 yardes	12 yardes		
Will'm Horfley and Will'm Ruſſell, gromes, to ether of them 4 y'ds	8 yardes		
John Marten, Edmonde Skaffe, and Will'm Longe, children, to every of them 3 yardes	9 yardes		
The Porters.			
Will'm Knevett, ſ'jeauntte, John Herde, Thomas Battſon, and Thomas Ball, yeomen, to every of them 4 yardes	9 yardes	3	9 yardes
	12 yardes		
Will'm Curtes and John Heyton, gromes, to ether of them 4 y'ds	8 yardes		
Purveiors of Cartes.			
Edmonde Myſſette, yeoman	4 yardes		
John Plume, grome	4 yardes		

The

Servauntes

The Gylder.

John Feltts, gilder　　　　4 yardes

The Dogge Keper.

John Beadle, dogge keper　　4 yardes

Sewers of the hawle.

Thomas Marvyn, John Stowe,
Clementte Norres, Randell
Thirkill, fewers of the
hawle, to every of them 7
yardes　　　　　　28 yardes　4　　12 yardes

Surviors of the Dreffor.

Goddarde Hall and Robarte
Jerningham, furveiors of
the dreffor, to ether of them,
7 yardes　　　　　　14 yardes　2　　6 yardes

The Waxe Chandeler.

Will'm Anftey, waxe chandeler　4 yardes

Servitors of the hawle.

Thomas Walker, Thomas
Tymperley, Leonarde Wil-
kinfon, Thomas Rowe, John
Fofter, John Savage, John
Redinge, Hughe Parye,
John Bifhoppe, James
Swifte, John Grete, Wil-
fride Eafton, George Reade,
Will'm Morton, Will'm
Fefye, Owen Burrowes,
Will'm Wekes, and John

Ventrife, to everye of them
4 yardes   72 yardes
    Meffingers.
John Davye, meffengere of the
comptinge houfe   4 yardes
    Wyne Porters.
Thomas Smithe, Davye Jones,
RobarteWinckeley, Robarte
Lovell, Thomas Crofte, Ed-
moonde Wafhell, John Sta-
cye, Thomas P'nell, Tho-
mas Richardefon, Richarde
Stertte, wyneporters, to
every of them 4 yardes   40 yardes
    The Fruterer.
Nicholas Harris, fruӽerer   4 yardes
    The Smithe.
Guyllam Votyer the Smithe   4 yardes
    Artificers and other Officers parteigninge
    to the Howfholde.
PeterRobbynfon, botell maker,   4 yardes
Thomas Dentte, purveyor of
rufhes   4 yardes
Edwarde Rowfley and Nicho-
las Calverley, yeomen, carte
takers, to ether of them 4
yardes   8 yardes
Rauffe Boughey, cowper of
the cellarre   4 yardes
Will'm Uftewayte, pewterer 4 yardes

                                                  Chrif-

Chriſtopher Porter, cowper of the howſholde	4 yardes
John Kingſton	4 yardes
Richarde Grene, partridge taker	4 yardes
John Grene, coſer maker	4 yardes
John Skinner, maſter ſkowrer	4 yardes
John Colman, tynker	4 yardes
Porters ſkowrers and turne broches, to every of them 1 y'de di. to the nomber of 31 p'ſons	46 yardes di.
Motley, woodberer	3 yardes

Penſioners of the Howſholde

Robarte Kynge, porter yeoman	4 yardes
John Blome, yeoman of the chan'dry	4 yardes
Robarte Elton, yeoman of the ſtable	4 yardes
John Dawnſtowe, yeoman of the chaundrye	4 yardes
John Dune, yeoman of the larder	4 yardes
Henry Fyſher, yeoman of the woodyarde	4 yardes
Chriſtopher Choninge, grome	4 yardes
John Bennett, yeoman porter	4 yardes
Rob'te Cowper, of the buttrye	4 yardes
Edwarde Jones	4 yardes

B b b 2   John

Servauntes

John Dyxe, yeoman of the ewerye	4 yards		
Richarde Elyott, fervitor of the hawle	4 yards		
Will'm Bate, yeoman of the woodyarde	4 yards		
Symonde Cleyboorne, grome of the woodyarde	4 yards		
James Pykes, barbor	4 yardes		
Roger Reper, yeoman, purveior of the pultrye	4 yards		
Henry Mylls, purveior of the fpicerye	4 yards		
Edmonde Felton, mafter cofferere and clarke	7 yards	2	6 yards
For Mr. Treaforer and Mr. Comptroller, to either of them, for trappors, 6 yardes	12 yards		
The Chapell.			
The fubdeane of the chapell	9 yards	1	3 yards
Sir Nicholas Archeholde, prefte	9 yards	1	3 yards
Sir Will'm Walker, prefte	9 yardes	1	3 yardes
Sir Roberte Chamberleine	9 yardes	1	3 yardes
Sir Will'm Gravefende, prefte	9 yardes	1	3 yardes
Sir John Angell, prefte	9 yardes	1	3 yardes
Will'm Hochine, gentilman	7 yardes	1	3 yardes
Thomas Byrde, gentylman	7 yards	1	3 yards
Richarde Bowre, gentilman	7 yards	1	3 yards
Roberte Pirrey, gentilman	7 yards	1	3 yards
Will'm Barbor, gent.	7 yards	1	3 yards
			Roberte

		Servauntes	
Roberte Richmounte, gent.	7 yards	1	3 yards
Thomas Wayte, gent.	7 yards	1	3 yards
Thomas Tallis, gent.	7 yards	1	3 yards
Nicholas Mellowe	7 yards	1	3 yards
Thomas Wrighte	7 yards	1	3 yards
John Bendebowe	7 yards	1	3 yards
Robert Stone, gent.	7 yards	1	3 yards
John Shepherde, gent.	7 yards	1	3 yards
Will'm Maperley, gent.	7 yards	1	3 yards
George Edwardes, gent.	7 yards	1	3 yards
Roberte Moorecocke, gent.	7 yards	1	3 yards
Will'm Hynns	7 yards	1	3 yards
Richarde Ayleworthe	7 yards	1	3 yards
Thomas Palfreman	7 yards	1	3 yards
Roger Cotton, gent.	7 yards	1	3 yards
Luke Cauftell, gent.	7 yards	1	3 yards
Richarde Farraunte	7 yards	1	3 yards
Edwarde Adame	7 yards	1	3 yards
John Singer, gofpeller.	9 yards	1	3 yards
Roberte Baffocke, f'jeaunte of the veftrye	7 yards	1	3 yards
James Cafter, gent.	7 yards	1	3 yards
Thomas Couflon, yeoman	7 yards		
John Lucum, yeoman	7 yards		
John Denman, yeoman	7 yards		
Walter Thuleby, yeoman	7 yards		
Morres Tedder, yeoman	7 yards		
Hughe Will'ms, yeoman	7 yards		
Richarde Tyll, com'on f'una'nte	3 yards		

		Servauntes	
12 children of the Kinges chappell, to evry of them 2 yards	24 yardes		
The com'on servaunte to the fayde children	3 yardes		
Clarcks of the Counceill.			
Armigill Wade	9 yardes	4	12 yardes
Barnarde Hampton	9 yardes	4	12 yardes
John Fothergyll, keper of the cownceiles recordes	7 yardes		
Gentilmen of the Previe Chambre.			
Sir Mores Bartlett, knighte	10 yardes	8	24 yardes
Sir Henry Nevell, knighte	10 yardes	8	24 yardes
Sir Will'm Fitzwill'ms,	10 yardes	8	24 yardes
Mr. Thomas Cotton	10 yardes	8	24 yardes
Will'm Som'er the Kinges foole, for his gowne and cooate	7 yardes	1	3 yardes
Gentilmen Ushers daylie Wayters.			
John Norris	9 yardes	3	9 yardes
Philippe Bauberye	9 yardes	3	9 yardes
Frauncis Everarde	9 yardes	3	9 yardes
John Franckewell	9 yardes	3	9 yardes
Hercules Raynsforthe	9 yardes	3	9 yardes
Gent. Ushers Qwarter Wayters.			
John Harmon	9 yardes	2	6 yardes
Will'm Tanner	9 yardes	2	6 yardes
Stephen Brackenbury	9 yardes	2	6 yardes
Thomas Nuporte	9 yardes	2	6 yardes
			Fowre

		Servauntes	
Fower yonge Lordes,			
The lorde Thomas Howarde	10 yardes	8	24 yardes
The lorde Gyles	10 yardes	2	6 yardes
The lorde Lumley	10 yardes	2	6 yardes
The lorde Mounte Joye	10 yardes	2	6 yardes
Sewers of the Chambre.			
Rycharde Forster	9 yardes	2	6 yardes
Richarde White	9 yardes	2	6 yardes
Robarte Alee	9 yardes	2	6 yardes
Turnor	9 yardes	2	6 yardes
Peers	9 yardes	2	6 yardes
Gromes of the Chambre.			
Thomas Garman	4 yardes		
John Johnson senior	4 yardes		
John Johnson junior	4 yardes		
Will'm Stoone	4 yardes		
Thylde	4 yardes		
Flemynge	4 yardes		
George Bayne	4 yardes		
Chapleyns.			
Sir Anthonye Ottwaye	9 yardes	3	9 yardes
Sir Edmonde Grindall	9 yardes	3	9 yardes
Serjeauntts at Armes.			
Richarde Rayneshawe	9 yardes	2	6 yardes
Will'm Clarke	9 yardes	2	6 yardes
Thomas Hales	9 yardes	2	6 yardes
Hughe Minors	9 yardes	2	6 yardes
Laurence Serle	9 yardes	2	6 yardes
Richarde Worley	9 yardes	2	6 yardes
Hughe Willoughbye	9 yardes	2	6 yardes
Henry Jones	9 yardes	2	6 yardes

The

Servauntes

The Garde.

John Peers, clarke of the
cheke, for 24 yeomen of the
garde, to every of them 4
yards   96 yardes

Kinges at Armes.

MasterGarter, principall kinge
at armes   9 yardes 4   12 yardes
Clarentius   9 yardes 3   9 yardes

Heralds at Armes.

Windesore   8 yardes 2   6 yardes
Richemonde   8 yardes 2   6 yardes
Somerfett   8 yardes 2   6 yardes

Purfyvantts at Armes.

Rouge Dragon   8 yardes 1   3 yardes
Rouge Crosse   8 yardes 1   3 yardes

Gromes of the Kinges Prevye Chambre.

John Phylpott   9 yardes 4   12 yardes
Christopher Salmon   9 yardes 4   12 yardes
John Fowler   9 yardes 4   12 yardes
Richarde Chyttwoodde   9 yardes 4   12 yardes
Thomas Streate   9 yardes 4   12 yardes
Davyd Vincente   9 yardes 4   12 yardes
Will'm Simbarke   9 yardes 4   12 yardes
Richarde Cooke   9 yardes 4   12 yardes
Will'm Thorppe   9 yardes 4   12 yardes
John Osborn   9 yardes 4   12 yardes
John Penne   9 yardes 4   12 yardes
Edwarde Harman   9 yardes 4   12 yardes
Walter Earle   9 yardes 4   12 yardes
        6   Clarckes

Servauntes

Clarckes of the Signett.

Richarde Taverner	9 yardes	{ 2	6 yardes
		1 clarkes	3 yardes
Will'm Honnynges	9 yardes	{ 2	6 yardes
		1 clarke	3 yardes
Gregory Raylton	9 yardes	{ 2	6 yardes
		1 clarke	3 yardes
Nicafius Yettfwertt	9 yardes	{ 2	6 yardes
		1 clarke	3 yardes
John Clyffe	9 yardes	{ 2	6 yardes
		1 clarke	3 yardes

The Lordes and Knyghtes of
the Kings Prevye Counceill.

The archebifhoppe of Caunterburye	16 yardes	12	36 yardes
The lorde chauncellor	16 yardes	12	36 yardes
The lorde treaforer	16 yardes	12	36 yardes
The lorde prevye feale	16 yardes	12	36 yardes
The duke of Suffolke	16 yardes	12	36 yardes
The earle of Arundell	16 yardes	12	36 yardes
The earle of Shrewfburye	16 yardes	12	36 yardes
The earle of Penbroke	16 yardes	12	36 yardes
The lorde chamberleine	16 yardes	12	36 yardes
The lorde Cobham	10 yardes	8	24 yardes
Mr. feacretory Peter	10 yardes	8	24 yardes
Mr. fecretorie Cicell	10 yardes	8	24 yardes
Mr. fecretorye Cheeke	10 yardes	8	24 yardes
Sir Edwarde Northe	10 yardes	8	24 yardes
Sir John Mafon	10 yardes	8	24 yardes
Sir John Baker	10 yardes	8	24 yardes

		Servauntes.	
Sir Rauffe Sadleyre	10 yardes	8	24 yardes
Sir Robarte Dowes	10 yardes	8	24 yardes
Lords and gent. of the Kinges Prevye Chambre.			
The earle of Worcefter	16 yardes	12	35 yardes
The lorde Thomas Graye	10 yardes	8	24 yardes
Sir Anthony Selenger	10 yardes	8	24 yardes
Sir Thomas Wrothe	10 yardes	8	24 yardes
Sir Anthonye Cooke	10 yardes	8	24 yardes
Mr. Wheler	10 yardes	8	24 yards
Sir Richarde Bluntte	10 yardes	8	24 yardes
Mr. Thomas Cotton	10 yardes	8	24 yardes
Cupberer.			
Mr. Fofter	9 yardes	4	12 yards
Kervers.			
The lorde Fitzwater	10 yardes	8	24 yards
Sir Edwarde Rogers	9 yardes	4	12 yardes
Mr. Carye	9 yardes	3	9 yardes
Sewers.			
Sir Perfivall Harte, fewers.	9 yardes	4	12 yardes
Sqwier for the Bodye.			
Mr. John Darcye, efqiviers for the bodye	9 yardes	3	9 yardes
Gentilmen Ufhers Quarter Wayters.			
Will'm Morice	9 yardes	2	6 yardes
Robarte Hodgkyns	9 yardes	2	6 yardes
6			Anthony

		Servauntes	
Anthony Wingfelde	9 yardes	2	6 yardes
Robarte Kinge	9 yardes	2	6 yardes
Sewers of the Chambre.			
Will'm Sackvylde	9 yardes	2	6 yardes
Randall Dodde	9 yardes	2	6 yardes
Edmonde Lyle	9 yardes	2	6 yardes
Officers at Armes.			
Norrey	9 yardes	3	9 yardes
Chester	8 yardes	2	6 yardes
Blewe Mantell	8 yardes	2	6 yardes
Paynters.			
Thomas Childe	4 yardes		
Rycharde Widers	4 yardes		
S'ieantts at Armes.			
John Smithe	9 yardes	2	6 yardes
John Saincte John	9 yardes	2	6 yardes
Walter Chankott	9 yardes	2	6 yardes
Richarde Borwell	9 yardes	2	6 yardes
John Knottsforthe	9 yardes	2	6 yardes
John Rechebell	9 yardes	2	6 yardes
The Kinges Chapleins.			
Mr. Latymer	9 yardes	3	9 yardes
Mr. Byll	9 yardes	3	9 yardes
Mr. Perne	9 yardes	3	9 yardes
Mr. Buttell	9 yardes	3	9 yardes
Mr. Rudde	9 yardes	3	9 yardes
The Kings Phisitions.			
Doctor Owen	6 yardes	3	9 yardes
Doctor Wendye	6 yardes	3	9 yardes

Ccc 2   The

		Servauntes	
The Potycarye.			
John Hemyngwey Poticarye	4 yardes	1	3 yardes
Surgeons.			
Thomas Vicars, ferjeaunte	4 yardes	2	6 yardes
Forrelte	4 yards	2	6 yardes
Ferres	4 yardes	2	6 yardes
Gromes of the Chambre.			
Rycharde Hodges	4 yardes		
John Baker	4 yardes		
Richarde Owtredde	4 yardes		
John Oker	4 yardes		
Anthony Grynham	4 yardes		
Nicholas Darbye	4 yardes		
Will'm Chatterton	4 yardes		
Laurence Huffey	4 yardes		
Will'm Aman	4 yardes		
Pages of the Chambre.			
John Haydon	4 yardes		
John Colier	4 yardes		
Will'm Worley	4 yardes		
Richarde Jones	4 yardes		
The Warderobe of the Roobes.			
Robarte Robotham, yeoman	9 yardes	4	12 yardes
Humfrey Adderley, grome	9 yardes	4	12 yardes
Thomas Jones, page	9 yardes	4	12 yardes
The Warderobe of the Bedds.			
Humfrey Orme, yeoman	7 yardes	1	3 yardes
Marmaduke Warderobe	7 yardes	1	3 yardes
Henry Plefington, grome	7 yardes	1	3 yardes
Richarde Beathell, grome	7 yardes	1	3 yardes
James Harman, page	7 yardes	1	3 yardes

Rauffe

		Servauntes	
Rauffe Rowlandefon, page	7 yardes	1	3 yardes
Robarte Childerney, fmithe	4 yardes		
The Meffingers of the Chambre.			
Adam Gafkin	4 yardes		
Robarte Capon	4 yardes		
Robarte Gromewell	4 yardes		
Will'm Herne	4 yardes		
Frauncis the pofte	4 yardes		
The Trumpetors.			
Benedicto Browne, f'jeaunte of trumpettors	7 yardes	2	6 yardes
8 trumpettors, to everye of them 4 yardes	32 yardes		
The Syngers			
John Temple	9 yardes	2	6 yardes
Richarde Atkinfon	9 yardes	2	6 yardes
Thomas Kente	9 yardes	2	6 yardes
Will'm Maperley	9 yardes	2	6 yardes
Will'm Tyleſley, keper of the ſtandinge warderobe at Windefore	4 yardes		
Robarte Hobbes, keper of the warderobe at Moore	4 yardes		
Will'm Griffithe, keper of the warderobe at Richemonde	4 yardes		
The matte maker yeoman	4 yardes		
Modena maker of the Kinges picture	4 yardes		

The

		Servauntes	
The hedd Officers of the Stable.			
Sir Edwarde Haftinges, Mᵗ of the Qwenes horffes	10 yardes	8	24 yardes
Henrye Lighe, cheffe avener	9 yardes	3	9 yardes
John Skinner, the feconde clarke of the avenrye	9 yardes	3	9 yardes
Nicholas Grene, the 3ᵗᵉ clarke of the avenrye	9 yardes	3	9 yardes
Edmonde Standen, clarke of the ftable	9 yardes	3	9 yardes
The Qwyries.			
Richarde Audeley	9 yardes	3	9 yardes
Sir Anthony Browne, knighte	9 yardes	4	12 yardes
Henrye Norrice	9 yardes	3	9 yardes
The lorde Chidiocke Pawlett	9 yardes	3	9 yardes
Sir Jaques Granado, knighte	9 yardes	4	12 yardes
Sir George Hawarde, knighte	9 yardes	4	12 yardes
Henrye Partridge	9 yardes	3	9 yardes
Barnardyne Granado	9 yardes	3	9 yardes
Serieaunte of the Cariage.			
John Ownftedde, ferjeaunte of the cariages	7 yardes	2	6 yardes
S'ieaunte Ferror.			
Thomas Dyxon, ferieaunte Ferror and Marfhall Ferror	7 yardes	2	6 yardes
Surveiors of the Stable.			
John Palmer	9 yardes	3	9 yardes
Mighell Grene	9 yardes	3	9 yardes
			George

		Servauntes	
George Stafforde	9 yardes	3	9 yardes
Will'm Brackenburye, gent. ryder	9 yardes	3	9 yardes

The Footemen.

Edmonde Bowteil	4 yardes
Thomas Edmondes	4 yardes
John Smithe	4 yardes
Richarde Clarke	4 yardes
Chriftopher Bothe	4 yardes
Humfrey Colley	4 yardes
Edmonde Duke	4 yardes

The Ryders.

John Nyxon	9 yardes	3	9 yardes
John Harrifon	9 yardes	3	9 yardes
Henrye Webbe	9 yardes	3	9 yardes
Anthonye Lamberte	9 yardes	3	9 yardes
John Webbe	9 yardes	3	9 yardes
Bartholomewe Jeekell	4 yardes		
Gylberte Comporte	4 yardes		
Henrye Hynde	4 yardes		
Henrye Marfhe	4 yardes		
Will'm Crotenden	4 yardes		
Nicholas Durraunte	4 yardes		
Will'm Dowley	4 yardes		

Officers of the Stable

John Johnfon, yeoman of the male	4 yardes
Thomas Griffithe, yeoman of the ftirroppe	4 yardes

Will'm

Will'm Harrifon, yeoman, fad-
leir ... 4 yardes
John Geynifhe, yeoman, peck-
man ... 4 yardes
Will'm Creffente, yeoman, bytt
maker ... 4 yardes

Yeomen Ferrors.
John Dixon ... 4 yardes
Peter Browne ... 4 yardes
John Golightlye ... 4 yardes
Will'm Golightlye ... 4 yardes

Yeoman of the Cloofe Carre.
John Darington, yeoman of
the clofe carre of the
roobes ... 4 yardes

Gromes of the ftyropp.
John Browne ... 4 yardes
Gilberte Johnfon ... 4 yardes
Will'm Hamerton ... 4 yardes
Stephen Prince ... 4 yardes

Grome of the Bottles.
John Henfhawe, grome of the
bottles ... 4 yardes

Gromes Ferrors.
John Elmfley ... 4 yardes
Will'm Harpen ... 4 yardes
Martyn Almayn ... 4 yardes
Thomas Marten ... 4 yardes

Gromes of the Cloffe Carre.
Richarde Laurence ... 4 yardes
George Stede ... 4 yardes

Sumptermen.

John Waterer	4 yardes
John Moore	4 yardes
Rauffe Johnfon	4 yardes
John Portes	4 yardes
Will'm Browne	4 yardes
John Hall	4 yardes
John Mapfter	4 yardes
Thomas Hawke	4 yardes

Muletters.

Robarte Oliver	4 yardes
John Dalton	4 yardes
Robarte Reade	4 yardes
John Bafeley	4 yardes
Piero Coffingarde	4 yardes
Robarte Barwike	4 yardes
Will'm Rofemary	4 yardes
Robarte Romaine	4 yardes
Cofine Damyan	4 yardes

Kepers of Courfers and Jen-
netts, &c.

Clemente Sandeforde	3 yardes
Thomas Bowbye	3 yardes
Henry Guyllam	3 yardes

Courfermen.

Will'm Gumbye	3 yardes
Reignolde Brewerton	3 yardes
Richarde Hall	3 yardes
John Forman	3 yardes
Thomas Childe	3 yardes
Andrewe Dewberye	3 yardes

VOL. XII.   D d d   John

		Servauntes	
John Robynſon	3 yardes		
Thomas Beere	3 yardes		
Thomas Wylde	3 yardes		
Roger Bayely	3 yardes		
Richarde Conwey	3 yardes		
John Medwin	3 yardes		
Richarde Smithe	3 yardes		
Morrice Smithe	3 yardes		
Richarde Atkinſon	3 yardes		
Lewes Pecocke	3 yardes		
Anthony Philpotte	3 yardes		
Robarte Cordell	3 yardes		
Rauffe Bolton	3 yardes		
John Preſton	3 yardes		
Roger Cheſter	3 yardes		
Robarte Thomas	3 yardes		
Andrewe Stephens	3 yardes		
George Oxon	3 yardes		
Richarde Herſeley	3 yardes		
John Aprice	3 yardes		
Chriſtopher Mawdeſley	3 yardes		
Thomas Gylmente	3 yardes		
John Robertts	3 yardes		
Mighell Weede	3 yardes		
Thomas Ogle, gentilman rider of the ſtable	9 yardes	4	9 yardes

Byſhoppes and Barons, &c.

Doctor Daye, biſhoppe of Chicheſter, preacher	10 yardes	8	24 yardes
The lorde Sainctjohn	10 yardes	8	24 yardes
The lorde Windeſore	10 yardes	8	24 yardes

The

		Servauntes	
The earle of Bathe	16 yardes	12	36 yardes
The lorde Burgaynye	10 yardes	8	24 yardes
The earle of Oxforde	16 yardes	12	36 yardes
The lorde Fitzwarren	10 yardes	8	24 yardes
The lorde Borrougbe	10 yardes	8	24 yardes
The lorde Barkeley	10 yardes	8	24 yardes
The earle of Suffex	16 yardes	12	36 yardes
The lorde Metravers	10 yardes	8	24 yardes
The lorde Scroope	10 yardes	8	24 yardes
The lorde Sturton	10 yardes	8	24 yardes
The lorde Stafforde	10 yardes	8	24 yardes
The lorde Fitzwater	10 yardes	8	24 yardes
Sᵗ Thomas Carden, knighte	10 yardes	8	24 yardes
Sᵗ James Crofts, knighte	10 yardes	8	24 yardes
Mr. Barnabye, gent. of the prevye chambre	10 yardes	8	24 yardes
Gentilmen Pencyoners.			
Thomas Afheley	9 yardes	3	9 yardes
Edwarde Horne	9 yardes	3	9 yardes
Edmonde Harvye	9 yardes	3	9 yardes
Edwarde Grimftone	9 yardes	3	9 yardes
Chriftopher Lydcooate	9 yardes	3	9 yardes
Will'm Palmer	9 yardes	3	9 yardes
Thomas Avercy	9 yardes	3	9 yardes
Symon Dygbye	9 yardes	3	9 yardes
Humfrey Coningfbye	9 yardes	3	9 yardes
John Fyfher	9 yardes	3	9 yardes
John Saundes	9 yardes	3	9 yardes
Marmaduke Boeke	9 yardes	3	9 yardes
George Befton	9 yardes	3	9 yardes
Henry Poole	9 yardes	3	9 yardes

George

	Servauntes		
George Throgmerton	9 yardes	3	9 yardes
Thomas Harvye	9 yardes	3	9 yardes
John Pyſter	9 yardes	3	9 yardes
John Digbye	9 yardes	3	9 yardes
Robarte Gage	9 yardes	3	9 yardes
Edworde Elrington	9 yardes	3	9 yardes
Edwarde Ferreis	9 yardes	3	9 yardes
Will'm Worthington	9 yardes	3	9 yardes
Will'm Almer	9 yardes	3	9 yardes
Baldewin Dowſe	9 yardes	3	9 yardes
Thomas Tierell	9 yardes	3	9 yardes
Nicholas Herne	9 yardes	3	9 yardes
Richarde Hardyne	9 yardes	3	9 yardes
Nicholas Sainctjohn	9 yardes	3	9 yardes
Humfrey Bate	9 yardes	3	9 yardes
Sir Edmonde Warren, knighte	9 yardes	3	9 yardes
The Henchemen.			
The yeoman of the Henchemen	5 yardes di.		
9 henchemen for there gowns, to every of them 4 yardes, and to every of them oone conate 1 yarde di.	49 yardes di.		
Oone ſervaunte for them	4 yardes		
Sᵗ Walter Myldemay, knighte	9 yardes	3	9 yardes
Sᵗ Thomas Moyle, knighte	9 yardes	3	9 yardes
The Myniſters of Weſtm' Churche.			
Twelve Prebendaries, to every of them 6 yardes	72 yardes		

12

		Servauntes	
12 Petie Canons, to everye of them 6 yardes	72 yardes		
A Gospellar	5 yardes		
The Episteler	5 yardes		
12 vykars, to every of them 4 yardes	48 yardes		
The Skoolemaster	4 yardes		
8 Qweristers, to everye of them oone yarde qr.	10 yardes		
2 Sexdeanes, to ether of them 3 yardes	6 yardes		
4 Bell Ringers	12 yardes		
The usher of the Skoole	4 yardes		
Balmayne the Frenche Skoole-master	9 yardes	3	9 yardes

The Officers of Westm' churche.

Three officers of the same churche, to every of them oone s'vaunte, to every oone servaunte 3 yardes		3	9 yardes

Knyghtes.

S' Thomas Hoolecrofte	9 yardes	4	12 yardes
S' Thomas Stradlinge	9 yardes	4	12 yardes
S' Humfrey Radcliffe	9 yardes	4	12 yardes
S' Fowlke Grevill	9 yardes	4	12 yardes
S' Nicholas Stourley	9 yardes	4	12 yardes
S' John Merckam	9 yardes	4	12 yardes
S' John Sainctelowe	9 yardes	4	12 yardes
S' John Will'ms	9 yardes	4	12 yardes

S'

		Servauntes	
S' Gyles Poole	9 yardes	4	12 yardes
S' Arthure Darcye	9 yardes	4	12 yardes
S' Robarte Drewrye	9 yardes	4	12 yardes
S' Will'm Rayncsforthe	9 yardes	4	12 yardes
John Amo, meffenger	4 yardes		
The deane of Windfore, re-geftre of thorder of the gartier	9 yardes	3	9 yardes
John Reade, keper of the ftandinge warderobe at Wellm'	7 yardes	1	3 yardes
The Marfhalfey.			
The knighte marfhall	9 yardes	3	9 yardes
20 fervaunts to attende upon him, for cleringe the waye, to every of them 1 yarde di.	30 yardes		
Trappors for the Haralds at Armes.			
M' Garter principall kinge at armes, for his horffe trappor	6 yardes		
M' Clarentius	6 yardes		
M' Norrey	6 yardes		
Windfore Harralde	4 yardes		
Richarde Harralde	4 yardes		
Somerfett Harralde	4 yardes		
Chefter Harralde	4 yardes		
Rouge Dragon	4 yardes		
Rouge Croffe	4 yardes		
Blewe Mantell.	4 yardes		

The

	Servauntes	

The Paynters.

Anthony Toto, f'jeaunte
  paynter — 7 yardes — 1 — 3 yardes
Nicholas Lyzarde, paynter — 4 yardes
Nicholas Modena, kerver — 4 yardes

The lorde treaforer marqwes
of Wincheftre, cheff mourner, for his mantell — 8 yardes

Therle of Shrewfburye, the
earle of Penbrooke, to ether
of them for there mantells
6 yardes — 12 yardes

    7 Pages of honoure.

4 pages of hono' that roode
upon the chariott horffes, to
every of them for there
gownes 4 yards, for there
cooates 1 yarde di. — 38 yardes di.

7 menne that leade the 7 chariott horffes, to every of
them oone gowne cont' 4
yardes. — 28 yardes

    Ryders of the Stable

Alexander Siggefale — 9 yardes — 3 — 9 yardes
Alexandre Zynzan — 9 yardes — 3 — 9 yardes
Hanyball Zinzan — 9 yardes — 3 — 9 yardes
Anthony Mouche — 9 yardes — 3 — 9 yardes

    Officers of the Jewell Howfe.

John Halil — 7 yardes — 1 — 3 yardes
John Kyrkbye — 7 yardes — 1 — 3 yardes
                            Edmonde

		Servauntes	
Edmonde Pygeon	7 yardes	1	3 yardes
Nicholas Briftowe	9 yardes	3	9 yardes
Laurence Bradfhawe, furveior of the kinges woorkes	7 yardes	3	9 yardes
Davy Marten the comptroller of the kinges woorkes	7 yardes	2	6 yardes
Nicholas Ellis, M' mafon	4 yardes		
John Ruffell, M' carpenter	4 yardes		
Richarde Pye, joyner	4 yardes		
John Pincherdowne, the kinges fjeaunte plumer	7 yardes	2	6 yardes
Peter Nicholfon Glafier	4 yardes		
Will'm Grene, cofermaker	4 yardes		
John Grene, coffermaker	4 yardes		
Anthony Silv', the chariott maker	4 yardes		
John Keyme, fmithe	4 yardes		
Thomas Mayneman	4 yardes		
The Kynges, Landres	7 yardes		
John Haywood, fewer of the chambre	9 yardes	2	6 yardes
S' Will'm Drewry, knighte	9 yardes	4	12 yardes
S' Will'm Goringe, knighte	9 yardes	8	24 yardes
M' Leonarde Chambrelen	9 yardes	3	9 yardes
M' Raufe Cotton, fewer	9 yardes	3	9 yardes
12 Beedmen of Weftm', to every of them 4 yardes	48 yardes		
S' Edwarde Haftinges, M' of the Qwenes horffe, for his trupper	6 yardes		
	6		S'

Servauntes

S' Edwarde Waldegrave, knighte, M' of the greate warderobe	10 yardes	8	24 yardes
Officers of the greate Warde-robe.			
The parfon of Sainte Andrewes	4 yardes		
Richarde Stoughton, clark of the greate warderobe	9 yardes	3	9 yardes
Stephen Hales, deputie to S' Rauffe Sadleire	9 yardes	3	9 yardes
Thomas Cotton	4 yardes		
Henry Stoughton	4 yardes		
John Bonyarde, yeoman tail-lor	4 yardes		
Thomas White, porter of the warderobe	4 yardes		
Thomas Laurence, meafurer of all the clothe	4 yardes		
To 5 other officers attend'unte in the greate warderobe all the tyme of the faide buriall, to every of them 4 yardes	20 yardes		
John Bridges	4 yards		
John Bonyarde	4 yardes		
Thomas Ackworthe	4 yardes		
Frauncis Poope	4 yardes		
Thomas Roofe	4 yardes		
Will'm Dyxe	9 yardes	3	9 yardes
Gregorye Richardfon	9 yardes	3	9 yardes

The Ten'nts of the greate
Wardcrobe.

Hughe Cooke	4 yardes
John Tregos	4 yardes
Arthure Pickman	4 yardes
John Kilbye	4 yardes
Thomas White	4 yardes
Phelippe Banbery	4 yardes
John Warde	4 yardes
Will'm Adamson	4 yardes
John Gurdler	4 yardes
Will'm Foller	4 yardes
Will'm Gryffyn	4 yardes
Will'm Simpfon	4 yardes
Will'm Walker	4 yardes
Richarde Crookes	4 yardes

Artificers pteynynge to the
Woorderobe.

John Bridges, the Kinges tay-lor	4 yardes
John Bonyarde, yeoman tay-lor	4 yards
Richarde Brickett, fkinner	4 yards
Hughe Efton, hofier	4 yards
Laurence Ball, fylkeman	4 yards
Henrye Arnolde, fhomaker	4 yards
John Aylonde, cutler	4 yards
Thomas Doughtye, gurdeler	4 yards
Will'm Browne, fpurrier	4 yards
Raphaell Hamonde, capper	4 yards
Launflett Stronge, glover	4 yards

Menne

		Servauntes	
Menne of Armes.			
Thomas Weſte	9 yards	3	9 yards
Walter Browne	9 yards	3	9 yards
Edmonde Hungerforde	9 yards	3	9 yards
Thomas Hungerforde	9 yards	3	9 yards
Edmonde Longe	9 yards	3	9 yards
Robarte Meneringe	9 yards	3	9 yards
John Cheyney	9 yards	3	9 yards
Will'm Gybbes	9 yards	3	9 yards
Anthony Harvye	9 yards	3	9 yards
Edwarde Barbor	9 yards	3	9 yards
Richarde Eldin	9 yards	3	9 yards
Rauffe Stafferton	9 yards	3	9 yards
Richarde Stafferton	9 yards	3	9 yards
Arthure Skarlett, oone of the Kinges trumpettors	4 yardes		
Clarkes of the Prevye Seale.			
Mr. Forthe	9 yards	3	9 yards
Mr. Hever	9 yards	3	9 yards
Mr. Turnor	9 yards	3	9 yards
Mr. Clarke	9 yards	3	9 yards
Mr. Cowper	9 yards	3	9 yards
Mr. Henry Sydney, of the prevy chambre	10 yardes	8	24 yards

To^ᵗ 9376 yardes

The totall of the Deliverey of the Quenes Matie Stoore for the forſayde Buriall.
Clothe of golde and ſylver tiſhewed withe golde and ſylver   20 yardes qr. di.

E e e 2   Clothe

Clothe of golde purple	51 yards di. di. qr.	
Clothe of golde blacke withe works	23 yardes	
Velvett blewe jeane	3 yards 3 qr.	
Damaſke blewe	2 yardes qr.	
Damaſke crimſin	2 yardes qr.	
Sarſcinett grene	3 yards 3 qr.	
Sarſcinett white, at 5s. 8d.	3 yards qr.	18s. 5d.
Satten white, at 11s.	4 yards	£.2. 4s. 0d.

XXVIII.

XXVIII. *Observations on the* Pusey Horn. *By the Right Honourable* Jacob *Earl of* Radnor.

Read November 11, 1790.

IN addition to the information respecting the Pusey Horn, published many years since by the Society, the traditional history respecting it may be thought worth noticing. It is as follows: Canute being encamped in the neighbourhood of Pusey, and the Saxons at a few miles distance, the king received intelligence from an officer of his army, who in the disguise of a shepherd had got into the enemy's camp, of an ambuscade formed by the Saxons to intercept him. This intelligence proved true; and the king in consequence escaping the danger, he gave this manor to the officer and his heirs for this service, to hold by the tenure of this horn, which has accordingly been preserved carefully by the proprietors ever since. The Danish camp called *Cherbury* castle, in the hamlet of Charney, and parish of Longworth, not a stone's throw from the boundary of Pusey, and the Saxon camp on the White Horse Hill at about seven miles distance, give an air of probability to the tradition. Its actual authenticity is not impeached by the letters of the inscription being (as they undoubtedly are) of a later date, for it might have been renewed in a subsequent age in the characters then in use, or upon the strength of the tradition, and by

way.

way of perpetuating it might have been then affixed to the
horn for the first time.

It has been underftood that the family affumed their name
from, and have always borne the fame name as the eftate,
and it is clear, that a century or two after the fuppofed
grant the name both of the parifh and family were *Pefei*, or
Pefie. The fame is true again in the fubfequent times, during
which both have been called, with fcarce any variation, *Pufey*;
but it is clear equally in my opinion, that the name of the grantee of the horn is according to the infcription, *Pecote*, though
neither in the account of Berkfhire in Domefday book (in
which there are three articles of *Pefei* in Gannesfelle hundred) does there appear fuch a parifh, nor at either of the
Pefeis fuch a proprietor, nor either in the annexed pedigree
(though it contains five generations antecedent to Richard,
living 25 Edward I.), nor in any of the writings of the family a fingle inftance of fuch a name as Pecote. This circumftance appears a ftrong confirmation of the idea, that the
infcription is the renewal of the original one, then perhaps
fo badly decyphered as to be erroneoufly fuppofed to be
Pecote, for otherwife the name, if then firft put upon the
horn, would probably have been either the one familiar at
the time, or at leaft one which was authorized by family
writings or records.

An infcription of the laft century (1655), on an altar
tomb in the church-yard of Pufey for " Richard Pufey,
alias Pefey, Pecote" can be quoted for nothing, except to
fhew, that the family could then read the infcription on the
horn, and had found by their title deeds, that the antient
was different from the modern fpelling of their name, and
that they claimed defcent from the grantee of the eftate, and
its

2

its feveral proprietors, notwithftanding the various ortho-
graphy of the name.

A manufcript memorandum dated 1674, of Mr. Dunch,
who enjoyed part of Pufey, fays, on the authority of Mr.
Fettiplace of Letcombe, a defcendant of the original grantee
of Pufey, that the grantees were named Pedecot ; to which
he adds, " briefly called Peafy;" but as this feems hardly
poffible to have been the abbreviation of the other name, he
probably meant to have faid " briefly called Pecote." This
tradition, however, with refpect to the name, feems fo un-
authorized, that probably it may be afcribed to the infcription on the horn, as the infcription may be to the bad de-
cyphering of the original infcription.

It appears by the account before publifhed, that a chan-
cery fuit had been carried on refpecting this eftate. The
following table of the family of Pufey is extracted from a variety of deeds, and from the period to which it is continued,
viz. to the fon of him who died in 1655, feems compiled with
a view of authenticating the pedigree at the time of that
fuit.

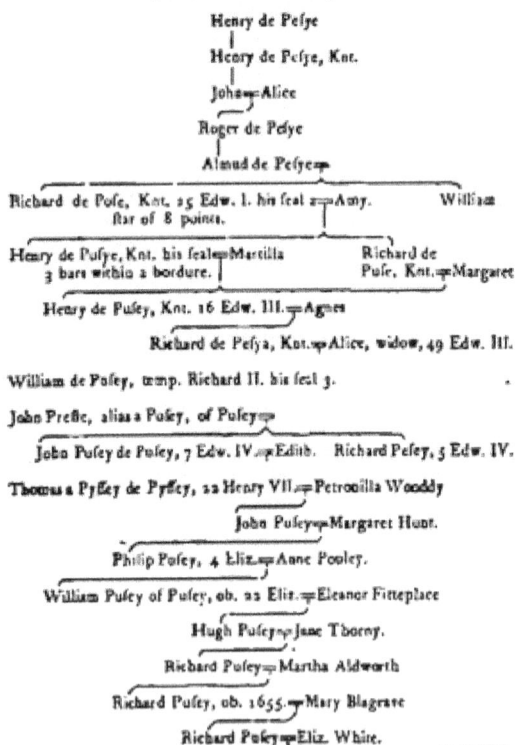

Henry de Pesye

Henry de Pesye, Knt.

John═Alice

Roger de Pesye

Almud de Pesye═

Richard de Pose, Knt. 25 Edw. I. his seal a═Amy. William
star of 8 points.

Henry de Pusye, Knt. his seale═Martilla Richard de
3 bars within a bordure. Puse, Knt. ═Margaret

Henry de Pusey, Knt. 16 Edw. III. ═Agnes

Richard de Pesya, Knt. ═Alice, widow, 49 Edw. III.

William de Pusey, temp. Richard II. his seal 3.

John Pessie, alias a Pusey, of Pusey═

John Pusey de Pusey, 7 Edw. IV. ═Edith. Richard Pesey, 5 Edw. IV.

Thomas a Pyssey de Pyssey, 22 Henry VII. ═Petronilla Wooddy

John Pusey═Margaret Hunt.

Philip Pusey, 4 Eliz. ═Anne Pooley.

William Pusey of Pusey, ob. 22 Eliz. ═Eleanor Fitteplace

Hugh Pusey═Jane Thorny.

Richard Pusey═Martha Aldworth

Richard Pusey, ob. 1655. ═Mary Blagrave

Richard Pusey═Eliz. White.

APPEN-

APPENDIX

AT A

COUNCIL OF THE SOCIETY

OF

ANTIQUARIES,

DECEMBER 11, 1776,

RESOLVED,

That fuch curious communications as the Council
fhall not think proper to publifh *entire* be extracted
from the Minutes of the Society, and formed into
an Hiftorical Memoir, to be annexed to each future
Volume of the Archaeologia.

A P P E N D I X.

The Life of Sir George Carve, after Earl of Totnes, by himself. Communicated by the Rev. Mr. Wrighte, Secretary.

Read January 9, 1794.

Anno.

1555. I was borne upon Wensday y* 29 day of May.

1564. Sent by my parents to y* universfyty of Oxford.

1573. Taken from y* universfyty.

1574. Sent for in to Ireland by y* old S' Peter Carew, and y* fame year a fervant to y* earl of Warwick.

1575. A voluntary in Ireland under the Lo. Deputy, Sir Henry Sydney.

1576. In y* abfence of my brother S' Peter Carew the younger, his lieutenant governor of the county of Cather Lughe, and vice conftable in Loghlin caftle.

1577. Rewarded for feruice done vpon y* rebels, w* a pention of 40* *per diem*, and ten horfe w*out cheque.

1578. A captayn at fea of the admirall fhippe under S' Humphrey Gilbert in his intended voyage to y* Weft Indies, and y* fame year fworne fervant to Queene Elizabeth..

1579. A captayn of foote in Ireland.

1580.

1580. Captain of Loghlin caftle, and of a troope of horfe; and by my brother's death lord of y' barony of Odrone; and y' fame year marryed.

1582. I went in to the Low Countries w'h Monfieur y' French Kings brother.

1583. Sheriff of y' county of Catherloge in Ireland.

1584. A gentleman penfioner in court to Queene Elizabeth.

1585. Knighted by S' John Perrot, and y' year I fould y' barony of Odrone.

1587. Mafter of the ordenance in Irelande, alfo y' year I was nominated, and had my inftructions to goe ambaffadour into France, but I excufed myfelf, and S' Ed. Wootton, afterwards lord Wootton, was imployed thither in my ftead.

1588. Sworne a counfellor of y' realme of Ireland.

1591. Lictenant of y' ordinance in England, and continued mafter of y' ordinance in Ireland a year after.

1592. Juftice of y' peace in divers fhires in England.

1594. I was nominated to goe ambaffador into Scotland to King James y' 6'h, but by favor of y' lord trefurer Burleigh I was difmift of y' imployment, and y' Lo Boroughs was fent in my roome.

1596. Mafter of y' ordenance in Cales voyadge.

1597. M' of y' ordenance in y' Ifland voyage.

1598. In France w'h y' principall fecretary S' Robert Cecill when he was ambaffador.

1599. M' of y' ordenance in y' army y' was affembled at London, the earl of Notingham being defigned general, and y' fame year I went into Ireland lord prefident of Mounfter

6　　　　　　　　　　　　　　　　1603.

1603. I was fent by y' king w'' fome others to bring Queene
Anne hither

1605. Vice chamberlayn, receiuor general, and fworn a coun-
celor to Queene Anne, and created a baron in parliament.

1608. M' of y' ordinance in England.

1609. Keeper of Nonfuch houfe and park, by grant from
Queene Anne, for term of her life.

1610. Governor of y' Ifle of Guernfey.

1611. Sent fole commiffioner into Ireland for reformation of
the army and improvement of his Ma'''' revenew.

1616. Sworne a privy counfellore to king James, and a commiffioner among others of the lords of the confeyl for
the government of the kingdom in the abfence of the
King when he went into Scotland

1618. Keeper of Nonfuch houfe and park, by grant of King
James for terme of my owne life.

1624. Sworne a counfellor of the warre by vertue of an act of
parliament.

1625. Sworne a privy counfellor to king Charles, and not
many dayes after fworne into his counfellors of warre,
and created earle of Totnes.

1626. Treafurer and receaver general to the Queene Henriette
Marie.

Examined Rog. Twyfden.

1629. He died fans iffue, March the 27th.

29 Sept.

29 Sept. 4 Edward IV. (A. D. 1465.) De Percuſſione Monetæ.

From Mr. A S T L E.

Proclamation for regulating the Price of Silver Bullion, and

the Value of the Money of the Kingdom.

Read April 3, 1794.

Rot. Clauſ. de Anno Regni Regis Edwardi Quarti Quarto. m. 20.

De Proclamationibus faciendis.

REX vicecomitibus London' ſalutem. Precipimus vobis quod ſtatim poſt recepcionem preſencium in ſingulis locis infra civitatem prediƈtam ubi melius videritis expediri publicam proclamationem faƈtam in forma ſequenti. Whereas late agoo owr Sov'aigne Lord the Kinge, Edward by the grace of God Kinge of Englaunde and of Fraunce, and Lord of Ireland, by conſideraċ'on of the ſcarcite of money within this his reaume, of lyklyhode amonges other thinges cauſed of lak of bryngyng of bolion into his myntes, which, as is conceived, is by cauſe that tho that ſhuld bringe bolion, may have more for their bolion in other princes myntes than in his. Willynge ſuche cauſes to be removed, and to encrece and multiplie his coigne to the com'ne wele of all this his land and ſubjeƈtis of the ſame, by proclamaċ'on in div's parties of this land, ordeigned and provided, that ev'y perſon that wold bringe ſilver in bolion plate or otherwiſe into his mynte within his Towre of London, where as afore tyme he ſhuld have taken and toke for lb. of ſilv' of the fyneſſe of a grote rennyng but xxjxs. ſterlingez, ſhall mowe nowe reſceyve clerely of ev'y lb.

weight

weight of fuche filv' at his feid mynte xxxiijs. fterlinges of the
fame fyneffe and allaye, fo clerely have more than he had by-
fore in ev'y unce by iiij d. and in grete in the lb. iiijs. as all att
large was declared in the fame proclamac'ons. The fame
our Sov'aigne Lord to thentent abovefeid, for many grete and
'fpi'all caufes and confeideracions conc'nyng the wele and
profperite of this land and his fubgettez of the fame, whos
welfare and increce is unto him the grettest comfort that may
be, hath now ordeigned and provided, and fo provideth and
ordeigneth, that immediately after the terme and fpace of xv
days next after this proclamacion every noble of gold which
nowe goith for vis. viiij d. fhall from thensforth be and renne
in all man' of paymentis to and for the value of viijs. iiij d. fterlings, and in likewife after the fame rate and afferant the half
noble and the ferthing of gold, that is to fey, the half noble
iiij s. iij d. and the ferthing of gold ii s. i d. Willing and in the
ftraytest wyfe com'aundyng all man' of men whatfoev' they be,
to obferve fulfille and kepe this his provifion and ordinaunce
made for the comune gude and welfare of all this his land as is
above reherfed. And to thentent to efchewe all man' difficul-
tez doubtez and ambiguitez that paraventur myght falle in
mennys myndez in this partie our feid Sov'igne Lord the
Kinge, accordyng to the cuftume that of old tyme bath bene
ufed in this his land, and yet is, willeth and ordeigneth that
iij grotes fhall make a fhillyng, vj half grotez a fhillyng, xij d.
whiche fhalbe called fterlings a fhillyng, xxiiij half penys a
fhillyng, xlviij ferthings a fhillyng, and xx s. fhall make a
pounde, and xiijs. iiij d. fhall make a mark. And over this
howe it be, owr feid Sov'igne Lord the Kinge div's tymez fith
the begynnyng of his reigne hath be moved for the com'une
and univ'fale wele of this his land, and fubgettis to the thingez
above reherfed, whiche after longe fadde and ripe delib'a-

cion and and coi'cacions had with men of grete wifedome and
experience in fuch behalfe as well marchauntez as other, hath
be and ben advifed and concluded by our feid Sov'aigne Lord
and the lordez of his counfell, for the wele and profitte of his
land and fubgettis. Yit that notwithftandyng it is con-
ceivid, that div'rs perfons for their private and finguler luere
eafle and fowe div'rs fedicious langage, to th'entent to lette
the feid ordinaunce made be fo grete advis and fo hurte the
common welfare of all this land entended by our feid fov'igne
and his counfeill. Wherefore the fame our Sov'igne Lord,
well and in the ftrayteft wyfe chargeth, that from hensforth
noo man' of man, of what eftate, degre, or condicion fo ever
he bee, take upon him by fuch man' o langage, or other
wyfe, to hurt trouble or lette or any occafion of lette,
geve unto the feid ordinaunce fo for the comune wele made
as is above reherfed, uppon the danger and perell that he
may falle in towardes the kinge, and upon payne of all that
he may forfaite unto him. And if there be eny perfone what-
forver he be, that thinketh that he hath fufficient matter and
reafons for hym neceffarily concludyng the feid ordinaunce not
to be for the comune wele of the lande and fubgettes, but rather
a loffe and hurte, the Kinge welle and ftraitly chargeth,
that he come before hym and his counfail, and declare and
fhewe them. And in cafe it can be underftand and founde fo
to be, our faid Sov'igne Lord the Kinge will with all diligence provide for a due and undelaied remedye in that behalfe. And he that fheweth and declareth fuche matter and
reafons fhall be benignely herd and have right a goode thanke.
Et hoc fub periculo quod incumbit nullatenus omittatis. T. R.
apud Redyng xxjx die Septembr'.

Per Breve de privato figillo.

Con-

Confimilia brevia diriguntur vicecomitibus, comitibus, &c. locorum fubfcriptorum, fub eadem data; videlicet.

Vic' Midd'.

Vic' Kant'.

Vic' Surr' & Suffex'.

Vic' Suth'.

Vic' Ville Suthampton.

Vic' Som' & Dorf'.

Vic' Devon'.

Vic' Cornub'.

Vic' Wilten'.

Vic' Oxon' & Berk.'

Vic' Ville Briftoll'.

Vic' Glouc'.

Vic' Wygorn'.

Vic' Warr' & Leyc'.

Vic' Northt'.

Vic' Civitatis Coventr'.

Vic' Bed' & Buk'.

Vic' Cantebr' & Hunt'.

Vic' Effex' & Hertf'.

Vic' Norff' & Suff'.

Vic' Notyng' & Derb'.

Vic' Ville Notyng'.

Vic' Lincoln'.

Vicecomitibus Civitatis Linc'.

Vic' Rotel'.

Vic' Hereford'.

Vic' Salop'.

Vic' Staff'.

Cancellario R' Com. Palatini R' Lancaftre'.

Cariffimo Confanguineo R'. Ricardo Comiti Warr', Cuftodi Quinq' Portuu' fuor', feu ejus Locum tenenti, ib.

Vic' Ville de Kyngefton fuper Hull.

Vic' Ebor'.

Vicecomitibus Civitatis Ebor'.

Vicecomitibus Norwic'.

Vic' Ville Novi Caftri fuper Tynam.

Vic' Weftm'l'.

Vic' Cumbr'.

Vic' Northumbr.

Vic' Civitatis Cantuar'.

Read May 15, 1794.

The Bracelet, Plate LI.fig. 1. was found upon the wrift of the fkeleton of a full fized man, about two yards under ground by the road fide in Weftwang field, in the Eaft Riding of the county of York, by fome workmen who were digging for materials to mend the road. The fkeleton was laid at full length with every bone in its proper place, and in good prefervation. Some teeth which dropped out of the fcull were perfectly frefh. In the intrenchments which divide and diffect in every direction the high wolds of that part of Yorkfhire, fkeletons, the heads of broken fpears, arrows, and other remnants of ancient weapons and armour are frequently found.

M. S Y K E S.

Extract of a Letter to the Prefident.

Read November 6, 1794.

My Lord,

I take the liberty of inclofing to your lordfhip a drawing of an ancient Sword or Dagger, lately found amongft a quantity of old iron in a fmith's fhop in Durham.   Plate LI fig. 4.

Length of the handle from A to B 5 inches.

Length of the blade from C to D 15 inches ;; width 1 in. ;.

Length of the guard from E to F 3 inches.

It is all of iron, of very rude workmanfhip, and, by the infcription on the blade, it is evident it has belonged either to *Antbony Beck* bifhop of Durham (Anno 1283) himfelf, or to fome one of his military attendants. The infcription is engraven of the original fize.

The

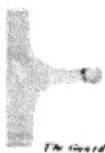

The Guard

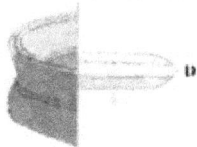

D

Fig 5 p 509

Fig 6 p 511

The handle is greatly bruifed and otherwife defaced through length of time, and now appears hollow, as reprefented in the drawing; but it is probable that there has been within the four iron bars or ribs a wooden handle, which has rotted away. This fword is now preferved in Durham cathedral, and is double edged.

The infcription is fac fimile; and if your lordfhip fhould be pleafed to think it worth communicating to the Antiquarian Society, to be engraved, it will greatly oblige,

Your Lordfhip's moft obedient,

Durham,   and devoted humble Servant,

Sept. 22, 1794.   JOHN LAMBERT.

Read December 11, 1794.

Burlington Street, December 11, 1794.

SIR,

Herewith I fend you a ring belonging to Lady Dorothea Hotham, and by her favour allowed to be exhibited by me at this meeting of the Society.

It was ploughed up about three years ago, in a field near Dalton Houfe, three miles from Beverley in Yorkfhire, the feat of the Hotham family.

The ftone fet in it is a fpecies of the Tricolor Sardonyx, and the impreffion on it a very beautiful Janus's head.

The characters round the ring are fuppofed to be the old French *.   I am, Sir,

Rev. Mr. Brand,   Your moft obedient humble Servant,

Secretary.   JOHN WOODD.

* See Plate LI fig. 5.

Read

—————

Read December 10, 1795.

Hedingham Castle, Essex, December 1, 1795.

The two Hawks' Rings, Plate LI. fig. 7, were found close to a hop ground about a quarter of a mile from this castle, and near the lodge of the ancient little park belonging to it, many years since converted into a farm.

This hop ground is in a low bottom, enclosed by two hills, with a stream of water constantly running through it, which, before the ground was employed in the present culture, was confined by sluices, forming several ponds, or stews, to preserve or fatten fish, a branch of luxury very necessary to our ancestors before the Reformation, and practised with an attention and expence now in disuse.

It is almost unnecessary to observe, that one of these rings, passed over the claws of a young hawk, would remain on its leg a permanent mark of the proprietor.

They are flat and circular, and appear to be of fine silver, one of them is also gilt; rings, indeed, of a form precisely similar to these, have been found of gold.

The inscription on both is the same, and on both equally legible,

" Ox—en—for—de,"

the manner in which the ancient family of De Vere, during so many centuries, possessors of this castle and honor, usually signed their title of earl.

They

They are infcribed on one fide only, the other being quite plain, but it is not unufual to fee them with an infcription on both [a].

The amufement of hawking feems fo generally neglected at this day, that if we except the partial attention beftowed upon it by the late earl of Orford, and perhaps a few more, it may be confidered as no longer entitled to a place in the lift of our field fports; yet, in moft of our modern leafes, a claufe is generally ftill to be found, referving to the landlord the free liberty of hunting, " *hawking*," and fowling, with other exceptions of a fimilar nature. I have the honor to be,

Sir,

Your very obedient humble Servant,

LEWIS MAJENDIE.

Read January 14, 1796.

Hedingham Caftle, Effex, January 1, 1796.

The Gold Ring, Plate LI.fig. 6, was difcovered about ten years fince in the Home Park at Windfor, by one of the labourers employed by his Majefty in lowering and removing the earth called the Bowling Green, immediately adjoining

[a] As in the ring found near Biggklefade, which was of gold, and infcribed on one fide " *fua Regit Anglie*," and, on the reverfe, " *n enmun Herferdie*." See Gentleman's Magazine for June 1795, page 474.

6.

the

the Eaft terrace of the caftle. Its form, and workmanfhip,
fhew it to be of no modern date.

The weight of the ring is four penny weights and four
grains ; the gold of which it is made does not appear to be
fine [a], but the inferiority of the material is fully fupplied by
the elegant workmanfhip beftowed upon it. The upper part
of the ring exhibits a neatly engraved pedeftrian armed figure with wings, reprefenting St. Michael flaying the dragon,
and the beaded wreath on the lower part, together with the
ornaments on each fide, are elegantly executed.

It may have belonged to fome foreign or Englifh knight of
the order of Saint Michael in France ; or, from the particular
place in which it was difcovered, it may without great improbability have been the property of one of thofe knights of
the garter who appear to have received the order of Saint
Michael [b] ; but, in either cafe, it muft be confidered as a
mere perfonal ornament of the wearer, that is, not as belonging to the ceremonial drefs of the order; for, although " a gold
ring" was one of the enfigns of the Equeftrian order among
the Romans [c], it clearly appears not to have conftituted
any part of the inauguration ceremony of the order of Saint

[a] An eminent goldfmith informs me, that though the precife quality of the
gold cannot be afcertained without an affay, he is of opinion that it is not fine,
or of more value than about three pounds per ounce.

[b] The order of St. Michael was inftituted in France by Lewis the Eleventh,
in 1469, into which many perfons of high diftinction in this country were admitted, as King Henry the Eighth, Sir Charles Brandon, afterwards duke of
Suffolk, both buried in St. George's chapel, Windfor. King Edward the Sixth,
Thomas duke of Norfolk, Robert earl of Leicefter, Sir Nicholas Clifford, Sir
Anthony Shirley, and others ; but of thefe all, except the two laft, were knights
of the Garter. See Afhmole and Anftis, paffim.

[c] Afhmole, edit. 1693, page 24, et feq.

Michael

Michael [*d*]; nor of that of the Garter [*e*], nor indeed of any of the other more modern orders of knighthood [*f*].

There is an oral tradition, that the spot where this ring was found was formerly the scene of tilts and tournaments before the sovereign of the order of the garter; if so, it is not improbable, that it may have dropped from the finger of one of the combatants during a contest of this nature, and have remained unnoticed for more than two centuries. The taste and neat execution of the workmanship will hardly authorize an opinion of more remote antiquity.

LEWIS MAJENDIE.

November 28, 1796.

Lieutenant Colonel Matthew Smith exhibited the Roman Patera engraved Pl. LI.fig. 2. dug up in August last, out of the earth in Great Tower-street, at the top of Beer-lane, a little below Barking church, in a bed of fine gravel, ten feet below the surface of the ground, which had been opened in order to make a sewer. The interior diameter is 6 inches and a half, depth 2 inches, height 2 inches 3 quarters. The inscription on the rim (fig. 3.) commemorates the potter.

[*d*] Anstis, vol. 1. p. 70, note p.
[*e*] Ashmole, p. 202, et seq.
[*f*] Ibid. p. 30.

Read January 27, 1796.

Fig. 8, Plate II. reprefents an ancient Inftrument of Brafs, refembling Gold, communicated by Philip Rafhleigh, Efq. M. P. found at the bottom of a mine near the river Fowey, ten fathoms under the furface of the earth, where a new work was begun for fearching after tin ore.

The fubftance of this inftrument, with a piece of amber fet at one end, and the great depth at which it was found, are evident marks of great antiquity, and leave but little doubt of its having belonged to ancient Britons or Druids. Great quantities of wood cover the banks of the river where this hook was found.

The celebrated golden hooks (as they have been ufually called), for pulling down and gathering mifletoe, were probably neither gold or made to cut, as the foftnefs of gold made that metal very unfit for fuch purpofes; the refemblance which this bears to gold might give it that name.

From thefe circumftances there is little reafon to doubt of this inftrument having been a Druid's hook, for gathering mifletoe.

. The circumftance of the *golden* fickle of the Druids refts entirely on the authority of Pliny, N. H. XVI. 96, where Dr.

6   Borlafe

Borlafe fuggefted no miftake [a] ; but Dr. Lort [b] fuggefted
a query, whether we fhould not read *area* inftead of *aurea*,
as Virgil [c] exprefsly fays, herbs for magical purpofes were
cut with *brazen* fickles, *falcibus ahenis*, where the name of the
metal cannot be affected by any various reading. The
polifh which the metal of thefe old Britifh inftruments takes
gives them the appearance of gold. Enough has been faid by
various writers on the mixed metal ufed by our anceftors,
which, according to Mr. Alchorne's analyfis, confifted chiefly
of copper interfperfed in particles of iron, and perhaps fome
zinck, but without containing either gold or filver [d] ; to
which Governor Pownall adds [e], that the apparent **proper-
ties** of the metal are, that it is of a texture which **takes an
exquifite** fine polifh, and in its colour exhibits more **of the
colour** of GOLD than of brafs or copper.

R. G.

Thurfday, June 4, 1795.

Owen Salufbury Brereton, efq. Vice Prefident, communicated a drawing of a ftone ornament in an outfide wall of the
Deanery houfe at Windfor, made by Henry Emlyn, efq. of
that place, architect. The date at the top is plainly 1500,
though part of the 5 has been defaced. The infcription is
perfect " Criftofero Urfwyk, decano." Plate LII.

[a] Antiq. of Cornwall, p. 288.　　[b] Arch. V. p. 111. note f.
[c] Æn. IV. 513.　　[d] Arch. III. p. 359.　　[e] Ib. p. 356.

　　　　　　Chrifto-

Chriſtopher Urſwic was inſtalled dean of Windſor in 1495, and lived many years in the next century. The portcullis and roſe are the well-known badges of Henry VII. The ſupporters, a griffin and greyhound belong alſo to that reign, as appears by the wooden cut of the royal arms prefixed to Henry the Seventh's Life in Hall's Chronicle.

INDEX.

INDEX.

LIST

LIST OF PLATES.

[427]

ERRATA.

Vol. XI. p. 430, l. 11, for "with what Mr. Deacon calls a red China plate," &c. read "with what Mr. Deacon's account (in an old hand, probably written by the person that found the scarabæus, and which is wrapped up with it) calls a red China plate," &c.

Vol. XII.
P. 36, l. 12, read masitandis.
P. 132, l. 1, for XIV. read XV.
P. 144, l. 6, for Edward read Henry.
P. 153, l. 10, for double read dotted.
P. 159, l. 15, " diam. height. di.   dia. height. di.
              " ft. in. ft. in.   ft. in. ft. in.   in
              " 3 3 13=0 4" should be 3 3 13 0=4
              " 2 4 14=6 2" should be 2 4 14 2=6+2
P. 195, l. 13, for Cirill read Ceril.
P. 207, l. 4, read 1795.
P. 297, l. 10, for entient read antient.

[429]

Prefents to the Society fince the Publication of the
Eleventh Volume of the Archaeologia.

Mr. John Carter.	Specimens of the ancient Sculpture and Painting now remaining in this Kingdom, from the earlieft period to the Reign of Henry VIII. Two Volumes, Folio.
William Owen, Efq.	The Second Part of his Welfh and Englifh Dictionary.
Society of Arts, Manufactures, and Commerce	The Twelfth Volume of their Tranfactions.
Royal Society of London.	Philofophical Tranfactions for 1794, Parts 1 and 2.
The Marquis of Hartford.	Tranfcript from a MS. in the public Library, Cambridge, concerning Grants of Lands in Norfolk and Suffolk in the Reign of Edward II. and feveral fucceeding Reigns.
John Caley and James Moore, Efqrs.	Firft Volume of Select Views in Scotland.
William Seward, Efq.	" Les Tombeaux des Rois, des Reines, & des autres, qui font dans l'Eglife Royale de Saint Denis." Paris, 1768 ; a Pamphlet.
Governor Pownall.	An Antiquarian Romance.
The Dean of Ripon.	A Drawing reprefenting the Ground Plan of the Collegiate Church of Ripon, 1794.
The Medical Society of London.	The Fourth Volume of their Memoirs.
Dr. Lettfom.	Grove Hill; an Horticultural Sketch, of which fifty copies were printed to give away.
Royal Humane Society.	The Firft Volume of their Tranfactions.
John Henniker Major, Efq.	Two Letters on the Origin, Antiquity, and Hiftory of Norman Tiles ftained with Armorial Bearings.
John Chamberlaine, Efq.	No V. of Portraits from the original Drawings of H. Holbein in his Majefty's Collection.

Vol. XII.   K k k.   William

William Seward, Esq.
: Anecdotes of some distinguished persons chiefly of the present and two preceding Centuries, 2 vols. 8vo.

Thomas Pownall, Esq.
: Descriptions and Explanations of the Remains of some Roman Antiquities dug up in the City of Bath in the Year 1790.

Mr. Deputy Nichols.
: Part of a general History of Leicestershire, intituled, "An History of Stapleford," in that county, folio.

Joseph Spilsbury, Esq.
: An ancient MS. folio, containing a general Collection of all the Offices in England, with their Fees in the Queen's Majesty's Gift, &c.

Mr. John Carter
: Nº I. of his ancient Architecture in England.

From the unknown Author.
: Annals of such Patriots of the distinguished Family of Fraser, Fryfell, Sim-fon, or Fitz-Simon, as have signalized themselves in the public Service of Scotland. Edinb. 1795, 8vo.

The Earl of Fife.
: The Second Volume of Cordiner's Ruins, &c. of Scotland, 4to.

Rev. Daniel Lysons.
: The Second and Third Volume of Environs of London, 4to.

Thomas Reid, M. D.
: Directions for warm and cold Sea Bathing, 8vo.

John Chamberlaine, Esq.
: Nº VI. of Portraits from Holbein's Drawings

William Seward, Esq.
: Vol. III. of Anecdotes of distinguished Persons.

Don Cœtani de Ancora.
: Xenocrates de Alimento ex aquatilibus, with Notes and Annotations, &c. Naples, 1794, 8vo.

Society of Arts, Manufactures, and Commerce.
: The Thirteenth Volume of their Transactions.

American Academy of Arts and Sciences.
: The First Part of their Second Volume of Memoirs, 4to.

Henry Emlyn, Esq.
: A Drawing of the Royal Arms of England cut in stone, over a window at a house called the New Commons at Windsor.

Royal Society of London.
: Philosoph. Transact. for 1795, Part I. and II.

John Chamberlaine, Esq.
: Nº VII. of Portraits after Holbein's Drawings.

Joseph Jekyll, Esq.
: A Folio Volume of MSS and Blazonings, found in a joint Collection of the late Sir Nathan Wrighte, Lord Keeper, and Sir Joseph Jekyll, Master of the Rolls.

Li-

Literary and Philosophical Society of Manchester.	Part Second of the Fourth Volume of their Memoirs.
Mr. Sherlock.	Three Numbers of Monuments, stained Windows, Brasses, &c. in Churches in the Environs of London.
Rev. Mark Noble.	An Historical Genealogy of the House of Stuarts, 4to.
Rev. Sir Rich. Kaye, Bart. Dean of Lincoln.	Two engraved Prints representing the Distribution of his Majesty's Maundy, drawn by Grimm, and engraved by Basire, 1789.
From the unknown Author.	On the Prosodies of the Greek and Latin Languages. London, 1796, 8vo.
Royal Society of Gottingen.	The Twelfth Volume of their Transactions.
J. M. Birchenstock, actual Aulic Counsellor of His Imperial Majesty, &c.	Two monumental Inscriptions, in the ancient lapidary Style, on the late King of Prussia and the late Arch Duke of Austria.
William Seward, Esq.	The Fourth Vol. of his Anecdotes of distinguished Persons.
Mr. Edward Jones, Bard to His Royal Highness the Prince of Wales.	Musical and Poetical Relics of the Welsh Bards, &c. London, 1794, folio; a new edition, doubly augmented and improved.
Mr. John Carter.	N° II. and III. of the ancient Architecture of England.
Edmund Malone, Esq.	An Inquiry into the Authenticity of certain miscellaneous Papers and legal Instruments, published December 24, 1795, and attributed to Shakspeare. Queen Elizabeth and Henry Earl of Southampton, &c. London, 1796, 8vo.
Rev. Aulay Macaulay.	The History and Antiquities of Claybrook in Leicestershire. London, 1791, 8vo.; also The Liturgy of the Church of England recommended, a Sermon preached at St. Mary le Bow, London, April 25, 1796, 4to.
The Rev. Dr. Layard.	A Sermon preached by him at the Anniversary Meeting of the Sons of the Clergy at St. Paul's, May 7, 1795.
Valentine Green, Esq.	The History and Antiquity of the City and Suburbs of Worcester, 2 Vols. 4to. London, 1796.

John

John Chamberlaine, Esq.	N° VIII. of Portraits after Holbein's Drawings.
Don Joseph Cornide.	Two Differtations written in Spanish on certain Iflands on the Coaft of Galicia, called Caffterides, and on the Pillar of Hercoles at the Entrance of the Port of Coruona, 8vo. Madrid, 1790.—4to. Ibid. 1792.
The Rev. Charles Turnor.	Monumenta illuftrium Virorum et Elogia, cura et ftudio Marci Zuerii Boxhorni. Amfterdam, 1630, folio.
Francis Doace, Esq.	Drawings from an Illumination prefixed to an antient MS. Book of Prayers.

WORKS

WORKS published by the SOCIETY of ANTIQUARIES of LONDON.

VETUSTA Monumenta, quæ ad Rerum Britannicarum Memoriam conservandam, Societas Tabulis aeneis incidi curavit; cum Explicationibus necessariis. Folio. Three Vols. Price *seventeen guineas* and a *half*. The Plates may also be had separately. See the following Lists of them.

Tables of English Silver and Gold Coins, from the Norman Conquell to the present Time; illustrated with 67 Copper-plates; together with the Weights, intrinfic Values of, and Remarks upon, the several Pieces. Quarto. Price in Sheets, 2*l*. 2*s*.

Five Differtations. Quarto; Price 7*s*: *viz.*
One on Domefday Book, and one on Danegeld, by P. C. Webb, Efq.
Two on the Heraclean Table, by Mr. Webb and Dr. Pettingal.
One on the *Vafcia*, by Dr. Pettingal.

Archæologia, or Miscellaneous Tracts relating to Antiquity; in Twelve Volumes, Quarto. Price in sheets 13*l*. 12*s*. 6*d*.; or, separately,

Vol. I.	15*s*.	Vol. VII.	1*l*. 1*s*.
Vol. II.	15*s*.	Vol. VIII.	1*l*. 1*s*.
Vol. III.	18*s*.	Vol. IX.	18*s*.
Vol. IV.	1*l*. 1*s*.	Vol. X.	1*l*. 5*s*.
Vol. V.	1*l*. 1*s*.	Vol. XI.	1*l*. 1*s*.
Vol. VI.	1*l*. 5*s*.	Vol. XII.	1*l*. 11*s*. 6*d*

The Account of the Comptroller of the Wardrobe of the Receipt and Expences of Edward I. in the 28th Year of his Reign, 1300; 10*s*. 6*d*.

A Collection of Ordinances and Regulations for the government of the Royal Houfhold, made in divers reigns from Edward III. to William and Mary. Alfo Receipts in ancient Cookery. Price in Sheets 15*s*.

The Military Antiquities of the Romans in Britain, by the late Major General Roy, F. R. S. F. S. A. accompanied with Maps, Plans of Camps and Stations, &c. folio. Price in Sheets 5*l*. 5*s*.

Some Account of the Collegiate Chapel of St. Stephen, Weftminfter. By John Topham, Efq. F. R. S. with Plans, Elevations, Sections, and Specimens of Architecture and Ornaments of fuch Parts of it as are now remaining. Folio. Price Two Guineas.

PRINTS.

Le Champ de Drap d'Or, or the Royal Interview of Henry VIII. and Francis I. between Guines and Ardres, in the year 1520. Price 2*l*. 2*s*.

Francis I's Attempt to Invade England, 1544; from an Hiftorical Painting at Cowdray in Suffex. Price 1*l*. 5*s*.

The Embarkation of King Henry VIII. at Dover, May 31, 1520, preparatory to his interview with the French King Francis I; from the original picture preserved in the royal apartments in Windfor Caftle. Price 1*l*. 11*s*. 6*d*.

The Proceffion of King Edward VI. from the Tower of London to Weftminfter; from an ancient Painting at Cowdray. Price 1*l*. 11*s*. 6*d*.

The Departure of King Henry VIII. from Calais, July 25, 1544.
The Encampment of King Henry VIII. at Marquifon, July 1544.
The Siege of Boulogne by King Henry VIII. 1544. Price 2*l*. 2*s*.—
. To thefe belong Five Hiftorical Differtations.

A CATALOGUE of PRINTS,

IN THE

VETUSTA MONUMENTA,

ENGRAVED AND PUBLISHED BY THE

SOCIETY of ANTIQUARIES of LONDON.

VOLUME I.

Numb.		Price.		
		l.	*s.*	*d.*
	THE general Title and Catalogue in Latin.	0	1	0
1.	A brafs lamp, found at St. Leonard's hill near Windfor.	0	1	0
2.	Ulphus's horn, preferved in the cathedral at York.	0	1	0
3.	The font at St. James's church, Weftminfter.	0	1	0
4.	The portrait of King Richard II. from an ancient picture lately in the choir of Weftminfter abbey.	0	2	0
5.	Three ancient feals, with their reverfes; the firft of Cottingham abbey in Yorkfhire; the fecond of Clare nall in Cambridge; and the third the chapter-feal of the church of St. Ethelfred at Ely.	0	1	0
6.	The ruins of Walfingham priory in Norfolk.	0	0	9
7.	Waltham Crofs.	0	1	0
8.	A Plan of the remaining walls and city of Verulam.	0	1	0
9—12.	Four views of the ruins of Fountain abbey, in Yorkfhire.	0	3	0
13, 14.	Three views of the gate of St. Bennet's abbey at Holm in Norfolk.	0	0	6
15.	The tomb of Robert Colles and Cecily his wife at Foulfham in Norfolk.	0	2	6
16.	The fhrine of King Edward the Confeffor in Weftminfter abbey.	0	2	0
17.	The North front of the gate at Whitehall.	0	1	0
18.	The North front of King's-ftreet gate, Weftminfter.	0	1	0
19.	Plans of the two preceding gates.	0	0	6
		1	0	3

	l.	s.	d.
Brought over	1	0	3

20. Coins of K. Henry VIII. Edward VI. Q. Elizabeth, and K. James I. Also a portrait of Q. Elizabeth, from a painting in enamel. } 0 | 1 | 0

21—26. The Tournament of K. Henry VIII. Feb. 12, 1510; from an ancient roll in the Herald's office. } 0 | 6 | 0

27. The ruins of Furness abbey in Lancashire. 0 | 1 | 6

28—33. The Baron's letter in the reign of K. Edward I. Feb. 12, 1300, to Pope Boniface VIII; with the seals appendent. } 0 | 6 | 0

34. An antique brass head dug up at Bath in 1727. 0 | 1 | 0

35, 36. Three views of Colchester castle in Essex, with the ground plot. } 0 | 2 | 0

37, 38. Tables of English gold and silver coins, shewing the several species coined in each reign. } 0 | 3 | 0

39. Tetbury castle in Staffordshire. 0 | 1 | 0

40. Melborn castle in Derbyshire. 0 | 1 | 0

41. Lancaster castle. 0 | 1 | 0

42. Pomefract castle in Yorkshire. 0 | 1 | 0

43. A gold seal of Pope Alexander IV; with gold and silver coins struck in France and Flanders, relating to the history of England. } 0 | 1 | 0

44. Knaresborough castle in Yorkshire. 0 | 1 | 0

45. A portrait of Dr. Tanner, Bp. of St. Asaph. 0 | 1 | 0

46. Tickhill castle in Yorkshire. 0 | 1 | 0

47. A plan of Roman roads in Yorkshire. 0 | 1 | 0

48. A Roman tessellated pavement, found near Cotterstock in Northamptonshire, 1736. } 0 | 1 | 6

49. An ancient chapel adjoining to the Bishop's palace at Hereford. } 0 | 1 | 0

50—52. Three Roman tessellated pavements found at Wellow near Bath, 1737. } 0 | 5 | 0

53, 54. Ancient seals and their reverses, from the Dutchy office of Lancaster. } 0 | 2 | 6

55. Gold and silver medals of Mary Queen of Scots, and Lord Darnley; with others of Queen Anne, Prince Henry, and K. Charles I. } 0 | 1 | 3

56. Gold and silver coins of several English kings, Prince Edward, and Q. Elizabeth. } 0 | 1 | 3

L l l 2

| | 3 | 2 | 3 |

Numb.		Price.		
		l.	*s.*	*d.*
	Brought over	3	2	3
57. A Roman fudatory found at Lincoln.		0	1	0
58—60. Ancient feals, from the Dutchy-office of Lancaster.		0	4	6
61. Winchefter crofs.		0	1	0
62. The decree of the Univerfity of Oxford in 1534, against the jurifdiction of the Pope in England.		0	2	6
63. A plan of the Tower Liberties, from a furvey in 1597.		0	2	0
64. Chichefter crofs.		0	1	0
65. Three views of the Roman *Retiarii*.		0	1	0
66—68. The portrait of Sir Robert Cotton, Bart. with two plates of fragments of an ancient MS. of the Book of Genefis, illuminated with elegant figures; and an hiftorical differtation thereon.		0	5	0
69. The ftandard of ancient weights and meafures, from a table in the Exchequer.		0	2	6
70. A view of the Court of Wards and Liveries, as fitting; with a brief hiftorical account of that court.		0	5	0
	Total	4	7	9

This FIRST Volume of the *Vetufta Monumenta* may be had complete for *four guineas.*

VOLUME II.

1—2. PLANS for re-building the city of London, after the great fire, in 1666.		0	2	0
3. A portrait of Mr. Holmes, keeper of the Records in the Tower.		0	1	0
4. Ancient deeds and feals.		0	1	0
5. A view of the Savoy from the river Thames.		0	1	0
6. The warrant for beheading King Charles I.		0	1	6
		0	6	6

6

		l.	s.	d.
	Brought over	0	6	6
7.	An ancient wooden church at Greenfted in Effex; the fhrine of St. Edmund the King and Martyr; and the feal of the Abbot of St. Edmund's Bury in Suffolk.	0	1	0
8.	Gloucefter crofs.	0	1	0
9.	Three tetfelated Roman pavements, found at Winterton in Lincolnfhire, 1747; with one at Roxby in that neighbourhood.	0	2	0
10.	Doncafter crofs.	0	1	0
11.	Sandal caftle in Yorkfhire.	0	1	0
12.	The Savoy hofpital in the Strand, with the chapel.	0	1	0
13.	Clitheroe caftle in Yorkfhire.	0	1	0
14.	A plan of the ground and buildings of the Savoy.	0	1	0
15, 16.	A view of the cathedral church and priory of Benedictines in Canterbury, with the effigies of Eadwin, a monk of that convent, between the years 1130 and 1174, both drawn by himfelf; with a printed account of the faid drawings.	0	3	0
17.	An ancient lamp in two views; a vafe, and two bells, all of brafs.	0	1	0
18.	Silenus and a lamp.	0	1	0
19.	Third feal of Canterbury cathedral, and a mantle-piece at Saffron Walden.	0	1	6
20.	Brafs trumpets, and other inftruments found in Ireland; and a fhield found at Hendinas in Shropshire; with an explanatory account.	0	2	0
21, 22.	An antique bronze figure, from the collection of the late Mr. Hollis, with an explanation.	0	5	0
23, 24.	Two views of the old palace at Richmond; with an account thereof.	0	5	0
25.	View of the palace of Placentia at Greenwich; with an account thereof.	0	2	6
26.	The Eaft window of St. Margaret's church, Weftminfter.	0	5	0
27.	View of the old palace at Hampton Court; with an account thereof.	0	4	0
28.	Portrait of Dr. Lyttelton, Bp. of Carlifle, mezzotinto.	0	5	0
		2	10	6

Numb.		Price.
		l. s. d.
	Brought over.	2 10 6

Seven Plates of ancient Monuments in Westminster Abbey, viz.

29. Front of the monument of Aveline Countess of Lancaster.
30. The cumbent figure of Aveline.
31. The undervaulting and ornaments of the tomb.
32. The North front of King Sebert's monument.
33. The figures of Sebert and Henry III.
34. Heads and ornaments on Sebert's monument.
35. The tomb of Anne of Cleves.

		0 10 6

36. The monuments of Raherus in St. Bartholomew's church, West Smithfield.
37. Specimens of architecture in the said church, with an account thereof.

| | | 0 6 • |

38. Fountain at Rouen, erected on the spot where the Maid of Orleans was burnt.

| | | 0 2 6 |

39. } Font at Winchester cathedral.
40. }

| | | 0 5 0 |

41, 42. Two views of the Palace of Beaulieu, or New Hall in Essex, built by King Henry VIII.

| | | 0 5 0 |

43. Roman pavements found in Pittmead, near Warminster. 0 5 0
44. Rom. pavements found at Cirencester and Woodchester. 0 5 0

45. Monument of Cardinal Beaufort in Winchester cathedral.
46. Monument of Bishop Wainflete in Winchester cathedral.
47. Figures of Cardinal Beaufort and Bishop Wainflete on their monuments.
48, 49. Parts and ornaments of the monuments of Cardinal Beaufort, Bishop Wainflete, and Bishop Fox.
50. Monument of Bishop Fox in Winchester cathedral.

| | | 1 5 0 |

51, 52. Two views of a reliquary in the possession of Thomas Astle, Esq.

| | | 0 6 0 |

53. Monument of Henry Bourgchier, the first Earl of Essex of that family, and of Isabel Plantagenet his wife, in the church of Little Easton, Essex.

| | | 0 3 0 |

54, 55. Ruthvell cross in Annandale.

| | | 0 5 0 |

| | Total | 6 8 6 |

This second Volume of the *Vetusta Monumenta* may be had complete for *six guineas*; or the two volumes together in boards for *ten guineas*.

VOLUME

VOLUME III.

This THIRD Volume of the *Vetusta Monumenta* to be had complete for *seven guineas and a half*; or the three volumes together in boards for *fourteen guineas and a half*.

Prints.

Prints engraved by the late Mr. GEORGE VERTUE, now the property of the SOCIETY OF ANTIQUARIES.

	Price.		
	l.	s.	d.
A PLAN of London in Queen Elizabeth's time, copied by Mr. Vertue 1748, in 8 plates.	0	6	0
View of St. Thomas' chapel in London bridge, 2 plates	0	4	0
Survey of the streets of London after the fire, 2 plates.	0	3	0
Two views of Old St. Martin's church in the Strand, with the ground plot.	0	2	6
Roman pavement at Stunsfield in Oxfordshire.	0	1	0
Two views of Mr. Lethieullier's mummy.	0	1	0

The first set of Mr. Vertue's historical prints, consisting of four plates, with descriptions.

Henry VII. and his Queen; Henry VIII. and Lady Jane Seymour. Procession of Queen Elizabeth to Hunsdon house. The cenotaph of Lord Darnley, with James I. when a child, and the Earl and Countess of Lenox, praying by it. The battle of Carberry Hill at large.	1	5	5

The second set, consisting of the five following prints:

Three children of Henry VII. Charles Brandon Duke of Suffolk, and Mary Queen of France. Frances Duchess of Suffolk, and Adrian Stoke her second husband. Lady Jane Grey. K. Edward VI. granting the palace of Bridewell for an hospital.	1	3	6
King Charles I. and his Queen.	0	5	0
Plan and elevation of the Minor Canons' houses at Windsor.	0	1	0
Lincoln's Inn chapel, with the ambulatory.	0	2	6
Plan of Whitehall.	0	2	0
Chichester cross.	0	2	0

Portrait of Sir John Hawkwood.	0	1	6
Four views of the ruins at Stanton Harcourt in Oxfordshire; drawn and etched by the Earl of Harcourt.	1	1	0

www.ingramcontent.com/pod-product-compliance
Lightning Source LLC
Chambersburg PA
CBHW022127020426
42334CB00015B/787